T0134709

# Human–Computer Interaction Series

**Editors-in-Chief**
Desney Tan
Microsoft Research, Redmond, WA, USA
Jean Vanderdonckt
Louvain School of Management, Université catholique de Louvain,
Louvain-La-Neuve, Belgium

*The Human–Computer Interaction Series,* launched in 2004, publishes books that advance the science and technology of developing systems which are effective and satisfying for people in a wide variety of contexts. Titles focus on theoretical perspectives (such as formal approaches drawn from a variety of behavioural sciences), practical approaches (such as techniques for effectively integrating user needs in system development), and social issues (such as the determinants of utility, usability and acceptability).

HCI is a multidisciplinary field and focuses on the human aspects in the development of computer technology. As technology becomes increasingly more pervasive the need to take a human-centred approach in the design and development of computer-based systems becomes ever more important.

Titles published within the Human–Computer Interaction Series are included in Thomson Reuters' Book Citation Index, The DBLP Computer Science Bibliography and The HCI Bibliography.

More information about this series at http://www.springer.com/series/6033

Rens Brankaert · Gail Kenning
Editors

# HCI and Design in the Context of Dementia

Springer

*Editors*
Rens Brankaert
University of Technology Eindhoven
Eindhoven, The Netherlands

Fontys University of Applied Sciences
Eindhoven, The Netherlands

Gail Kenning
University of New South Wales
Sydney, Australia

University of Technology Sydney
Sydney, Australia

ISSN 1571-5035 ISSN 2524-4477 (electronic)
Human–Computer Interaction Series
ISBN 978-3-030-32837-5 ISBN 978-3-030-32835-1 (eBook)
https://doi.org/10.1007/978-3-030-32835-1

© Springer Nature Switzerland AG 2020
This work is subject to copyright. All rights are reserved by the Publisher, whether the whole or part of the material is concerned, specifically the rights of translation, reprinting, reuse of illustrations, recitation, broadcasting, reproduction on microfilms or in any other physical way, and transmission or information storage and retrieval, electronic adaptation, computer software, or by similar or dissimilar methodology now known or hereafter developed.
The use of general descriptive names, registered names, trademarks, service marks, etc. in this publication does not imply, even in the absence of a specific statement, that such names are exempt from the relevant protective laws and regulations and therefore free for general use.
The publisher, the authors and the editors are safe to assume that the advice and information in this book are believed to be true and accurate at the date of publication. Neither the publisher nor the authors or the editors give a warranty, express or implied, with respect to the material contained herein or for any errors or omissions that may have been made. The publisher remains neutral with regard to jurisdictional claims in published maps and institutional affiliations.

This Springer imprint is published by the registered company Springer Nature Switzerland AG
The registered company address is: Gewerbestrasse 11, 6330 Cham, Switzerland

# Contents

# Contributors

**Konstantin Aal** Information Systems and New Media, University of Siegen, Siegen, Germany

**Arlene Astell** KITE, University Health Network, Toronto, Canada;
Department of Occupational Sciences & Occupational Therapy and Department of Psychiatry, University of Toronto, Toronto, Canada;
School of Psychology & Clinical Language Sciences, University of Reading, Reading, UK;
Rehabilitation Sciences Institute, University of Toronto, Toronto, Canada

**Saskia Bakker** Experience Design, Philips, Eindhoven, The Netherlands

**Jeanette Bell** University of Technology Sydney, Ultimo, Australia

**Alethea Blackler** QUT Design Lab, Queensland University of Technology, Brisbane, Australia

**Inge Bongers** Tranzo, School of Social and Behavioral Sciences, Tilburg University, Tilburg, The Netherlands

**Rita Maldonado Branco** Research Institute for Design, Media and Culture (ID+), Aveiro, Portugal

**Rens Brankaert** Department of Industrial Design, Eindhoven University of Technology, Eindhoven, The Netherlands;
School of Allied Health Professions, Fontys University of Applied Sciences, Eindhoven, The Netherlands

**Sarah Campbell** Digital World Research Centre, University of Surrey, Guildford, UK

**Paula Castro** Federal University of São Carlos, São Carlos, Brazil

**Li-Hao Chen** Department of Applied Arts, Fu Jen Catholic University, Taipei, Taiwan

**Theopisti Chrysanthaki** Digital World Research Centre, University of Surrey, Guildford, UK

**Teresa Cid** INTRAS, Valladolid, Spain

**Emily Corrigan-Kavanagh** Digital World Research Centre, University of Surrey, Guildford, UK

**Michael Craven** Nottinghamshire Healthcare NHS Foundation Trust, Nottingham, UK

**Maria da Graça Campos Pimentel** University of São Paulo, São Paulo, Brazil

**Shital Desai** Department of Design, School of Arts, Media, Performance and Design (AMPD), York University, Toronto, Canada

**Suzanne Dillon** University of Technology Sydney, Ultimo, Australia

**Steve Donovan** Citrus Suite, Liverpool, UK

**Erica Dove** KITE, University Health Network, Toronto, Canada;
School of Psychology & Clinical Language Sciences, University of Reading, Reading, UK;
Rehabilitation Sciences Institute, University of Toronto, Toronto, Canada

**Berry Eggen** Department of Industrial Design, Eindhoven University of Technology, Eindhoven, The Netherlands

**Jac Fennell** Cardiff Metropolitan University, Wales, UK

**Sarah Foley** University College Cork, Cork, Ireland

**David M. Frohlich** Digital World Research Centre, University of Surrey, Guildford, UK;
Federal University of São Carlos, São Carlos, Brazil

**Dennis Frost** University of Technology Sydney, Ultimo, Australia

**Julie Gosling** Nottinghamshire Healthcare NHS Foundation Trust, Nottingham, UK

**Stephen Grady** University of Technology Sydney, Ultimo, Australia

**Dew Harrison** University of Wolverhampton, Wolverhampton, UK

**Niels Hendriks** Dementia Lab, Inter-Actions, LUCA School of Arts, Genk, Belgium

**James Hodge** Newcastle University, Tyne, UK

**Maarten Houben** Department of Industrial Design, Eindhoven University of Technology, Eindhoven, The Netherlands;
Tranzo, School of Social and Behavioral Sciences, Tilburg University, Tilburg, The Netherlands

**Wijnand IJsselsteijn** Human Technology Interaction, Eindhoven University of Technology, Eindhoven, The Netherlands

**Gail Kenning** Ageing Futures Institute, University of New South Wales, Sydney, Australia;
Faculty of Arts and Social Sciences, Faculty of Engineering and IT, University of Technology Sydney, Ultimo, Australia

**Tuck Wah Leong** University of Technology Sydney, Ultimo, Australia

**Raquel Losada** INTRAS, Valladolid, Spain

**Yuan Lu** Department of Industrial Design, Eindhoven University of Technology, Eindhoven, The Netherlands

**Laurie Miller** Neuropsychology Unit, Royal Prince Alfred Hospital and University of Sydney, Camperdown, Australia

**Mirella Minkman** Centre of Expertise Long-Term Care, Vilans, Utrecht, The Netherlands;
TIAS School for Business and Society, Tilburg University, Tilburg, The Netherlands

**Chris Morland** Citrus Suite, Liverpool, UK

**Kellie Morrissey** University of Limerick, Limerick, Ireland

**Henk Herman Nap** Centre of Expertise Long-Term Care, Vilans, Utrecht, The Netherlands;
Human Technology Interaction, Eindhoven University of Technology, Eindhoven, The Netherlands

**Kristina Niedderer** Manchester Metropolitan University, Manchester, UK

**Zena O'Connor** Design Research Associates, Sydney, Australia

**Joana Quental** Research Institute for Design, Media and Culture (ID+), Aveiro, Portugal;
Department of Communication and Art, University of Aveiro, Aveiro, Portugal

**Laura Ramos** School of Computer Science, Faculty of Engineering and Information Technology, University of Technology Sydney, Ultimo, Australia

**Óscar Ribeiro** Department of Education and Psychology, University of Aveiro, Aveiro, Portugal;
Centre for Health Technology and Services Research (CINTESIS), Porto, Portugal

**Karin Slegers** Department of Communication & Cognition, Tilburg School of Humanities and Digital Sciences, Tilburg University, Tilburg, The Netherlands;
Institute for Media Studies, Mintlab, KU Leuven, Leuven, Belgium

**Sandra Suijkerbuijk** Centre of Expertise Long-Term Care, Vilans, Utrecht, The Netherlands;
Human Technology Interaction, Eindhoven University of Technology, Eindhoven, The Netherlands

**Myrte Thoolen** Department of Industrial Design, Eindhoven University of Technology, Eindhoven, The Netherlands

**Jeffrey Thurlow** University of Technology Sydney, Ultimo, Australia

**Cathy Treadaway** Cardiff Metropolitan University, Cardiff, Wales

**Ans Tummers-Heemels** Human Technology Interaction, Eindhoven University of Technology, Eindhoven, The Netherlands

**David Unbehaun** Information Systems and New Media, University of Siegen, Siegen, Germany

**Elise van den Hoven** School of Computer Science, Faculty of Engineering and Information Technology, University of Technology Sydney, Ultimo, Australia;
Department of Industrial Design, Eindhoven University of Technology, Eindhoven, The Netherlands;
Duncan of Jordanstone College of Art and Design, University of Dundee, Dundee, UK

**Daryoush Daniel Vaziri** University of Applied Sciences Bonn-Rhein-Sieg, Sankt Augustin, Germany

**Daniel Welsh** Open Lab, Newcastle University, Newcastle, UK

**Rainer Wieching** Information Systems and New Media, University of Siegen, Siegen, Germany

**Andrea Wilkinson** Dementia Lab, Inter-Actions, LUCA School of Arts, Genk, Belgium

**Chih-Siang Wu** DreamVok, Taipei, Taiwan

**Volker Wulf** Information Systems and New Media, University of Siegen, Siegen, Germany

**Chen-Fu Yang** DreamVok, Taipei, Taiwan

**Isabela Zaine** Digital World Research Centre, University of Surrey, Guildford, UK;
University of São Paulo, São Paulo, Brazil

# Chapter 1
# Framing in Context

**Gail Kenning and Rens Brankaert**

> *For me context is the key—from that comes the understanding of everything.*
> —Kenneth Noland, American artist, 1988

## 1.1 Introduction

Human–computer interaction (HCI) researchers, designers and practitioners are increasingly turning their attention to addressing pressing societal issues. One of the major global challenges facing the twenty-first century is the ageing population. This brings about both challenges and opportunities and will motivate societal change. Older people currently make up a larger portion of the population than ever before. More people living into advanced old age means that incidences of dementia, for which advanced age is a major factor, will increase. Dementia is a term for a range of diseases and conditions and dementia care is complex and multifaceted. Dementia impacts individuals, families and communities and is prompting a re-evaluation of local and global care systems. Until relatively recently, research has predominantly focused on the biomedical aspect of dementia, aiming to find a cure and prolong

G. Kenning (✉)
Ageing Futures Institute, University of New South Wales, Sydney, Australia
e-mail: Gail.Kenning@unsw.edu.au

Faculty of Arts and Social Sciences, Faculty of Engineering and IT, University of Technology Sydney, Ultimo, Australia

R. Brankaert
School of Allied Health Professions, Fontys University of Applied Sciences, Eindhoven, The Netherlands
e-mail: R.Brankaert@fontys.nl

Department of Industrial Design, Eindhoven University of Technology, Eindhoven, The Netherlands

© Springer Nature Switzerland AG 2020

R. Brankaert and G. Kenning (eds.), *HCI and Design in the Context of Dementia*, Human–Computer Interaction Series,
https://doi.org/10.1007/978-3-030-32835-1_1

life. However, there is no cure on the horizon and the focus now is shifting to how to support and care for people, currently living with dementia, to achieve the best quality of life possible. This book focuses on how HCI and design can address this challenge and support people living with dementia, it focuses on those who have dementia and stakeholders in their care.

People living with dementia are part of a complex ecology of care. They are members of familial, local and social communities; serviced by local and national healthcare systems; impacted by the economic, legal and citizenship systems; and users of the everyday environment and so, effected by decisions made in relation to infrastructure and urban planning. This complexity and 'messiness' of the everyday design space for people living with dementia can be accommodated in the wide range of approaches used in HCI and design and be embraced by researchers and designers willing to collaborate and work across fields and disciplines. However, to do this, researchers and designers need to take into account the multivariate stakeholders and the dynamic systems, structures and environments in which dementia care exists, and work *in context.*

This book introduces a range of perspectives, approaches and methods for HCI researchers, designers and practitioners with or without experience of working in the *design for dementia* space. It will provide information that will enable them to design and fulfil projects that can contribute to the much needed support of people living with dementia and stakeholders in their care, and develop knowledge and skills that are transferable to other marginalized groups. The contributions critically explore projects, case studies, theories and practices at the intersection of design, HCI and dementia. Each chapter in this book shows how *context* is key to good design and technology development. The authors, who are HCI researchers, designers and practitioners, discuss how they have negotiated the complexities of working with participatory approaches to deliver usable, inclusive and accessible *in context* research, projects, technology and design outcomes to support people living with dementia.

The projects discussed in this book relate to specific research and design in the context of dementia. However, the processes, methods and methodologies; the tools, guidelines and principles; the inclusive, reciprocal and compassionate approaches; and the artefacts, systems and services are transferrable. There are ideas, concepts and principles that can be used more widely in the area of care; with people with cognitive and physical access needs; and by those both experienced and new to the area of *in context* design. This book is an accessible resource for developers and designers working across disciplines and design spaces. The book is divided into four sections; Inclusion and recognition, Design approaches, Design and experience and Design in the field.

## 1.2 Setting the Scope

We will begin with an overview of why *context* is important for HCI and discuss the relationship between HCI and design. We will then provide insights into why ageing and dementia is a socially significant issue in the twenty-first century and how HCI and design can support the well-being of people with dementia and stakeholders in their care. We will briefly discuss some of the language and terminology used in the design for dementia care space and discuss the rationale for an *in context* design approach.

### *1.2.1 Context and HCI*

As society moves from an experience economy towards a transformation economy, designers, researchers and practitioners are increasingly addressing *global* societal challenges, that call for *local* understandings and solutions, and use *local* infrastructures (Brand and Rocchi 2011). These societal challenges are complex and dynamic and impact on the everyday lives of people. They also present opportunities and challenges for design and the development of technologies. But to understand *how*, *why* and *when* they impact and *what* can be done to support people, we need to understand the context in which these challenges exist. To ignore the context in which people live poses risks that can lead to misinformation, misinterpretation, inappropriate design and wasted resources, at a time when they are increasingly limited.

For researchers or practitioners more familiar with fundamental research or technological approaches that seek to address precise hypothesis and limit variables, working *in context* can be challenging, and may sometimes appear counterintuitive. But, to provide appropriate and effective design and technological solutions that impact quality of life, in its many different forms, researchers and designers *need* to embrace the complexities and 'messiness' of everyday life. They need to use research approaches and practices that enable them to understand *context* as an inextricable part of the process of engaging directly with people and their needs. To impact quality of life, HCI and design projects need to be conducted *in context*.

Inclusivity, accessibility and usability are societal priorities, and ongoing priorities in the field of HCI. The multidisciplinary field developed because of the need to ensure that computers and digital technologies were accessible to a general public and not only to experts or engineers. Now, HCI researchers and developers address a broad spectrum of human experiences and activities and support social and civil needs through the development of interactive technologies (Grudin 2017). As new challenges arise, the HCI community engages across fields and disciplines, beyond HCI and the universal needs of computer interaction, to address the needs of specific user groups and the challenges they face in relation to everyday technology use. As HCI recognizes users as a heterogeneous group with individual needs, wants and desires, the domain has increasingly begun to explore human perspectives and how to foster interaction and experience through technology, by embracing design research and employing design practices.

### *1.2.2 HCI and Design*

From a background of shaping the appearance of products, design is now being re-conceptualized as a discipline that empowers human beings through the development of artifacts, systems and services that contribute to meaning making in the everyday, supports individuals and communities and impacts social and behavioral change (Krippendorff 2006). Designers are taking on some of the greatest challenges facing society this century by working in transdisciplinary ways, and by operating across disciplinary boundaries. Design has become a field of research that critically pushes forward, intersects with other research disciplines such as health, psychology, engineering and computer science and offers new perspectives, approaches and innovative solutions.

Designers deal with challenges that involve multiple viewpoints, that are sometimes seemingly conflicting and opposing, and are able to integrate them into a single concept (Martin 2009). Designers do this by identifying needs, conceptualizing and building and testing prototypes to arrive at new ideas (Krogstie 2012). Design draws on processes that facilitate understandings of cognitive and emotional responses to aesthetics and technology (Norman 1988). To understand the needs of users and stakeholders, designers take into account discourse, disciplinary understanding and the experiences of people by using sensitive and inclusive approaches (Thompson Klein 2004).

Design research uses design artefacts and systems in *research–through–design* approaches, to address challenges and investigate context (Zimmerman et al. 2007). The strength of this approach, according to Gaver (2012), lies in its ability to 'continually and creatively challenge status quo thinking'. To support the ongoing shift of HCI in reaching a wider range of populations and being inclusive and accessible, design research can provide valuable insights and approaches that focus on individuals and human perspectives. Through the use of design artefacts and systems, researched *in context*, design can support HCI as it responds to social challenges.

One of the key challenges in society today is how technology can support older people and people living with dementia. As computers and technology are ubiquitous in the everyday, older adults, many with cognitive or physical limitations, chronic diseases or frailty, will increasingly access and use technologies that are unfamiliar and challenging for them to use.

### 1.2.3 Ageing and Dementia

Scientific and medical advances and improvements in living conditions means a higher proportion of the population than ever before will live into old age and advanced old age (United Nations 2015; World Health Organisation 2017). Many people will grow older in relatively good health, with vitality. But with more people entering advanced old age, the incidences of age-related challenges increases, the most significant being dementia (Prince et al. 2016). This has extensive social and economic implications in exerting stress on existing healthcare systems and social structures.

Dementia impacts all aspects of society and life and there are many different stakeholders invested in the care of people living with dementia. The dementia care space is made up of a complex network of stakeholders, legacy systems and approaches to care that include, clinical, medical, healthcare, social, cultural, economic and policymaking communities. Dementia, while a global issue, is embedded in society differently across nations, countries, states, provinces and districts. Dementia care is administered through different bodies, departments and organizations,. In addition, dementia care and support takes place in a variety of settings and environments, with people living alone at home, with a caregiver or their family; in nursing homes and aged care facilities; in private residential facilities; in institutionalized hospitals and emergency care departments; and in palliative care homes.

Dementia is not a specific identifiable disease, but an umbrella term for a range of diseases and conditions of which Alzheimer's disease is the most common form (60–80% of cases), followed by vascular dementia (5–10%) (Alzheimer Association 2019). Dementia is progressive and irreversible. The impact varies significantly from person to person and according to the type of dementia present (Alzheimer Association 2019). There is no cure on the horizon, and none expected in the upcoming years. Therefore, prevention strategies that address lifestyle choices such as diet, exercise and smoking and potential risk factors such as low education, stress and high blood pressure are being explored (Cummings et al. 2018; Dockrill 2018). But, because of the complexity of the condition, it is likely that only a limited number of dementia cases can be prevented (de Bruijn et al. 2015). Furthermore, prevention research is still in its early stages, especially with regard to Alzheimer's disease (Graham et al. 2017).

Dementia often impacts memory, cognitive and physical functioning, judgement, communication, a person's ability to perform everyday activities, and may impact personality and behavior (Alzheimer Disease International 2019). Support is often needed for everyday tasks and activities, including wayfinding and orientation, food shopping and preparation, maintaining social connection, legal and financial challenges, and, in the later stages of the disease, with personal hygiene and care. To access services, people may need support with reading, comprehension and in the use of communication technologies and online systems (Topo 2008). Processes, systems and the environment need to be adapted and improved to enable them to cope with cognitive and physical changes brought on by dementia.

Globally and locally healthcare and dementia care have undergone fundamental, philosophical and radical changes, resulting in person-centered approaches and the promotion of self-management in care. Person-centered approaches originated in psychotherapy and were translated into dementia and aged care (Kitwood 1997), before being used in healthcare more generally, in the form of patient-centered care (Manthorpe and Samsi 2016). These approaches focus on personal well-being, self-esteem, identity and personhood, and give rise to an increased interest in non-clinical and non-medical approaches that will improve quality of life (Crampton and Eley 2013; Prince et al. 2016). Importantly, person-centered approaches can cater to the needs of the individual, and the highly personal way in which dementia manifests.

Philosophies of care are now focusing on person-centered approaches and on providing people currently living with dementia and those invested in their care, support and strategies to enable them to cope with dementia, to improve their lived experience and well-being and to experience the best quality of life possible. Design and technology can be used to address the challenges of living with dementia now and in the future. But, to contribute meaningfully designers and researchers need to engage with the complexities of engaging in this area.

### *1.2.4 Moving HCI and Design Forward in the Context of Dementia*

As dementia care transitions from a primarily epidemiological perspective and outlook towards an experience-oriented view, it means that people with dementia are no longer perceived as a homogenous group, or judged in terms of the characteristics of their condition. Rather, they are assessed as individuals with their own wants, needs, beliefs, dreams and desires. This perspective is increasingly being taken into account in the research, design and development of technology in the HCI domain (Lazar et al. 2017, 2018; Morrissey et al. 2017). Such approaches promote inclusive and *socially just* perspectives for collaborating with people with dementia in HCI research, through a research and design approach of *with* rather than *for*.

In HCI and design research, there are various methods for involving users. Co-creation (Sanders and Stappers 2008) and participatory approaches (Muller 2003; Robertson and Simonsen 2013) allow potential users, and the people impacted by the outcomes of a research or design project, to be part of the design process. The involvement of people with dementia is of particular importance in the quest to design usable, desirable, empowering and acceptable new technologies for them. However, dementia has unique characteristics, and all people with dementia are impacted by the condition differently, therefore direct and active involvement needs to be facilitated to ensure that design artefacts (technologies, objects, experiences or services) address their needs (Branco et al. 2015; Brankaert and Den Ouden 2017; Hendriks et al. 2014; Lindsay et al. 2012; Wallace et al. 2013). To do this, it is important to engage with all of those who will be impacted by the design artefacts, and to include them as experts in the lived experience of dementia.

As HCI and design communities rise to the challenge of supporting vulnerable groups, approaches are needed that take into account human perspectives, nuances and intricacies. More conventional methods used in HCI, such as *controlled labs*, do not provide the means to deal with the complexities of life in the everyday, neither do they allow for an ecologically valid *in context* research (Koskinen et al. 2011). However, a *designerly* perspective can support an understanding of context, including how individuals are located within physical environments, their interactions, their ever-changing relationships and their engagement with material objects and 'things'. Together HCI and design can engage in new processes *in context* and develop recommendations for new technology and service development. These approaches allow us to investigate the impact of technology on the environment, the network of relationships and the people involved.

### *1.2.5 Language and Terminology*

This book brings together the experience of researchers, designers and practitioners with varied expertise, from across a range of disciplines, from Asia, Europe, Australia and North America. Not only are the philosophies, practices, regulations and economics related to dementia care different for each country, so is the terminology used. As Jac Fennell discusses in Chapter 1.4 language and terminology can be both uniting and divisive and aid and hinder communication. Cathy Treadway in Chapter 1.3 also discusses the importance of language and makes reference guides available from organizations in the UK and Australia in her work. We also hear this echoed in the work of Frost et al. in Chapter 1.5 and the voices of people living with younger onset dementia, who make clear they do not want to be called *sufferers*.

In this book we have, where possible, supported authors in the use of terminology familiar to them. This means that people in professional and informal care roles may be referred to throughout the book as carer, caregiver, caretaker, family member, care staff and each author will clarify their use of these terms. Similarly, residential aged care may be referred to as nursing homes, aged care facilities or residential care homes. As editors we have asked authors not to use terminology that may be considered offensive to individuals, such as 'the demented' or 'dementia sufferer', and use labels like 'patient' only when appropriate, for example, if the project is conducted in a clinical or medical setting. Mostly people with a diagnosis of dementia are referred to as people with dementia or people living with dementia.

This book aims to appeal to a range of people in the area of HCI and design. We recognize that our audience is likely to identify in both HCI and design as researchers, designers, practitioners, students, care professionals or any combination of these. Similarly, we use terms such as designers to refer to design researchers and design practitioners, and HCI researchers to refer to HCI researchers and HCI practitioners.

## 1.3 Book Structure

In this book, we set out to address the challenges and opportunities of *design for dementia* and working in the *dementia care space*. The chapters provide concrete and practical examples for designers and researchers interested in HCI, design, dementia and addressing complex societal challenges.

***Inclusion and recognition***
We begin by exploring how people living with dementia and stakeholders in their care can be included and recognized in the design and research process to ensure they have a voice in the artefacts, systems, processes and technologies designed. We also begin by exploring how HCI and design can contribute to the dementia care space and the assumptions made in this field. This section of the book reflects on how research and design practices can accommodate a wide range of participants and their needs. These chapters provide fundamental insights into good practice when working with people with dementia, and what is considered respectful. They provide a context and frame for inclusive engagement in HCI, design and research in general.

The needs of the participants are explored, from different perspectives by Kenning and Treadaway. Kenning, in Chapter 1.1, suggests that giving consideration to reciprocity when engaging with sensitive user groups is a way of reducing the likelihood of participants feeling—or being—*used* or exploited in participatory research and design processes. She proposes thinking in terms of *give and take*. She encourages researchers and designers to ensure the *experience* of participating in the research and design process is meaningful in itself or has a lasting impact. Treadaway, in Chapter 1.3, uses a *Compassionate Design* approach to develop playful artefacts for people with advanced dementia. She explores personalization as a means of ensuring an inclusive and respectful approach. By acknowledging the unique characteristics of people, and paying attention to their relationships, Treadaway suggest that we can design meaningful interventions for some of the most disenfranchised members of the community.

IJsselsteijn et al. reflect on the design process in Chapter 1.2. They show how approaches to technology and design, adopted by main stream technology developers and major European programs, can lead designers and developers into a trap of what they suggest are *technology temptations*. They aim to combat the frequently dominant focus on disability and the perceived need for functional support by advocating for *Warm Technology*. This approach is affirming of old age, empowers people in need and provides meaningful interventions for people with dementia and those around them. They introduce three design cases to show what *Warm Technology* can offer. This chapter aims to promote reflection on what we would want technology to be in the context of dementia, and makes suggestions as to how we might get there.

Finally, Frost et al. and Fennell highlight the importance of language when engaging in the design for dementia space. In Chapter 1.5, Frost et al. discusses the impact of Younger Onset Dementia (YOD). Through the words and voices of people living with Younger Onset Dementia, we hear their calls to be treated with dignity and respect, particularly in the language used to discuss their condition. They show how their life circumstances differ from those with dementia in old age and highlight the importance of this being a consideration in anything designed for their use. Frost et al. show how researchers and people with dementia can engage in authentic partnerships, as exemplified by the co-authoring of the chapter for this book. The stories provided by the people with dementia inspire further research and design in this specific domain of YOD. Fenell, in Chapter 1.4 offers an example of how language can impact designers and the design processes. In proposing a *space for uncertainty* Fenell shows that the space that was originally set aside for designers to reflect on how they might currently contribute to the context of dementia, prompted the design professionals to reflect on how language shapes thinking, and subsequently impacts design. It explores how using non-inclusive language impacts the decisions made in a design or research process.

***Design approaches***

This section explores how to work with people in an appropriate way in HCI research and design in the context of dementia. The contributions look at tools, methods, methodologies, perspectives and approaches for working with people living with dementia. It examines how we ensure the proposed technology or design meet the specific needs, wants and abilities of potential users. The chapters provide current perspectives on what inclusion, intuitiveness and co-design mean today in design, technology development and research practice. The wide variety of perspectives show how diverse projects can include marginalized groups of people in the design and development process and presents guiding principles that can be taken into practice.

Hendriks et al. and Branco et al. take us on a journey through their co-design research. They focus on what methodologies and approaches can be used to engage directly with people with dementia and stakeholders in their care, to ensure that participants are empowered to engage to the best of their abilities. In Chapter 2.1, Hendriks et al. begin by recounting their research journey to find *a single method* for involving people with dementia in their design process. Their eventual findings run counter to their original aims by indicating that there is no *one* way of working with people with dementia. They conclude that a very individualized and relational way of working is key to working with this group. The findings are summarized in four guiding principles for designers and researchers. Branco et al. focus on defining design approaches and methodologies for this context in Chapter 2.2. They return to the seminal theories of Kitwood to explore how his guiding principles of Positive Person Work (Kitwood and Bredin 1992) can be interpreted and translated into design practice. Translating these principles into design practice inspires designers to be considerate of the people they include, and importantly provides ways of working for those new to *design for dementia*.

Ramos et al., Blackler et al., and Astell et al., explore how reviewing existing technologies, theories and frameworks can be used to understand users' specific needs and responses in the context of dementia. Ramos et al. in Chapter 2.3 focus on how design and research can support memory. They develop guiding principles that highlight the considerations needed when designing to support *Prospective Memory,* based on a review of projects by designers and HCI researchers working in this area.

In Chapter 2.4 Blackler et al. use the *Intuitive Interaction Framework* (IIF) to assess the intuitiveness of people with dementia when interfacing with interaction design in technology. They focus on novel and familiar interaction paradigms for conventional technologies and discuss three case studies that showcase IIF as a practical tool for researchers and designers. Astell et al., in Chapter 2.5, introduce the *TUNGSTEN* method which was developed as a guide for researchers to collaborate with older adults and people with dementia on technology research projects. The method which includes tools for researchers and designers, sets out a number of steps to illustrate how a few simple yet critically important steps can ensure there are benefits for researchers and participants.

***Design and experience***

In this section, we shift focus from inclusive design and research approaches and perspectives to concrete examples of what HCI and Design can do to support the lives of people living with dementia. It shows how designers and researchers can learn from the people we engage with and be guided in their research and design processes. It shows how we can also learn from other fields and disciplines. It highlights the potential of media creation and capture, the simplicity of easy-to-use technologies and foregrounds the importance of engaging with the senses in the context of dementia. This section ends with an overview on intergenerational engagements to promote connection through technology use.

Frohlich et al. in Chapter 3.1 highlight the potential of *assistive media* in the context of dementia. They build on the findings from Art Therapy, active and passive Music Therapies and Reminiscence Therapy to develop a framework for how media can be used to create therapeutic experiences. The framework for assistive media, introduced in this chapter, examines aspects of storytelling and the relationships between media, author and audience and maps potential scenarios for media use. Media experiences are also the focus of Hodge and Morrissey's project in Chapter 3.4. They share their experiences of working closely with people and families living with dementia on media creation projects. In one project, virtual reality (VR) is used to create bespoke environments modeled in 3D for people with dementia to enjoy. Another project questions the suitability of 3D modelled environments and involves accompanying families on day trips to *capture* meaningful moments together. The findings recognize the role of caregivers *and* acknowledge *their personhood* as people, as separate from their caregiver role. Foley and Welsh, in Chapter 3.5 show that technology design can counteract stigma and provide opportunities for skill-building and connecting generations through a learning process. They introduce two innovative intergenerational case studies of technology that values and supports connecting people in the context of dementia. In the first project, *Ticket-to-Talk* provides a series of carefully selected prompts for younger and older people to talk about together. *Printer Pals* uses what might be considered the *first wave* of HCI design, in the form of a printer, to deliver messages between people, to trigger curiosity and discussion.

Finally, Houben et al. and O'Connor focus on exploring the senses, and in particular sound and vision, respectively. Houben et al., in Chapter 3.2., engage in a series of workshops with people living with dementia to understand how sounds and soundscapes can add meaning to the lives of people with dementia. The *Soundboard* is used as an interactive activity to explore everyday sounds. The chapter focuses on how the activity is set-up and managed to build knowledge related to everyday sounds, from interacting and engaging with people with dementia. The study offers five guidelines for an engagement to understand people's likes and dislikes, wants and needs and to support design in this space. Following on with a focus on the senses, O'Connor's expertise is in understanding color and how it impacts on the senses and emotions. In Chapter 3.3, she explores how understanding environmental visual literacy can support HCI developers and designers to understand the impact of color in the care environment and improve, for example, orientation, user experience and inclusiveness for people with dementia. O'Connor presents four principles for color use that can be adopted by researchers and designers in HCI.

***Design in the field***

In the last section, we explore examples of technology and services that use co-design to promote autonomy for people living with dementia. The chapters include a focus on the development of artefacts to enable, for example, people living with dementia to arrange social events for themselves, and to select and play their own choice of music. Similarly, exergames are shown to be empowering for individuals and group as they come to understand the rules of engagement. The last two chapters in this book show how multidisciplinary partnerships and engaging with multiple stakeholders can be fruitful for design and research. This section provides examples of technology and service proposals to aid people living with dementia and their care network and highlights the wide range of ways that future researchers, designers and technology developers in HCI and design can create new opportunities in people's everyday lives.

Niedderer et al. and Thoolen et al., use an iterative design approach to understand how to promote autonomy with people living with dementia. In Chapter 4.3, Niedderer et al. share details of an inclusive co-design process conducted as part of a large European consortium (MinD). The chapter focuses on maintaining the social connections of people with dementia. This resulted in the co-production of *Let's meet up*, an interactive interface supporting people with dementia to enable them to connect with others via video calling and encouraged them to undertake activities with other people. This design process provides insights into how projects can work with multiple stakeholders towards a synthesized design proposal. Co-design also comes to the fore in the contribution of Thoolen et al., in Chapter 4.1. This chapter showcases *Sentic*, an interactive music player with interchangeable modules to adapt the interface to suit the abilities of the person with dementia. It was developed over the course of five workshops, using a sensitive co-design process. The findings highlight how design aesthetics contribute to the adoption of technology, and shows how adaptive technologies have potential for people living with dementia because they can accommodate a variance in people's abilities over time. Unbehaun et al., in Chapter 4.2 shares a design study of an information and communication technology (ICT)-based system to support activity and mobility for people with dementia and their care network by offering an exergames program. Over a 4-month trial of their system the motivation, collaboration and cooperation among the parties involved increased by using the system. Importantly, people were not only engaging with the games but also looking forward to the participatory sessions and valued the social component of the exergames, showing potential for these types of intervention in the context of dementia.

As we come towards the end of the book Suijkerbuijk et al. and Chih-Siang et al. show the opportunities and challenges of engaging with partners from differing disciplines and industry. Building further on the nature of collaborative projects, experiences from several European projects Suijkerbuijk et al. show the complexities of working with different people from different backgrounds on the development of technology and services for people living with dementia in Chapter 4.5. They explore how designers and researchers from other disciplines are not necessarily receptive to user-centered perspectives and that design can advocate for the importance of active user involvement in the context of dementia. Chih-Siang et al. show how working in projects carefully structured to support collaboration between disciplines and industry can have highly successful outcomes in Chapter 4.4. They discuss examples of two service design cases in Taiwan, where the challenges of an ageing population are acute. These collaborations took place between a care organization and designers engaged in the *5% initiative*, in which they donate 5% of their time towards a societal challenge. The initiative produced *FooKit* a cooking kit to ensure older people could get nutritious meals, and a customized tourism service for people with dementia to visit a local zoo, without the usual crowds beings present. The service cases show the variety of roles taken on by the designer throughout the design process.

## 1.4 Conclusion

We have provided an overview of the societal challenges that come with an ageing population and increasing incidences of dementia. In addition, we present a wide range of current approaches and philosophies of dementia care; the complexity of the dementia care space; the many different stakeholders, fields and disciplines impacted; and most importantly how HCI and design can contribute to the lives of people living with dementia. We have provided an overview of the many different ways that HCI developers, designers and researchers are already contributing to *Design for Dementia,* the *dementia care space,* and the *quality of lives* of people living with dementia and stakeholders in their care. We now invite you to take a look at the contributions of experts in this area, their approaches to research and design and the opportunities to contribute new perspectives to address challenges *with* and *for* people with dementia. All contributors are currently active and working in this field, and their insights and findings are widely applicable to other domains. We hope, however, that this is just the start and that you will be inspired to engage and contribute to the much needed design and research in this area.

## References

Association Alzheimer (2019) Alzheimer's disease facts and figures. Alzheimer's Dement 2019 15(3):321–387

Alzheimer's Disease International (2019) World Alzheimer Report 2019: attitudes to dementia. London: Alzheimer's Disease International

Branco RM, Quental J, Ribeiro Ó (2015) Getting closer, empathising and understanding: setting the stage for a codesign project with people with dementia. Interact Des Architect 26:114–131

Brand R, Rocchi S (2011) Rethinking value in a changing landscape and business transformation. Future Studies—Philips Design. Philips, Eindhoven. https://doi.org/10.1016/j.fbp.2016.06.016

Brankaert R, den Ouden E (2017) The design-driven living lab: a new approach to exploring solutions to complex societal challenges. Technol Innov Manage Rev 7(1):44–51

Crampton J, Eley R (2013) Dementia-friendly communities: what the project "Creating a dementia-friendly York" can tell us. Working Older People 17(2):49–57. https://doi.org/10.1108/13663661311325463

Cummings J, Lee G, Ritter A, Zhong K (2018) Alzheimer's disease drug development pipeline: 2018. Alzheimer's Dement: Transl Res Clin Interv 4:195–214. https://doi.org/10.1016/j.trci.2018.03.009

de Bruijn RFAG, Bos MJ, Portegies MLP, Hofman A, Franco OH, Koudstaal PJ, Ikram MA (2015) The potential for prevention of dementia across two decades: the prospective, population-based Rotterdam study. BMC Med 13(1):132. https://doi.org/10.1186/s12916-015-0377-5

Dockrill P (2018) One of world's biggest drug companies just abandoned Alzheimer's and Parkinson's research. https://www.sciencealert.com/one-world-s-biggest-drug-companies-abandoned-alzheimer-s-parkinson-s-disease-pfizer. Accessed 5 Dec 2018

Gaver W (2012) What should we expect from research through design? In: Proceedings of the 2012 ACM annual conference on human factors in computing systems—CHI '12. https://doi.org/10.1145/2207676.2208538

Graham WV, Bonito-Oliva A, Sakmar TP (2017) Update on Alzheimer's disease therapy and prevention strategies. Annu Rev Med 68:413–430. https://doi.org/10.1146/annurev-med-042915-103753

Grudin J (2017) From tool to partner: the evolution of human-computer interaction. Synth Lect Hum-Cent Inf 10(1):i–183. https://doi.org/10.2200/S00745ED1V01Y201612HCI035

Hendriks N, Huybrechts L, Wilkinson A, Slegers K (2014) Challenges in doing participatory design with people with dementia. In: Proceedings of the 13th participatory design conference on short papers, industry cases, workshop descriptions, doctoral consortium papers, and keynote abstracts—PDC '14—volume 2. https://doi.org/10.1145/2662155.2662196

Kitwood T (1997) Dementia reconsidered: the person comes first. Open University Press, Buckingham England, Philadelphia

Kitwood T, Bredin K (1992) Towards a theory of dementia care: personhood and well-being. Ageing Soc 12:269–287

Koskinen I, Zimmerman J, Binder T, Redström J, Wensveen S (2011) Design research through practice from the lab, field, and showroom. Morgan Kaufmann, Waltham, MA

Krippendorff K (2006) Chapter 07: Design methods, research, and a science for design. In: The semantic turn: a new foundation for design. https://doi.org/10.1201/9780203299951

Krogstie J (2012) Bridging research and innovation by applying living labs for design science research. In: Lecture notes in business information processing, vol 124. Springer, Berlin, Heidelberg, pp 161–176

Lazar A, Edasis C, Piper AM (2017) A critical lens on dementia and design in HCI. In: Proceedings of the 2017 CHI conference on human factors in computing systems—CHI '17. ACM Press, Denver. https://doi.org/10.1145/3025453.3025522

Lazar A, Toombs AL, Morrissey K, Kenning G, Boger J, Brankaert R (2018) HCIxDementia workshop: engaging people living with dementia. In: Extended abstracts of the 2018 CHI conference on human factors in computing systems—CHI ′18, New York. ACM Press, New York, USA, pp 1–7. https://doi.org/10.1145/3170427.3170613

Lindsay S, Brittain K, Jackson D, Ladha C, Ladha K, Olivier P (2012) Empathy, participatory design and people with dementia. In: Proceedings of the 2012 ACM annual conference on human factors in computing systems—CHI ′12. ACM Press, New York, p 521

Manthorpe J, Samsi K (2016) Person-centered dementia care: current perspectives. Clin Interv Aging 11:1733–1740. https://doi.org/10.2147/CIA.S104618

Martin RL (2009) The design of business: why design thinking is the next competitive advantage. Harvard Business Press, Boston

Morrissey K, McCarthy J, Pantidi N (2017) The value of experience-centred design approaches in dementia research contexts. In: Proceedings of the 2017 CHI conference on human factors in computing systems—CHI ′17. ACM Press, Denver. https://doi.org/10.1145/3025453.3025527

Muller MJ (2003) Participatory design: the third space in HCI. Hum-Comput Interact Handb 4235:1051–1068. https://doi.org/10.1145/153571.255960

Norman DA (1988). The Design of Everyday Things. New York: Basic Books. ISBN 978-0-465-06710-7

Prince M, Comas-Herrera A, Knapp M, Guerchet M, Karagiannidou M (2016) World Alzheimer Report 2016 improving healthcare for people living with dementia. Coverage, quality and costs now and in the future. Alzheimer's Disease International (ADI). https://doi.org/10.13140/RG.2.2.22580.04483

Robertson T, Simonsen J (2013) Participatory design. An introduction. In: Robertson T, Simonsen (eds) Routledge international handbook of participatory design. Routledge, pp 1–17. https://doi.org/10.4324/9780203108543

Sanders E, Stappers PJ (2008) Co-creation and the new landscapes of design. CoDesign 4(1):5–18

Thompson Klein J (2004) Prospects for transdisciplinarity. Futures 36(4):515–526

Topo P (2008) Technology studies to meet the needs of people with dementia and their caregivers: a literature review. J Appl Gerontol 28(1):5–37. https://doi.org/10.1177/0733464808324019

United Nations, Department of Economic and Social Affairs, Population Division (2015). World Population Ageing 2015 (ST/ESA/SER.A/390). http://www.un.org/en/development/desa/population/publications/pdf/ageing/WPA2015_Report.pdf

Wallace J, Wright PC, McCarthy J, Green DP, Thomas J, Olivier P (2013) A design-led inquiry into personhood in dementia. In: Extended abstracts on human factors in computing systems on—CHI EA ′13. ACM Press, New York, p 2883. https://doi.org/10.1145/2468356.2479560

World Health Organisation (2017) Global strategy and action plan on ageing and health. Geneva. Licence: CC BY-NC-SA 3.0 IGO

Zimmerman J, Forlizzi J, Evenson S (2007) Research through design as a method for interaction design research in HCI. In: Proceedings of the SIGCHI conference on human factors in computing systems—CHI ′07. ACM Press, pp 493–502. https://doi.org/10.1145/1240624.1240704

# Part I
# Inclusion and Recognition: In the Context of Dementia

# Chapter 2
# Reciprocal Design

**Gail Kenning**

## 2.1 Introduction

Design and technology development is increasingly focusing on how to contribute to twenty-first century-living and the challenges and opportunities that individuals and organisations face (Krippendorff 2006). Designers and Human–Computer Interaction (HCI) developers are engaging in user-centred approaches, which means working with a wide range of individuals who may benefit from, or be prospective users of, the products, systems, processes, research or technologies produced. Some of the greatest challenges that designers and developers can contribute to are in the area of ageing and health care, and in particular the care of people living with dementia (Kenning 2019). As designers and developers engage in user-centred approaches directly with people living with dementia and stakeholders in their care, they are using *participatory* and *co-design* approaches, working in experience-driven *living labs* and creating *labs without walls* in context (Brankaert and den Ouden 2017; Hendriks et al. 2014; Morrissey 2017).

Working directly with people living with dementia with cognitive and physical limitations and stakeholders in their care, who are often operating in a highly emotionally charged environment, requires careful consideration. The design of a project or study requires careful attention of, not only the internal project needs, but also the needs of participants engaged in the participatory process. So, working in this way, what are the ethical imperatives that designers and developers new to the area need to consider? This chapter explores how participatory design processes that allow designers and developers to gain knowledge from the lived experience of those

G. Kenning (✉)
Ageing Futures Institute, University of New South Wales, Sydney, Australia
e-mail: Gail.Kenning@unsw.edu.au

Faculty of Arts and Social Sciences, Faculty of Engineering and IT, University of Technology Sydney, Ultimo, Australia

© Springer Nature Switzerland AG 2020 
R. Brankaert and G. Kenning (eds.), *HCI and Design in the Context of Dementia*, Human–Computer Interaction Series,
https://doi.org/10.1007/978-3-030-32835-1_2

living with dementia, can provide reciprocal engagements to ensure participants directly benefit from the participatory experience. It suggests that this mutually beneficial relationship needs to be recognised and included as part of the design and development process.

## 2.2 Background

Before examining how reciprocity can operate in relation to participatory design, it is useful to look at the context, challenges and opportunities for designers and developers coming into this space. We will begin by exploring why the contribution they can make is so important, and how they can work with best practice approaches when engaging with users with specific care needs.

### *2.2.1 Ageing Population*

As the median age of the population increases and more people than at any time before live into old age, concerns arise with regard to how to support and care for older members of the community and the potential demands the older population may have on health care systems (Australian Government Department of Health 2015, 2018; World Health Organisation 2017). While poor health is not synonymous with older age, ageing increases the likelihood of infirmity and disease, including chronic conditions such as dementia. The likelihood is, that it will be older people with advanced, critical, high or chronic care needs who need care in hospital and aged care facilities. The majority of older people, with low-care needs, will continue to live in the community, in assisted living places or at home (Commonwealth of Australia 2019 p. 28). Homes, houses, infrastructure, and communities need to adapt to suit the needs of the old and very old in the community, and additional resources will be needed in the form of more people, support structures, technologies and smart design solutions.

### *2.2.2 Quality of Life*

The general health and well-being of the older population can be supported not only by the clinical, medical and health care systems, but also through non-clinical and medical approaches that are supportive and cost effective (Baird and Thompson 2018). Increasingly, governments, researchers, health professionals, organisations and care industries are recognising that ill health and living with chronic conditions do not necessarily exclude people from experiencing a good quality of life (Biggs and Powell 2001). Having a good quality of life can mean being supported to, for example retain mobility, stay connected with others, remain physically and mentally active and alert, engage in activities and events where they can be meaningfully occupied and have social interaction (Renehan et al. 2012). As a result, as discussed in Chap. 1, greater consideration is now being given to older care needs in the community and how the spaces, places, tools and technologies used by the general population can be adapted to support the changing needs of an older population. Furthermore, the incidences of age-related conditions such as dementia are likely to increase as the population ages. Therefore, support is also needed to improve the quality of life of those living with dementia and stakeholders in their care (family members, carers, volunteers and communities). This presents challenges and opportunities for designers and developers to create, design and adapt systems, processes and artefacts that can support people and positively contribute to their quality of life in the every day.

### 2.2.3 Understanding Needs

To make this much-needed contribution to the lives of older people and people living with dementia, designers and developers need to understand how ageing and dementia impact on the population. This includes the need for societal changes, for example to infrastructure, health care systems and structures, labour and the workforce. Designers and developers also need to understand the impact dementia has on individuals and stakeholders in their support and care. While dementia has for so long been understood from a biomedical perspective, increasingly aged and dementia care have provided alternative perspectives on dementia, focusing on personhood and individual needs and wants (Kitwood 1997; Kontos and Martin 2013; Zeisel 2009). Designers and developers working with user-centred approaches are also recognising the need to engage with the psychosocial aspect of dementia and understand the *lived experience* of people living with dementia and of being a stakeholder in their care (Morrissey et al. 2016).

### 2.2.4 Participatory Approaches

In design and technology development, co-design and participatory approaches are increasingly being used to engage directly with potential users and gain their input into the design and development process. Similarly in the spaces of aged care, health care, social care and primary care, participatory approaches are increasingly being used to understand the people, context and needs of those who may benefit or use the artefacts produced from the design or development process (Cunningham and Reay 2019; Gaver et al. 2004). These approaches often use feedback mechanisms such as focus groups, user testing, interviews, and increasingly they involve workshops, creative approaches and innovative methodologies, such as *Bodymapping*, *Handmapping* and the Visual Matrix (Bennett et al. 2019; De Jager et al.

2016; Kenning et al. 2020; Manley and Roy 2016). These approaches engage participants in the design process in varying degrees by eliciting proactive engagement and responses that inform the design and development outcome. However, when working with people with advanced dementia, whose needs may be greatest, participants may be unable to articulate their wants and needs through the usual channels available to them, such as talking, writing and signing. Here the use of creative engagement and approaches can open up possibilities for participatory engagement in the design process (Hendriks et al. 2014; Maldonado Branco et al. 2017; Morrissey 2013). But this opens up questions about the ethical imperatives that arise for designers and developers working with participants on design projects, where they may not be capable of anticipating or imagining the end product of the design process they are engaging in (Kenning 2017d; Treadaway et al. 2018).

The impetus for designers and developers to engage with users in the design process comes from a need and want to understand the user perspective, to design and develop systems, environments and artefacts that meet the needs of the user(s) and, for the most part, positively contribute to society and societal needs (Krippendorff 2006). However, alongside altruistic drivers for engaging in design and development to support the needs of older people and people with dementia, designers and developers also gain financial benefit, do projects or research that benefits their own career, knowledge institutions and organisations they work for, and develop knowledge and understandings that can be used on other projects at a later time. Therefore, this chapter discusses an approach to design and development that aims to ensure that the contribution that participants make in enabling designers and developers to gain knowledge from their lived experience, is acknowledged and reciprocated. This means aiming for all participants in the participatory design process to benefit from it.

### *2.2.5 Reciprocal Engagement*

Participants engage in participatory research and design projects for a variety of reasons as shown by a wide range of research and design projects in Europe, US, Canada and Australia (Hendriks et al. 2014; Morrissey et al. 2016; Suijkerbuijk et al. 2015; Treadaway and Kenning 2015b). Their engagement may be altruistic, to support research or design in specific areas, such as dementia. They may engage because they have an invested interest, such as experience with dementia as a carer or professional. Some participants are brought to projects through the organisations they work, volunteer for or engage with. Sometimes they may be introduced to projects through the management of the care facility in which they live or work. Some participants have a full understanding of the design and development process they are engaging with. They are able to recognise, for example that the design and development process may not have immediate outcomes and can share in the anticipation and imagining of what the outcomes might be. However, others, particularly people living with advanced dementia, may not be able to fully conceptualise the entire design and development process, or anticipate or imagine the potential outcomes (Viard et al. 2014). Such participants may not be cognisant of the nuances of the research or design process being undertaken. But, this does not necessarily minimise the contribution they can make, and importantly, excluding participants because of such limitations potentially reduces the agency and autonomy of people who are least heard in society. Often people with dementia, like other groups of people with specific access needs, are most disadvantaged by the systems and processes that aim to listen to, engage with, understand and empathise with them. Therefore, ways and means need to be found to ensure that they *can* participate and can engage and contribute to the best of their abilities (Maldonado Branco et al. 2017).

When working with people living with dementia or participants who may not be able to recognise how what they are doing in the here and now relates to future outcomes, their personal benefit for engaging in participatory design is potentially compromised. For example, if the only outcomes of a project are to produce a specific prototype, then if participants are not able use the prototype, or understand, comprehend or recognise how what they are doing contributes to the design or development process, where is their immediate benefit for taking part? How can designers and developers ensure they are not exploiting participants to achieve their own goals?

Reciprocity, sometimes discussed in terms of mutuality, is a well-established concept and has been studied in the area of psychology, ethics, communication, network theory, pedagogy, game theory and design (Dale 2017; Graumann 1995 p. 4; Ison and Sugden 2018). It forms the basis of macro and micro negotiations and exchanges between parties. It may be positioned as 'paying back what we have received' or 'give and take'. In our everyday negotiations reciprocity takes many forms. We are often aware that some of our own needs can be fulfilled by others, and recognise that the needs of other people can be fulfilled by us. So, in the case of design and development with people living with dementia, designers and developers recognise that they need to understand how dementia is experienced and the context in which people live, engage and are supported. What do people with dementia, engaged in participatory design processes, need in return?

In aged and dementia care environments research is increasingly showing that older people and people living with dementia often lack stimulation, social engagement and connection and meaningful activities. There are fewer opportunities to interact with new people or engage in new activities. The types of activities and engagements that are undertaken in participatory processes can fulfil these needs and establish a reciprocal relationship with participants. Stakeholders may also benefit, by seeing the participant engaging with others, being stimulated, having autonomy and being respected. We will now look at a case study that uses reciprocity throughout the design process.

## 2.3 Making It Together: A Reciprocal Case

The *Making It Together (MIT)* design research study explored how people living with advanced dementia in residential aged care facilities and stakeholders in their care, can work closely with researchers and designers in a participatory project. The aim was to design a series of objects and activities that would occupy, entertain, engage, promote *in the moment* pleasure and contribute to their quality of life. To understand the needs and wants of people living with advanced dementia the project offered six workshops (three in each facility) to engage staff, family members and people living with dementia in a series of activities. The methodology was selected to provide designers and developers with an participants' abilities and experiences, and to provide feedback on a range of sensory objects, activities, and prototypes. The workshop format facilitated stimulation and engagement for participants, and provided them with opportunities for social connection. The *MIT* project has been discussed in other publications (Kenning 2018), but in this chapter we will focus primarily on the aspect of reciprocity.

### *2.3.1 Participants*

Two residential aged care facilities were selected for inclusion in the study following discussion between researchers and care staff. One was in South West Sydney and another, used for its potential to offer different perspectives, was in a small regional town in northern New South Wales, Australia. Participants were selected using a qualitative purposive methodology to recruit 'information-rich cases yielding insights and in-depth understanding rather than empirical generalisations'. People living with dementia were selected following discussion between residential aged care facility staff, family or legal guardians and researchers. They included six females and two males (four from each residential aged care facility) between the ages of 66–96 years of age. The criteria for selection of participants were as follows.

- A diagnosis of mid to advanced dementia.
- Able to engage in a workshop for a period of 1–2 hours.
- Would benefit from engaging with people, objects and activities.
- Were unlikely to experience undue stress or anxiety from participation.
- Were able to communicate verbally or non-verbally.

Stakeholders were invited to participate. This meant there was either a staff member, volunteer or family member acting as a support person for each person with dementia. Three staff members were involved in each of the workshops (not all participants had family members who could attend). Three daughters of family members attended three of the workshops, and volunteers attended other workshops in their absence. The criteria for stakeholders were as follows.

- A volunteer or member of care staff employed at either residential aged care facility and familiar with the client participant(s).
- A family member or carer of a participating person living with dementia.

The residential aged care facilities provided researchers with information about participants, from their care profile, and gave brief characteristics of how their dementia might influence their behaviours. All had advanced dementia; several wore hearing aids; one person suffered post-traumatic stress disorder; one person was often withdrawn and preferred to be alone or with one other person; two people had been teachers and liked talking about their experiences; one person had confabulating tendencies; one 93-year old participant often became anxious because she thought her mother was waiting for her and that she needed to go, and another participant had an intent focus on money and always offered to pay for things.

### *2.3.2 Consent*

Consent for all participants was arranged in consultation with the residential aged care facilities. The organisations had access to family and legal guardians. Participants with advanced dementia also gave their personal consent at each workshop. Consent was requested only for the immediate activity being undertaken, and not for the entire design project. Consent was reassessed at the beginning and throughout each workshop, using a process consent approach as discussed by Dewing (2007). This approach recognises that verbal and non-verbal behaviours and responses can be indicative of stress and anxiety, and can constitute a withdrawal of consent. It also asserts, that consent may be reinstated if participants exhibit behaviours and responses consistent with wanting to re-engage and become involved in activities.

### *2.3.3 The Design Process*

The workshops were intended as opportunities for participants to engage with and respond to a range of visual and tactile stimuli and prototypes, and to engage with each other. Researchers were able to observe participants and stakeholders and gain an understanding of physical and cognitive abilities; gauge responses to material, objects and activities; assess likes, dislikes and levels of interest or disinterest; and provide a fun, enjoyable and creative event.

Three workshops were conducted in each of the residential aged care facilities each had discrete aims. But, the overall aims of the workshops were as follows.

- Develop co-design and participatory approaches for engaging with people living with dementia, allowing them access to the design process.

- Enable people living with dementia and stakeholders to provide input to a series of developed prototypes or finished products to be given to participants, or developed further after the study finished.
- Establish a framework for how co-design and participatory design processes can be evaluated for people with advanced dementia based on verbal and non-verbal behaviours and responses.
- Provide opportunities for participants to have fun, feel engaged and interact with others.

The first workshops were designed to enable researchers to engage with participants as they explored materials, objects and activities (visual and tactile probes) to understand their likes, wants, needs and abilities. Each participant was given a personalised *fiddle bag*, consisting of a strong canvas bag containing an array of materials, objects and activities. The objects and activities in the bag had been selected for each participant based on the profiles provided by the care staff. The *fiddle bags* were designed to be a fun activity, providing participants with an element of surprise as they took objects out of the bag for further investigation. Researchers observed participants' responses to the materials, objects and activities and assessed the extent to which they were liked or disliked; encouraged interaction with other participants; or stimulated discussion, storytelling or laughter.

In the second workshops, participants were given prototypes made by designers in the weeks between workshops one and two. They included a *musical cushion*, a *gear assembly kit*, a *piano,* made from dessert spoons and a *flower arranging picture kit.* Participants were invited to interact with the objects and activities and provide feedback. The responses to the objects were observed and assessed. The feedback included verbal and non-verbal responses indicating whether the participants liked or disliked the objects and activities, talked about them, told stories or suggested changes they would make (Fig. 2.1).

The prototypes given to participants in workshop two were made by designers informed by the participant's responses to the objects and activities in the *fiddle bags* from workshop one. Not all designers working on prototypes had attended the first workshop. This was to minimise the potential stress on participants caused by having many *new* people in the room. All designers had been provided with images, video and audio recordings of the workshops, along with researchers' notes and debrief recordings, the care profiles of participants, and the stakeholder and researcher analysis of participants' responses to materials and objects, and to other people in the room.

After workshop two, the prototypes were further developed by designers and taken to the final third workshop. The workshops examined the extent to which participants engaged with the advanced prototypes made by designers, and the extent to which the prototypes brought pleasure or facilitated engagement with others. Participants were asked to engage with and critique the artefacts and to provide information and feedback on their level of interest in them.

**Fig. 2.1** Participants with advanced dementia engage with a series of prototypes in the workshops

### *2.3.4 Data*

The workshops were audio and video recorded for post-event analysis; researchers made journal notes and kept observation schedules in which they observed facial expressions, gestures, emotions and bodily movement. Researchers also observed how long participants engaged with objects and the intensity of the engagement. In addition, staff, volunteers and family members were given a series of colourfully designed A5 booklets, with a range of questions and space for non-prompted comments. As they talked, with the participants, about each of the sensory objects in their *fiddle bag* (workshop 1), the prototypes (workshop 2) and the advanced prototypes (workshop 3), they made notes. They talked to participants about the objects asking, for example 'Do you like this'? 'Would you change this'? 'What would you change'? They made notes if the participant began to tell stories, made associations with the object, began to sing or simply became engrossed in the activity. Gestures and signs were often used, such as a thumbs up, or thumbs down, a smile or a grimace on their face.

### *2.3.5 Analysis*

Data, in the form of text, images, objects and audio and video recordings, were thematically analysed using a range of software including Word, Excel, Nvivo version

10 and video analysis software. Deductive themes were established prior to the stakeholder workshops. These deductive themes were based on existing academic and industry literature in relation to evaluation of creative activities and design research, and the researchers' prior experience. They were given to researchers attending the workshops and used as a foundation for observation of participants. Researchers also engaged in an exploration of inductive themes emerging from the analysis of the data using Nvivo software. Findings related to the objects and activities produced as a result of the workshops are discussed in a number of publications (Kenning 2016, 2017b, 2018) and so will not be discussed here. However, how reciprocity unfolded throughout the project has not been assessed in detail and will be explored here.

### 2.3.6 Case Study Rationale and Development of Reciprocal Approach

The rationale for using a reciprocal approach, although it was not explicitly named as such at the outset of the project, was based on a number of factors. Care staff at the organisations had expressed concern as to how participants living with advanced dementia would respond to the proposed workshop environment, as they usually engaged with them one-to-one. Therefore, in our efforts as researchers to understand how people living with advanced dementia responded to objects, activities and materials, and with care staff and each other, there was an imperative to ensure that they were comfortable and relaxed. We were aware that participants from the care facilities often had few visitors, and lacked ongoing stimuli and things to do. We also recognised that as the aims of the project were to develop activities and artefacts that could promote well-being and enjoyment, then the research process also needed to be enjoyable for those involved. We were also aware of the time commitment that the care organisation had invested in the project. Management and care staff, who were very busy, had to reorganise workloads and staff schedules, and provide additional personal care in getting participants to the workshop in a timely manner and ready to engage. The reciprocal approach needed to be extended, where possible, to include stakeholders who would take pleasure in seeing participants engaged and socially connected.

Recognising the need for reciprocity, researchers then began to explore how to facilitate a reciprocal engagement. The workshop activities needed to be designed, to facilitate feedback with regard to the prototypes being developed allowing, through observation, for researchers to find out individual and group responses to objects and activities. The workshops also needed to fully engage participants. Research and design projects engaging with people living with advanced dementia, in particular, show the importance of sensory engagement for stimulation and communication (Treadaway and Kenning 2018). Therefore, it was decided that the workshops would be *hands on* and sensory to enable people to engage with material objects, and things that they can touch, smell and hold. The content, and approaches used, were informed by existing research and the experience of the researchers who had worked on participatory projects with people with dementia, and had a deep understanding of how engaging with tactile and material objects can reveal tacit knowledge, and other 'ways of knowing', promote affective responses, and can 'communicate differently' (Gandolfo and Grace 2009; Kenning 2015; Kenning and Treadaway 2017; Schofield-Tomschin and Littrell 2001; Treadaway and Kenning 2015a; Treadaway et al. 2016).

The rationale for engaging with material objects and activities in this way, was also because there was a high likelihood that the participants with advanced dementia would not be able to relate to abstract concepts, understand diagrams or models, or decode texts or drawings of designs. In addition, as some participants experienced memory loss, there was a likelihood that some would not be able to maintain focus on chronological developments of the design process or engage in anticipating and imagining project outcomes.

The participatory design process used in the workshops promoted a sense of autonomy and agency in the participants. For example, in the first workshop, each participant had their own *fiddle bag* and was able to direct how the objects were taken out of the bag and handed to them by the researcher or stakeholder. Alternatively, they could engage directly with the *fiddle bag* and take objects out or put them back in the bag as they desired. This, taking things out of the bag and putting them back, stimulated comments, discussion and storytelling as participants recognised objects and associated them with places, people and events, or were curious and raised questions about the objects.

The objects and materials chosen to be explored in the *fiddle bags* were personalised to each participant based on information provided by the care facility. This included background information about participants, likes and dislikes, employment history, family circumstances and cultural background. The personalization worked in two ways. For example, some objects and activities were familiar to the participant and promoted recognition. This stimulated responses such as stories and associations. This could be used as feedback for the developments of the prototypes. However, the familiar objects also offered comfort and security, and promoted confidence *in the moment* as participants engaged with them. Other objects selected for participants, were novel and innovative, they promoted curiosity, were sometimes challenging and stimulated strong reactions. This too acted as feedback to the researchers. It also prompted laughter within the group of participants For example, when one male participant was given oversized knitting needles to engage with, he responded emphatically with 'I don't knit!'

Care staff had been concerned whether the group workshop format would work for people with advanced dementia because of the potential for over-stimulation and the risk of having 'too much going on'. However in practice, while participants showed signs of being tired towards the end of the two hours, only one person withdrew and that was only for a short period of time. All participants enjoyed sharing the objects and activities, and importantly, engaging with other participants—which did not occur often. The design of the project had allowed for sustained periods of enjoyment as participants engaged in the workshops, with other participants, with stakeholders and with the objects. They enjoyed both the company and the sensory stimulation. The designers gained insights into the abilities and potentialities of people living with advanced dementia. They produced nine prototypes as part of the project, based on the responses of participants to the sensory objects in workshop one. Two of the prototypes are being further developed. Four of the designers have continued to work in the area of dementia as designers, psychologists, HCI developers and researchers. This project set-up also formed the basis of a number of other projects including 'A day in the life' and 'Co-design for everyday support of person-centred and relationship centred care' (Kenning 2017a; Kenning et al. in press).

## 2.4 Principles for Reciprocal Design

As a result of the participatory design process in this study, there were a number of principles that encouraged and supported reciprocity and may be considered part of a reciprocal approach. The reciprocal approach extended not only to the participants living with dementia, but also to the care staff and the host organisation. The primary principles were to ensure that all participants were treated with respect and dignity (Kitwood 1997). The principles in practice in the project were as follows.

- Ensuring everyone is 'listened' to—The workshops were set up to ensure that everyone was able to have input. For those who were not able to verbally articulate their responses, time was given to ensure that they could communicate in their own way, for example through gestures, sounds or facial expressions.
- Acknowledging all contributions—The level of participation varied. Some participants were able to articulate clearly their likes and dislikes, tell stories, express opinions and engage directly. For others, their responses were much more nuanced, with small gestures, one or two words or bodily responses. It was important to acknowledge all contributions, whatever the scale or intensity of the response.
- Acknowledging their expertise—The project recognised everyone in the room as an expert. The experts included those with a lived experience of having dementia, as care staff, as volunteer, as family member, or as designer and researcher. The *360 degree view* from these experts provided insights into the design and development of the final prototypes.
- Making time and space to listen—The workshops were paced. Giving people time to think, formulate responses and to listen. This meant that at times the same response or story was repeated over, and that the discussion often went 'off topic'. This was considered part of the process of engagement.
- Flexibility—In care organisations priorities change quickly. Participants were sometimes unable to attend, rooms were changed, care staff were not available and the times of the workshops were changed at short notice. Flexibility was needed throughout the project, in both attitude and in the everyday engagement. The reciprocity was extended to the care organisation who always made the best

efforts to follow the agreed program. When this was not possible researchers were accommodating and worked with management and staff to find the best solution for all.

- Recognising long and short term needs—The project sought to understand how design could benefit each of the participants in the longer term production of objects and activities to stimulate and entertain. However, it was important to recognise that the participant may not be able to engage in conceptualising future needs. Therefore, engaging with participants *in the now* and recognising immediate needs of participants was an important aspect of the process.

## 2.5 Discussion

For many people working, in aged care, health care and dementia care settings, reciprocity is already how they engage with people in their everyday. However, for those from a research, engineering, medical or clinical background, engaged in methodologies such as Randomized Controlled Trials (RCTs), this may not be the case as the needs of individual participants are not foregrounded in the project design or research set-up. However, as researchers, designers and developers increasingly engage in collaborative and interdisciplinary work with participants, the needs of a range of stakeholders must be taken into account, and increasingly this means adopting user-centred approaches that seek to not only to understand the user, but also to empathise and recognise the context in which they exist and act.

Employing reciprocal approaches in design and development requires a level of flexibility in the design process to accommodate changing needs. More traditional research methodologies, such as RCTs, are not able to cater to this level of flexibility. Similarly, in the everyday environment projects are subject to time and budget restraints that may pose limitations on the ability for researchers, designers and developers to fully take into account the needs of participants, particularly if they do not fully align with the overall project outcomes. However, for projects that are exploratory, examining what can work, when and how, there are benefits from working with a reciprocal approach. Projects benefit from the contribution of committed, enthused participants with lived experiences who can share their insights. Facilitating reciprocity can support autonomy and agency, provide opportunities for social connections, and acknowledge and compensate for participant's contribution in design and research.

Reciprocity is an approach that gives consideration, not only to the internal or project needs of designers and developers, but also respectfully understands the perspectives of people with dementia, family and carers, and the effort it may take for them to be engaged in research. The principles of reciprocity recognise the need for communication and the need for design projects to be inclusive and enabling. In this project a reciprocal design approach benefited all involved. The designers completed the design prototypes and gained insights into the needs and wants of people living with advanced dementia, how the design process can be adapted and how we interact with and learn from each other. The participants enjoyed a series of engagements and experiences, that they talked about afterwards, and some of the activities from the workshop, exploring sensory objects, became part of their regular activities program.

## 2.6 Conclusion

With a growing and changing population of older people and people living into advanced old age—and increasingly more people who can give us insights into what it is like to live to 100, there are opportunities and challenges for HCI and design. Using approaches that allow for designers to gain an understanding of what it is to be old or to live with dementia is crucially important. It is also important that designers and developers are able to move beyond understanding and are able to empathise. This can be achieved through engaging with the context of where, when and how people need support. With more designers and developers coming into the area to offer longer term support and explore how design and technology can help and support individuals and society, it is also important for designers and developers to recognise the needs and wants of those they are working with in the *here and now in reciprocal ways*.

## References


Australian Government Department of Health (2015) National framework for action on dementia 2015–2019. Australia. https://agedcare.health.gov.au/ageing-and-aged-care-older-people-their-families-and-carers-dementia/national-framework-for-action-on-dementia-2015-2019

Australian Government Department of Health (2018) Aged Care Funding Instrument (ACFI) Reports. Ageing and aged care. https://agedcare.health.gov.au/tools-and-resources/aged-care-funding-instrument-acfi-reports

Baird A, Thompson WF (2018) The impact of music on the self in dementia. J Alzheimers Dis 61(3):827–841. https://doi.org/10.3233/JAD-170737

Bennett J, Froggett L, Kenning G, Manley J, Muller L (2019) Memory loss and scenic experience: an arts based investigation. Forum: Qual Soc Res 20(1)

Biggs S, Powell JL (2001) A Foucauldian analysis of old age and the power of social welfare. J Aging Soc Policy 12(2):93–112

Brankaert R, den Ouden E (2017) The design-driven living lab: a new approach to exploring solutions to complex societal challenges. Technol Innov Manage Rev. https://timreview.ca/article/1049

Commonwealth of Australia (2019) Medium and longterm pressures on the system: the changing demographics and dynamics of aged care. Canberra

Cunningham H, Reay S (2019) Co-creating design for health in a city hospital: perceptions of value, opportunity and limitations from ‘Designing Together’ symposium. Des Health 3(1):119–134

Dale EJ (2017) Reciprocity as a foundational concept in teaching philanthropic and nonprofit studies. Philanthropy Educ 1(1):64–70

De Jager A, Tewson A, Ludlow B, Boydell K (2016) Embodied ways of storying the self: a systematic review of body-mapping. FQS 17(2)

Dewing J (2007) Participatory research: a method for process consent for people who have dementia. Dement: Int J Soc Res Pract 6:11–25

Gandolfo E, Grace M (2009) …it keeps me sane…women, craft wellbeing. Vulgar Press, Carlton North

Gaver W, Boucher A, Pennington S, Walker B (2004) Cultural probes and the value of uncertainty. Interact—Funology 11(5):53–56

Graumann CF (1995) Commonality, mutualities, reciprocity: A conceptual introduction. In: Marková I, Graumann CF, Foppa K (eds) Mutualities in dialogue. Cambridge University Press, Cambridge, New York, pp xvii, 282 p

Hendriks N, Huybrechts L, Wilkinson A, Slegers K (2014) Challenges in doing participatory design with people with dementia. In: Proceedings of the 13th participatory design conference on short papers, industry cases, workshop descriptions, doctoral consortium papers, and keynote abstracts—PDC ′14, vol 2, pp 33–36

Ison A, Sugden R (2018) Reciprocity and the paradox of trust in psychological game theory. J Econ Behav Organ 167:219–227. https://doi.org/10.1016/j.jebo.2018.04.015

Kenning G (2015) 'Fiddling with threads': craft–based textile activities and positive well-being. Text: J Cloth Cult 13(1):50–65

Kenning G (2016) Making it together: person centred design to promote positive wellbeing. Paper presented at the art of health and wellbeing 2016, Sydney

Kenning G (2017a) 'A day in the life': participatory design research for aged care. Paper presented at the Australian association of gerontology. The Golden Age, Perth

Kenning G (2017b) Making it together: apart. Aust J Dement Care 6(5):32–36

Kenning G (2017d) Reciprocal design: inclusive design approaches for people with late stage dementia. Paper presented at the design 4 health 2017, Melbourne. https://research.shu.ac.uk/design4health/wp-content/uploads/2012/09/D4H2017-Proceedings-Master-File-PDF2.pdf

Kenning G (2018) Reciprocal design: inclusive design approaches for people with late stage dementia. Des Health 2(1):1–21. https://doi.org/10.1080/24735132.2018.1453638

Kenning G (2019) Chronic health: if not us then who? A review of an exhibition exploring the assistive, speculative, provocative and challenging role of design for health—Embassy of health, dutch design week. design for health. Des Health 3(1):162–179. https://doi.org/10.1080/24735132.2019.1592357

Kenning G, Treadaway C (2017) Conversations at the edge of play. Continuum 31(6). https://doi.org/10.1080/10304312.2017.1370075

Kenning G, Visser M, Zijlema A (in press) Co-design to explore the everyday of person-centred and relationship centred care. Sydney

Kitwood TM (1997) Dementia reconsidered: the person comes first. Open University Press, Buckingham England, Philadelphia

Kontos PC, Martin W (2013) Embodiment and dementia: exploring critical narratives of selfhood, surveillance, and dementia care. Dementia 12(288):288–302

Krippendorff K (2006) The semantic turn: a new foundation for design. CRC/Taylor & Francis, Boca Raton

Maldonado Branco R, Quental J, Ribeiro Ó (2017) Personalized participation: an approach to involve people with dementia and their families in a participatory design project. CoDesign 13(2):127–143. https://doi.org/10.1080/15710882.2017.1310903

Manley J, Roy AN (2016) The visual matrix: a psycho-social method for discovering unspoken complexities in social care practice. Psychoanal, Cult Soc 22(2):132–153

Morrissey K (2013) Emerging values in participatory design and dementia: explicating, operationalising and redfining. Paper presented at the ACM CHI, Paris, France. di.ncl.ac.uk/vulnerability/files/2013/02/Morrissey_DFWP20131.pdf

Morrissey K, Wood G, Green D, Pantidi N, McCarthy J (2016) 'I'm a rambler, I'm a gambler, I'm a long way from home': the place of props, music, and design in dementia care. Paper presented at the DIS '16 designing interactive systems. Brisbane, QLD, Australia, pp 1008–1020

Morrissey K, McCarthy J, Pantidi N (2017) The value of experience-centred design approaches in dementia research contexts. Paper presented at the CHI conference on human factors in computing systems—CHI '17 (CHI '17)

Renehan E, Dow B, Lin X, Blackberry I, Haapala I, Gaffy E, Cyarto E, Brasher K, Hendy S (2012) Healthy ageing literature review. www.health.vic.gov.au/agedcare/maintaining/downloads/healthy_litreview.pdf

Research—a qualitative living lab protocol. Paper presented at the 5th living lab summer school 2014, Amsterdam

Schofield-Tomschin S, Littrell MA (2001) Textile handcraft guild participation: a conduit to successful aging. Cloth Text Res J 2001(19):41–51. https://doi.org/10.1177/0887302X0101900201

Suijkerbuijk S, Brankaert R, De Kort YAW, Snaphaan LJAE, Den Ouden E (2015) Seeing the first-person perspective in dementia: a qualitative personal evaluation game to evaluate assistive technology for people affected by dementia in the home context. Interact Comput 27(1):47–59n

Treadaway C, Kenning G (2015a) Designing sensory e-textiles for dementia. Paper presented at the the third International Conference on Design Creativity (3rd ICDC), Bangalore, India. https://repository.cardiffmet.ac.uk/dspace/handle/10369/7470

Treadaway C, Kenning G (2015b) Sensor e-Textiles: person centred co-design for people with later stage dementia. Working with Older People 20(2):76–85

Treadaway C, Kenning G (2018) Sensory e-textiles and playful objects: designing for advanced dementia care. Paper presented at the 4th Neurological Disorders Summit (NDS- 2018), Los Angeles, USA

Treadaway C, Kenning G, Prytherch D, Fennell J (2016) Laugh: designing to enhance positive emotion for people living with dementia. Paper presented at the 10th design and emotion conference, Amsterdam, September 2016

Treadaway C, Fennell J, Taylor A, Kenning G (2018) Designing for playfulness through compassion: design for advanced dementia. Paper presented at the design 4 health, Sheffield

Viard A, Piolino P, Belliard S, de La Sayette V, Desgranges B, Eustache F (2014) Episodic future thinking in semantic dementia: a cognitive and fMRI study. PLoS One 9(10)

World Health Organisation (2017) Global strategy and action plan on ageing and health. Retrieved from Licence: CC BY-NC-SA 3.0 IGO

Zeisel J (2009) I'm still here: a breakthrough approach to understanding someone living with Alzheimer's. Avery, New York

# Chapter 3
# Warm Technology: A Novel Perspective on Design for and with People Living with Dementia

**Wijnand IJsselsteijn, Ans Tummers-Heemels, and Rens Brankaert**

## 3.1 Introduction

With the rapid increase of life expectancy worldwide, there is an urgent need to think more imaginatively and more inclusively about aging. Old age is not a singular stage of life for everyone aged over 65, as some developmental models suggest, rather it is a rich, multiform, non-linear, culturally contextualized, and deeply personal process.

As people age, some may see themselves having to confront a life with dementia. Having dementia, however, does not define a person. When focusing scholarly and design efforts on improving the lives of people living with dementia, it becomes acutely clear that aging should not be assessed in terms of deterioration, even though it may be a part of aging for some. Consequently, design efforts to support people living with dementia should not only focus on the support, substitution, or amelioration of functional decline, but on better ways of affirming old age—enabling people to remain open and attached to the world and to other people, and, as Lynne Segal (2014) so beautifully put it, *"staying alive to life itself"*. In this light, there is a need to rethink the role of design and technology in old age, and to challenge the dominant but problematic rhetoric of technology as a solution to the *"burden of*

W. IJsselsteijn · A. Tummers-Heemels
Human Technology Interaction, Eindhoven University of Technology, Eindhoven, The Netherlands
e-mail: W.A.IJsselsteijn@tue.nl

A. Tummers-Heemels
e-mail: A.I.M.Tummers-Heemels@tue.nl

R. Brankaert (✉)
Department of Industrial Design, Eindhoven University of Technology, Eindhoven, The Netherlands
e-mail: R.Brankaert@fontys.nl

School of Allied Health Professions, Fontys University of Applied Sciences, Eindhoven, The Netherlands

© Springer Nature Switzerland AG 2020

R. Brankaert and G. Kenning (eds.), *HCI and Design in the Context of Dementia*, Human–Computer Interaction Series,
https://doi.org/10.1007/978-3-030-32835-1_3

*care"* that comes with an aging population (Greenhalgh et al. 2012; Fitzpatrick et al. 2015). In this chapter, a new way of looking at technology in the context of dementia is proposed by introducing the concept of *Warm Technology*, a framing of technology that intentionally challenges the prevalent connotation of technology as rational and efficient, yet complicated, impersonal, and uncaring of the individual. Before discussing Warm Technology, we will analyze some of the issues that limit progress in designing for dementia. In particular, we will focus on the temptations that engineers and designers fall prey to when designing technology for people living with dementia, leading to solutions that are not well-matched to people's actual needs and potential. By way of alternative, examples of Warm Technology will be provided along with a rationale of how to design this type of technology in an inclusive and respectful way.

## 3.2 The Paradox of Technology

The present time shows significant technological progress and an increase in technological functionality. In fact, technological innovation is progressing so rapidly that people may fall behind in their ability to manage it. Increasingly, people are living with technologies that may be technically reliable, but are complex or counterintuitive to use in daily life. A fundamental paradox of technology is its simultaneous ability to both connect people and to isolate them, to provide information and to misinform, to enhance productivity and to stifle it, to make people feel comfortable with it, and to alienate them from it.

When confronted with the significant challenges of an aging population, policymakers are, understandably, looking at technology as a way forward. Technology may offer valuable means of supporting independence and social connectedness, promoting a sense of self-efficacy and personal dignity, and providing support in continued mastery over their environment. Regardless, the paradoxical nature of technology outlined above is amplified as people age. Research indicates that older adults experience more physical limitations in using technology because of, for example, systems that require fine-grained motor control, physical strength, or high visual acuity. They feel stigmatized by technology that emphasizes their frailty, such as large red alarm buttons to be worn as a necklace or mobility support designed as medical devices. They may experience difficulties in learning how to use new technologies because they are too complex. Older adults are sometimes justifiably skeptical about the benefits of new technologies. Don Norman, author of *The Design of Everyday Things* (1988), a pioneer in design and Human–Computer Interaction and VP of Apple, himself in his mid-80s at the time of this writing, observes:

> Despite our increasing numbers the world seems to be designed against the elderly. Everyday household goods require knives and pliers to open. Containers with screw tops require more strength than my wife or I can muster. (We solve this by using a plumber's wrench to turn the caps.) Companies insist on printing critical instructions in tiny fonts with very low contrast. Labels cannot be read without flashlights and magnifying lenses. And when companies do design things specifically for the elderly, they tend to be ugly devices that shout out to the world "I'm old and can't function!" We can do better. (Norman 2019).

The vulnerabilities associated with dementia likely aggravate these issues. Older adults living with dementia represent a growing and highly diverse group. Their familiarity with technology is different in part because the dominant technology of people's formative years may differ substantially (Docampo Rama et al. 2001). They will have varied levels of computer literacy depending on their age, education, prior occupation, and life experiences. Challenges that come with dementia, such as memory loss, difficulties in planning, sequencing and processing information, reduced problem-solving abilities and problems with language, to a greater or lesser degree, pose limitations on the technologies people living with dementia are likely to use and willing to embrace.

## 3.3 Refocusing Our Design Efforts

The primary focus of technology development to date has been on the delivery of remote care and in enabling independent living. The majority of these Ambient Assisted Living (AAL) and telecare systems focus on functional support to ameliorate or overcome the limitations and frailty associated with dementia. Such functional support includes safety and security in the form of, for example, fall detection monitors; lifestyle monitoring including tracking physical activity in the home; physiological measurements such as blood pressure and other vitals; and medication monitoring and reminders. In reviewing the existing literature on technology and dementia, a number of observations can be made. Firstly, it is challenging for researchers and developers to involve people with dementia in the design and development process. While some studies manage to involve people living with dementia, much work in this area gains input from users or stakeholders, such as caregivers or family members, who are *around* the person with dementia (Orpwood et al. 2004). This is reflected in the type of technology requirements that are elicited, typically addressing the independence of the person living with dementia by supporting Activities of Daily Living (ADLs), and alleviating the *"burden of care"*, for example, through remote monitoring applications. Important as these are, the needs expressed by people with dementia themselves show a different focus. Suijkerbuijk and colleagues (2019) present a recent review of studies actively involving people with dementia. These approaches reveal the need for social and meaningful activities, for company and social connection, to be accepted and respected as they are, and to be seen as a unique and complete human being (Orrell et al. 2008; Van der Roest et al. 2009; Miranda-Castillo et al. 2010; van Wijngaarden et al. 2019). This shows a shift of perspective, away from a narrow medical focus, to a more holistic approach that focuses on a meaningful and fulfilling life, being able to deal with and adapt to the condition, and not having dementia define the essence of someone's life or their sense of self (Lazar et al. 2017).

Secondly, there are significant challenges associated with moving technologies from the design stage to implementation, where they are in day-to-day use over longer periods of time. There is a systematic research-to-practice fissure for many technology propositions, including those aimed at supporting informal carers (Gitlin et al. 2015). A recent review on the adoption of AAL technologies (Peek et al. 2014) demonstrates that most studies tend to focus on the pre-adoption phase of technology, that is, probing the attitudes toward and expectancies around technology, rather than the actual use of technology at home. Many studies fail to look at the lived experience of people with dementia or to address their needs with technology.

In sum, there is a need to radically rethink technology propositions for people living with dementia in order to live well, and the implications this has for how technologies are developed. In order to adequately include the experiences, views, and needs of people living with dementia participatory practices and co-design approaches need to be adopted (Brankaert 2016; Suijkerbuijk et al. 2019). This has clear added value over and above randomized controlled trial approaches that are used to assess clinical efficacy and care efficiency. A more holistic approach is needed that prioritizes a person's lived experience and is sensitive to the complex and subtle dynamics, tradeoffs, modifications, and dilemmas that technology may introduce, as people are trying to make sense of their condition.

In this chapter, the concept of Warm Technology illustrates a way to refocus efforts away from seeing dementia as a predominantly clinical matter with its associated focus on functional support, and toward improving well-being and quality of life. The goal is to have technology be instrumental to living as well as possible, and to address the majority of concerns, needs, and wishes of people with dementia in their everyday lives. Before turning to Warm Technology in more detail, we will first analyze why many of the technological efforts to date have not been successful in reaching this goal.

## 3.4 Temptations of Technology

Much of the technological innovation in the context of dementia to date has been technology-driven, despite frequently stated ambitions and claims of its user-centeredness. This technology-centricity is, at least in part, responsible for the paradox of technology we mentioned earlier. There are five trends, or, from a technology developer's point of view, we might suggest they are "temptations", traceable in many technology proposals. We might compare these technology temptations to the Sirens' songs from Homer's *The Odyssey.* The Sirens' songs were so attractive to the ear that it lured sailors to sail their ships close by to hear the songs, only to have their ships crash upon the rocks. The story's main character, Odysseus, wanted to hear the Siren's songs so he had his crew sail the ship past them. In order not to endanger his ship and his crew he had them put wax in their ears, and asked to be bound to the ship's mast himself, only to have his ropes tightened should he beg to be released. Similarly, technology offers various temptations to many designers and developers. These temptations are powerful, omnipresent yet not always evident, and difficult to challenge. In our current society, digital technology is a strong enabling force and can be extremely useful and powerful when appropriately applied. However, more often than not, projects addressing innovations for older adults, and particularly in dementia care, tend to use the technological possibilities as their point of departure. This is not to say that technology temptations are the product of some explicit tech-push agenda. We frequently fall prey to these temptations even despite ambitions of user-centeredness and best intentions to create technological designs that make a positive difference in people's lives. Only by becoming aware of these temptations, can we relate explicitly to them, and make conscious, well-informed, and critical choices throughout our technology design work. So how can designers and developers resist such "temptations" in their work?

**Temptation #1: Technology for Everything** The first temptation is to see technology as a relevant solution to most if not all challenges facing older adults. This includes a wide variety of situations from food and medication intake, to social contact, to the need to be physically active. The mixed results reported in literature on technology-based interventions, including AAL, telecare, and supporting technologies, raise questions as to the efficacy of all these technical interventions and show that technology does not always offer the right or best possible solution. For example, a need to be physically more active might be addressed through a playful gamification app, or an elaborate exergame, but in all likelihood, day-to-day physical activity may be better served through a tailored and subtle restructuring of a person's habitual, physical, and social living environment. Technology, in this situation, might be operating separately from the activities of daily life, or be integrated and become a natural part of it. The first question that needs to be asked is whether technology is at all relevant to the challenge and context at hand. This is not to be opposed to technology—quite the contrary—but if the same or better results can be achieved by non-technological means, technology should be taken out of the equation, and be used only where it can make a demonstrable positive difference.

**Temptation #2: Screens Everywhere** A Google search on "technology in dementia care" yields search results that are predominantly screen-based, such as iPads, laptops, smartphones, and the occasional robot—all with suspiciously healthy and happy-looking seniors using them. This admittedly impressionistic account of technology in dementia care is nonetheless representative of today's dominant approach to technology design. Screen-based interfaces represent interactions with software that can serve a multitude of functions. These devices are widely available, affordable, and easily scalable. However, despite these advantages, for the purposes of dementia care these screen-based devices also have properties that limit their suitability. Touch-based interfaces facilitate interaction with virtual objects using one or two fingers via a glass pane. The world that surrounds us and shapes our perceptual-motor experiences, however, is not confined to a smooth, cold, light-emitting, glass pane. In everyday life, we use our hands to manipulate and feel the physical world around us. We touch and hold objects, we feel their weight and balance, their texture and temperature. We rub, prod, push, feel, stroke, cuddle, and caress. The versatility inherent in these dexterous skills, and the richness of our tactile sensitivity is largely underutilized in screen-based approaches, where visual information lives behind the glass of a display. With increasing age, both visual sensitivity and motor skills tend to become compromised, which is yet another reason to invest in designs that support multimodal informational redundancy and the familiar richness of working with our hands (Brankaert 2016).

**Temptation #3: Sensors Everywhere** As older adults have a desire to remain independent in their homes and communities, novel home-based sensors or monitoring technologies are increasingly introduced to provide care and assist family caregivers. Smart home solutions are used to sense the environment in the form of, for example, video cameras, motion sensors, or pressure sensors. Sensors are also used on the person's body as activity trackers or, blood pressure sleeves, for example. These sensors can be used to serve a variety of functions to capture *"rational"* data, including remote health monitoring, medication reminder services, alarms, predictive diagnostics, or coaching. However, issues around consent, privacy, and dignity are rarely discussed. Furthermore, opaque causality chains based on sensing and actuation that occurs in smart homes can lead to incomplete and incorrect mental models or so-called "superstitious" learning—that is, misunderstanding or misattribution of the connection between the cause of an action and its experienced outcomes. This will also have likely detrimental effects to a person's sense of agency and control over technology, and may result in decreased self-efficacy and a sense of learned helplessness.

Aside from these implementation issues, more fundamental questions arise about who these sensor systems are actually serving. In many known examples, it is not the person who is being monitored who benefits from the system, but rather the person doing the monitoring—the care organization, care professionals, or informal carers. While there may be good reasons to utilize sensors in order to ensure the health and safety of older adults, there are a number of issues that affect the cost-benefit tradeoff of the extensive use of sensors in private home environments. Instead of focusing on physical or functional support, technology could also emphasize the more individual, emotional, and social aspects of human beings in need of support (Pudane et al. 2019).

An example of adverse effects of extensive behavior monitoring and intervention is provided by the iconic video "Uninvited Guests" (Superflux 2015), where the video's main character, Thomas, aged 70, is expected to use smart objects to track his behavior (specifically, eating, sleeping, and physical activity) and receives timely reminders through his smart watch from his children remotely monitoring his behavior. While each of the goals related to health behavior make individual sense, the video demonstrates the combined impact of impersonal monitoring technologies, a paternalistic and privacy-invasive approach to behavior intervention, and an overall focus on health behaviors and functions, rather than a more holistic approach to quality of life. In this video, Thomas is clearly not enjoying the nagging presence of the "friendly" reminders, leading to understandable reactance on his part, eventually tricking the system, and his remote children, rather than changing his behavior.

**Temptation #4: Using Interpreted "Natural" Interaction** In Human–Computer Interaction, "natural" interaction is somewhat of a "holy grail". In relation to interactive technologies, "natural" interaction is understood to be the ability to closely emulate and support inherent human interactional qualities and abilities, such as voice interfaces, gestural interfaces, or touch interfaces, rather than using arbitrary conventions and procedures for interaction. However, several issues arise in the current application of "natural" interaction (Norman 2010). For example, voice commands, that are being integrated into our everyday systems through smartphones and laptops, are ephemeral and do not provide visual cues about their current state or possible choices in relation to their responses. Similarly, gestural sensing such as with the Microsoft Kinect, while fun to interact with, lacks functional applications. Additionally, these systems provide limited feedforward to what is possible with the system, and we have to rely on memory to interact with them. This leads to problems in knowing what commands to use, of recognition by the system, error recovery, decreased task efficiency, and overall ambiguity. People with dementia often experience challenges with motor skills, language, and memory, and so the difficulty in interacting with these "natural" interfaces is amplified.

**Temptation #5: Integrating Services into a Single Application** Finally, many projects aim to focus on interoperability or integrating multiple services and technologies into a single system or interface. There are many examples available that describe technology integration efforts, resulting in telecare and smart home solutions to enhance older adults' independence and quality of life. A typical example of an integrated system is described by Nourizadeh et al. (2009): *"The system ... is equipped with technologies to monitor them and detect any abnormal state in their health situation, like bed and chair sensors, a mini PC connected to a TV, medical sensors, a wireless camera network. The system detects health abnormalities at an early stage through the frequent monitoring of physiological data."* Systems such as these aim to increase independence and to ultimately create health care savings. However, convincing underlying arguments as to why these systems should be connected and what makes them more easily accessible, remain unknown.

Often, multi-purpose systems such as a PC or iPad are used for integration purposes. However, such powerful, versatile, multi-purpose interfaces have an inherent drawback: complexity. The more services are integrated into a single device, the more complex an interface is likely to be, as it needs to manage different modes of operation. In addition, it requires a generic input or interaction style that may suit some applications and contexts-of-use more than others. Bill Buxton, in his classic text on the complexity of so-called "super-appliances" (Buxton 2001), likened such multi-purpose interfaces to Swiss army knives, in that they support a multitude of functions such as a saw, a spoon, a nail file, or corkscrew, but perform none of these functions particularly well. Moreover, each of these functions would typically be needed in a different task context—the workshop, the kitchen, the bathroom, etc. If technology for people living with dementia is designed well for specific needs and contexts, it tends to work better and is more likely to be useful.

## 3.5 Warm Technology

People with dementia are still often challenged by loss-of-control and stigmatization, whereas they would benefit from a more accepting environment. They sometimes feel as if they are not considered a "complete human being" (van Wijngaarden et al. 2019). Technology focused on functional support, as exemplified earlier in this chapter, tends to address deficits and deterioration and emphasizes the frailty and cognitive limitations of people with dementia. This starting point can lead to an inherent disempowerment, and an implicit lack of respect in data collection practices toward people with dementia and in the resulting designs made for them. The associated overgeneralization and underlying assumptions raise concern, since this impersonal approach does not generally promote well-being nor preserve dignity. There is an opportunity as well as an urgency for technology to address the needs of people with dementia, in providing a supporting role in dementia care, by a focus on enhancing the psychosocial qualities of life and well-being. To this aim, and in response to the temptations outlined above, we offer an alternative perspective with Warm Technology. This technology aimed at improving quality of life by supporting and enhancing human potential, social connectedness, dignity, and self-reliance. Warm Technology challenges traditional notions of technology as rational and efficient, yet impersonal, complicated, or uncaring. Warm technology also challenges the unproductive view that older age is primarily a phase of ill-health, inactivity, and steady decline. We have identified five elements that, taken together, define Warm Technology. They are

(1) A focus on the possible, the potential, and the wealth of skills and experiences older individuals possess or may wish to develop;
(2) Support for social and emotional needs, enhancing feel-good moments;
(3) Technology that is familiar, personally empowering, non-intimidating, and highly user-friendly, thus increasing self-reliance and self-efficacy;
(4) Aesthetically pleasing, non-stigmatizing design solutions, acknowledging the rich diversity in older age;
(5) Personalized designs, utilizing and supporting the richness of natural human sensory and motor system, and acknowledging personal context and history.

The technology resulting from this approach we see as enabling, user-friendly, personal, affect-centered, and non-stigmatizing, and therefore more likely to be accepted and to make a positive difference in the lives of people living with dementia.

### *3.5.1 Designing Warm Technology*

Design of Warm Technology emphasizes the inclusive perspective argued for throughout this book. This approach is based on user-centered design, and involves treating people with dignity and respect, and developing mutual trust and an understanding of personal histories, context and preferences. This means including people with dementia as co-designers of the technology, using iterative engagement and ensuring there are many touchpoints with people with dementia (Brankaert et al. 2015). Additionally, a design-driven "Living Lab" approach is used to allow for experimentation, with evaluation conducted in a real-life context (Brankaert and Den Ouden 2017). For these evaluations, appropriate methods are selected and adapted for inclusion of people with dementia. In developing Warm Technology a person-centered care philosophy is adhered to (Ross et al. 2015), which arose from the disabilities field and can be characterized by the motto *"no decision about me, without me"*. Here, person-centered care positions the person receiving care as an equal partner in planning and executing care. So, to develop Warm Technology we need to consider the lived experience of people with dementia and, like person-centered care in care practice, take the perspective of people being cared for as a starting point. Furthermore, Warm Technology builds on the principles of value-sensitive design (Friedman et al. 2009), which promotes dignity, autonomy, privacy, freedom, compassion, trust and meaningful relational connections (Foley et al. 2019). Thus, this approach emphasizes the individuality and uniqueness of each person living with dementia.

Conducting user engagements in Living Lab environments fosters an attitude of reflection, experimentation, and openness in the home or care environment to enable designers and developers to quickly learn from technology implementation (Brankaert and Den Ouden 2017). Using adapted research techniques, such as interviews, observations or probes, we can work with people living with dementia, and analyze their experiences and understand their adoption of technology in context. Both Nygård (2006) and Bartlett (2012) emphasize the importance of giving people with dementia a sense of control during research by, for example, allowing them to decide whether, when, where, or how to provide input to research.

Issues relating to ethics when working with vulnerable people, such as people with dementia, require careful consideration. Special attention needs to be given to the process of gaining informed consent. This needs to be transformed from a one-off information exchange resulting in consent being given to a continuous dialog (Coughlan et al. 2013). Furthermore, as dementia is progressive, the participant's desire to take part, or their satisfying the participatory conditions, may change significantly over the course of the research. Those who retain the duty of care in relation to participation need be to actively involved in the process, and continuously monitor the status of consent in order to safeguard the integrity and interests of the participant at all times. Challenges in adapting well-established research and informed consent methods to fit the needs and abilities of people with dementia is, in part, the reason why there has been a scarcity of first-hand perspectives in technology design for people with dementia to date (see also Scholzel-Dorenbos et al. 2010; Span et al. 2013).

### 3.5.2 *Warm Technology: Three Design Cases*

Health care professionals often voice concerns that technology will replace interpersonal contact in care. These worries may arise because of a lack of knowledge and awareness of the wide range of opportunities offered by humane and dignified technological applications for people living with dementia. Three Warm Technology design examples are showcased below that illustrate the potential and opportunities of this approach.

**Stay-Tuned Radio** In the earlier stages of dementia people can feel lonely, there are often fewer people around and grown-up children might have left home and live far away. But, the need for social connection remains, and social interaction is greatly beneficial for people with dementia. Family members can, from their side, feel the urgency and longing to be connected to their relatives with dementia, to be able to maintain social bonds and satisfy mutual emotional attachment.

The "Stay-Tuned" radio is a communication system designed by Marjolein Wintermans—den Haan (Wintermans et al. 2017). The device integrates WhatsApp®, a popular messaging application, with a familiar 60 s radio exterior (Fig. 3.1). Family members can record voice messages and send them to the radio via WhatsApp®. Small pictures of family members appear on the front panel of the radio and the person with dementia can select one of these pictures with the left knob and listen to the messages from that person. They can adjust the volume with the right knob. The interaction is kept simple and familiar and is reminiscent of a radio interface, building further on their technology experiences in their formative years. A person with dementia is able to listen to messages, music, or other personalized sound clips from their family members, and interact with the radio by themselves. This system caters to the needs of both the person with dementia and family members.

**Fig. 3.1** The Stay-Tuned Radio

**Fig. 3.2** The Homing Compass

**Homing Compass** The "Homing Compass" is a simple navigation system with one simple feature, its arrow always points homewards (Brankaert and Suijkerbuijk 2019; Fig. 3.2). Traditional GPS solutions for people living with dementia are tracking devices that primarily facilitate the needs of family members and caregivers to enable them to trace a person with dementia. The person with dementia is not an active part of the engagement, but becomes the object to be tracked. The "Homing Compass" is inclusive for people with dementia as it provides a user interface to navigate home by themselves, while still being traceable if needed. The design's exterior is reminiscent of wayfinding devices such as a compass to aesthetically support the acceptance and usability of the system. It has a pleasurable tactile quality and a sturdy, high-quality look-and-feel. Additional features such as a map, auditory feedback and alternate route selection were initially considered in the design process, but removed from the device to retain its simplicity. In understanding and supporting the strengths and possibilities of people with dementia, we need to offer challenging physical as well as emotional stimuli and do so in a simple, non-intimidating way. This solution helps people cope with the disorientation that can occur in an unfamiliar place.

**VITA Music Pillow** VITA is a music pillow for people living with dementia to provide them with access to sound and music (Fig. 3.3). VITA stimulates social connectedness, storytelling, and the experience of touch, through sound (Houben et al. 2020). It has a fabric-based interface, with six soft-touch sensors integrated into the pillow that people with dementia or their carers can touch to activate the playing of music and sound files. The audio is carefully selected together with family members to facilitate positive mental associations and provide a meaningful experience for people living with dementia. VITA has a web interface for caregivers to select and upload suitable music and sound fragments, including personal messages. The interfaces enable different sound palettes to be selected to cater to the needs of different users through a single VITA. The interface circumvents the complexity that is commonly present when accessing audio, such as smart devices, PCs, or radio systems.

**Fig. 3.3** The VITA sound interface pillow

### *3.5.3 Challenges for Warm Technology*

The design cases provide examples of how the Warm Technology approach may support user-friendly, inclusive and non-stigmatizing technology for people living with dementia, developed in close cooperation with them. Nevertheless, we see there are also several challenges for Warm Technology. Firstly, the route from research and prototype development to a product on the market is difficult, particularly because of not wanting to lose the strengths inherent in person-centered work. The expectations in relation to the development of some of the existing prototype technologies designed for people with dementia need to be managed. Many of these are still under development and time to market can be very slow, up to 10 years. Furthermore, potentially, driven by market mechanisms, products coming to market can only become viable by focusing on implementation and scale as opposed to what makes it meaningful for people living with dementia.

Secondly, there are clear challenges regarding the evaluation of the use and acceptance of technologies outside of a research context. Short-term studies of technology deployment and use allow insights into people's general attitudes and opinions toward technology, and may help to identify potential usability issues. However, how researchers and designers "prime" or introduce people to the technology inextricably impacts the technology's evaluation. Therefore outcomes of studies need to be interpreted with care, being aware of the fact that findings from a research study, where technology has been carefully introduced, do not necessarily apply to technology that as gone to market. Despite several efforts over the past years, there is a paucity of research on how to implement technological innovations in the everyday lives of people with dementia, particularly when there are organizational issues with implementing technology such as lack of time and motivation in caregivers that need to be overcome.

Thirdly, Warm Technology and its implications for design are still under development. Currently, it offers an appealing perspective to work toward. However, the ways in which to operationalize it in service delivery, functionality and aesthetics of technology will require further work. Moreover, the manifestations of Warm Technology and the extent to which it is successful in achieving its stated goals of social connectedness, self-efficacy, well-being, and quality of life need further investigation as well. The overarching aim is to focus on supporting and enhancing human potential, augmenting feelings of well-being in using technology that is personalized, respectful and user-friendly, encouraging a positive outlook on technology design for dementia, and a recognition of the enormous potential in this area.

## 3.6 Conclusion

Returning to the story of Odysseus, we want designers and developers to be inspired but also to be critical of their own work and not to be tempted by the Siren songs of technology. We need to realize technology is no panacea, and be aware of the frequent mismatch between the dominant solutions offered in AAL and telecare technologies today—through screens, sensors, "natural" interactions, and technology integration—and the personal needs of people living with dementia.

In this chapter, we presented the concept of Warm Technology, which redirects our focus from providing efficient and clinical support in view of the limitations and ongoing deterioration associated with dementia, to a more emancipated notion of aging, and a technology design process that is sensitive to the possibilities and unique qualities of old age—personal, affective, social, contextualized, and embodied. To research, develop, implement, and scale Warm Technology concepts for people with dementia, Eindhoven University of Technology (TU/e) initiated the cross-disciplinary Dementia and Technology Centre of Expertise (www.Dementiaandtechnology.com). This center is a research collaboration and networking hub with a focus on Warm Technology to improve the quality of life of people living with dementia. In our work, we collaborate with other research centers and care organizations, establishing Living Labs that enable the inclusion of the people with dementia early in the design process.

In sum, Warm Technology aims to address a gap in the development of current technology for people living with dementia. To understand the potential of Warm Technology for design an open attitude is needed to see the positive impact that technology can have on the emotions and well-being of people who are endeavoring to age successfully and to live happy and fulfilled lives. At a societal level, we need to remove the stigmatization associated with dementia, and regard people with dementia with dignity, recognizing their personhood (Kontos and Martin 2013), and bringing humanity and compassion to aging, rather than focusing on the rhetoric of fighting, beating or overcoming dementia. We need to recognize that for the foreseeable future dementia exists in society and is the reality for individual people. Warm technology offers a way forward to design technology, that will enhance the ability of people with dementia to live well, with an increased quality of life.

## References


Bartlett R (2012) Modifying the diary interview method to research the lives of people with dementia. Qual Health Res 22(12):1717–1726. https://doi.org/10.1177/1049732312462240

Brankaert R, Den Ouden PH, Brombacher AC (2015) Innovate dementia: the development of a living lab protocol to evaluate interventions in context. Info 17(4):40–52. https://doi.org/10.1108/info-01-2015-0010

Brankaert R (2016) Design for dementia: a design-driven living lab approach to involve people with dementia and their context. Technische Universiteit Eindhoven, Eindhoven

Brankaert R, Den Ouden PH (2017) The design-driven living lab: a new approach to exploring solutions to complex societal challenges. Technol Innov Manage Rev 7(1):44–51

Brankaert R, Suijkerbuijk S (2019) Outdoor life and technology with dementia. In: Astell A, Smith S, Joddrell P (eds) Using technology in dementia care: a guide to technology solutions for everyday living. Jessica Kingsley Publishers, London, pp 53–64

Buxton B (2001) Less is more (more or less). In: Denning PJ (ed.) The invisible future—the seamless integration of technology in everyday life. McGraw-Hill, New York, pp 145–179

Coughlan T, Mackley LK, Brown M, Martindale S, Schloegl S, Mallaband B, … Hine N (2013) Current issues and future directions in methods for studying technology in the home. PsychNology 11(2):159–184

Docampo Rama M, de Ridder H, Bouma H (2001) Technology generation and age in using layered user interfaces. Gerontechnology 1(1):25–40. https://doi.org/10.4017/gt.2001.01.01.003.00

Fitzpatrick G, Huldtgren A, Malmborg L, Harley D, Ijsselsteijn W (2015) Design for agency, adaptivity and reciprocity: reimagining AAL and telecare agendas. In: Designing socially embedded technologies in the real-world. Springer, London, pp 305–338

Foley S, Pantidi N, McCarthy J (2019) Care and design: an ethnography of mutual recognition in the context of advanced dementia. In: Proceedings of the 2019 CHI conference on human factors in computing systems—CHI '19 May 04, 2019, Glasgow, Scotland UK. ACM, New York, USA. https://doi.org/10.1145/3290605.3300840

Friedman B, Kahn PH, Borning A (2009) Value sensitive design and information systems. In: The handbook of information and computer ethics, vol 2003. Wiley, Hoboken, pp 69–101

Gitlin LN, Marx K, Stanley IH, Hodgson N (2015) Translating evidence-based dementia caregiving interventions into practice: state-of-the-science and next steps. Gerontologist 55(2):210–226

Greenhalgh T, Procter R, Wherton J, Sugarhood P, Shaw S (2012) The organizing vision for telehealth and telecare: discourse analysis. BMJ Open 2(4):e001574. https://doi.org/10.1136/bmjopen-2012-001574

Houben M, Brankaert R, Bakker S, Kenning G, Bongers I, Eggen B (2020). The role of everyday sounds in advanced dementia care. In: Proceedings of the 2020 CHI conference on human factors in computing systems—CHI '20. ACM, New York, USA, 1–14. https://doi.org/10.1145/3313831.3376577

Kontos P, Martin W (2013) Embodiment and dementia: exploring critical narratives of selfhood, surveillance, and dementia care. Dementia 12(3):288–302

Lazar A, Edasis C, Piper AM (2017) A critical lens on dementia and design in HCI. In: Proceedings of the 2017 CHI conference on human factors in computing systems—CHI '17, ACM, New York, USA, pp 2175–2188. https://doi.org/10.1145/3025453.3025522

Miranda-Castillo C, Woods B, Orrell M (2010) People with dementia living alone: what are their needs and what kind of support are they receiving? Int Psychogeriatr 22(4):607–617

Norman D (1988) The psychology of everyday things. Basic Books, New York

Norman D (2010) Natural user interfaces are not natural. Interactions 17(3):6–10

Norman D (2019) I wrote the book on user-friendly design. What I see today horrifies me. Fast Co. https://www.fastcompany.com/90338379/i-wrote-the-book-on-user-friendly-design-what-i-see-today-horrifies-me. Accessed 19 Nov 2019

Nourizadeh S, Deroussent C, Song YQ, Thomesse JP (2009) Medical and home automation sensor networks for senior citizens telehomecare. In: 2009 IEEE international conference on communications workshops, pp 1–5. IEEE. https://doi.org/10.1109/ICCW.2009.5208093

Nygård L (2006) How can we get access to the experiences of people with dementia? Suggestions and reflections. Scand J Occup Ther 13(2):101–112

Orpwood R, Bjorneby S, Hagen I, Maki O, Faulkner R, Topo P (2004) User involvement in dementia product development. Dementia 3(3):263–279

Orrell M, Hancock GA, Liyanage KCG, Woods B, Challis D, Hoe J (2008) The needs of people with dementia in care homes: the perspectives of users, staff and family caregivers. Int Psychogeriatr 20(5):941–951

Peek S, Wouters EJ, van Hoof J, Luijkx KG, Boeije HR, Vrijhoef HJ (2014) Factors influencing acceptance of technology for aging in place: a systematic review. Int J Med Inf 83:235–248

Pudane M, Petrovica S, Lavendelis E, Ekenel HK (2019) Towards truly affective AAL systems. In: Ganchev I et al (eds) Enhanced living environments, LNCS 11369, pp 152–176. https://doi.org/10.1007/978-3-030-10752-9_7

Ross H, Tod AM, Clarke A (2015) Understanding and achieving person-centred care: the nurse perspective. J Clin Nurs 24(9–10):1223–1233

Segal L (2014) Out of time: The pleasures and the perils of ageing. Verso, London and New York, pp 3–4

Span M, Hettinga M, Vernooij-Dassen M, Eefsting J, Smits C (2013) Involving people with dementia in the development of supportive IT applications: a systematic review. Ageing Res Rev 12(2):535–551. https://doi.org/10.1016/j.arr.2013.01.002

Suijkerbuijk S, Nap HH, Cornelisse L, IJsselsteijn WA, de Kort YAW, Minkman MMN (2019). Active involvement of people with dementia: a systematic review of studies developing supportive technologies. J Alzheimer's Dis 69(4):1041–1065. https://doi.org/10.3233/JAD-190050

Superflux (2015) Uninvited Guests, a film created by Superflux Lab for the ThingTank project. For further information visit: superflux.in/work/uninvited-guests. https://vimeo.com/128873380

Van der Roest HG, Meiland FJM, Comijs HC, Derksen E, Jansen APD, van Hout HP J, Jonker C, ... Droes RM (2009) What do community-dwelling people with dementia need? A survey of those who are known to care and welfare services. Int Psychogeriatr 21(5):949–965

Van Wijngaarden E, Alma M, The A-M (2019) "the eyes of others" are what really matters: the experience of living with dementia form an insider perspective. PLoS ONE 14(4):e0214724. https://doi.org/10.1371/journal.pone.0214724

Wintermans M, Brankaert R, Lu Y (2017) Together we do not forget: co-designing with people living with dementia towards a design for social inclusion. In: Proceedings of the design management academy 2017. International Conference, Hong Kong, vol 2, pp 767–782

# Chapter 4
# Personalization and Compassionate Design

**Cathy Treadaway**

## 4.1 Introduction

This chapter discusses the importance of personalization when designing products for dementia care. It presents arguments for keeping the person at the heart of the design process and research methods that enable this to happen.

### *4.1.1 Context*

Dementia is without doubt one of the major health challenges facing society today (Patterson 2018). The increasing number of people living with the disease into the more advanced stages presents a looming crisis for the care sector. The lack of specialized dementia care service provision and the increasing economic impact of large numbers of people with high levels of dependency has become a major concern for many countries around the world (Prince et al. 2015). Creating designs to assist in the activities of daily living and support the well-being of people living with dementia is imperative as there are few drugs available that can ameliorate the distressing symptoms of confusion, agitation and memory loss that characterize the disease (Livingston et al. 2017).

One of the difficulties in designing for people affected by dementia is the complexity of the condition. The term 'dementia' is used to describe collectively over 100 different diseases of the brain, each presenting and progressing differently (Alzheimer's Research UK 2016); Alzheimer's disease is the most common form of dementia. Individuals are affected uniquely by the disease depending on personal circumstances, past experiences and social relationships. Although memory loss is most commonly

C. Treadaway (✉)
Cardiff Metropolitan University, Cardiff, Wales
e-mail: CTreadaway@cardiffmet.ac.uk

© Springer Nature Switzerland AG 2020

R. Brankaert and G. Kenning (eds.), *HCI and Design in the Context of Dementia*, Human–Computer Interaction Series,
https://doi.org/10.1007/978-3-030-32835-1_4

associated with dementia, perceptual and behavioural changes can predominate in some forms of the disease. This wide variety in the characterization of dementia explains why it is vital to focus on the needs of the individual and not the symptoms of the disease and explains why a focus on 'personalization' in the context of design is so important.

Keeping the person living with dementia at the heart of the design process is crucial if designs are to be appropriate and useful. Including dementia 'experts by experience'—those living with the disease and those that are involved intimately with their care, helps to provide unique insights into the needs of individuals and their specific design requirements. This approach can enable highly personalized designs to be created (Hendricks et al. 2017).

### *4.1.2 Keeping the Individual at the Heart of the Design Process*

Including people living with dementia in research is widely acknowledged as being vital for the success of any design outcome, however, this has not always been the case. Until the 1990s the prevailing medicalized view of dementia perceived people living with the disease as 'sufferers' in need of a cure. Research tended to be done *to* rather than *with* people living with dementia and prioritized the physical, rather than psychosocial aspects of the disease (Higgins 2013). Fresh perspectives on dementia were introduced into care practice as a result of the work of Tom Kitwood and others, who promoted the concepts of 'person-' care (Kitwood 1997; Kitwood and Brendin 2008). This radical and inclusive viewpoint has had a profound beneficial impact on healthcare strategies and research approaches, valuing the inclusion of those living with dementia in studies.

Kitwood's theories have recently been extended and revised to reflect changing societal attitudes (Dewing 2008; Brooker and Kitwood 2019). Dementia has more recently been reconceptualized as a disability, recognizing a person's citizenship and need to promote and protect their human rights. There is a growing awareness of the need to preserve the dignity, autonomy and quality of life of individuals affected by the disease (Milne 2010; Brooker and Kitwood 2019). Language used in the context of dementia reflects these changing attitudes. In the UK the DEEP Language Guide, developed by people living with dementia in conjunction with the UK Network of Dementia Voices, is an essential resource for those working in the field of design for dementia (DEEP 2014).[1] The guide proposes forms of words that are acceptable, positive and empowering to people living with dementia and so challenges the negative stereotypes that have prevailed in society for so long.

[1] http://dementiavoices.org.uk/wp-content/uploads/2015/03/DEEP-Guide-Language.pdf (accessed 05.05.2019).

### *4.1.3 Ethical Considerations*

Including people living with dementia in research recognizes their human right to be involved, and values them as individual citizens with their own unique perspectives and opinions. Gaining informed consent for their inclusion in research, however, poses complex ethical issues as someone living with dementia may have limited mental capacity, memory loss and communication difficulties (Mullins 2018). Although it may be possible to gain approval for inclusion of a person living with dementia from relatives and carers, it is important to recognize that the proxy may override the person's view, were they able to express it. Also, a person living with dementia does not *automatically* lack capacity to consent for themselves. It may be possible to identify their wishes, even for those living with the later stages of the disease. This can be done with the guidance of a relative or carer who knows the person well, via an empathic and sensitive interpretation of physical and facial expressions (body language). A 'process method', in which informed consent is sought each time a person takes part in a research activity, can enable a person living with dementia to be included in a study. Process methods may include visual rather than written information as non-verbal communication tools (Higgins 2013). The important aspect of this approach is that 'people who lack capacity remain at the centre of decision making and are fully safeguarded' (NMC 2008 cited in Higgins 2013).

## 4.2 Person and Relational Care

The importance of personhood in relation to design for dementia cannot be overstated, as it is key in maintaining a person's dignity and value (Kontos and Naglie 2006). Dementia changes the person's cognitive functioning, behaviour, as well as memories of lived experiences. However, there is a common misperception that the disease 'destroys the person' (Sabat and Harré 1992; Holton 2016) and that they become 'lost', 'absent' or 'no longer there'. These attitudes can lead to relationship breakdown, marginalization, isolation and neglect and so need to be challenged (Eckman et al. (1991) cited in Kontos and Naglie 2006). This assumed 'loss of selfhood' arises from the impact of the disease on cognition, memory and communication, which are so highly valued in our contemporary hypercognitive western culture (Dewing 2008). Sabat and Harré (1992), contend that 'loss of self' arises primarily from how others view and treat the person living with dementia. The effect of this on a person is devastating, exacerbating the distressing symptoms of the disease such as agitation, anxiety and depression. There is a clear need to find ways to maintain personhood and reaffirm a person's sense of identity (Kontos and Naglie 2006).

### 4.2.1 Personhood—What Is It? Why Does It Matter?

Although some aspects of personhood are constructed socially, provided and guaranteed by the presence of others (Wallace et al. 2013), our self-identity is preconscious, embodied and can persist far into the end stage of the disease (Sabat and Harré 1992; Kontos and Martin 2013; Hughes 2014). Our embodied selves do not require the cooperation of others to exist nor do they require memory recall. We are situated embodied agents whose lived experience is sedimented into our very beings, physically and emotionally through our contact with others and the world around us (Hughes 2014). This can be observed in the expressiveness of the body via gesture and body movement; communicating personality, character and cultural experience that is unique and individual (Kontos and Naglie 2006).

### 4.2.2 Memory and Identity

Lived experience shapes body and mind simultaneously by providing us with both *explicit* and *implicit* memories (LeDoux 1998). Explicit memories (those that can be expressed and communicated) can be shaped by thought and words and it is this type of memory that is most likely compromised by dementia. However, implicit memories, both emotional and procedural (muscle memories which are acquired through repeated activities of daily living), can be retained late into the disease. These help to contribute to the unique self-identity that makes a person who they are, even when they can no longer remember for themselves. A person's individual preferences are shaped by a lifetime of sensory experiences and intuition (preconscious and automatic responses). These contribute details about an individual, as do the constantly changing challenges and experiences of living with the disease. No person remains the same through a lifetime; we are constantly changing and evolving in response to the context in which our lives unfold.

Our identity is also shaped by the context of our lives and the things we own, the environment and culture in which we live and how it is reflected back to us. Those people who make up the social circle of a person living with dementia are crucially important. They are the guardians and maintainers of personhood and can be considered 'active participants' in a two-way process that is relational and dynamic (Wallace et al. 2013). Some aspects of 'self' are constructed socially, through conversation, storytelling, reminiscence and reflection with others. In addition, an individual's possessions and clothing can act as mediators, communicating vital detail about a person's identity over time and through the progression of the disease.

A person living with dementia is not 'lost' as a result of living with the disease; they remain corporeally the same person and, as citizens of 'a just and civilized society', have rights to be recognized, included and treated with compassion (Hughes 2014 pp. 75). Finding ways to uncover, preserve and communicate the personhood of a person living with dementia enables others to continue to see the person and not the disease. Design has a significant role to play in helping to achieve this. Integration of technology: electronics, smart materials, digital fabrication and programmable technologies, now enable products and environments to be designed that have the potential to be bespoke or easily personalisable. The following section focuses on ways in which designers are incorporating technology to create personalized products for people affected by dementia.

## 4.3 Technology and Personhood

Digital and communications technologies provide designers with an array of useful tools to enable products to be customized, through the inclusion of highly relevant personal content including photographs, music files and text. Physical computing, wireless technologies and robotics can be used to create bespoke physical objects to assist in activities of daily living and to support the well-being of people affected by dementia (Hendricks et al. 2017; Kenning 2017; Treadaway et al. 2018b). Published product design research for dementia focuses on several key areas: assistive and enabling technologies (memory aids and tracking devices), reminiscence (apps and resources for sharing personal histories), performative and sensory enriched environments (communication apps, devices to stimulate dance, Snoezelen spaces) and activities (playful objects, music and sensory devices). A number of common themes emerge from research findings including the ethical dilemmas that dementia research poses[2]; the emotional impact of undertaking the research on all involved and the legacy it leaves behind; the importance of contextual understanding and appropriate design for the stage of dementia that the participants are living with; the need to build relationships to foster empathy and trust, and most significant of all, the need to create highly personalized design solutions.

### *4.3.1 Personalized Reminiscence*

There is a bewildering array of smartphone and tablet apps designed to support the functional and cognitive aspects of daily life for people living with dementia at the early to mid-stages. Some of these are designed specifically to help a person retain their identity through personalized multimedia story making. In 2016, the UK Government and leading dementia charities launched a new platform called Dementia Citizens to 'help people with dementia and those who care for them, using apps on smartphones and tablets'[3] (Critten and Kucirkova 2017). In particular two apps have been developed and promoted via this platform: 'Book of You' and 'Playlist for

[2]See Hughes (2014) 'How we think about dementia' for further guidance on ethical issues.

[3]https://www.nesta.org.uk/blog/dementia-citizens-learning-from-a-citizen-science-platform-for-dementia-research/ acc 02.02.19.

Life'. Both are designed for use by people living with dementia and their carers to stimulate moments of positive remembering through selected favourite music and personal history information and images.[4]

Digital personalization is a technique enabled by touchscreen devices such as smartphones and tablets, that provide access to multimedia formats (video, still photographs, audio recording). These devices provide a number of ways of recording, compiling and replaying media, delivering multiple prompts to elicit memory (Ibid). The apps provide a creative platform to design personalized multimedia stories to stimulate and share long-term memories of people who live with mild to moderate dementia. They aim to help a person retain a sense of self-identity through the story and then be able to share it with others. These apps work best when the person living with dementia is supported by a sensitive caregiver who is a sympathetic listener and will not add to or interrupt the storytelling. They require a degree of digital competence and dedicated time, to practice and get used to the software.

Reminiscence activities can be highly beneficial for people in the earlier stages of the disease, however, as memory is increasingly impacted, they may highlight what has been *lost* and cannot be recovered as a result of dementia. Consequently, there is a need to also celebrate the *present*—especially as it becomes increasingly difficult or confusing to try and remember the past.

#### 4.3.1.1 Objects that Contribute to Sensory Enriched Environments

'In the moment' experiences are vital for people when memory fails and the ability to perceive the reality others experience is challenged by the disease. Non-verbal methods of interaction become increasingly vital, as do ways of stimulating the senses through sight, hearing, smell and tactile interaction (Lykkeslet et al. 2014). Without encouragement, a person living with dementia can become increasingly locked within their own universe and lose connection with others and the world around them (Ibid). Products and environments that stimulate the senses have been found to soothe, engage and support pleasurable experience and so enhance the well-being of people in the mid to late stages of the disease (Bennett et al. 2016; Treadaway and Kenning 2016; Jakob and Collier 2017). Digital technologies such as music players, sensory e-textiles, interactive objects that respond to movement or emit light, can be incorporated into environments and can be programmed for individual preferences, such as choice of music or favourite colour (Treadaway and Kenning 2016).

[4]There are many other similar apps including: Our Story; My Story; Book Creator; Story Maker; CIRCA project; Living in the moment project.

#### 4.3.1.2 Products to Engage and Give Pleasure and Meaning

People living with the mid to late stages of dementia often become anxious, agitated or alternatively increasingly passive and disengaged from the world. Finding ways to soothe a person who is experiencing 'ill-being' or boredom as a result of the disease, can be a real challenge since there may be multiple factors involved. Objects and engagement with activities can provide successful alternative ways of soothing a person without the need to resort to medication (Cohen-Mansfield et al. 2012). Examples include interactive sensory textiles (Treadaway and Kenning 2016), soothing objects, (Treadaway and Kenning 2016; Treadaway et al. 2019), music boxes and playful objects (Morrissey et al. 2016; Branco 2017; Treadaway et al. 2018c). By integrating technology, these objects can become personally meaningful, enabling a person to respond emotionally even if they are unable to remember the past significance of the object or song, etc. (Wallace et al. 2013; Bennett et al. 2016; Treadaway et al. 2018c).

#### 4.3.1.3 Approaches to Design

Designers working successfully in this field use participatory and co-design research methods with a strong focus on empathy and inclusion (Hendriks et al. 2014; Branco et al. 2017). Experience Centered Design (ECD) is a design approach that has been used successfully to ensure that concepts are appropriate to the individual needs of a person living with dementia (Morrissey et al. 2017). This method aims to illuminate the participants lived and felt experience resulting in designs that are an empathic response to their needs and wishes. Co-design and design probes are used to provide a richer understanding of the *experience* of personhood in dementia and inform the development of sensitive and meaningful designs. Wallace's work in designing digital jewellery exemplifies this co-creative approach (Wallace et al. 2013). The use of probes helps to mediate a close relationship between researcher and the person living with dementia, helps to structure the inquiry and to scaffold the reflection and dialogue which unfolds throughout the process. The relational aspect of working in this way echoes the social construction of personhood through storytelling, reflection and dialogue (Sabat and Harré 2008).

Kenning's 'Making it Together' project found that active participation of people living with dementia in design research provided reciprocal benefits for both designers and participants (Kenning 2017). The designers were able to grow their skills, knowledge and understanding of dementia empathically with the participants who enjoyed the creative stimulation, building their self-esteem and thereby supporting their wellbeing. Reciprocal design celebrates the value of making together as a deeply insightful method of design inquiry for dementia.

Following diagnosis, people living with dementia may live for many years with gradually increasing levels of dependency and everyday care needs. Simultaneously, their capacity to make their own decisions about care and lifestyle choices diminishes as the disease progresses. Understanding how life changes for a person living with

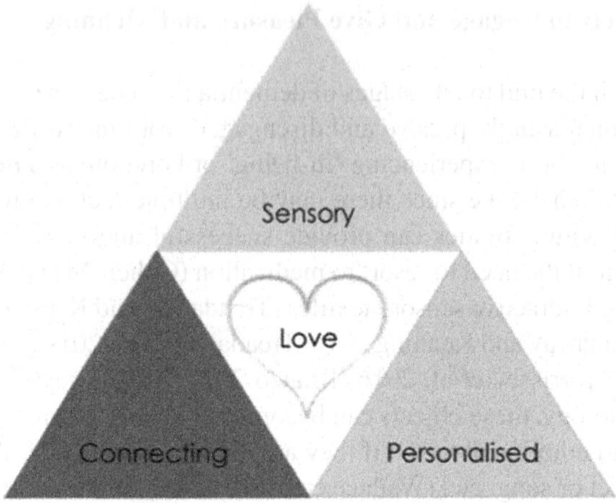


**Fig. 4.1** Compassionate design

dementia is essential if designers and technologists are to create appropriate and *care-full* designs that help people live well with the disease until the end of life. When people are in the later stages of dementia it is increasingly difficult for them to communicate their personal preferences within the co-design process. Finding ways to keep them central in a loving, caring and positive way is vital to developing appropriate and useful products. Compassionate Design[5] (Treadaway et al. 2018a) is an approach directly informed by dementia experts and people living with advanced dementia, that places loving kindness at the heart of the design process (Fig. 4.1). It prioritizes three key areas in design development, focusing on personalization, *sensory* stimulation and encouraging *connection* (with others and the world around them). The following section describes LAUGH design research that developed and tested the Compassionate Design approach.

### *4.3.2 LAUGH Project: A Case Study Using Compassionate Design*

The LAUGH research project was a three-year qualitative study that developed a range of hand-held playful objects for people living with advanced dementia[6] (Treadaway et al. 2019). The research aimed to inform the creation of stimulating, pleasurable and soothing objects to help in the care of people living with advanced dementia. The research was underpinned by Compassionate Design, focussing design thinking

[5]Free to download from: https://www.laughproject.info/wp-content/uploads/2018/04/Compassionate-Design_toolkit.pdf.

[6]LAUGH project 2015-2018 Funder by UK Arts and Humanities Research Council Grant ref: AH/M005607/1.

on the three key themes of personalization, sensory stimulation and connections with others and the world. The initial participatory research examined the role of hand-use and the importance of procedural and emotional memory in promoting subjective well-being, playfulness and pleasure (Treadaway et al. 2018b). This knowledge was used to shape designs for highly personalized playful objects for a small group of residents in two residential dementia care homes.

The participants, their caregivers and families, worked closely with the research team to ensure that the designs were personalized, safe and easy to use. Most, although not all of the designs, included technology that extended their sensory properties (music, vibration, lights) and enabled them to be highly personalized. Examples of playful objects that were developed included: an interactive steering wheel for a man who had been a roadside recovery driver and mechanic (Fig. 4.2); a set of 'giggle balls' that giggle with children's laughter when held in the hand, for a woman who had been a keen bowls player (Fig. 4.3); a retro telephone in a box that plays Spanish conversation and songs, for a woman who had lived in Spain (Fig. 4.4) and a soft textile object 'HUG' (reminiscent of a baby with a beating heart and music player) for a grandmother who had become withdrawn and unresponsive (Fig. 4.5). Several of the designs included small microcontrollers with speakers that contained a personalized music playlist of favourite songs. Carers and relatives noted that the personalization of the designs had stimulated positive emotion and, in some cases, provoked surprising and intense moments of sensory reawakening in which past memories were recalled and expressed (Treadaway et al. 2018c).

#### 4.3.2.1 How to Personalize: Developing 'Portraits'

Each of the LAUGH designs was informed by detailed *portrait* of the person living with dementia, developed in collaboration with family members, care staff and the person themselves (Fig. 4.6). Building relationships with research participants, including people living with dementia, their caregivers and family members, is important for gaining their trust—essential when gleaning detailed information to help to personalize designs. Designers often use *personas* (fictional descriptions of likely end users) to help focus design development. *Personas* are used to help to ensure the suitability of a design for a particular market sector or type of customer. In the LAUGH research, *portraits* rather than *personas* were developed, in order to ensure that designs were bespoke. Portraits comprised of visual sketches and brief written texts capturing elements of a person's life history and preferences, including their favourite colours, music playlists, favourite hobbies, pets, holiday locations, etc. They also included their current preferences, evolved as a result of ageing or living with dementia. For example, increased sound volume for someone with impaired hearing, brighter colours for a person with visual impairment or reduced sensory information to avoid overload and confusion. In addition, a drawn portrait of the face of the person was made by one of the research team. The process of creating this pencil sketch helped to stimulate a deeper feeling of connection and commitment to

Fig. 4.2 LAUGH steering wheel

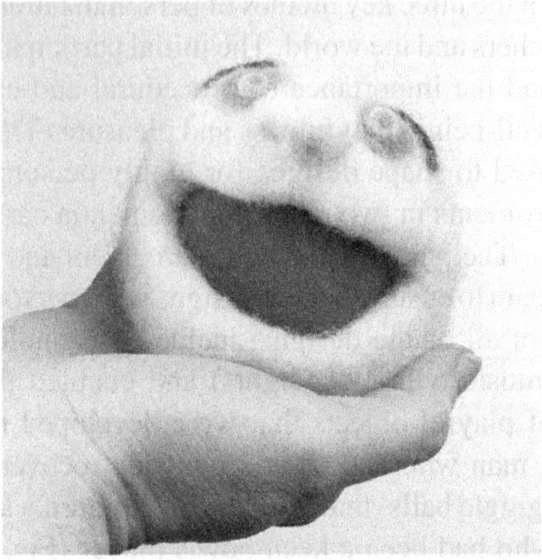

Fig. 4.3 LAUGH giggle balls

Fig. 4.4 LAUGH telephone

Fig. 4.5 LAUGH HUG

the individual participants, focusing mindful attention on the person's past history as well as their current life with dementia.

Trying to knit together and briefly summarize information about an individual's many years of lived experience is not simple. Nevertheless, the process can reveal a whole range of potential themes to inspire the design process. It also provides a creative starting point that keeps the person living with dementia at the very heart of the process. Collecting portrait information also stimulates communication with relatives and carers, keeping them involved in the process as well as helping to promote the importance of personhood. Highly personalized designs also help to celebrate and emphasize an individuals' continued value as a human being throughout their dementia journey; the resulting designs are more likely to engage their interest.

is 97 and has lived in residential care for 12 years. She was born and grew up in Spain and Spanish is her mother tongue although she has lived in Wales most of her life. Her parents died when she was a child and she was adopted by a Spanish family with three other children.

was in the WRAF during the war and worked in the Officer's Mess. After the war her family ran a fish and chip shop and in later working life she was a school cook.

She enjoyed gardening (flowers) and playing bingo. Her favorite pet was her white cat called Sheba.

is very 'potchy' and active but has problems with her vision and so needs bright colours with high contrast. She particularly likes blues and violets. Her favorite smell is lavender.

likes chatting and needs attention and conversation. She likes balls to play with and loves people sitting with her. She doesn't watch TV but likes music especially old songs.

She doesn't like: to feel constrained, dislikes blankets and things over her legs and being cuddled.

is 83 and has only recently been moved to residential care from hospital. working life has involved driving and working as a car mechanic. He worked for the RAC, drove taxis and worked as a garage mechanic.

He is currently very 'potchy' and seems to be comforted by tactile sensory stimulation which calms his agitation. doesn't like bright lights.

has five children and seven grandchildren. As a family they enjoyed holidays with their caravan and boat and going fishing. He still enjoys being taken out. He loves the sea air and the smell of the countryside.

enjoys watching TV and listening to music. His favorite programmes include Top Gear and comedies such as One Foot in the Grave, Last of the Summer Wine, Only Fools and Horses and Allo Allo.

His hands are constantly moving and he continues to be dexterous but needs guidance and help doing things. His eyesight is not so good.

enjoys music – especially country music and music of the 1960s.

**Fig. 4.6** LAUGH portraits

## 4.4 Conclusion

In preparation for creating products and technologies suitable for use by people living with dementia, a designer needs to be well informed about the disease: understand its complexity, stages and progression; how it may impact a person's perceived reality; influence relationships and inhibit communication and ways in which it is unique to each individual. In addition, an asset-based approach that focuses on the individual and acknowledges aspects of a person *less* affected by the disease can be inspirational, emotionally uplifting and help to preserve the dignity of those affected by dementia.

What is required is a 'strong focus on remaining skills that the individual has, as opposed to what skills or experiences have been lost' (Kalsy-Lilico cited in Critten and Kucirkova 2017 p. 4). Compassionate and empathic approaches can help inform the development of designs that are appropriate and acceptable, both for the person for whom they are designed and the environment into which they will be placed. Keeping the person living with dementia at the heart of the design process, acknowledging their needs, preferences and human rights, ensures that designs for products, systems or environments are ethical, safe and useful.

## References

Alzheimer's Research UK (2016) All about dementia. A. Society. Cambridge, Alzheimer's Research UK. AAD-1114-1116, p 20

Bennett P, Hinder H, Cater K (2016) Rekindling imagination in dementia care with the resonant interface rocking chair. In: CHI EA '16 proceedings of the 2016 CHI conference extended abstracts on human factors in computing systems. ACM, San Jose, California, USA

Branco RM (ed) (2017) Dementia lab: stories from design and research 2. Dementia Lab, Germany

Branco RM, Quental J, Ribeiro Ó (2017) Personalized participation: an approach to involve people with dementia and their families in a participatory design project. CoDesign 13:127–143

Brooker D, Kitwood TM (2019) Dementia reconsidered, revisited: the person still comes first. Open University Press, London, England

Cohen-Mansfield J, Marx MS, Freedman LS, Murad H, Thein K, Dakheel-Ali M (2012) What affects pleasure in persons with advanced stage dementia? J Psychiatr Res 46(3):402–406

Critten V, Kucirkova N (2017) 'It brings it all back, all those good times; it makes me go close to tears'. Creating digital personalized stories with people who have dementia. Dementia 0(0):1471301217691162

DEEP (2014) Dementia words matter: guidelines on language about dementia. DEEP Guides. UK, DEEP The UK Network of Dementia Voices, p 4

Dewing J (2008) Personhood and dementia: revisiting Tom Kitwood's ideas. Int J Older People Nurs 3(1):3–13

Hendriks N, Wilkinson A (eds) (2017) Dementia lab: the role of design. Dementia Lab, Belgium

Hendriks N, Huybrechts L, Wilkinson A, Slegers K (2014) Challenges in doing participatory design with people with dementia. In: Proceedings of the 13th participatory design conference: short papers, industry cases, workshop descriptions, doctoral consortium papers, and keynote abstracts—volume 2. ACM, Windhoek, Namibia, pp 33–36

Higgins P (2013) Involving people with dementia in research. Nurs Times 109(28):20

Holton R (2016) Memory, persons and dementia. Stud Christ Ethics 29(3):256–260

Hughes JC (2014) How we think about dementia: personhood, rights, ethics, the arts and what they mean for care. Jessica Kingsley, London

Jakob A, Collier L (2017) Sensory design for dementia care—the benefits of textiles. J Text Res Pract 5(2):232–250. https://doi.org/10.1080/20511787.2018.1449078

Kenning G (2017) Making it together: reciprocal design to promote positive wellbeing for people living with dementia. University of Technology Sydney, Sydney, Australia

Kitwood T (1997) Dementia reconsidered: the person comes first. Open University Press, London

Kitwood T, Bredin K (2008) Towards a theory of dementia care: personhood and well-being. Ageing Soc 12(3):269–287

Kontos P, Martin W (2013) Embodiment and dementia: exploring critical narratives of selfhood, surveillance, and dementia care. Dementia 2013:12

Kontos PC, Naglie G (2006) Expressions of personhood in Alzheimer's: moving from ethnographic text to performing ethnography. Qual Res 6(3):301–317

LeDoux JE (1998) The emotional brain: the mysterious underpinnings of emotional life. Weidenfeld & Nicolson, London

Livingston G, Sommerlad A, Orgeta V, Costafreda SG, Huntley J, Ames D, Ballard C, Banerjee S, Burns A, Cohen-Mansfield J, Cooper C, Fox N, Gitlin LN, Howard R, Kales HC, Larson EB, Ritchie K, Rockwood K, Sampson EL, Samus Q, Schneider LS, Selbæk G, Teri L, Mukadam N (2017) Dementia prevention, intervention, and care. The Lancet

Lykkeslet E, Gjengedal E, Skrondal TH, Storjord MB (2014) Sensory stimulation-a way of creating mutual relations in dementia care. Int J Qual Stud Health Well-being 9. https://doi.org/10.3402/qhw.v9.23888. https://doi.org/10.3402/qhw.v9.23888

Milne A (2010) The 'D' word: reflections on the relationship between stigma, discrimination and dementia. J Mental Health 19(3):227–233

Morrissey K, Wood G, Green D, Pantidi N, McCarthy J (2016) I'm a rambler, I'm a gambler, I'm a long way from home: the place of props, music, and design in dementia care. In: Proceedings of the 2016 ACM conference on designing interactive systems. ACM, pp 1008–1020

Morrissey K, McCarthy J, Pantidi N (2017) The value of experience-centred design approaches in dementia research contexts. In: Proceedings of the 2017 CHI conference on human factors in computing systems. ACM, pp 1326–1338

Mullins J (2018) A suitcase of memories: a sensory ethnography of tourism and dementia with older people. Ph.D., Cardiff Metropolitan University

Patterson C (2018) World Alzheimer's Report 2018. Alzheimer's Disease International, London September 2018

Prince M, Wimo A, Guerchet M, Ali G, Wu Y, Prina M (2015) World Alzheimer Report 2015: the global impact of dementia—an analysis of prevalence, incidence, cost and trend. London

Sabat SR, Harré R (1992) The construction and deconstruction of self in Alzheimer's disease. Ageing Soc 12(4):443–461

Treadaway C, Kenning G (2016) Sensor e-Textiles: person centered co-design for people with late stage dementia. Working with Older People 20(2):76–85

Treadaway C, Fennell J, Prytherch D, Kenning G, Prior A, Walters A (2018a) Compassionate design: how to design for advanced dementia. Cardiff Metropolitan University, Cardiff

Treadaway C, Taylor A, Fennell J (2018b) Compassionate design for dementia care. Int J Des Creativity Innov 7(3):1–14

Treadaway C, Fennell J, Prytherch D, Kenning G, Walters A (2018b) Designing for well-being in late stage dementia. In: Coles R, Costa S, Watson S (eds) Pathways to well-being in design: examples from the arts and humanities. Routledge, London, pp 136–151

Treadaway C, Fennell J, Taylor A, Kenning G (2019) Designing for playfulness through compassion: design for advanced dementia. Design for Health, pp 1–21

Wallace J, Wright PC, McCarthy J, Green DP, Thomas J, Olivier P (2013) A design-led inquiry into personhood in dementia. In: Proceedings of the SIGCHI conference on human factors in computing systems. ACM, Paris, France, pp 2617–2626

# Chapter 5
# Making Space for Uncertainty

**Jac Fennell**

## 5.1 Introduction

This chapter presents research undertaken as part of the LAUGH project[1] to explore design processes and the design of hand-held playful objects for people living with advanced dementia. The chapter reports on a workshop with designers that enabled them to draw on their experience and training in design, provided creative opportunities to reflect on their personal values and challenged preconceptions about designing for dementia care. The chapter contends that design specialists benefit from opportunity to have their design-thinking 'disrupted' in order to reflect on and reconsider their unconscious biases, attitudes and values. It presents evidence that interdisciplinary co-design with experts is vital when working in design areas of high sensitivity, where common language needs building, ethical issues need addressing and deep insights into complex design problems are required.

## 5.2 Challenges for Designers

Dementia is a complex, highly emotive disease, requiring sensitivity, empathic understanding and compassion within a design context. Globally, the number of people with the disease is expected to double every 20 years. By 2050 it is projected there will be 115 million people with dementia worldwide (Prince et al. 2015). The cost

[1] *The LAUGH research project was funded by UK Government through an AHRC Standard Grant Ref: AH/<005607/1.*

J. Fennell (✉)
Cardiff Metropolitan University, Wales, UK
e-mail: JFennell@cardiffmet.ac.uk

© Springer Nature Switzerland AG 2020

R. Brankaert and G. Kenning (eds.), *HCI and Design in the Context of Dementia*, Human–Computer Interaction Series,
https://doi.org/10.1007/978-3-030-32835-1_5

both economically and emotionally is significant and increasing (Alzheimer's Society 2016; Bray et al. 2019; Cheston and Christopher 2019). Providing new ways to care for people living with the advanced stage of the disease is imperative in a world in which carers are hard to find and informal carers are overburdened.

Dementia affects memory, perception, cognition and behaviour and there is currently no cure for the disease. Current care practice involves physical day-to-day care but often neglects a holistic approach that considers a person's emotional and psychological wellbeing. Often prescribed medication is used to treat the so-called perceived 'challenging behaviours' that are considered symptomatic of the disease. Finding new non-pharmacological approaches to care, so that people are able to live well with the disease, is where designers can offer their support. In recent years, design researchers have offered many ideas that support people to live well with the disease (for example, Bennett et al. 2016; Branco et al. 2017; Jakob et al. 2017; Treadaway et al. 2018), but the process of designing for dementia is not easy. It is a challenging and complicated disease to understand how best to design for.

The need for designers to be educated on dementia is important, especially as there are many differences between each stage of the disease. In the earlier stages, there may be very minor changes to the person's abilities, such as loss of memory of recent events, forgetting conversations and words, and becoming confused (Alzheimer's Society 2019). At this stage, a person's independence can be supported by focussing on what they can do. As dementia is a progressive condition, damage to the brain will cause change in a person's mental abilities, and the more advanced stages of dementia can be more challenging for both the person affected by disease and their support network. In the later stages, a person may experience greater memory loss and struggle with daily activities. They will experience more changes in their behaviour and find it difficult to communicate. For designers, understanding these differences in the stages of dementia is vital for understanding how best to design appropriate solutions that meet people's current needs and desires.

Designing appropriate, safe and beneficial products and services presents a challenge for designers with limited knowledge of dementia. Designers who have not had direct experience of the disease are often informed through medical and clinical viewpoints and are unaware of the embodied nature of the condition, the variations that exist from person to person, and the limitations and possibilities. Further challenges arise for designers exploring co-design approaches when engaging with people living with advanced stages of the disease, who are chair or bed-bound and may have severe communication difficulties.

The methods used when designing for dementia need to be carefully considered. Where user-centred design approaches are considered pertinent for gaining user insight, they may not be appropriate for people with dementia who may have cognitive impairment and limited verbal communication. Instead, designing for people living with dementia requires focus on the experiential and sensory perceptions of dementia (Lazar et al. 2017). Design researchers have responded to this need by adopting methods that support understanding a person's experience and are exploring new ways to connect, communicate and design with people affected by the disease (Branco et al. 2017; Morrissey and McCarthy 2015; Niedderer et al. 2017; Treadaway et al. 2016a, b). Experience Design approaches support this enquiry and the more recent development of the Compassionate Design methodology, illustrated through a toolkit for designers (Treadaway et al. 2018), offers real-world insight for connecting with people living with the more advanced stages of the disease. Advances in the adoption and development of such design methodologies to support connecting, communicating and understanding people offer new insight into the complexities of the disease and how to successfully design for it.

## 5.3 Approaches for Designing for Advanced Dementia

This chapter explores some of the challenges designers face when designing for advanced dementia by reporting on findings from the LAUGH research project. The project developed a collection of playful objects to support wellbeing of people living with advanced dementia. The intention was to interrogate the design process to inform the design industry to ensure that designs are appropriate for this demographic.

The approaches used to gather data in this research were qualitative and inclusive, placing people at the heart of the process. Initial data was gathered though interviews with a series of dementia experts and people living with the early stages of the disease. In addition, participatory co-design workshops were held in which expert participants, including health and care professionals, scientists and technologists, were encouraged to engage in practical and creative activities (Treadaway et al. 2016a, b). These creative activities were embedded in the workshops to engage participants, disrupt preconceptions and challenge conventional thinking: to take participants out of their comfort zone and encourage creativity. Qualitative data was gathered via audio and video recordings, photography and concept boards. A thematic analysis, informed by a literature review and dementia expert interviews, was used to interrogate the data and inform design development (Treadaway et al. 2016a).

The approaches enabled the research team to hear the voice of the experts, with humility. They helped maintain deep focus on people living with advanced dementia, provoking the innovative thinking required to meet such a complex design challenge. It provided the dementia experts opportunities to speculate on possible design solutions and feedback on emerging ideas. Insights gained through the process contributed to the ideation phase of design development and later used to critique the evolving design concepts. In addition, the dementia experts assisted with rapid feedback and refinement of emerging design ideas through each of the participatory events.

The participatory methods used ensured that the scope and reach of the research impacted on the many different disciplines represented by the workshop participants. The design research team became one of many expert voices as they worked alongside and accommodated the ideas of other non-design specialists during the co-design events. The flow of ideas between the design research team and dementia experts enabled a space for questioning of accepted norms and speculative opportunities for design.

As the project developed, it became evident that the skills and technical expertise of design specialists were also required to further hone and refine the co-produced concepts being developed and give them physical form and robustness. It was this critical phase, of using design-thinking to discuss dementia—an essential part of the study's design process, where the need to allow for uncertainty was evident. This particular phase of the project offers insight as to why a space for designers to reflect and question their personal values and unconscious bias is important when designing for dementia.

## 5.4 Using Design-Thinking to Discuss Dementia

The Design Challenge workshop invited a multidisciplinary group of designers and technologists who had not been involved in the earlier workshops, to contribute their expertise, approaches to the creative process and differing viewpoints on design. The aim was to explore design for dementia and 'disrupt' or challenge existing design-thinking. Creative practitioners, technologists and professional designers (n-10) were brought together specifically to explore design speculations emerging from the previous LAUGH co-design workshops, discussed in the previous section. The group included product, textile and interaction designers, and a computer scientist and psychologist working in design research. They were aged 20–40 years and the majority were female. The group were familiar with the workshop setting, they had all been or were currently involved in design research projects and they had knowledge of, or were skilled in, design-thinking techniques (Curedale 2018). Prior to the event, workshop organisers were aware that the group were likely to have little experience of dementia. Participant introductions during the workshop exposed their limited knowledge of dementia which predominantly came from (distant) family members living with the disease and/or hearing about dementia in the media. As in previous project workshops, qualitative data from the Design Challenge was gathered via audio and video recordings, and concept boards.

The event was divided into three activity sessions using envisioning techniques to generate ideas. These included: association exercises, dot voting and storyboarding. Each session was followed by a group discussion with opportunity to reflect and focus ideas ready for the next activity. The intention was to move from the broad themes identified by the experts in previous co-design workshops and generate sketches or paper prototypes for playful products. The use of envisioning techniques enabled the multidisciplinary group to explore ideas through their discipline (and experience and preconceptions) under a shared design narrative. The focussed activities around concept generation offered prime opportunity to explore and discuss many issues in dementia care. They encouraged participants to think divergently and the structure of the event was designed to challenge each designer's established patterns of thinking, design processes, deeply held values and unconscious bias.

## 5.5 Safe Spaces to Explore Uncertainty

The Design Challenge had been set up with the intention of creating a secure 'space for uncertainty' for participants. However, the activity sessions were familiar to many of the designers and they were confident about moving forward with design concepts. Nevertheless, it was evident from the outset that, apart from the research team, understanding of the disease was limited, which had implications for product design and development. The 'place of uncertainty' that was being sought in the design process coalesced in the debrief sessions at the end of each workshop activity. Time had been allocated for group discussion to give participants opportunity to feedback on the dialogue and design concepts emerging from smaller group activities and further critique of work presented by others. However, significant was the questioning from workshop participants that occurred frequently during these group discussions about dementia. This, and the types of questions asked is evidence of people being uncertain about the subject they were designing for.

The workshop not only allowed time and space to explore uncertainty around designing for dementia, but also contributed to a change in thinking from the designers. Discussions at the beginning of the workshop highlighted a consensus from the participants that they should be designing new products to support reminiscence and memory recall. Through discussion and guidance from the researchers that this is inappropriate for designing for advanced dementia, the participant's approach changed towards thinking about products that supported in-the-moment playfulness. The value of being playful was a finding from the researcher's prior work (Treadaway et al. 2016a, b) and was used to guide participants towards more appropriate designs. Educating the design participants this way not only influenced the design outcomes but also changed preconceived views favouring reminiscing, which may not have met the needs of people affected by dementia.

Further uncertainty was evident from the many questions about the suitability of design concepts. One participant questioned how simplified designs should be following advice from a member of the research team that simpler designs are effective. This advice came from key findings from previous LAUGH workshops with dementia experts revealing people with mid to late stage dementia benefit from one-step repetitive activities, for example, sanding back and forth on wood (Treadaway et al. 2016a, b). Sharing knowledge from previous workshops supported the Design Challenge participants when they were uncertain of the needs of the people they were designing for and sought confirmation from the research team regarding suitability. This questioning the appropriateness of design ideas is evidence that there were times of uncertainty during the activities and only following this, once questions had been answered, were designers able to develop ideas.

## 5.6 Empathic Understanding

The Design Challenge participants were encouraged to be empathic and raised questions regarding the need to design for their future-self. The idea of designing for their future-self developed from a debate that to design for dementia, designers need to understand the disease and in doing so, may influence how they might prepare for their own future. Fulton Suri (2003) explains empathy as 'achieving a greater awareness, an extended imagination and sensitivity to another person's world in a powerfully memorable way'. To be able to build empathy, it is important that designers 'engage, listen and understand the outlook of other people' (Strickfaden et al. 2009). The workshop participants questioning designing for their future-self supported empathic understanding of the disease and their understanding of how other people might feel through self-projection and considering living 'in their shoes.'

For designers to feel *with* the person they are designing for, rather than *for*, supports a way of knowing about people and things outside of our own personal world (Hickman 2005). Designers are unlikely to have experienced living with dementia themselves so their understanding is limited. To fully empathise, opportunity to question and reflect upon preconceived understandings is crucial. With limited knowledge about the disease, empathic visualising and imagining, and questioning appropriateness and acceptability, support designers in becoming fully aware of the challenges and issues surrounding the people they are designing for. By considering their future-selves, the designers gained valuable insight and were more responsive to understanding the challenges of designing for dementia. As a result, discussion quickly progressed to consider the potential of future technology when designing for dementia. This connection to designing for their future sparked a flurry of design concepts.

Design concepts resulting from these discussions included an idea based on a vintage telephone (see Fig. 5.1). This concept provided a platform for broad discussion about services, technology and social media, and helped participants understand embodied issues related to dementia care. The telephone concept was developed to prototype stage after the Design Challenge workshop and was informed by preferences and the life history of a person in the advanced stages of the disease (see Fig. 5.2). The telephone prototype rings spontaneously and plays a music track from a pre-programmed favourite playlist. As this prototype was developed for a lady who had grown up in Spain and whose first language was Spanish, her telephone plays Spanish music and conversation.

## 5.7 (Un)Common Language

Alongside questioning of suitability of designs and designing for future-self, notable was the frequency of discussion and uncertainty around the language used to talk about dementia. Questions about language featured in all of the group discussions

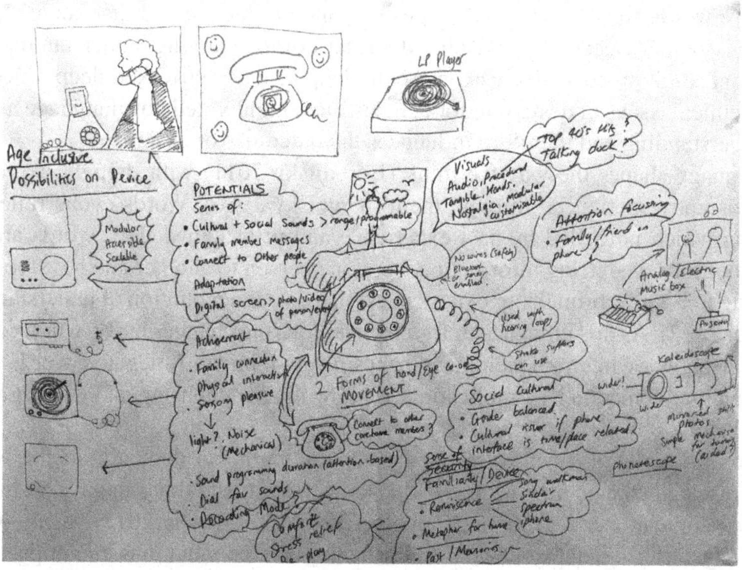


Fig. 5.1 Sketches of telephone concept from design challenge workshop

Fig. 5.2 Telephone prototype developed following the design challenge workshop

during the Design Challenge. Language use and terminology for dementia inherited from various disciplines (scientific, clinical, medical, technological and design fields) and applied to people living with dementia in a care environment may not be appropriate. It became evident that it could not be assumed that the use of ethically sensitive words would be viewed as positive and productive and that language use was an issue that needed to be dealt with as part of the learning, understanding and communication process. Discussion around language use provoked deep reflection on the ethical issues of designing for dementia and highlighted how language affects our understanding and therefore influences the outcomes of design.

Language shapes the way we think (Boroditsky 2011) with thought expressed in words and experienced through them (Vygotsky 1986). Words evoke reflective thinking which is fuelled by past experience and prior knowledge. Words are not just a tool for transferring information from one person to another and how we form meaning for words through our experiences, shapes our negotiation of understanding (Mercer 2002). As this influence of framing and filtering changes how we think about words and how we interpret their meaning, using predominantly negative words when talking about dementia has implications on how the people using and hearing those words react.

Appropriate words need to be used when talking about dementia as the words people use can change how people understand and act, and this can have an impact on how people affected by dementia feel (Alzheimer's Society 2018). Using words that imply suffering, depersonalise and have negative connotations can impact how people affected by the condition feel. Instead, positive uplifting words that empower and respect the individual will influence how the world sees them. This view supports Kitwood's (1997) person-centred approach of seeing the person before the condition, where a more meaningful and non-stigmatising terminology gives voice and respect to the person affected by the condition.

Changing use of a word is challenging when they have become ingrained into everyday life through extensive use and supported through media exposure (Jellinger 2010). An example is the word 'sufferers', which is still extensively used to describe people affected by dementia. An international movement, led by prominent figures in dementia (Alzheimer's Society 2018; Dementia Voices DEEP 2014; Swaffer 2014), has campaigned against using negative words like 'sufferers' to develop a positive language and attitude when talking about dementia. A set of guidelines on terminology considered appropriate has been developed and approved by people living with dementia and published by Alzheimer's Society (2018). Dementia Friends sessions, also initiated by Alzheimer's Society, educate people in adopting appropriate terminology through their dementia awareness sessions. Their aim is to change the way people think, act and talk about dementia so that those affected by the condition are able to live in their community without fear or prejudice. Adopting this positive language to talk about dementia supports the societal change needed in understanding the condition.

In the Design Challenge workshop, the term 'sufferers' was used frequently by the designers. Each of the three workshop activities brought intense discussions around the language and terminology associated with dementia where, at that point, the designers were unaware of how inappropriate words can cause considerable offense to those living with the disease or working in the field. The research team routinely use the guidelines published by Alzheimer's Society (2018) and advocated their consideration and use by participants of the workshop. Inappropriate language continued to be used at various points during the workshop and became a source of irritation. One participant commentated:*we need to be sensitive but bold enough to allow us to innovate and not be held back by the use of words*. And another stated: *words can stop us communicating in an environment like this*.

Much time was spent discussing terminology and the ethical implications of incorrect language. The frequency of these discussions in the data highlights the importance of appropriate vocabulary when designing for dementia and the need for designers to have flexibility to embrace the way in which semantics convey ethical understanding. By insisting on the correct vocabulary and sharing understanding together, the research team was able to provoke deep reflection by the designers on the ethical issues around dementia. Sensitivity, awareness and respect are needed when discussing the disease, and these discussions established a new 'place for uncertainty' for designers who had not previously considered the wider implications of inappropriate words in a design context.

In these moments of uncertainty, it was evident that clarity was needed to move on in the design process: concept generation was halted and reassurance was given from the research team around suitability of words. The research team presented a simplified understanding of the problems of language with an agreed understanding that there are more complex issues involved but there was a need to move on to explore new boundaries with less restriction. Facilitating clarity and a common ground during uncertainty is critical in supporting designers when designing for complex issues. Presenting clearly defined and simplified understanding of complex issues helps move the process forward, as well as giving designers opportunity to reflect upon their own biases and preconceptions. Language may not seem important but encouraging designers to reflect upon the insensitive use of it moved the discussion towards a stronger empathic understanding of the design problem, and this was crucial to producing better solutions.

## 5.8 Discussion

### *5.8.1 Opportunities for Reflection and Challenging Preconceptions*

A number of key themes related to designing for advanced dementia arose from the Design Challenge workshop. These included the need to challenge a designer's existing viewpoint and understanding of dementia; the benefit of offering time to discuss uncertainty in a safe and familiar environment; the need to design for our future-selves and the value of creating a shared common language for dementia. Workshop participants' experiences confirmed that having space and time to reflect and share thoughts around these themes supported their learning and understanding of dementia.

When designing in a complex field such as dementia, it is beneficial to make space for uncertainty and create time for reflection. Reflection is immersed in our ways of experiencing and seeing the world. Fostering moments of reflection creates sense and knowledge, and people who are encouraged to reflect carefully about what they are doing and experiencing learn in a more profound way (Schön 1983). As learning happens through self-discovery and self-appropriation of the information presented, 'learning belongs ultimately to the learner' (Schön 1987).

Through the act of designing, designers are exposed to many variables making them responsive to embracing new learning. Schön describes this as having a conversation with the situation, which has comparisons to experience design approaches used in HCI (Sengers et al. 2005). Schön (1983) acknowledges designers discover more about the problem through trying to solve the problem, and the process of designing embraces the complexity of the problem through constant negotiation and solving of additional problems that emerge along the way. McCarthy and Wright (2004) and Dourish (2001) acknowledge the importance of the evolving, dynamic dialogue of experience that develops through reflection and addressing unknowns. Explicit, transferable theories provide background information but dialogue and reflection of the unknown present new opportunity for designers through reflection-in-action (Schön 1983).

The Design Challenge supported many instances of reflection-in-action where addressing unknowns through conversation encouraged reflection on known phenomenon. Design participants appreciated having time to talk about their experiences and share their uncertainties about designing for dementia through the debrief sessions at the end of each activity. Making complex topics more accessible to designers is vital, and allowing opportunity in the design process to understand subject complexities is valuable to all involved. It gives confidence to people new to the subject through informed discussion—but allowances for uncertainty are needed too—to produce richer empathic understanding. Discussion between designers (with limited knowledge) and the research team (with expert knowledge) produced an all-round richer understanding of the complexities of designing for advanced dementia. This allowed designers to 'push beyond their own empathic horizon' (McDonagh and Thomas 2010) to consider the views of experts by experience. It may have taken the designers out of their comfort zone but it gave opportunity to critically reflect upon their own prejudices and biases.

Critical reflection on use of language formed a significant part of the Design Challenge. People's views are shaped by the language they use and when this has been reinforced by historic misappropriation of words, it can be incredibly difficult to change. This was evident in the Design Challenge where inappropriate use of language highlighted the importance of creating appropriate shared narratives when designing for complex subjects. Lengthy discussions on language influenced and impacted the initial aim of the workshop (to explore design concepts) and caused negativity and disruption. Project facilitators acknowledging participant's lack of understanding and uncertainty about a subject will note it is an important distraction that needs addressing to allow progression. Failure to address uncertainty as it arises in the design process may be detrimental to fulfilling end-user needs.

*Designing* offers solutions to problems and *designers* are taught to be curious and to ask questions. Offering space and time to be inquisitive about design problems gives designers opportunity to be reflective on past experience and receptive to new information. Reflective thinking disturbs and disrupts judgment through with a willingness to engage in further inquiry (Dewey 1997). The Design Challenge encouraged reflective thinking and self-discovery through embracing uncertainty. There were many moments of questioning and testing of ideas around possibilities and potential, of challenging the designers understanding of dementia care practices and critiquing societal norms. This often led to frustration around the constraints over what is possible, halted by the current system of dementia care (guided by knowledge from the research team). It created moments of despair for the immense challenge facing society and fear of facing their future-selves. Ultimately, these discussions led to hope and belief that design can play a pivotal part in supporting people to live well in their challenging journey through the disease.

When designing for a new subject field, such as dementia, being aware of and allowing space to understand the subject is crucial learning for designers. To fully appreciate the complexities of designing for dementia, designers need opportunity to disrupt and challenge (or be challenged on) their understanding of the disease. The Design Challenge highlighted the importance of challenging a designer's understanding and unconscious bias and by including experts by experience in the design process, ensured experts by design were challenged. Designers must learn about the subject they are designing for and their views need to be questioned. Reflection brings 'unconscious aspects of experience to conscious awareness, thereby making them available for conscious choice' (Sengers et al. 2005). This encourages designers to adapt and develop their experience with new knowledge as well as challenge their own preconceptions. Supporting reflective dialogue during the Design Challenge not only brought new knowledge to design participants, but positively influenced the design offerings. Overall, this approach to disrupt thinking can benefit designing for other complex subject areas too. Making space to explore a designer's uncertainties in a safe environment with others who have deep subject knowledge facilitates shared language and deeper understanding to inform the development of appropriate design concepts.

## References

Alzheimer's Society (2016) Fix dementia care: NHS and care homes. Alzheimers.org.uk. https://www.alzheimers.org.uk/download/downloads/id/3026/fix_dementia_care_nhs_and_care_homes_report.pdf. Accessed 17th Oct 2019

Alzheimer's Society (2018) Positive language: an Alzheimer's society guide to talking about dementia. Alzheimers.org.uk. https://www.alzheimers.org.uk/sites/default/files/2018-09/Positive%20language%20guide_0.pdf. Accessed 24th April 2019

Alzheimer's Society (2019) The progression of Alzheimer's disease. Alzheimers.org.uk. https://www.alzheimers.org.uk/about-dementia/symptoms-and-diagnosis/how-dementia-progresses/progression-alzheimers-disease. Accessed 17th Oct 2019

Bennett P, Hinder H, Cater K (2016) Rekindling imagination in dementia care with the rocking chair. In: Proceedings of the CHI conference of human factors in computing systems. ACM, pp 2020–2026

Boroditsky L (2011) How language shapes thought. Sci Am 304(2):62–65

Branco RM, Quental J, Ribeiro Ó (2017) Personalised participation: an approach to involve people with dementia and their families in a participatory design project. CoDesign 13(2):127–143

Bray J, Brooker D, Latham I, Wray F, Baines D (2019) Costing resource use of the Namaste care intervention UK: a novel framework for costing dementia care interventions in care homes. Int Psychogeriatr 1–10

Cheston R, Christopher G (2019) Dementia in context. In: Confronting the existential threat of dementia. Palgrave Pivot, Cham

Curedale R (2018) Design thinking: process and methods, 4th edn. Design Community College Inc., Los Angeles

Dementia Voices: DEEP (2014) DEEP guide: dementia words matter. Dementiavoices.org.uk. https://www.dementiavoices.org.uk/wp-content/uploads/2015/03/DEEP-Guide-Language.pdf. Accessed 27th April 2019

Dewey J (1997) How we think. Dover Publications, New York

Dourish P (2001) Where the action is: the foundations of embodied interaction. MIT Press, Cambridge, MA

Fulton Suri J (2003) Empathic design: informed and inspired by other people's experience. In: Koskinen I, Battarbee K, Mattelmäki T (eds) Empathic design: user experience in product design. IT Press, Helsinki, p 52

Hickman R (2005) Why we make art and why it is taught. Intellect, Bristol

Jakob A, Manchester H, Treadaway C (2017) Design for dementia care: making a difference. In: Proceedings of the NORDES 2017: design + power, 7th Nordic design research conference

Jellinger K (2010) Should the word 'dementia' be forgotten? J Cell Mol Med 14(10):2415–2416

Kitwood TM (1997) Dementia reconsidered: the person comes first. Open University Press, Buckingham

Lazar A, Edasis C, Piper AM (2017) A critical lens on dementia and design in HCI. In: Proceedings of the CHI conference of human factors in computing systems. ACM, pp 2175–2188

McCarthy J, Wright P (2004) Technology as experience. MIT Press, Cambridge, MA

McDonagh D, Thomas J (2010) Rethinking design thinking: empathy supporting innovation. Australas Med J 3(8):458–464

Mercer N (2002) Words and minds: how we use language to think together. Routledge, London

Morrissey K, McCarthy J (2015) Creative and opportunistic use of everyday music technologies in a dementia care unit. In: Proceedings of the ACM SIGCHI conference on creativity and cognition. ACM, pp 295–298

Niedderer K, Tournier I, Colesten-Shields D, Craven M, Gosling J, Garde JA, Bosse M, Salter B, Griffioen I (2017) Designing with and for people with dementia: developing a mindful interdisciplinary co-design methodology. In: Proceedings of the IASDR international conference, pp 816–837

Prince M, Wimo A, Guerchet M, Ali GC, Wu YT, Prina M (2015) World Alzheimer report 2015. The global impact of dementia: an analysis of prevalence, incidence, cost and trends. Alzheimer's Disease International (ADI), London

Schön D (1983) The reflective practitioner: how professionals think in action. Basic Books, New York

Schön D (1987) Educating the reflective practitioner. Jossey-Bass, San Francisco

Sengers P, Boehner K, David S, Kaye JJ (2005) Reflective design. In: Proceedings of the 4th decennial conference on critical computing: between sense and sensibility. ACM, pp 49–58

Strickfaden M, Devlieger P, Heylighen A (2009) Building empathy through dialogue. In: Proceedings of the eighth international conference of the European academy of design. Design Convexity, p 451

Swaffer K (2014) Dementia: stigma, language, and dementia-friendly. Dementia 13(6):709–716

Treadaway C, Prytherch D, Kenning G, Fennell J (2016a) In the moment: designing for late stage dementia. In: Proceedings of 50th anniversary design research society conference. Design research society, 27–30 June 2016

Treadaway C, Fennell J, Kenning G, Prytherch D, Walters A (2016b) Designing for wellbeing in late stage dementia. In: Proceedings of the WELL-BEING 2016: co-creating pathways to well-being, the third international conference exploring the multi-dimensions of well-being, Birmingham City University, 5–6 Sept 2016

Treadaway C, Fennell J, Prytherch D, Kenning G, Prior A, Walters A, Taylor A (2018) Compassionate design: how to design for advanced dementia—a toolkit for designers. Cardiff Metropolitan University, Cardiff

Vygotsky LS (1986) Thought and language, revised by A. Kozulin. MIT Press, Cambridge, MA

# Chapter 6
# Approaches for Authentic Engagement: Younger Onset Dementia

**Dennis Frost, Suzanne Dillon, Stephen Grady, Jeffrey Thurlow, Tuck Wah Leong, and Jeanette Bell**

*If you've met one person with dementia, then you've only met one person with dementia.*
Professor Tom Kitwood, 1997.

## 6.1 Introduction

As Professor Kitwood (1997) asserts, dementia is a deeply personal experience affecting an individual in many ways—physiologically, psychologically, and socially. How individuals experience dementia is unique (Kitwood 1997). Thus, it makes sense that any efforts to understand the experiences of people with dementia should consider a bespoke approach; one that is not only cognizant of the individual's situation and

The HCI researchers would like to thank the study participants and co-authors of this chapter. To ensure that the voices of the participants are represented, minimal editing has been carried out with regards to the comments and writings of the study participants and authors.

D. Frost · S. Dillon · S. Grady · J. Thurlow · T. W. Leong · J. Bell (✉)
University of Technology Sydney, Ultimo, Australia
e-mail: Jeanette.Bell@me.com

D. Frost
e-mail: Dennis.Frost@bigpond.com

S. Dillon
e-mail: SD132209@gmail.com

S. Grady
e-mail: Grady.Steve@gmail.com

J. Thurlow
e-mail: Thurlowjeffrey@yahoo.com.au

T. W. Leong
e-mail: TuckWah.Leong@uts.edu.au

© Springer Nature Switzerland AG 2020

R. Brankaert and G. Kenning (eds.), *HCI and Design in the Context of Dementia*, Human–Computer Interaction Series,
https://doi.org/10.1007/978-3-030-32835-1_6

circumstances but at the same time, thoughtful, sensitive, and respectful. Adopting a bespoke approach is only a recently explored idea, especially in Human–Computer Interaction (HCI) which also research and design digital technologies in, and for, dementia settings. Bespoke approaches move the current corpus of research methodologies forward that the HCI community uses when researching and designing in dementia settings.

In this chapter, we present our bespoke approach when working with people with Younger Onset Dementia (YOD). Specifically, we focus on how to include those individuals with YOD as co-researchers and co-designers. This is because, currently, individuals with YOD are an underrepresented group in social, medical, and government systems (Thompson 2011; Sansoni et al. 2016; Rossor et al. 2010) with most efforts directed at Late-Onset Dementia (LOD). The chapter focuses on the unique challenges and different circumstances of those with YOD, when compared to those of LOD in HCI research. Our research approach led to insights into ways that HCI researchers can adapt and improve their research and design methods when working in collaboration with those living with YOD.

We begin this chapter with a brief overview of YOD and discuss how and why we, as researchers, set out to establish a research collaboration with people living with YOD with the aim to understand their needs and preferences when engaging in research and design projects. The outcomes of this collaboration will be discussed from two perspectives—the HCI researchers and the people living with YOD. We will also present a number of recommendations for HCI researchers and designers to consider when working specifically with people with YOD.

## 6.2 Context

Digital technologies can be used to support people with later onset dementia in a variety of ways, including, for example, surveillance technologies to monitor for falls or to more easily find and track those who get lost. However, there are other more relevant and immediate issues and challenges to address for those living with YOD—before surveillance measures are required. This is because, unlike LOD, those with YOD live with quite different and unique circumstances, which we will be discussed shortly. But first we would like to briefly provide the background to our research goals, beginning with an acknowledgement of the positioning and aims of the Dementia Alliance International (DAI), the key international advocacy body for dementia, which states.

DAI is a not-for-profit organization with membership exclusively for people with dementia from around the world and is widely accepted as "the global voice of dementia". DAI advocates for taking a human rights approach when researching in the field of dementia (DAI 2017). The wish from this community is to "see the person, not the dementia".

With this in mind, the design of technologies used to specifically support those living with YOD must be accomplished through research methods that allow for appropriate and sensitive ways to elicit stories from those living with YOD in order to build understandings of their distinctive lived experiences. At the same time, it is also imperative that we consider how to include YOD individuals at each step of the research and design process. While many within the HCI community have discussed ways to include those living with dementia in the technology design process (Vines et al. 2013; Wallace et al. 2013), there is a dearth of guidance for researchers working with people with YOD. So, one of our goals was to collaborate with the YOD community to understand the kinds of methods which would be most appropriate to understand their unique experiences of dementia, especially in the earlier stages of YOD, and also explore how to best engage them in the technology design process.

Our review of the HCI literature related to designing digital technologies and working with those with YOD and the broader YOD setting, revealed remarkably limited efforts to date (Rossor et al. 2010). As we suspected, most research efforts in HCI, as well as other fields such as medical, economic, and social sectors have been focused on dementia in the elderly (Brown et al. 2017; Withall et al. 2014). So, what is YOD and how different is it from LOD? We start by characterizing YOD and what this means in the daily life for a person diagnosed with dementia in an earlier phase of life.

### *6.2.1 Younger Onset Dementia—Life Circumstances*

There are both differences and similarities in how dementia is experienced between YOD and LOD. One major difference is the life-stage of the person with YOD, making the circumstances of YOD markedly different from that of LOD. We will start by unpacking these differences and highlight the significance of using the most appropriate methods of research in this sensitive setting.

The diagnosis of YOD is often quite unexpected when a person is aged in their thirties, forties, or fifties. The medical classification of YOD (under 65 years) also imposes a "sociological partition" that is reflective of an employment age. Largely, the age a person is diagnosed with dementia has no specific biological significance as there is a range of dementia symptoms across this arbitrary divide (Rossor et al. 2010).

YOD usually occurs in an earlier period of the life cycle stage, and it is this aspect that raises a number of issues that include social, physical, and financial implications. For example, individuals diagnosed with YOD are generally fit and in good physical health and may not experience the co-morbidities associated with LOD (Sansoni et al. 2014). The diagnosis, coupled with a lack of support services greatly impact the person with YOD; more so than that of the LOD (Withall et al. 2014; Thompson 2011). From a financial perspective, the person diagnosed with YOD is generally still employed and engaged in all aspects and demands of life (Withall et al. 2014; Van Vliet et al. 2012). Many will be the main income earner and some may even be a parent of young children (Rossor et al. 2010), but suddenly forced to leave paid employment because of their diagnosis of dementia. With this, many YOD families will experience financial difficulties arising from the loss of income as well as having to meet additional care costs (Sansoni et al. 2014). The issues discussed here also implicate the carer of a person with YOD; with the carer often facing higher levels of anxiety, depression, and even marital problems when compared to carers of older people with dementia (Arntzen et al. 2016).

Furthermore, there is a stigma associated with dementia that is widespread and often unknowingly reinforced by inappropriate language in dementia discourse (Swaffer 2014). People with YOD do not want to be known as *sufferers* or be framed or be made to feel to be a *burden*. Individuals with YOD are seeking opportunities to *live well with dementia*. Dementia organizations provide Language Guidelines (Alzheimer Australia 2017) to promote the consistent use of appropriate language. Further on in this chapter the YOD team also give their personal insights into experience of living with the stigma of dementia.

### 6.2.2 Lived Experiences of YOD

While research has contributed to a significant understanding of the needs and experiences of those with dementia (Cahill et al. 2004; Kitwood 1997; Downs 1997), there are still very few empirical accounts of the experiences of the younger individuals living with dementia. First-hand accounts of YOD are rare and found mainly in personal publications (Swaffer and Rahman 2015; Swaffer 2016; Bryden 2012). It is suggested that the lived experiences of YOD are not only markedly different from dementia seen in the elderly, but also there is a greater negative impact on their lives and that of their families (Greenwood and Smith 2016). This compounds the need to have appropriate research methods to better understand these experiences. An important step is to first understand how research is currently conducted in the dementia setting and assess the appropriateness of these methods in context of YOD, given their vastly different circumstances.

### 6.2.3 Current Methods in Dementia Research

Researchers in dementia settings often assign a caregiver, partner, or guardian to act as a proxy for the person with dementia, as the decline in cognition affects the ability of someone with advanced dementia to provide lucid accounts of their experiences. Talking to a proxy for the person with dementia is a well-established approach. However, researchers also suggest that this social science approach has tended to marginalize the experiences of those with dementia (Downs 1997; Dewing 2002; Moore and Hollett 2003). Recently, social researchers (Tanner 2012; Cahill et al. 2004) have challenged the use of a proxy and sought to empower people with dementia by allowing them to be directly involved in the research and design process.

During our reconnaissance work, the people we met with YOD also expressed the desire for greater agency and autonomy in the research process; to become co-researchers, and to not use proxies in any interactions. This led to a realization that we needed to re-evaluate, reconsider, and even evolve our methodological approach to be more inclusive and appropriate. We decided on a combination of ethnography and Participatory Action Research (PAR). This combination offers a collaborative and inclusive approach that has also been used by others in HCI (Green and Kirk 2018; Brereton et al. 2014). As the research progressed, the ethnography lessened and it was much more PAR.

### 6.2.4 *Participatory Action Methods (PAR)*

Baum et al. describe PAR as a methodology that pays careful attention to power relationships, advocating for power to be deliberately shared between the researcher and the researched and blurring the line between the two until the researched become the researchers (Baum et al. 2006). This approach is particularly helpful for marginalized groups to strengthen relationships and engage communities in the research process, where it is owned by the communities (Berg and Lune 2004). We were particularly inspired by the collaborative possibilities of PAR and introduced this as an approach to strengthen the inclusivity and agency of those with YOD.

## 6.3 Taking a Collaborative Approach

To best understand how to engage in research in the dementia setting, we, the researchers, undertook a number of reconnaissance activities to observe and interact with individuals living with dementia. As discussed, our participants with YOD had a strong interest in becoming co-researchers (refer to Fig. 6.1) and did not want an intermediary (proxy) acting on their behalf which, is an approach most commonly used in dementia research (Bell and Leong 2017).

### 6.3.1 *Getting to Know Each Other*

In this section, we describe the journey that led to HCI researchers and individuals with YOD working together in a research partnership. We begin with how we approached those with YOD, how trust emerged over time and present first-hand YOD insights and recommendations to the HCI community.

Early in this research journey, we saw value in adding a reconnaissance phase into our research plan to learn more about the needs of those with YOD, before leaping into the empirical research. We also saw this to be an opportunity to build

**Fig. 6.1** A member of the research team engaged in workshop activities looking at technology and YOD

relationships and trust. This was our way of addressing the sensitivity and complexity in YOD. These activities included face-to-face visits, regular skype and phone calls, and social activities such as BBQs, lunches, social outings, and a 3-day road trip (Fig. 6.2).

The time spent in this initial phase was focused on getting to know the 'person' and not their dementia. Conversations included everyday activities, chatting

**Fig. 6.2** Train travel on a 3-day roadtrip to Dubbo, in rural Australia. Travelling together provided deeper researcher insights into YOD

about hobbies, pets, stories of their younger lives, their children, family, and partners. As researchers, we also shared similar stories our family experiences with dementia. This degree of familiarity was somewhat unexpected, yet in hindsight, an essential part of sharing personal stories and building trust over time.

During this exploratory phase, we noticed the participants' prolific use of technology such as smartphones and digital watches. They used these technologies for a variety of activities including posting updates on social media, blogging, texting, scheduling, and using GPS for navigation. As the involvement of the participants in this research grew, they indicated a wish for our work to present opportunities for digital technology designs to support YOD.

### *6.3.2 Participants as Co-researchers and Collaborators*

Given our commitment to Participatory Action Research (PAR), we, the researchers, made it clear, from the beginning of our journey with our YOD participants that we were open to them joining the study as co-researchers and collaborators. This meant considering how they could participate and contribute to the research through all phases of the project. In fact, we learned that many of the individuals we met were already active in the area of dementia research; to stay abreast with current advances in dementia knowledge.

As co-researchers, they felt that they were able to provide open and unsolicited feedback on how they were experiencing dementia, as being a part of the research. Their engagement with a number of dementia organizations to develop policies on various issues such as palliative care, end-of-life planning, and decision-making rights also brought rich perspectives to the research. Treating each participant as a co-researcher meant that we shared relevant findings and thoughts about research with the individual participants. This sharing ensured that they were not only kept informed but also had the opportunity to clarify the findings and add to the findings. This was the beginning of the collaborative research partnership with those living with YOD.

### *6.3.3 The YOD Research Team*

The spirit of this inquiry is grounded in a philosophy of inclusion. "Nothing about us without us" has been adopted by many marginalized groups and emancipatory movements, including by those who advocate for individuals living with dementia. This slogan conveys the message that no policy should be reached without full participation and representation of all relevant stakeholders. Individuals with YOD are very capable of representing themselves, or speaking up for those who are no longer able to do so. The research team was fully committed to the DAI position statement that "We are legally entitled to be included, and not just consulted, or represented by others afforded" (DAI 2017). Which is why we sought individuals living

**Fig. 6.3** The YOD research team working together in a technology design workshop

with dementia to collaborate with us to understand how they experience YOD, and how technology could support their day-to-day life.

The individuals in our team (and co-authors of this chapter) as seen in Fig. 6.3 are: Dennis Frost, Suzanne (Suzie) Dillon, Stephen Grady and Jeffrey (Jeff) Thurlow. We also acknowledge the valuable contributions of their partners (Ann Grady, Sebastian Caruso) and friends (Kas Hilton) in building the deep insights and strengthening the context of the YOD story.

Next, we present some of the responses of those living with YOD when asked to offer their perspective on living with dementia to researchers in HCI. We will conclude with suggestions and recommendations for those wishing to work in the YOD research and design setting with messages and insights offered by those living with YOD to the HCI community.

## 6.4 The Perspective of Individuals Living with YOD

In this next section, a personalised narrative style is used with quotes from those in our team who were living with dementia. This style of has been carefully considered and chosen to enrich the context and amplify the voice of those who have been generous in sharing their messages.

The pictorial responses (refer to Figs. 6.4, 6.5, and 6.6) are emergent findings from an exercise in diarising the YOD experience, and demonstrates 'individuality' regarding ways to communicate back to researchers. After this, we provide the personal YOD insights shared which emerged in response to two questions we posed

**Fig. 6.4** The research team explored the day-to-day lives of YOD. Offering a choice of methods to diarise YOD experiences

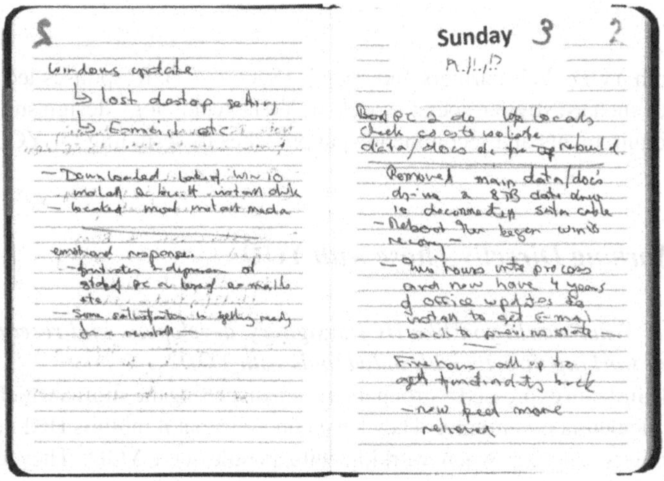


**Fig. 6.5** Handwritten diary entries was a preferred method of communication by one team member when logging the experience of YOD

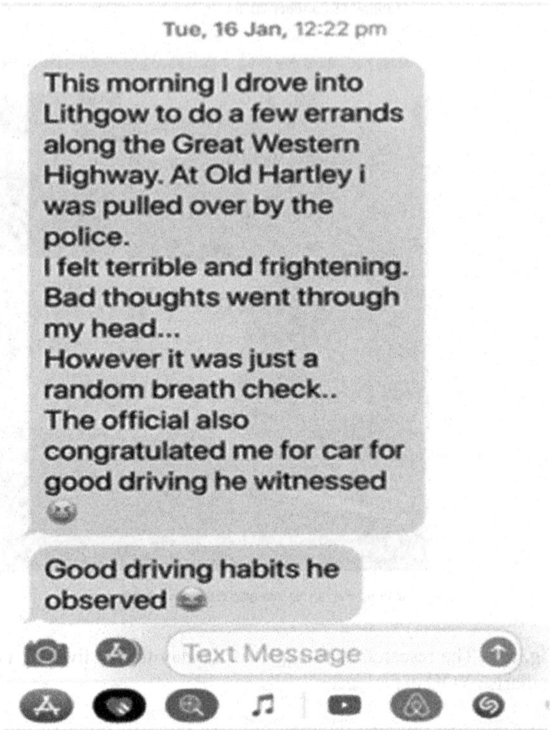


**Fig. 6.6** SMS Text was the preferred method for another individual who found handwriting challenging

to those with YOD, their partners and friends (Sect. 6.4.1). Responses led to emergent themes such as; stigma, social aspects of YOD, technology design suggestions, end-user requirements and recommended approaches to designing for YOD.

### 6.4.1 Working Directly Those with YOD

***Question 1: What would you like HCI designers, developers, and researchers to know about working directly with individuals with YOD?***

Overall, the team expressed a strong interest in dispelling the stigma which tends to shroud the dementia community. They have concerns that it inhibits HCI designers' and researchers' success when working with people with YOD. They make the following suggestions:

> Clear the stigma. Most of what people *know* about dementia is wrong or heavily influenced by a *clinical* view that concentrates on some of the symptoms but ignores the people.

The team emphasized humanity and highlighted their ability to contribute while still living with dementia:

> We can still contribute to society… We are able to do things and enjoy things. The main thing is 'we're real people.', and that 'we aren't suddenly incompetent mentally' with this diagnosis.

Our team also highlighted the importance of understanding their individual living situations, suggesting that this can inform how the HCI community can help:

> YODs still have young families, are often still working and are well below retirement age. This has a devastating effect by forced early retirement & subsequent burden on family finances.

A strong focus on how language was used was evident in their responses, for example:

> I would suggest that within the domain of *living with dementia*, we are not the consumers (a term often used), groups like the *care providers* are the real consumers; not only of our limited and dwindling financial assets but of our very lives. Put simply do not use these terms! Also, so not use words such as demented, sufferers, burden. We wish to 'live well' with dementia.

### 6.4.2 Perceptions of Dementia

The key message that emerged in response to Question 1, was around "perceptions of dementia". Often the image of dementia is that of an elderly person in the late stage of dementia. This person is assumed to be physically frail, confused and dependent on a carer for their most basic needs. This widely shared perception of dementia is of concern to those living with YOD as they do not fit these profiles. This is an important issue for HCI designers to contemplate when working in this area of research. The authors of this chapter who live with YOD are very clear that they would like the HCI community to consider their perspective. They are asking the research community address the stigma, starting with addressing the type of language that reinforces this stigma.

### 6.4.3 Current HCI Design

***Question 2: You are invited to join a project to design technologies for individuals living with YOD; what would you like HCI designers to know about an individual living with YOD in the context of technology design?***

Being included in all steps of the research and design process is a key theme. The YOD group have been largely overlooked in most areas of research and design;

> What we need is for designers not to make assumptions about our needs but to remember to ask what we need.

This was a critical gap that emerged in the review of literature in HCI design and in dementia A key point raised by our YOD team members is that they wished to be included in the design process, and to have a strong sense of agency in the process.

> I would suggest that when people design and build new solutions, [that] they are operating on a subconscious belief that the end users will adapt to their solution, rarely is it the other-way around.

### 6.4.4 Designing for Two

The literature shows that designers primarily focus on solutions that support the carer. *Designing for Two* references the observed lack of technology for individual use by people with dementia. The YOD team want the HCI designers to pause and consider the role of the carer as separate from the YOD person themselves, for example, they suggest;

> Include features for *respite & self-care*, *me* time, for those with YOD, and carers.

They suggested HCI designers ask:

> Does [the technology] benefit both the user and their companion or caregiver?

### 6.4.5 Adding Substance to the Technology

Our research team suggested that designers need to think more deeply about the application of the technology in a real-world situation. In other words, how well aligned is the technology solution to the needs of the person with dementia? They offered a way to check on this aspect:

> Take an inclusive participatory design approach. Engaging users in the design process will enable the end-product to more closely align with user needs.

They suggested that features that would benefit them personally include;

> Designing things to help keep that independence in differing forms is a big thing. What do I want? Location apps, assistant apps, reminder apps – those sorts of things are very big for us. To help us structure our day, reminders for when we leave our home, do we have our keys, everything we're supposed to have when we go out.

and

> Having a mode on your phone, or a device that I can say "yes, I'm having a good dementia day" or "no, I'm not having a good dementia day" and if it's the latter it jumps into a mode to provide more assistance.

### 6.4.6 Learning the "How-To" of the Technology

Our YOD team members suggest that HCI designers must consider the individual nature of dementia and the very differing abilities of individuals. They advised:

> We can still learn, but learning is not as easy as it used to be. It requires a lot of repetition. We find it really difficult when faced with jargon. Keep it simple.

Here they offer are a few recommendations on the usability of the technology:

> The tool should be useful to its full potential with minimal training or familiarity with tech tools as a prerequisite. If something new is built on a familiar framework or way of doing things, not only will it be easier to adapt to, but the chances of being able to continually engage with it will also increase.

They continued:

> Directions need to be short, simple and uncomplicated.
>
> Multi step directions may not be remembered in the order they are given. Left/right, up/down, north/south can all be frequently reversed.
>
> It may be of great value if you can *componentize* your prototypes so each aspect can be tested by people living with dementia, both as a component and as a whole.

### 6.4.7 Other Aspects to Consider

The YOD research team was keen to point out, dementia is more than memory loss. It's complex and each individual will experience their life with dementia in vastly different ways. Issues with sensory functions can impact the usability of a technology:

> sense of taste, smell, sight, hearing and touch can be altered

and

> speech is frequently affected as there is difficulty with finding appropriate words
>
> *Therefore, they ask HCI designers to consider:*
>
> Emotion plays a significant role in how people make decisions; If there are prompts, what tone do the prompts use? For example, are the prompts neutral in language and tone, or are they associated with a particular mood? How will that mood align with the user as they experience the prompts?

## 6.5 Discussion

The insights presented in this chapter emerged over the course of a two-year longitudinal fieldwork study. Most qualitative research of dementia provides guidance on how to conduct research with older adults living with dementia, and classifies them as a vulnerable group. However, this "vulnerability" is due to the fact that those are individuals living with more advanced stages of dementia and thus, requiring the assignment of a proxy in dementia research. But, this is at odds with our experience of conducting research with people living with YOD. The "emerging" literature on YOD aligns with the experience and position taken by the authors of this chapter who live with dementia. These younger individuals living with dementia are independent, often still working, engaged with life, live with less severe cognitive decline and are very capable of providing informed consent on their own behalf. They are actively involved with their health decisions, reflective about their situation, and *tech savvy*. They are fiercely independent and vocal about their rights and agency. Given the lack of guidance on how to work with such individuals, it was beneficial to invest the time to build familiarity and sensitivity into the engagement process with these individuals. Therefore, we have listened and adapted our approach to research based on the needs of the YOD community. Having discussed the YOD perspective, we would now like to offer the HCI researcher perspective.

### *6.5.1 What We Learned as HCI Researchers*

Firstly, we reiterate that those living with YOD have expressed the need for appropriate research methods that are inclusive and respectful for their desire for agency and autonomy. Secondly, they want to be actively participating as co-researchers in research, because they want to shape the narrative of their own experiences with dementia. As HCI researchers and designers, we realized that to better understand this position, we needed to take time before rushing into the study design and fieldwork.

We learned from the literature and from engaging directly with those living with dementia, that each person will experience dementia in their own way—with varying abilities. With this, researchers must adapt their methods to first understand, and second find ways to best meet the needs of participants. For example, the approach taken by researchers (Bell and Leong 2019) enabled participants to self-select the particular probes and reporting mediums (i.e., Figs. 6.4, 6.5 and 6.6) that best supported their preferences and retained abilities. The participants could also personalize their probes. This revealed how the use of a proxy when researching with a person in the early stage of life with dementia is not only unnecessary but also in fact, undesirable. However, having a support person present during research activities remains an option. This choice is for the person with dementia to make, not the researcher.

The limitations on this account of YOD is that our team living with YOD are from similar cultural and ethnic backgrounds. They are well-educated professionals and have sound socioeconomic status. On reflection, this may be why they were more *visible*, allowing us to connect and recruit them into this research. Their backgrounds may also suggest why they have a strong sense of agency and why they volunteer in public positions to advocate for those with similar experiences of YOD. Furthermore, their particular career backgrounds, some being academics, may suggest why they feel strongly about being co-researchers.

### 6.5.2 Considerations for Future Researchers

To engage seriously in research in the area YOD requires a great deal of tenacity, empathy, sensitivity, and personal awareness. The reciprocity experienced by being open as a researcher to letting people into your life can be very emotionally satisfying and moving. Bell and Leong work in the area of YOD, produced the following recommendations for HCI researchers in YOD settings (Bell and Leong 2019).

> **Time**: Be mindful and respectful of how a person with dementia perceives and values their time (dementia time). They may not remember the past in the order it happened. They are also aware of their cognitive decline and are explicitly choosing how they best invest their precious time.
>
> **Flexibility**: Look for opportunities to be flexible in the design process and implementation of the research. This will support the varying needs and abilities of the individuals with dementia to communicate and engage in a way most comfortable for them.
>
> **Varying abilities**: Be mindful of the variation in abilities of a person with YOD. Individuals might have particular types of tasks that will challenge them unnecessarily. For example, if diarizing is being used to capture experiences - having to record handwritten entries may be stressful for a person who is losing this ability. However, they may enjoy providing diary updates by recording a voice message.

In summary, we learned that dementia is complex and affects the abilities of people in unique ways. We used elements from participatory action research and ethnographic methodologies to guide our collaboration and to ensure the inclusivity and agency of everyone involved. As HCI researchers, we must be adaptive and flexible to the needs of those with YOD, to respond and utilize their retained abilities, and adjust to their dementia-related challenges. Therefore, it was necessary to introduce flexibility and provide options when designing data-capture tools throughout the research. We stress again the benefit of adapting, trialing, and refining the tools during the research process to support the needs and goals of the YOD community.

Having the individuals with YOD work directly with—and trialing the research tools first, taught us about the need to consider the ethical and physical demands we might impose on our participants. We are reminded to use appropriate language in instructions, and of the difficulties that individuals might have with particular types of tasks due to unique changes in their brain and cognitive processes, and unpredictable changes dementia has on the individual (Bell and Leong 2017).

## 6.6 Conclusion

This chapter describes a unique collaboration between HCI researchers and a number of individuals living with YOD, in a research project to better understand the experiences of living with dementia. Over the course of the fieldwork, we faced challenges in using existing HCI methodologies—when applied to YOD research. To overcome this, we turned to those who live with YOD for guidance. This collaboration produced rich and personal YOD insights in addition to guidance for HCI researchers and designers wanting to work in the area of YOD technology design.

### *6.6.1 Contributions of This Chapter*

We suggest that the learnings from this chapter can be applied beyond research within YOD settings, to how we conduct research with general populations as well. Given this, we would urge researchers to be more reflective and pay particular attention to how we design probes for our participants to "communicate" with us during an inquiry process—with some discussions or even negotiations with the participants before the design of the probes. Furthermore, it may be pertinent for researchers to consider ways to provide more freedom and autonomy to participants at every step of the HCI research and design process.

**Acknowledgements** We would like to gratefully thank the families and friends of those living with YOD who welcomed us into their lives and offered their rich life stories and insights to support the HCI Research Community. Thank you also to Sebastian Caruso, Kas Hilton, Ann Grady, and Max Wild for their valuable input and support for this project.

## References

Alzheimer Australia (2017) Dementia language guidelines. https://www.fightdementia.org.au/resources/dementia-language-guidelines. Accessed 10 Jun 2017

Arntzen C, Holthe T, Jentoft R (2016) Tracing the successful incorporation of assistive technology into everyday life for younger people with dementia and family carers. Dementia 15:646–662

Baum F, MacDougall C, Smith D (2006) Participatory action research. J Epidemiol Community Health 60: 854–857

Bell J, Leong TW (2017) Collaborative futures: a technology design approach to support living well with dementia. In: Proceedings of the 29th Australian conference on computer-human interaction. ACM, pp 397–401

Bell J, Leong TW (2019) Collaborative futures: co-designing research methods for younger people living with dementia. In: Proceedings of the 2019 CHI conference on human factors in computing systems. ACM, p 352

Berg B, Lune H (2004) Cap. 7: action research. Qualitative research methods for the social sciences. vol 5, pp 247–268

Brereton M, Roe P, Schroeter R, Hong AL (2014) Beyond ethnography: engagement and reciprocity as foundations for design research out here. In: Proceedings of the SIGCHI Conference on Human Factors in Computing Systems (CHI'14). ACM, pp 1183–1186

Brown L, Hansnata E, La HA (2017) Economic cost of dementia in Australia

Bryden C (2012) Who will I be when I die? Jessica Kingsley Publishers

Cahill S, Begley E, Topo P, Saarikalle K, Macijauskiene J, Budraitiene A, Hagen I, Holthe T, Jones K (2004) 'I Know Where this is Going and I Know it won't Go Back' hearing the individual's voice in dementia quality of life assessments. Dementia 3:313–330

DAI (2017) Dementia Alliance International. https://www.dementiaallianceinternational.org/

Dewing J (2002) From ritual to relationship: a person-centred approach to consent in qualitative research with older people who have a dementia. Dementia 1:157–171

Downs M (1997) The emergence of the person in dementia research. Ageing Soc 17:597–607

Green D, Kirk D (2018) Open design, inclusivity and the intersections of making. In: Proceedings of the 2018 designing interactive systems conference. ACM, pp 173–186

Greenwood N, Smith R (2016) The experiences of people with young-onset dementia: a meta-ethnographic review of the qualitative literature. Maturitas 92:102–109

Kitwood T (1997) The experience of dementia. Aging Mental Health 1:13–22

Moore TF, Hollett J (2003) Giving voice to persons living with dementia: the researcher's opportunities and challenges. Nurs Sci Q 16:163–167

Rossor MN, Fox NC, Mummery CJ, Schott JM, Warren JD (2010) The diagnosis of young-onset dementia. Lancet Neurol 9: 793–806

Sansoni J, Duncan C, Grootemaat P, Capell J, Samsa P, Westera A (2016) Younger onset dementia: a review of the literature to inform service development. Am J Alzheimer's Dis Other Dementiasr 31:693–705

Sansoni J, Duncan C, Grootemaat P, Samsa P, Capell J, Westera A (2014) Younger onset dementia: a literature review. University of Wollongong: Centre for Health Service Development. http://ro.uow.edu.au/ahsri/373

Swaffer K (2014) Dementia: stigma, language, and dementia-friendly. Sage Publications Sage UK, London, England

Swaffer K (2016) What the hell happened to my brain?: living beyond dementia. Jessica Kingsley Publishers

Swaffer K, Rahman S (2015) What the hell happened to my brain?: living beyond dementia. Jessica Kingsley Limited

Tanner D (2012) Co-research with older people with dementia: experience and reflections. J Mental Health 21:296–306

Thompson D (2011) Service and support requirements for people with younger onset dementia and their families. Social Policy Research Centre, University of New South Wale, Sydney

Van Vliet D, De Vugt ME, Aalten P, Bakker C, Pijnenburg YA, Vernooij-Dassen MJ, Koopmans RT, Verhey FR (2012) Prevalence of neuropsychiatric symptoms in young-onset compared to late-onset Alzheimer's disease–part 1: findings of the two-year longitudinal NeedYD-study. Dement Geriatr Cogn Disord 34:319–327

Vines J, Mcnaney R, Clarke R, Lindsay S, Mccarthy J, Howard S, Romero M, Wallace J (2013) Designing for-and with-vulnerable people. CHI'13 extended abstracts on human factors in computing systems. ACM, pp 3231–3234

Wallace J, Wright P C, McCarthy J, Green D P, Thomas J, and Olivier P. 2013. A design-led inquiry into personhood in dementia. In Proceedings of the SIGCHI Conference on Human Factors in Computing Systems (CHI'13). ACM, 2617–2626.

Withall A, Draper B, Seeher K, Brodaty H (2014) The prevalence and causes of younger onset dementia in Eastern Sydney. Aust, Int Psychogeriatr 26:1955–1965

# Part II
# Design Approaches: In the Context of Dementia

# Chapter 7
# Against Dedicated Methods: Relational Expertise in Participatory Design with People with Dementia

**Niels Hendriks, Karin Slegers, and Andrea Wilkinson**

## 7.1 Introduction: Dementia and Participatory Design

Talking about involvement in the design process brings one to participatory design (PD). PD deals with the blurring of the borders between the designer and other stakeholders involved in the design process. This blurring of borders between the designer and those one designs for, transforms the latter into an active user—from design recipient to design decision maker (Binder 1996; Luck 2003).

To involve a person with dementia in the design process is challenging, however, due to a series of physical, psychiatric and cognitive ailments (American Psychiatric Association 2000) as well as a society that still holds a rather negative view of the agency of people with dementia (Binney et al. 1990; Bond 1992). All these ailments and perceptions lead to challenges in involving people with dementia in the design process. Span et al. (2013) found that only a limited group of researchers actually attempted to involve people with dementia in the design process. Morrissey (2017), Rodgers (2017), Branco et al. (2017), Kenning (2018) and Smeenk (2017) are only a small group of the designers and researchers doing so. All of these researchers and designers report similar reasons as to why people with dementia are not involved in

N. Hendriks (✉)
Dementia Lab, Inter-Actions, LUCA School of Arts, Genk, Belgium
e-mail: Niels.Hendriks@kuleuven.be

K. Slegers
Department of Communication & Cognition, Tilburg School of Humanities and Digital Sciences, Tilburg University, Tilburg, The Netherlands
e-mail: Karin.Slegers@luca-arts.be

Institute for Media Studies, Mintlab, KU Leuven, Leuven, Belgium

A. Wilkinson
Dementia Lab, Inter-Actions, LUCA School of Arts, Genk, Belgium
e-mail: Andrea.Wilkinson@luca-arts.be

© Springer Nature Switzerland AG 2020

R. Brankaert and G. Kenning (eds.), *HCI and Design in the Context of Dementia*, Human–Computer Interaction Series,
https://doi.org/10.1007/978-3-030-32835-1_7

the design process. Along with budget and time restrictions Smeenk et al. (2017) sees as a first reason the absence of adequate PD or co-design methods. Rodgers believes this comes from the fact that 'many codesign techniques and tools, however, assume particular skills, expertise, and processes that rely on certain levels of communication, cognitive, and creative skills on the part the participants' (Rodgers 2017, p. 192) and that these skills are often absent when working with people with dementia. For this reason, the existing co-design tools and techniques are not appropriate. Morrissey too acknowledges this, as she sees that most designers typically turn to workshop approaches and focus too much on output. She feels designers need to reflect on 'what we [designers] consider as communicative in order to open up our notions of participation and authorship in dementia' (Morrissey 2017, p. 64) and search for ways to engage people with dementia in the design process. The research question we focus on in this chapter consequently starts from the idea of recognizing a person with dementia as a partner in the research and design process, and focuses on these *ways of engaging*. As such, this chapter describes the search for a set of methods, tools and techniques that supports the involvement of people with dementia in the design process.

## 7.2 From One Size-Fits-All Approach to Building Personal Relationships

The answer to the question at stake has been developed in three case studies, a series of workshops and an educational module for design students. The next section will show how the question has been answered through the different case studies.

### *7.2.1 AToM—In Search of a Dedicated Method*

The aim of the AToM (A Touch of Memory) project was to setup an intelligent network of objects (sensors, smart devices, etc.) and people (formal carers, partners, etc.) working together to ameliorate the life of a person with dementia. At the time we carried out this project, a series of guidelines was created, adapted from literature describing the involvement of people with amnesia and aphasia (two common symptoms related to dementia) and literature on involvement of older adults and people with dementia. These 29 guidelines were tested and refined during the AToM-project. The guidelines focused on, amongst others, the role of the moderator of a PD session, the different participants, or the way the results of a participatory session could be analyzed (see Hendriks et al. 2013). The approach of searching for dedicated methods was revised after failed attempts at applying these in a design project and a search for new and refined sets of methods in a series of workshops began (Fig. 7.1).

**Fig. 7.1** A series of workshops: against dedicated methods and method stories at CHI16

At these workshops (see Hendriks et al. 2015) researchers and designers were brought together to discuss the methods that could be fitting to involve people with sensory and cognitive impairments (such as dementia) in the design process. All workshop organizers were working on technology-oriented projects dealing with people with cognitive and sensory impairments and wanted, through these workshops, to learn from the experiences of others as the workshop format stimulated sharing of experiences and debate on the challenges each participant perceived. A total of 42 researchers and designers participated in the workshop series. The conclusion from these workshops was that dedicated methods were not the path to follow, but instead more individualized ways of working (adapted to the abilities and disabilities of those involved) were needed. To learn from the experience of others was considered to be fruitful, however, the final part of each workshop, which tried to abstract general guidelines from each individual's experience clashed with the nuanced experiences (based on individual context or who one worked with) that each researcher or designer wanted to bring to the table.

### *7.2.2 Dementia Lab: Personalized Ways of Working*

Despite the fact that attempts to generate a certain form of a generalized way of working was still the goal of the next project, a more qualitative and individualized way of working gradually became part of the way of working set forth. This next project, Dementia Lab[1], had as a goal to support occupational therapists of a local *Public Centre for Social Welfare* in Belgium. The occupational therapists visited people with dementia living at home to see how they could support their living at home and home-based care. The goal of this project was to explore design's potential to support the occupational therapists and the person with dementia. We set up a PD process with people with dementia where people with dementia and designers would collaboratively create the artefacts. Slowly, we learned that working together with people with dementia required a strong engagement of the designer and researcher. In one instance, this led to going grocery shopping, cooking and eating together with a person with dementia and visiting them for several weeks afterwards. In another instance, working on a calendar together with a woman with dementia had the designers meet in at her home each Monday morning for over three months. These types of investments—personal contact, frequent visits, and a focus that was not always on the design element at hand—were later analyzed as being crucial for facilitating the participation of the person with dementia.

### 7.2.3 *AtHome: Embeddedness and Relationship Building*

Despite our positive experiences of being able to work more personally, there was still a feeling that a more hands-on way of working would be valuable as we felt that there was an artificial separation between the places of care and living, the nursing care home or the homes of the person with dementia where the designers and the people with dementia would meet, and the place where most of the design work took place, the offices and workshop of the designers and researchers. Other 'material' elements, apart from the space where the design work happened, were also of importance. The fact that working together with a person with dementia was only carried out in certain time-restricted and clearly agreed moments of time is just one example. These time-restrictions led to many appointments going to waste because, for example, the person with dementia was not in the mood to work together, or the person with dementia would, in some cases, become nervous or even agitated. Each visit meant entering the world of the person with dementia and 'intruding' into their lives and places of living and care. The fact that one intrudes their space, leads to potential power imbalances that may negatively affect the involvement of the person with dementia. In our next project, AtHome, we aimed to reduce this feeling of being an intruder. This started by building a relationship with a person with dementia (see also Hendriks et al. 2018). This relationship forms the basis of our defining ways to facilitate the participation of the person with dementia.

[1]The Dementia Lab project is not to be mistaken with the Dementia Lab Conference. While the Dementia Lab project was a one-off project, the name Dementia Lab was used to cluster all efforts on design and dementia at the institute of two of the authors. As the conference was founded by these authors, the conference self-evidently was named Dementia Lab Conference.

Building a relationship cannot be done hastily. For these reasons, in AtHome we were embedded in a care facility. The AtHome project had as an aim to research how artistic and designerly practices can enhance the feeling of home for a person with dementia in a nursing care home. Methodologically, AtHome explored how this longitudinal embeddedness would support the involvement of people with dementia. This brought the authors at least once a week for more than three years to the care facility and saw them working in a room close to or in the dementia ward. After AtHome we concluded that longitudinal involvement and relationship building should form the basis of facilitating a person with dementia's involvement (read in more detail in Hendriks et al. 2018).

### *7.2.4 Educational Module: Person-Centered Care as Framework*

As a way to transfer the findings of these projects to education, an educational module for design students was set up. Each year, for over four years, eight to 15 master's degree students from various design disciplines participated in the educational module, sometimes supplemented by a professional designer. In the course of 15 weeks, each student worked closely with one person with dementia and designed an artefact that would make their life more pleasant. All classes, workshops, design work and moments of interaction between the design student and the person with dementia in this module took place in dementia wards of several care facilities. In the educational module, it became clear that the search for a dedicated passe-partout way of working that could be applicable in designing together with a person with dementia should be abandoned. As discussed in the next section, designers using more dedicated approaches were negative about such an application as, amongst other things, it lacked practical responses to the situations at hand or the guidelines were too rigid. In lieu of the dedicated passe-partout way of working, we came to believe that the collaboration between a person with dementia and the designer should be based on the relationship they have. Through this relationship, the designer can define and facilitate ways of involving the person with dementia.

As can be seen, the initial attempt at finding a dedicated method was abandoned in favor of a more personal or individual approach. Before going deeper into what this personal approach entails, the next section will first explain why we kept attempting to, for a long time, hold on to a dedicated, one-size-fits-all way of working.

## 7.3 From Methodism to a Focus on Relational Way of Working

Multiple reasons exist to not focus on a dedicated universal method. In a previous publication we described how dementia is an umbrella term encompassing a series of different types of dementia and the individual way in which dementia unfolds does not allow for a *one-size-fits-all* approach (Hendriks et al. 2015). While there are approximate distinctions between different phases (ALZ.org 2007) there is no single way, to describe how dementia will unfold and affect the life of an individual. Furthermore, it is unfitting to not validate the person with dementia as the unique human being they are. In addition, designers who provided the 29 guidelines, referenced previously, felt they were not sufficient and gave specific reasons (Hendriks 2019). They advised: (1) the guidelines are a checklist that can be used to see whether the designer thought about a certain aspect (or not) but it is not a real *way of working*; (2) what is actually needed, is a method that can be used *in the field*. (3) The guidelines do not help designers *in the moment*, at the time when something goes wrong or in cases in which the designer has something planned but the moment asks for a certain improvisation on the spot. (4) Not every guideline is relevant; thus it is better to have a more dynamic set of rules that is adaptable towards a specific context (residential vs. home care; early stage vs. late stage; capability to verbally communicate vs. having a severe form of aphasia); (5) the format (a list of *rules*) wasn't always useable and was found to be too generic.

The ambition of wanting to find a dedicated method, as was the initial ambition, came from what can be labeled as method-ism. *Method-ism* is described as the use of methodologies, tools and techniques in a rational and detached way (Introna & Whitley 1997) leading to knowledge and understanding. Method-ism can be understood as a recipe that is applied rigorously in the hope of leading to a satisfying outcome. However it does not enforce the need to take into account the situation or context of use. According to Heidegger (1962), tools only make sense in use and thus the way a tool is applied will depend on the use context and the understanding of the context that arises. Moreover, this process also happens in reverse: when using a tool, understanding and knowledge will change. Introna and Whitley (1997), therefore, also see the application of a method as having a cyclical element wherein the method, tools and techniques are adapted according to the understanding and knowledge that is generated at hand. In other words, what they suggest is that a method is not something that should be strictly followed, but it is more of a toolbox that gets adapted in relation to the situation at hand and the understanding and knowledge that gradually grows.

The way in which the initial question of finding methods, tools and techniques in this chapter was answered started off from the principles of *method-ism* but took on a different approach, namely, a relational way of working; seeing methods more as *toolboxes* (open, ad-hoc assemblages). This relational way of working is explained in the next section.

### 7.3.1 *Relational Way of Working*

The search for a dedicated method was abandoned and the starting point of the design process became the individual way of working with the person with dementia. In individually working with a person, a relationship is built-up. The knowledge, experience and expertise arising out of this relationship is the starting point that define and establishes ways of involving the person with dementia. To go from this dedicated and universal way of working, and a form of *method-ism*, to a more relational way of working is of course not something that happened overnight, but is the result of multiple (smaller) insights that came throughout the years (and the various projects, workshops and educational modules described above) and it is, in hindsight, hard to discern when this insight exactly came about. There are however some elements that became catalysts. In the various workshops we abandoned the idea of a dedicated method but acknowledged the value of the different individual stories each participant brought to the table. Moreover, the focus of the workshops was altered as we focused on how the details of the individual stories (of designers working with a person with dementia) helped others to set up or adapt their way of working. In addition, in the Dementia Lab project one specific anecdote became of great importance in how the relational way of working came about. In this project and in one particular example we worked closely together with a former (female) cook. Our way of working was to cook and eat together and through this process integrate, evaluate and adapt some design artefacts along the way. Looking at this process retrospectively, when being present as people preparing and eating food together we were not perceived as designers or researchers, but as nice people (friends) who were willing to visit and cook. When one of the researchers tried to redefine the relationship and stepped out of this role of the *friend who came over to cook* and became a researcher who started to observe activities and was explicitly not cooking, but taking notes and observing what the woman with dementia was doing, this irritated the woman with dementia who indicated 'you are not here to observe me'.

Not only do these experiences lead to a change of focus, from dedicated ways of working to a more relational way of working, but also reflects the work of other researchers and designers. These researchers and designers defined various methods, tools and techniques for involving people with dementia in this relational way of working. Caris-Verhallen et al. (1999) experimented with proximity and touch; Branco et al. (2016) used openness (elements of the artefacts left open to be filled in); Wallace et al. (2013) took on artefacts as mediators in communication; Morrissey (2017) focused on touch, movement, song and dance; Kenning (2017) used a variety of tools from surveys to like dislike-tools to enable less direct ways of encouraging involvement. These researchers and designers show that it is through building close relationships with people with dementia that these methods, tools and techniques came into fruition. It is from these close relationships that the designers and researchers gained relational expertise through the knowledge they have acquired in frequent interactions with people with dementia (Dindler & Iversen 2014). The designers and researchers then use this relational expertise to select, adapt and appropriate existing tools and techniques to facilitate the collaboration with the person with dementia. In addition, by building up the relational expertise with one person with dementia, the designer is better suited in defining design decisions implicitly: based on, for example, non-verbal expressions (nods, smiles, muscle tension, being focused or not) or how a designer interprets the response of the person.

Although they do not always name it as such, the above-mentioned designers and researchers use the relational expertise as their foundation to facilitate involvement. The novelty of this chapter lies in providing guiding principles to put this relational way of working into practice, something that was lacking in the literature. As can be read in the next paragraph, the guiding principles were based on marrying the elements that are specific to the (participatory) design domain (PD) and elements that are specific to person-centered care (PCC), a care paradigm that is often adopted in dementia care.

### *7.3.2 Relational Way of Working Put into Practice*

The relational way of working was tested and refined throughout the educational module and the AtHome-project (all findings in the following section are, however, only related to the educational module). This resulted in four guiding principles that serve as concrete foundational elements, or *handles*, on which to build a relationship, gain relational expertise and facilitate the involvement of people with dementia. These guiding principles differ from guidelines or a set rules. Guiding principles are not intended to be rules to govern (or strict guidelines), but more of a compass or set of values that can be seen as a framework. For this reason, some guiding principles are less *directive* than the above-mentioned guidelines.

The guiding principles described here were based on marrying elements from PCC with elements specific to participatory design. The reasoning behind this is that PCC is a care paradigm that supports caregivers to set up, engage in and nurture meaningful relationships and interactions with people with dementia. Three central elements of person-centered care were used: reflection (on your interactions with the person with dementia (for example Passalacqua & Harwood 2012), the use of storytelling (as a way to create the story of the person with dementia and to narrate the encounters with the person with dementia) and the use of role-play (to acquire a better patient understanding via elements of drama (Kontos et al. 2010). While PCC focuses on relationship building, PD focuses on the value of the designed artefacts and the explicit sharing of power and how these designed artefacts can play a role herein. We will explain each of the four guiding principles and narrate how they were put into practice into a design process.

### 7.3.3 Creating Choices Through Reflective Designerly Actions

In PCC there is some focus on reflective actions; analyzing one's fears or challenges and evaluating how one experiences and responds to, for example, positive, resistive, or awkward behaviors of a person with dementia. This (self) reflection happens both individually as well as in a group of peers. In PD, such reflection could be used to create choices, to open up more potential design paths. In the educational module (self) reflection happened in videos as each designer made short video reflections after each interaction with a person with dementia and reviewed these videos multiple times throughout the design process and in group discussions with peers, carers and the authors of this paper. The confrontation with their own words (when reviewing the video-reflections) and the suggestions, critique and reflections of others helped the designers to be critical towards their own design choices and opened up new potential paths for design. Reflecting on the different interactions with the people with dementia helped them to make small discoveries and *handles* to open up new design paths. Most of the times these *handles* were not clear *in the moment*, but became of importance after the reflection through the videos and group conversations. These *handles* could be rituals or habits (for example, humming along with folk songs or the continuously touching of clothing), historic events (having survived a bombardment) or objects that were evident of being of great importance or triggering an intense response with the person with dementia. These *handles* were used as a way to *draw* a person in the design process.

This can be exemplified by the story of designer Mira, who, after some weeks working with Jeanne, was unsure which paths would be interesting to follow. She experimented with board games, but, after reviewing her own interactions (through the video reflections) she realized there was one particular element she had forgotten to explore. 'We read glossy magazines together. I thought she read it for the showbiz. (…) I only realized later on, that I should use clothing and glossy magazines to capture her attention. In quite subtle ways I could have noticed her enthusiasm for clothing (…). I then gathered piles of books on fashion of the 60s and 70s and used this to define what she thought was beautiful or what type of style she liked most.' Mira realized, only after looking back on her own work, that this was a path to follow after she noticed that in her video reflections she often casually referred to the magazines and how Jeanne was enjoying them.

### 7.3.4 Making Selections Through Storytelling

Storytelling is used in PCC to enable caregivers to make explicit the story of how they perceive a person with dementia. In this way, carers gain insight in how they perceive a person with dementia and they are asked to critically look at how this perception influences the way they take care decisions and interact with them. Making design selections on the other hand, deals with the fact that each design process has a multitude of potential paths the design process can take, but one will have to make selections and chose only one path the design process will take. Storytelling helps the designer make these selections.

An example could be found in the story of Bea. In the first two weeks of the design process in the educational module, students were required to create stories. These stories were told through sketches, photo-stories and more poetic materializations such as soundscapes or small clay statues. These sketches, photo-stories and materializations showed how the designer perceived the person with dementia, what their vision on and relationship with them is. In a clay statue, designer Bea expressed the sadness she experienced in Jean, the person with dementia she collaborated with. The statue shows Jean crying, something he did very often. Later, she understood that this crying was not (only) an expression of him feeling unhappy, but a way to express negative as well as positive emotions. In the course of the weeks, she learned to understand and use his responses (crying, holding hands, etc.) in their encounters and this helped her to, in this way, make selections in the potential design decisions she could take.

### *7.3.5 Making Design Choices Concrete Through Role-Playing*

Role-playing in PCC is used to reflect on and improve ways in which a caregiver interacts with a person with dementia. In the educational module role-playing was used to enact how the designs (from concepts, over sketches or prototypes) could work in day-to-day situations. These role-plays supported the designer in evaluating the collaboratively-made design decisions. In the educational module, role-play happened on two levels. On the one hand, sessions were set up wherein the designer *performs* how a certain design choice would work out for the person with dementia in real-life situations, involving the person with dementia (played by the designer or one of their peers), the carers and peers, all reflect and critique on what has been enacted. The other form of role-play sees the designer stepping into the lived reality of the person with dementia and integrates the *what if's* of the design decision into this role-play. As an example, designer Xavier used the act of smoking together and stimulating (or role-playing) a *good old boy's* atmosphere to set the correct tone to reflect, together with resident Gust, on what his design could mean. Xavier therefore used smoking and talking about 'Cigarettes, women and being a male. Haha, I know. (…) He smokes, just like I do. I waited for him when he was allowed to go for a smoke and would join him. Then I would "randomly" show him my designs and have him … well, respond to it. In the meantime, we talked about "women" and going out. Otherwise he wasn't interested.' Xavier role-played this *old boy's atmosphere* and suggested what the design (a playful day schedule) could mean and in this way had his resident collaborate. It is thus through role-playing that design choices are collaboratively made.

### 7.3.6 Evaluating Design Decisions Together

The designer wants to understand the use-context of the person with dementia. Through this embedded approach with the person with dementia, they are able to evaluate design decisions and look at the integration of the design in daily life and care. The evaluation happens through use and by making design decisions transparent by, for example, creating posters that make explicit how the design decisions came about. Evaluating design decisions becomes part of the act of making. Making happens through use, taking artefacts into the context of daily life and care and adapting them on the spot. This process of making and adapting is based *on the spot* evaluations.

Designer Karen worked together with Ann, a person with dementia who was confined to her wheelchair and hardly responded to any visual or verbal stimuli. Karen tried to understand what type of textures and material elements would give Ann the most pleasant experience and gave Ann different types of fabrics to hold. While Ann held the fabrics, Karen interpreted her non-verbal responses and adapted her designs *on the spot*. Such an approach is not a prototyping workshop where we see a non-designer actively cutting, pasting and gluing the material of their liking, but still, there a making process, within Ann's the abilities, that happens through use. Sketches of designs created together with and for Karen can be seen in Fig. 7.2.

## 7.4 Conclusion

The research question central to this chapter was to find a set of tools and techniques that could be produced to support the involvement of people with dementia in the design process. It started from a dedicated, universal approach. First, a series of design guidelines based on participatory projects involving people with aphasia, amnesia and elderly was defined. However, an analysis of the design work indicated that passe-partout way of working was not possible for every person with dementia. One of the main conclusions was that a more individualized way of working was needed. This individualized way of working supports the build-up of a personal relationship between the person with dementia and the designer. It is based on this personal relationship that the design decisions are collaboratively taken and ways to facilitate involvement of a person with dementia are defined. This chapter defines four guiding principles that help to setup this personal relationship, gain relational expertise and make design decisions collaboratively.

Future research will look into several challenges that come with such a relational way of working. We foresee challenges on the level of feasibility: how can results from such an individual approach be used for a larger group of people with dementia

**Fig. 7.2** Sketches of a prototype created together and for Ann

and is this way of working too costly, taking up too much time of the designer and researcher? In addition, ethical issues arise: how *deep* as a designer do you step into this relationship and how do you discern your role as 'human being' from that of a designer or researcher and what is the best way to end a relationship, what is the exit strategy when the formal project time is over?

## References


ALZ.org (2007) Stages of Alzheimer's & Symptoms | Alzheimer's Association. Geraadpleegd 8 januari 2018, van https://www.alz.org/alzheimers_disease_stages_of_alzheimers.asp#late

American Psychiatric Association (2000) Diagnostic and statistical manual of mental disorders: DSM-IV-TR®. American Psychiatric Publishing

Binder T (1996) Learning and knowing with artifacts: an interview with Donald A. Schön. AI Soc 10(1):51–57. https://doi.org/10.1007/BF02716754

Binney EA, Estes CL, Ingman SR (1990) Medicalization, public policy and the elderly: social services in jeopardy? Soc Sci Med 30(7):761–771

Bond J (1992) The medicalization of dementia. J Aging Stud 6(4):397–403

Branco RM, Quental J, Ribeiro Ó (2016) Playing with personalisation and openness in a codesign project involving people with dementia. In: Proceedings of the 14th participatory design conference: full papers, vol 1, pp 61–70. https://doi.org/10.1145/2940299.2940309

Branco RM, Quental J, Ribeiro Ó (2017) Personalised participation: An approach to involve people with dementia and their families in a participatory design project. CoDesign 13(2):127–143. https://doi.org/10.1080/15710882.2017.1310903

Caris-Verhallen WM, Kerkstra A, Bensing JM (1999) Non-verbal behaviour in nurse–elderly patient communication. J Adv Nurs 29(4):808–818

Dindler C, Iversen OS (2014) Relational expertise in participatory design. In: Proceedings of the 13th participatory design conference: research papers, vol 1, pp 41–50. https://doi.org/10.1145/2661435.2661452

Heidegger M (1962) Being and time. 1927 (trans: Macquarrie J, Robinson E). Harper, New York

Hendriks N (2019) The involvement of people with dementia in the design process (University of Leuven). Geraadpleegd van https://lirias.kuleuven.be/retrieve/534184

Hendriks N, Huybrechts L, Slegers K, Wilkinson A (2018) Valuing implicit decision-making in participatory design: A relational approach in design with people with dementia. Des Stud 59:58–76. https://doi.org/10.1016/j.destud.2018.06.001

Hendriks N, Slegers K, Duysburgh P (2015) Codesign with people living with cognitive or sensory impairments: a case for method stories and uniqueness. CoDesign 11(1):70–82. https://doi.org/10.1080/15710882.2015.1020316

Hendriks N, Truyen F, Duval E (2013) Designing with dementia: guidelines for participatory design together with persons with dementia. In: Kotzé P, Marsden G, Lindgaard G, Wesson J, Winckler M (red) Human-computer interaction—INTERACT 2013. Springer, Berlin, Heidelberg, pp 649–666

Introna LD, Whitley EA (1997) Against method-ism: exploring the limits of method. Inf Technol People 10(1):31–45

Kenning G (2017) Making it together: reciprocal design to promote positive wellbeing for people living with dementia. Geraadpleegd van UTS website: https://gailkenning.files.wordpress.com/2017/10/making-it-together-final-reduced-size.pdf

Kenning G (2018) Reciprocal design: inclusive design approaches for people with late stage dementia. Des Health 2(1):1–21

Kontos PC, Mitchell GJ, Mistry B, Ballon B (2010) Using drama to improve person-centred dementia care. Int J Older People Nurs 5(2):159–168

Luck R (2003) Dialogue in participatory design. Des Stud 24(6):523–535. https://doi.org/10.1016/s0142-694x(03)00040-1

Morrissey K (2017) “I’m a rambler, I’m a gambler, I’m a long way from home”: exploring participation through music and digital design in dementia care (University College Cork). Geraadpleegd van https://hdl.handle.net/10468/3524

Passalacqua SA, Harwood J (2012) VIPS communication skills training for paraprofessional dementia caregivers: an intervention to increase person-centered dementia care. Clin Gerontol 35(5):425–445. https://doi.org/10.1080/07317115.2012.702655

Rodgers PA (2017) Co-designing with people living with dementia. CoDesign 0(0):1–15. https://doi.org/10.1080/15710882.2017.1282527

Smeenk W, Sturm J, Eggen B (2017) Empathic handover: how would you feel? Handing over dementia experiences and feelings in empathic co-design. CoDesign 1(1): 1–16

Span M, Hettinga M, Vernooij-Dassen M, Eefsting J, Smits C (2013) Involving people with dementia in the development of supportive IT applications: a systematic review. Ageing Res Rev 12(2):535–551

Wallace J, Wright PC, McCarthy J, Green DP, Thomas J, Olivier P (2013) A design-led inquiry into personhood in dementia. In: Proceedings of the SIGCHI conference on human factors in computing systems, pp 2617–2626. https://doi.org/10.1145/2470654.2481363

# Chapter 8
# Materializing Personhood: Design-Led Perspectives

**Rita Maldonado Branco, Joana Quental, and Óscar Ribeiro**

## 8.1 Introduction

The ideas presented in this chapter were developed as part of a doctoral project to design appropriate personalized strategies for ludic communication between people with dementia and those in their close social circle, while inviting them to participate in the process (Branco 2018). The research questioned how the values of person-centered care (Brooker 2007; Killick and Allan 2001; Kitwood 1997) based on respecting and maintaining personhood and social relationships could be used and reflected in the designed artefacts and in the configuration of participatory design processes involving people with dementia.

R. M. Branco (✉)
Research Institute for Design, Media and Culture (ID+), Aveiro, Portugal
e-mail: Ritamaldonadobranco@gmail.com

J. Quental
Research Institute for Design, Media and Culture (ID+), Aveiro, Portugal
e-mail: Joana.Quental@ua.pt

Department of Communication and Art, University of Aveiro, Aveiro, Portugal

Ó. Ribeiro
Department of Education and Psychology, University of Aveiro, Aveiro, Portugal
e-mail: Oribeiro@ua.pt

Centre for Health Technology and Services Research (CINTESIS), Porto, Portugal

© Springer Nature Switzerland AG 2020

R. Brankaert and G. Kenning (eds.), *HCI and Design in the Context of Dementia*, Human–Computer Interaction Series,
https://doi.org/10.1007/978-3-030-32835-1_8

## 8.2 Personhood and Positive Person Work

The concept of personhood, originally associated with dementia care by Kitwood (1997), refers to a relational sense of self which is conveyed by others, highlighting that we can only be truly a person if we are recognized as such by others, and that our sense of self is maintained through being in relationships, and thus in communication. Kitwood (1997, pp. 89–92) described ten types of interaction toward people with dementia that address their psychological needs, preserve personhood, and enhance well-being, naming them *Positive Person Work.* He viewed this approach as being in opposition to *Malignant Social Psychology* (Kitwood 1997, pp. 45–49), a group of 17 interactions that he perceived as a threat to personhood. Positive Person Work includes recognition, negotiation, collaboration, play, timalation (referring to sensorial stimulation), celebration, relaxation, validation, holding, and facilitation. In fact, Kitwood (1997) mentioned two more interactions: creation and giving. While the first ten are initiated by the carer, positioning the person with dementia as a receiver, the second two arise spontaneously from the person with dementia, to whom the carer should respond in an empathic and encouraging way. In this chapter, we focus on these initial ten interactions.

### *8.2.1 Designing for Positive Person Work*

The relationship between humans and material objects are described by Verbeek (2012) as mediation. In his view, 'material objects play a role in the relations between humans and their world, helping to give shape to the nature of their experiences and activities' (p. 167), and that 'an intervention in the material world is always an intervention in the human world' (p. 172). Likewise, Niedderer (2007) discusses the role potential artefacts have in mediating social interaction, suggesting a triangulated interaction. Among other design research concerned with designing for positive experiences and subjective well-being (Hassenzahl 2010; Pohlmeyer and Desmet 2017), Pohlmeyer (2013) analyzes possible roles that design can have in promoting happiness. She recognizes artefacts as direct sources of happiness; artefacts as enablers of an activity that contributes to well-being; artefacts as symbolic representations of something valuable to people; and artefacts as support and encouragement to motivate and guide people to happiness-enhancing activities.

Drawing on these ideas, we propose three main functions that artefacts can have in promoting Positive Person Work interactions (Fig. 8.1): (1) artefacts can act as *symbols*, if their pragmatic and hedonic attributes correspond and symbolically suggest the values and attitudes inherent to the Positive Person Work interactions; (2) artefacts can be *catalysts* of Positive Person Work, providing the interactions directly to the person with dementia; and (3) artefacts can *support* others to initiate Positive Person Work with the person with dementia, mediating these interactions and acting as vehicles for communication.

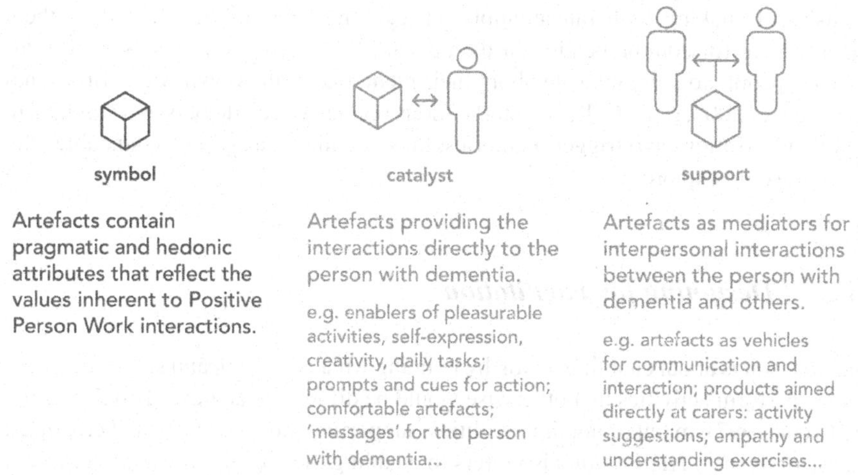

symbol
Artefacts contain pragmatic and hedonic attributes that reflect the values inherent to Positive Person Work interactions.
catalyst
Artefacts providing the interactions directly to the person with dementia.
e.g. enablers of pleasurable activities, self-expression, creativity, daily tasks; prompts and cues for action; comfortable artefacts; 'messages' for the person with dementia...
support
Artefacts as mediators for interpersonal interactions between the person with dementia and others.
e.g. artefacts as vehicles for communication and interaction; products aimed directly at carers: activity suggestions; empathy and understanding exercises...


**Fig. 8.1** Roles of artefacts in promoting Positive Person Work

It is important to note that although artefacts might have the potential to promote these interactions, and thus positive experiences for people with dementia and those taking part in the interaction, the experience also depends on how each individual person perceives and uses the artefact. Desmet and Hekkert suggest 'Experience is not a property of the product but the outcome of human-product interaction, and therefore dependent on what temporal and dispositional characteristics the user brings into the interaction' (2007, p. 7). We begin by providing an overview of the ten Positive Person Work interactions and reflecting on how artefacts can promote these interactions.

### *8.2.2 Designing for Recognition*

In this context, *Recognition* refers to the acknowledgement of the person with dementia as a person, and the affirmation of her or his own uniqueness (Brooker 2007; Kitwood 1997; Van Weert et al. 2006). Designing for *recognition* implies that what is designed demonstrates respect and dignity for the person, both in the proposed use and mediated interactions, and aesthetically. *Recognition* can be used as a design strategy to affirm the person's identity and uniqueness. Artefacts can be triggers to support talking about identity and idiosyncrasies. This can be further reinforced if artefacts invite and allow for personalization, such as including the person's names, emphasizing her or his characteristics and virtues, using known references, and promoting activities that are meaningful. The use of references, from the past or from popular culture, to elicit autobiographical memories is a frequent strategy in designing for people with dementia, especially if the aim is to engage them in activities and conversation. Here, *recognition* is related to reminiscence, 'the voluntary or involuntary action of recollecting memories from one's past' (Afonso et al. 2016, p. 2), which consists of 'making deliberate attempts to trigger memories of the past and use them as a vehicle for communication in the present. Reminiscence provides opportunities for people to communicate about their memories in their own way' (Bruce and Schweitzer 2008, p. 170). These interventions regularly use artefacts as a stimulus to start conversations and trigger memories, thus making it easily understandable why design would explore it.

### 8.2.3 Designing for Facilitation

*Facilitation* is about enabling action by noticing what is missing and supporting people to perform activities that otherwise would be difficult to achieve (Brooker 2007; Kitwood 1997), maintaining their abilities, supporting independence, and creating a sense of agency. *Facilitation* also refers to enabling the creation of *meaning*, which according to Hassenzahl (2010), lies in the hedonic characteristics of an artefact (i.e., its aesthetics, attractiveness, capacity to stimulate and to communicate one's identity). In fact, Hughes (2014) describes people with dementia as 'aesthetic beings', referring to their embodied engagement with all the dimensions of the world, not only through understanding, but also through the senses. Designing for people with dementia can be envisaged as an opportunity for supporting this aesthetic approach and creating aesthetic experiences. In addition, aesthetic decisions can support functionality and ease of use, by making artefacts culturally and personally relevant and less stigmatizing: creating a familiar and recognizable appearance; utilizing contrasting colors to help to distinguish different elements; creating consistency among different elements; emphasizing the essential functions and features and avoiding unnecessary complexity (Gowans et al. 2007; Pullin 2009; Timlin and Rysenbry 2010; Zeisel 2009).

It is important to envisage possibilities and uses that can support differing abilities, across the progression of dementia, and to understand what can be helpful and enabling, or confronting and diminishing. For example, while a person in more advanced stages of dementia might need a specific artefact to undertake a certain activity, someone in the early stages might find the same artefact stigmatizing. This might, therefore, require the design of different solutions or artefacts to adapt to these changes. Artefacts that assist care and support the carer also fit into this concept of *facilitation*.

### 8.2.4 Designing for Negotiation

*Negotiation* consists of providing opportunities for exercising control and choice (Brooker 2007; Kitwood 1997), through being consulted about needs and preferences in daily life, or through stimulating personal and creative expression (Allan 2001).

Artefacts can play a role in triggering conversation and create space for dialog (Wallace et al. 2013) and can be catalysts of choice, despite the difficulties in communicating verbally, understanding, and remembering. The ability to recognize rather than remember is key and so multiple-choice formats are often less compromising and easier for people with dementia (Sabat 2014). Artefacts can be designed to provide several options and possibilities, allowing people to choose and can include elements that can be moved around, offer different aesthetic possibilities such as color, or provide different possibilities for use. Another way of designing for *negotiation* is to leave space in artefacts to stimulate self-expression and creativity or that support artistic activities (Killick and Craig 2011).

### 8.2.5 Designing for Collaboration

*Collaboration* means working together, involving the person with dementia 'as full as equal partner' (Brooker 2007, p. 94), instead of being a passive receiver of care. In the original definition by Kitwood (1997), *facilitation* and *collaboration* are interrelated. However, we chose to differentiate them, by emphasizing the enablement of people with dementia to undertake actions in *facilitation* and highlighting the promotion of joint actions in *collaboration*. Here, artefacts promote moments of togetherness and enable the person with dementia to participate in shared activities such as practical daily tasks or leisure. Designing experiences that involve cooperation, such as teamwork or artefacts that require interdependence, such as when the artefact needs more than one person to use or activate it, are possible ways to design for *collaboration*. Games are good examples of products that prompt social interaction and sense of togetherness, across different generations (Wildevuur et al. 2013). While inappropriate game experiences, which sometimes might be too challenging and competitive, may lead to frustration, appropriate games have the potential to improve the quality of life of people with dementia (Anderiesen et al. 2015).

### 8.2.6 Designing for Play

*Play* refers to spontaneity and self-expression (Kitwood 1997), and it is related to creativity, fun, and humor (Brooker 2007), which often have an important role in dealing with the adversities of dementia. Play can also stimulate imagination, positive enjoyment and active engagement, while promoting connectedness and bonding with others (Killick 2012). In order to design for *play*, artefacts need to promote fun through playful and sensorial experiences, encourage self-expression such as the sharing of stories, opinions, interpretations, feelings, or be related to artistic or creative activities. Caillois (1961) differentiates two types of play suggesting that *paidia is* free and spontaneous play and *ludus* is a more structured, game-like kind of play. Both can be taken into account and combined in designing for people with dementia.

While it is important that artefacts have familiar and recognizable appearances to facilitate understanding and use, ambiguous and versatile artefacts might trigger curiosity and openness, as they do not imply a right or wrong way to use them (Gaver 2009). Furthermore, deliberately designing an artefact that makes space for appropriation can be a way to add personalized, idiosyncratic elements that are relevant and meaningful for the person with dementia. Artefacts that allow spontaneous exploration with one's hands, involving fiddling and fidgeting, can be pleasurable particularly for people with advanced dementia (Treadaway et al. 2019). While, as mentioned, competitive games are not always suitable for people with dementia, the structure, rules, and material elements of the game can prompt playful activities, moments of sharing, and creative self-expression. For example, simple operational rules can guide action and challenge people to participate; turn-taking can ensure equal participation in a collective activity, supporting more passive players to contribute; behavioral rules can encourage a playful and open attitude, as well as role-playing; and game materials can be *things-to-think-with*, and help to bridge gaps in communication (Brandt 2011).

### *8.2.7 Designing for Timalation*

*Timalation* is a term coined by Kitwood which involves the provision of sensuous and sensory stimulation, without requiring intellectual understanding: 'The significance of this kind of interaction is that it can provide contact, reassurance and pleasure, while making very few demands' (Kitwood 1997, p. 91). Artefacts can be used as catalysts for sensorial stimulation, designing sensorial elements to provide a more active and energetic stimulation or in calmer moments, helping people to slow down and relax (Treadaway et al. 2015). Artefacts can support communication between persons with dementia and others, helping carers to develop a sensitivity to communicate non-verbally (Treadaway et al. 2019). Additionally, they can support *embodied selfhood*, 'the idea that bodily habits, gestures, and actions support and convey humanness and individuality' (Kontos 2014, p. 123).

Designing for *timalation* also means that the sensorial aspects of products need to be emphasized. It is also possible to consider the senses in relation to all kinds of products, placing attention on the textures and smell of materials, possible sounds arising from the use of the artefact, as well as the visual elements, so that artefacts can have rich sensory qualities, despite their function (Lupton and Lipps 2018; Sonneveld and Schifferstein 2008). However, overstimulation needs also to be considered.

### 8.2.8 Designing for Celebration

*Celebration* does not only refer to special occasions, but the experience of joy at any moment in life by promoting a friendly atmosphere. According to Kitwood (1997), this is a form of interaction where the differences between people with or without a diagnosis become less noticeable. Brooker (2007) suggests *celebration* is also 'recognizing, supporting and taking delight in the skills and achievements of the participant' (p. 92). Creating artefacts that enhance celebratory moments and focus on celebrating the person and what is meaningful to her or him, as well as her or his achievements, can be ways of designing for celebration. Furthermore, using humor, surprise, fun, and music can support the experience of celebration and joy through artefacts.

### 8.2.9 Designing for Relaxation

*Relaxation* consists of slowing down and creating a calm atmosphere (Brooker 2007; Kitwood 1997). Dementia symptoms can generate a lot of anxiety and agitation (Zeisel 2009), therefore people often need help to relax. Kitwood (1997) points out that some people with dementia are only able to relax when near others because of their high social needs. Artefacts can play a crucial role as catalysts of *relaxation*, mainly by providing comfort, warmness, and encouraging people to slow down, while being entertaining and appeasing. Friendly and familiar-looking artefacts can avoid stress, and a choice of soft tones and textures, that are pleasing to touch, or provide appropriate lighting can promote a relaxed environment (Bennett et al. 2016; Biamonti et al. 2014). Artefacts can also support carers in providing *relaxation* by inducing a calm atmosphere, or by suggesting to carers that they adapt to the pace of people with dementia. Even if slowing down is not the primary aim, the engagement in relaxation activities often makes people comfortable and at ease, distracting them from obsessive thoughts or behaviors (Branco 2018).

### 8.2.10 Designing for Holding

*Holding* 'means to provide a safe psychological space, a *container*' (Kitwood 1997, p. 91). Van Weert et al. (2006) adds empathy to the definition of *holding* so that the feelings of the person are accepted and responded to, with warmth and affection, and Brooker (2007) includes the provision of security and comfort as part of this kind of interaction. While promoting a relaxed environment, familiar and comfortable objects might foster a feeling of safety. Calming cues might help the person to reduce anxiety and feel secure. Personal belongings can also be reassuring and help to maintain some sense of autonomy (Treadaway et al. 2019). However, even if artefacts can be designed to promote a safe and comforting environment, *holding* is essentially a human interaction, which cannot be substituted for by artefacts. Therefore, it might be more relevant to design artefacts to support carers to provide this secure and comfortable environment. This can be done by either developing tools that help them to understand what and who causes the person to feel safe or unsafe, relaxed or stressed, and why, or by prompting collective activities that are suitable and pleasurable for the person. This approach encourages people with dementia to feel included and validated, which can be even more meaningful if occurring with those in their close social circle (Branco 2018).

### *8.2.11 Designing for Validation*

*Validation* refers to the acknowledgement and sensitivity of the experience, emotions, and subjective truth of the other, and of responding accordingly, at a *feelings* level. It requires empathy to seek an understanding of a person's frame of reference (Brooker 2007; Kitwood 1997). Similarly to *holding* and perhaps even more so, *validation* is a deep human interaction. An artefact can have a tender, affectionate appearance and language, and can be personalized, but for this kind of interaction people are needed. If artefacts create opportunities for people with dementia to be included in an activity, encouraging them to participate at their own pace and way, this might encourage others to listen and respect their contributions, relate to them, and validate them. Another approach consists of designing for empathy (Devecchi and Guerrini 2017; Gamman et al. 2015) and supporting carers to have an empathic and emotional understanding of the perspective of the person with dementia.

## 8.3 Codesigning with Positive Person Work

Along with design research about the participation of people with dementia in the design process (e.g., Branco et al. 2017; Hendriks et al. 2014, 2015, 2018; Kenning 2018; Lazar et al. 2017; Lindsay et al. 2012; Morrissey et al. 2017; Orpwood 2009; Wallace et al. 2013), studies about the involvement of people with dementia in research (Cowdell 2006, 2008; Dewing 2007), and research relating to communicating with people with dementia (Downs and Collins 2015; Killick and Allan 2001), Positive Person Work can be used in codesign processes involving people with dementia. For example:

- Including people with dementia as active participants in the design process, showing respect, greeting participants by their name, being sensitive to how they communicate, observing, listening carefully and non-judgementally, are all ways of taking *recognition* into account.

- Finding ways to *facilitate* participation through adapting the process to suit participants, setting up meetings that are not too long, having a warm and open attitude, avoiding activities that require abstract thinking, having good quality prototypes to try out, and redesigning tools and materials to support participation.
- Activities and materials can also be designed to promote *negotiation*, encouraging the exercise of choice, and providing opportunities for recognition rather than recall.
- The *collaboration* of family members and formal caregivers is also important to encourage participation, interaction, and bonding, although it should be ensured that people with dementia still have space to contribute by themselves.
- Codesign activities can constitute moments of fun and self-expression, thus embedding *play*.
- *Timalation* relates to paying attention to non-verbal gestures and expressions, and what they communicate about how a person is feeling, and the use of tangible and sensorial materials.
- Codesign activities should also focus on *celebrating* participants' abilities, their life history and personal references, as well as congratulating and valuing their contributions.
- It is important to ensure a *relaxed* and easy-going atmosphere, respecting the pace of participants.
- Creating a comfortable, non-judgemental, and friendly environment, demonstrating a caring and comforting attitude are also ways to encourage the person to feel secure enough to participate, thus taking *holding* into consideration.
- *Validation* demands an empathic attitude as shown:
  - during the planning, by understanding if what is being asked of participants is appropriate, and consulting family or formal carers about topics that might be confronting or elicit negative emotions;
  - during participatory events, by observing and paying attention to signs of tiredness, anxiety, boredom and or frustration and responding to participants' reactions and feelings; and being open to stop or postpone a meeting if it is not a good day and the person wishes to, even if not all the goals for that sessions are fulfilled.
  - after the research project is finished, by planning exit strategies.

## 8.4 Positive Person Work as Evaluation

In the present research, a codesign process was carried out based on the ten themes of Positive Person Work. It involved people with dementia and their families, and yielded several artefacts, either designed *from scratch* for a particular person or family, or through the personalization of previously conceived artefacts. These outputs were produced and delivered to the participating families, as well as used in

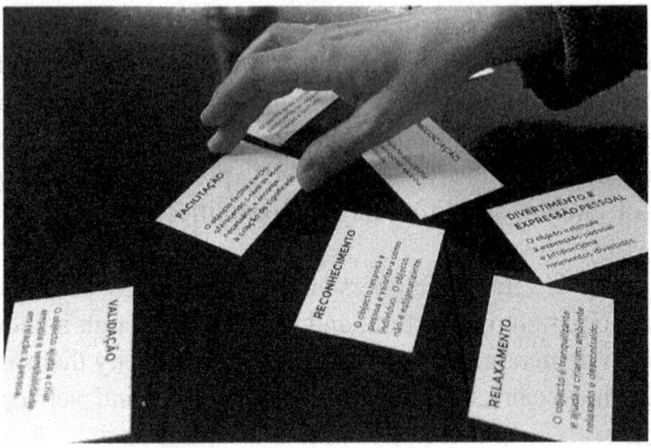


**Fig. 8.2** Choosing interaction-cards for the Positive Person Work evaluation exercise

institutional settings. While it is not possible to provide details of the process here, it is useful to show how the themes of Positive Person Work can be used to evaluate the artefacts produced. Family members and healthcare professionals evaluated how the artefacts were used and experienced, based on interviews and on a card sorting exercise devised to understand if participants perceived and associated the Positive Person Work interactions with the artefacts. Interviewees were invited to select the interaction they associated with the artefact from a series of cards that contained details of each interaction, and to explain their choice (Fig. 8.2). In addition, healthcare professionals were asked to reflect on ways in which the artefacts mediated these interactions (Fig. 8.3), and acted as

1. direct catalysts of the interaction with the person with dementia;
2. as support for the carers to deliver the interaction;
3. as a symbol of the values inherent in the interactions.

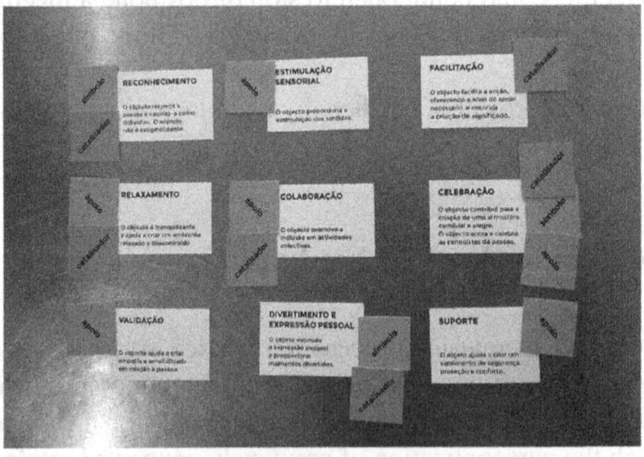


**Fig. 8.3** Positive Person Work evaluation exercise, including the associated roles of artefacts in promoting Positive Person Work

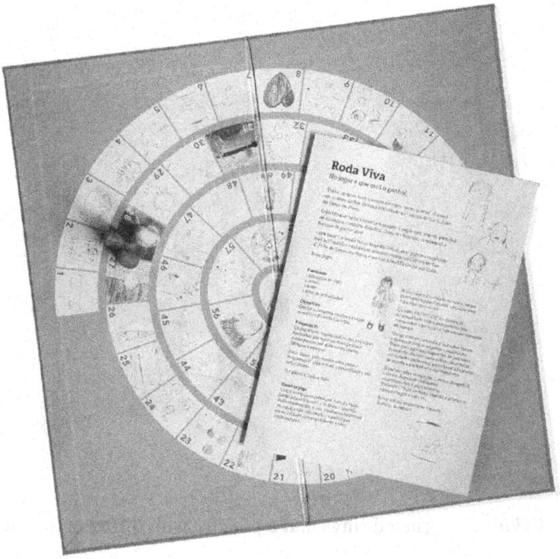


Fig. 8.4 A personalized board game

Although the sample was not large enough to draw specific conclusions, these exercises served as a basis for discussing and reflecting on the association between Positive Person Work and the design of artefacts for and with people with dementia. In order to illustrate this evaluation exercise based on Positive Person Work, we will focus on two of the products that were analyzed by family members and healthcare professionals:

1. *The Board Game* (Fig. 8.4) is a simple game that can be personalized. It was designed to provide opportunities for families to engage with their relative in a collective activity, by compiling details of some of the activities delivered by the institutions, and presenting them in an easy format to enable families to do them at home (Branco et al. 2015).
2. *The Tactful Things* (Fig. 8.5) consist of two artefacts that make use of textiles to deliver appropriate and appealing tactile and visual stimulation. These artefacts were designed to respond to a specific person's need to touch and hold things with her hands, and to the observation of her particular gestures to sensory fabrics. They also referenced the person's past devotion to knitting and lace-making (Branco et al. 2016).

When asked to associate the Positive Person Work interactions with the two artefacts, none of the participants had difficulties in selecting several. Some participants chose all the interactions they considered the artefact could mediate, even if they noted that the interactions could be hindered by the setting or how the use of the artefact was supported. Other participants selected only those that they believed were occurring more obviously through the use of the artefact. In considering both artefacts, *recognition*, *holding*, and *relaxation* were the interactions selected most often by participants.

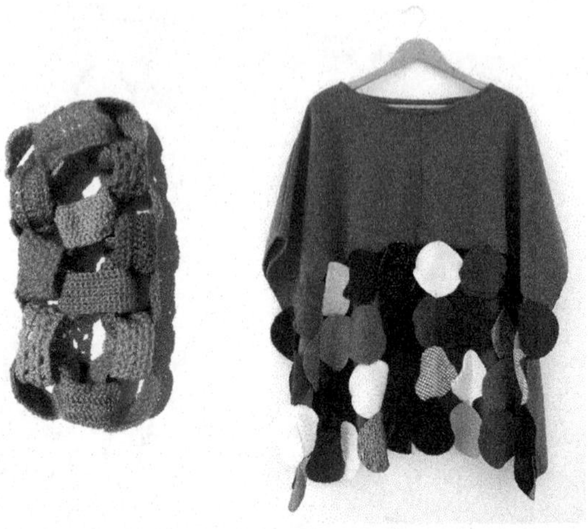

**Fig. 8.5** *The Tactful Things*: crocheted rings and a poncho with different textures and colors

Participants mainly associated *recognition* with the inclusion of personal content and activities, which was seen as a way to make it more meaningful and to validate the person with dementia. While *The tactful things* were created based on the gestures and preferences of a specific person, *The board game* allowed for personalization, promoting life history through references to people's identity and stories:

…it makes her identify herself with the game, to see herself as a person. It stimulates the memories of who they truly are. (relative, family B, 24.03.2017)

*Holding* was associated with the comfort and relaxation provided by *The Tactful Things* and with familiar themes and activities in *The Board Game*. These were regarded as crucial in making people feel secure in participating, in the promotion of a comfortable and friendly environment and in playing with those who are close, by encouraging bonding, and the feeling of safety that can emerge from it:

The game ends up facilitating that [holding] due to the themes. … When he doesn't control the game, he might feel insecure and inhibited. In the case of *The Board Game*, the themes are familiar to him. (relative C, family A, 05.03.2017)

The creation of an easy-going atmosphere was also regarded as being closely connected to *relaxation*. The ludic function of *The Board Game* was believed to directly contribute to making participants at ease, encouraging their participation without feeling judged, and constituting an entertaining occupation. However, it was noted that this is conditioned by how others facilitate the use of the artefacts. Participants believed *The Tactful Things* helped *relaxation*, due to the touch and warmth they provide, as well as the choice of soft and pleasant textures which were linked to comfort:

the fact that it promotes some comfort will help the person's restlessness, and support the person to stay calmer, more relaxed. (psychologist A, 15.03.2017)

*Timalation* was an obvious choice for all participants regarding *The Tactful Things*, due to its multi-sensorial qualities. Nonetheless, *timalation* was also associated with *The Board Game* because of the variety of activities in the game, and the possibility offered for reminiscing indirectly impacting the senses.

*Play* was linked to the artefacts because of their ludic appeal, and the enjoyment observed when people used them. In the case of *The Board Game*, its potential to create a fun environment and enjoyable moments was emphasized. The playful appearance of the playing pieces and dice also contributed to creating a playful mood among the participants. In addition, the professionals also called attention to the possibility for personal expression that the game allowed, through some of the tasks and particularly the sharing of stories.

*Facilitation* was associated with the artefacts' capacity to support the person in using their abilities. *The Board Game* was thought to unblock communication and promote the sharing of stories. The use of different types of prompts and cues, which need to be in part stimulated by the person conducting the activity, proposed themes that otherwise may not be talked about. *The Tactful Things* facilitated exploration, by supporting the natural need of people in more advanced stages of dementia to move and hold things with their hands.

Although *The Board Game* was thought to promote a joyful and convivial atmosphere due to its ludic function, a sense of *celebration* also relies on how the activity is conducted. *Celebration* was associated with people's references and preferences, as well as to the development of artefacts that do not make cognitive demands, such as *The Tactful Things*, which rewarded all kinds of responses:

> I also chose celebration because it is something that does not expect anything from the person on that task. Everything is possible. … Whatever she does will be positive and has value. (psychologist A, 15.03.2017)

Participants chose *collaboration* as an interaction occurring during the use of *The Board Game* because it promoted a collective activity that brings together groups of people, whereas *The Tactful Things* are more suited to individual use or just one carer. Participants agreed that *The Board Game* encouraged *collaboration* in a very natural way, because of its *ice-breaking* qualities, which supported group cohesion and well-being.

The presence of others and the dynamics of the activity are crucial in the development of *validation.* The space created for personal expression, and specifically the turn-taking aspect of *The Board Game*, encouraged people to listen, respect, and acknowledge the stories and choices of others. In the case of *The Tactful Things*, *validation* was related to the opportunities for interaction and non-verbal communication between the person with dementia and others that the artefacts permitted:

> Although she doesn't speak, there are other things that communicate at a higher level. It was noticeable that she understood that there was empathy and sensitivity towards her. She felt recognized. (psychologist E, 23.03.2017)

Finally, *negotiation* was the least selected interaction. According to the participants, neither *The Board Game* nor *The Tactful Things* offered many options for people to choose from. However, *negotiation* was associated to the presence of multiple-choice and with the opportunities for personal expression stimulated by the artefacts.

## 8.5 Conclusion

The values and strategies of each Positive Person Work interaction are combined and overlapped in a complex web of relations. This does not mean that all artefacts should include all interactions. For example, although sometimes *play* can be *relaxing*, these two interactions correspond to different forms of engaging, one more active and stimulating, the other calmer and more tranquil. Moreover, similar strategies can be used to reach different goals. For example, *timalation* can support both playful and relaxing interactions.

While initially the interactions related to artefacts are interpreted from the point of view of the designer, the evaluation brings the user's perspective to the fore. In this project, this shift brought about important considerations and conclusions (see tables below Figs. 8.6 and 8.7). It was insightful to understand what design intentions became apparent and how they were perceived. For example, it was surprising that *holding* was one of the most favored interactions when, from a design point of view, it was more difficult to find design strategies to deliberately mediate and promote it through an artefact. Similarly, *relaxation* was associated with the use of all artefacts because they provided ludic occupation, whereas from the design perspective relaxation was mainly associated with the specific intention to slow down and relax.

The perspective of use also reinforced the role of the caregiver in ensuring a beneficial use of the artefact, and in promoting these interactions. Despite the value attributed to the artefacts, even when families were involved in the process, the artefacts were not sufficient to provide *the experience* of these interactions, and could even have undesired effects. The designed artefacts aimed to create opportunities for people to communicate; however, they always relied on caregivers in their use. In fact, the range of experiences in the use of artefacts shared by participants revealed the many different ways of approaching them. The artefacts were dependent on the operationalization of the activity and the capacity of the facilitator to adapt use, observe, and respond to people's reactions. The institutional setting, that included healthcare professionals and more people with similar mental health conditions, facilitated a beneficial use of the artefacts. At home, while many families have the need and will to communicate and have meaningful moments with their relative, the setting, the emotional charge and the lack of sensitivity, among other reasons, make it more difficult to use the artefact in an enjoyable way. Many times, family members recognized that they were unsure of how to approach the artefact, and how to deal and respond to some reactions of their relatives.

In order to tackle these issues, it was proposed that different ways of using the artefacts are provided, from those with more to less demanding needs, so that carers are aware of different possibilities for use. In this way, they can adapt use to suit their

DESIGNING FOR POSITIVE PERSON WORK

### Recognition

The artefact respects and dignifies the person. It is not stigmatising. The artefact supports and values her/his uniqueness and identity.

- Respect and dignity (both in function and aesthetics).
- Personalisation and reminiscence.
- Inclusion of personal references and preferences.
- Activities that acknowledge people's stories and characteristics.

### Timalation

The artefact provides and emphasises sensorial experiences.

- Using all the senses to communicate.
- Providing pleasurable aesthetic experiences (energising or relaxing).
- Supporting embodied selfhood.
- Paying attention to sensorial attributes (visual, textures, materials, etc).
- Supporting participation in activities that stimulate the senses.
- Using artefacts as prompts to talk about and reminisce about the senses.

### Facilitation

The artefact enables the person to use their abilities and to unblock communication. The artefact encourages the creation of meaning.

- Promoting sense of agency and autonomy.
- Physical, cognitive and cultural accessibility; simplicity; aesthetics to support functionality.
- Considering the progression of dementia.
- Prompts, cues, reminders; products that assist care.
- Might be dependent on others to encourage the interaction.

### Celebration

The artefact contributes to create a convivial and joyful atmosphere. The artefact supports and celebrates personal abilities and achievements.

- Celebrating the person and what is important to her/him – inclusion of personal references and preferences.
- Conveying joy, humour, surprise, fun.
- Using music.
- Artefacts that do not make cognitive demands, thus acknowledging all kinds of responses.
- Reliant on how others conduct the activity.

### Negotiation

The artefact provides opportunities for control and choice.

- Supporting consultation.
- Using of multiple-choice.
- Stimulating creativity and self-expression.

### Relaxation

The artefact promotes relaxation or a relaxing environment.

- Promoting a comfortable, warm and easy-going environment.
- Relaxing or ludic function.
- Encouraging self-expression without judgement.
- Familiar and friendly look; soft and pleasing tones and textures.
- Helping carers to slow down.
- Conditioned by how others participate and conduct the activity.

### Collaboration

The artefact promotes inclusive joint activities.

- Supporting participation in shared activities (daily tasks or social activities).
- Promoting collective activities (e.g. games).
- Interdependence.
- Ice-breaking qualities
- Supporting co-creation.

### Holding

The artefact helps to create feeling of safety, security, reassurance.

- Promoting a relaxed, familiar and comfortable environment.
- Using personal belongings and references and familiar themes and activities.
- Including calming messages or cues.
- Encouragement of bonding.
- Reliant on how others conduct the activity.

### Play

The artefact stimulates self-expression. The artefact makes use of humour and provides enjoyable moments.

- Stimulating spontaneity and self-expression (sharing stories or more artistic).
- Creativity, fun, humour.
- Ambiguity and versatility.
- Friendly and playful appearance.
- Game materials as cues for participation and playful mood.
- Attention to overstimulation.

### Validation

The artefact encourages the development of empathy and sensitivity.

- Creating space for personal expression.
- Encouraging to listen, respect and acknowledge the stories and choices of others – turn-taking.
- Including personal references.
- Tender and affectionate look and language.
- Designing for empathy.
- Reliant on the presence of others and on how they conduct the activities.

**Fig. 8.6** Synthesis of main reflections on designing for Positive Person Work

CODESIGNING WITH POSITIVE PERSON WORK

### Recognition

Showing respect.

Greeting participants by their name.

Listening carefully and non-judgementally.

Being sensitive to how participants communicate.

Attending to participants' uniqueness by being open to share control about the process and accept their preferences of participation.

### Timalation

Using tangible and sensorial materials and prototypes.

Giving stimuli and carefully observing their reactions, gestures and non-verbal communication.

Particularly important to include and connect with people with advanced dementia.

### Facilitation

Adapting the process to participants.

(Re)designing tools and materials to support participation.

Avoiding activities with abstract thinking.

Bringing tangible things to try.

Having warm and open attitude.

Attention to the duration of meetings.

### Celebration

Focusing on participants' abilities.

Celebrating participants' uniqueness.

Congratulating and valuing participants' contributions.

### Negotiation

Designing activities and materials that encourage the exercise of choice.

Providing options for recognition rather than recall.

### Relaxation

Ensuring a relaxed and easy-going atmosphere.

Respecting the pace of participants.

### Collaboration

Setting participatory design events as opportunities for joint activities.

Including family members and/or formal caregivers can be important to encourage participation (but ensuring that people with dementia have space to contribute by themselves).

### Holding

Creating a comfortable, non-judgemental and friendly environment.

Encouraging the person to feel secure and at ease to participate.

Observing, trying to understand how the person is feeling and responding to it.

Avoiding confrontational situations

### Play

Planning codesign activities as moments of fun and self-expression.

Providing participants an enjoyable time as a consequence of their participation.

Valuing particitation in codesign activities as an outcome, even if it does not yield expected outputs.

### Validation

Empathic attitude.

Responding to participants' reactions and feelings.

Understanding if what is being asked is appropriate and comfortable for participants.

Consulting family or formal carers about topics that might confront or elicit negative emotions.

Paying attention to signs of tiredness, anxiety or frustration.

**Fig. 8.7** Synthesis of main reflections on codesigning with Positive Person Work in consideration

relative with dementia, and not get attached to a particular way of using the artefact. Artefacts might be accompanied with simple recommendations on how to engage with a person with dementia in an activity, how to stimulate her or him to participate, how to respond, and what attitudes to avoid, among others. In this way, the artefacts could also be ways of sharing communication strategies, which can be of overall relevance when caring for someone with dementia (Downs & Collins 2015; Killick & Allan 2001).

This analysis of the artefacts by participants validated our proposal to associate the Positive Person Work interactions with the design of artefacts. Therefore, we believe that to have them in consideration in the design process is a valuable source of inspiration and a direction to contribute to a positive experience of use, as well as a way to gather discerning feedback on the outputs of design. Positive Person Work interactions can also be a useful and important guide for planning and involving people with dementia in codesign processes. Without intending to be prescriptive or to propose a single way of designing for people with dementia, these reflections are aimed at supporting a more conscious, ethical, and aesthetic approach to designing for and with people with dementia and their carers.

**Acknowledgements** The authors would like to thank all the participants, from families and institutions, for their availability and contributions. This work was funded by the Foundation for Science and Technology in the scope of Ph.D. grant PD/BD/105810/2014.

## References

Afonso RM, Selva JPS, Postigo JML (2016) Reminisce interventions in elderly people. Encycl Geropsychol 200:1–8. Springer, Singapore. https://doi.org/10.1007/978-981-287-080-3_260-2

Allan K (2001) Communication and consultation: exploring ways for staff to involve people with dementia in developing services. The Policy Press, Bristol

Anderiesen H, Scherder E, Goossens R, Visch V, Eggermont L (2015) Play experiences for people with Alzheimer's disease. Int J Des 9(2):155–165

Bennett P, Hinder H, Cater K (2016) Rekindling imagination in dementia care with the resonant interface rocking chair. In: CHI EA '16 proceedings of the 2016 CHI conference extended abstracts on human factors in computing systems. ACM, New York, pp 2020–2026. https://doi.org/10.1145/2851581.2892505

Biamonti A, Garmegna M, Imamogullari B (2014) A design experience for the enhancement of the quality of life for people with Alzheimer's disease. In: Franqueira T, Sampaio J (eds) Proceedings of the what's on: cumulus spring conference. Aveiro, pp 285–299

Branco RM (2018) Codesingning communication in dementia: participatory encounters with people with dementia and their families towards personalised communication strategies. Faculdade de Belas Artes da Universidade do Porto, Porto. https://hdl.handle.net/10216/110846

Branco RM, Quental J, Ribeiro Ó (2015) Getting closer, empathising and understanding: Setting the stage for a codesign project with people with dementia. Interact Des Arch J—IxDA 26:114–131. http://www.mifav.uniroma2.it/inevent/events/idea2010/index.php?s=10&a=11&link=ToC_26_P&link=26_7_abstract

Branco RM, Quental J, Ribeiro Ó (2016) Tactile explorations in a codesign project involving people with dementia. In: Desmet P, Fokkinga S, Ludden GDS, Cila N, Van Zuthem H (eds) Celebration contemplation proceedings of the 10th international conference on design and emotion. Amsterdam, pp 642–650

Branco RM, Quental J, Ribeiro Ó (2017) Personalised participation: an approach to involve people with dementia and their families in a participatory design project. CoDesign 13(2):127–143. https://doi.org/10.1080/15710882.2017.1310903
Brandt E (2011) Participation through exploratory design games. In: Rasmussen LB (ed) Facilitating change: using interactive methods in organisation communities and networks. Polyteknisk Boghandel og Forlag, Lyngby, pp 213–256
Brooker D (2007) Person-centred dementia care: making services better. Jessica Kingsley Publishers, London
Bruce E, Schweitzer P (2008) Working with life history. In: Downs M, Bowers B (eds) Excellence in dementia care: Research into practice, 1st edn. McGraw-Hill International, Maidenhead, Berkshire, pp 168–186
Caillois R (1961) Man, play and games (trans: Barash M). University of Illinois Press
Cowdell F (2006) Preserving personhood in dementia research: a literature review. Int J Older People Nurs 1(2):85–94. https://doi.org/10.1111/j.1748-3743.2006.00016.x
Cowdell F (2008) Engaging older people with dementia in research: myth or possibility. Int J Older People Nurs 3(1):29–34. https://doi.org/10.1111/j.1748-3743.2007.00096.x
Desmet P, Hekkert P (2007) Framework of product experience. Int J Des 1(1):1–10
Devecchi A, Guerrini L (2017) Empathy and design. A new perspective. Des J 20(sup1):S4357–S4364. https://doi.org/10.1080/14606925.2017.1352932
Dewing J (2007) Participatory research. A method for process consent with persons who have dementia. Dementia 6(1):11–25. https://doi.org/10.1177/1471301207075625
Downs M, Collins L (2015) Person-centred communication in dementia care. Nurs Stand 30(11):37–41. https://doi.org/10.7748/ns.30.11.37.s45
Gamman L, Ehn P, Davis S, Wong V (2015) OPEN MIND: shake up taboo by design! In Lee Y, Tsang A, Fung K(eds) Presented at the open design forum: co-creating our open societies through design, Hong Kong, pp 80–122
Gaver W (2009) Designing for Homo Ludens, Still. In: Binder T, Malborg L, Löwgren J (eds) (Re)Searching the digital Bauhaus. London, pp 163–178
Gowans G, Dye R, Alm N, Vaughan P, Astell AJ, Ellis M (2007) Designing the interface between dementia patients, caregivers and computer-based intervention. Des J 10(1):12–23. https://doi.org/10.1080/rfdj20.v010.i01;wgroup:string:publication
Hassenzahl M (2010) Experience design: technology for all the right reasons. Morgan & Claypool, San Rafael, Calif. https://doi.org/10.2200/s00261ed1v01y201003hci008
Hendriks N, Huybrechts L, Slegers K, Wilkinson A (2018) Valuing implicit decision-making in participatory design: a relational approach in design with people with dementia. Des Stud 59:58–76. https://doi.org/10.1016/j.destud.2018.06.001
Hendriks N, Huybrechts L, Wilkinson A, Slegers K (2014) Challenges in doing participatory design with people with dementia. In: Winschiers-Theophilus H, D'Andrea V, Iversen OS (eds) PDC '14 proceedings of the 13th participatory design conference, vol 2. ACM, New York, pp 33–36. https://doi.org/10.1145/2662155.2662196
Hendriks N, Slegers K, Duysburgh P (2015) Codesign with people living with cognitive or sensory impairments: a case for method stories and uniqueness. CoDesign 11(1):70–82. https://doi.org/10.1080/15710882.2015.1020316
Hughes JC (2014) The aesthetic approach to people with dementia. Int Psychogeriatr 26(9):1407–1413. https://doi.org/10.1017/s1041610214001100
Kenning G (2018) Reciprocal design: inclusive design approaches for people with late stage dementia. Des Health 2(1):142–162. https://doi.org/10.1080/24735132.2018.1453638
Killick J (2012) Playfulness and dementia: a practice guide. Jessica Kingsley Publishers, London
Killick J, Allan K (2001) Communication and the care of people with dementia. Open University Press, Maidenhead
Killick J, Craig C (2011) Creativity and communication in persons with dementia: a practical guide. Jessica Kingsley Publishers, London
Kitwood T (1997) Dementia reconsidered. Open University Press, Maidenhead

Kontos PC (2014) Selfhood and the body in dementia care. In: Downs M, Bowers B (eds) Excellence in dementia care: research into practice, 2nd edn. Open University Press, Maidenhead, Berkshire, pp 122–131

Lazar A, Edasis C, Piper AM (2017) A critical lens on dementia and design in HCI. In: CHI '17 proceedings of the CHI conference on human factors in computing systems. CHI, New York

Lindsay S, Brittain K, Jackson D, Ladha C, Ladha K, Olivier P (2012) Empathy, participatory design and people with dementia. In: Konstan JA, Chi EH, Höök K (eds) CHI '12 proceedings of the conference on human factors in computing systems. ACM, New York, pp 521–530. https://doi.org/10.1145/2207676.2207749

Lupton E, Lipps A (2018) The senses: design beyond vision. In: Lupton E, Lipps A (eds). Cooper-Hewitt Smithsonian Design Museum & Princeton Architectural Press, New York

Morrissey K, McCarthy J, Pantidi N (2017) The value of experience-centred design approaches in dementia research contexts. In: CHI '17 proceedings of the CHI conference on human factors in computing systems. ACM, New York, pp 1326–1338. https://doi.org/10.1145/3025453.3025527

Niedderer K (2007) Designing mindful interaction: the category of performative object. Des Issues 23(1):3–17. https://doi.org/10.1162/desi.2007.23.1.3

Orpwood R (2009) Involving people with dementia in the design process: Examples of iterative design. In: Topo P, Östlund B (eds) Dementia, design and technology. Dementia, Amsterdam, pp 79–95. https://doi.org/10.3233/978-1-58603-950-9-79

Pohlmeyer A (2013) Positive design: new challenges, opportunities, and responsibilities for design. In: Marcus A (ed) Design, user experience, and usability. User experience in novel technological environments, vol 8014. Springer, Berlin, Heidelberg, pp 540–547. https://doi.org/10.1007/978-3-642-39238-2_59

Pohlmeyer A, Desmet P (2017) From good to the greater good. In: Chapman J (ed) Routledge handbook of sustainable product design. Routledge, Taylor & Francis Group, London, pp 469–486

Pullin G (2009) Design meets disability. MIT Press, Cambridge, Massachusetts

Sabat SR (2014) A bio-psycho-social approach to dementia. In: Downs M, Bowers B (eds) Excellence in dementia care: research into practice, 2nd edn. Open University Press, McGraw-Hill Education, Maidenhead, Berkshire, pp 107–121

Sonneveld MH, Schifferstein HNJ (2008) The tactual experience of objects. In: Schifferstein HNJ, Hekkert P (eds) Product experience. Elsevier, Amsterdam, pp 259–285. https://doi.org/10.1016/b978-008045089-6.50005-8

Timlin G, Rysenbry N (2010) Design for dementia: Improving dining and bedroom environments in care homes. Helen Hamlyn Centre, Royal College of Art, London

Treadaway C, Fennell J, Taylor A, Kenning G (2019) Designing for playfulness through compassion: design for advanced dementia. Design for Health 7(3):1–21. https://doi.org/10.1080/24735132.2019.1593295

Treadaway C, Kenning G, Coleman S (2015) Sensor e-Textiles: designing for persons with late stage dementia. In: Christer K (ed) Presented at the 3rd European conference on Design4Health

Van Weert JCM, Janssen BM, Van Dulmen AM, Spreeuwenberg PMM, Bensing JM, Ribbe MW (2006) Nursing assistants' behaviour during morning care: effects of the implementation of snoezelen, integrated in 24-hour dementia care. J Adv Nurs 53(6):656–668. https://doi.org/10.1111/j.1365-2648.2006.03772.x

Verbeek P-P (2012) Humanity in design: a few notes on the relations between anthropology and materiality. In: Gunn W, Donovan J (eds) Design and anthropology. Ashgate, Surrey

Wallace J, Wright PC, McCarthy J, Green DP, Thomas J, Olivier P (2013) A design-led inquiry into personhood in dementia. In: Mackay WE, Brewster S, Bødker S (eds) CHI '13 proceedings of conference on human factors in computing systems 2013.ACM, New York, pp 2617–2626. https://doi.org/10.1145/2470654.2481363

Wildevuur S, van Dijk D, Hammer-Jakobsen T, Bjerre MÄyväri A, Lund J (2013) Connect: design for an empathic society. In: Wildevuur S, van Dijk D, Hammer-Jakobsen T, Bjerre M, Äyväri A, Lund J (eds). BIS Publishers, Amsterdam

Zeisel J (2009) I'm still here. Avery, Penguin Group, New York

# Chapter 9
# Prospective Memory Failure in Dementia: Understanding and Designing to Support

**Laura Ramos, Laurie Miller, and Elise van den Hoven**

## 9.1 Introduction

The increased prevalence and awareness of dementia is driving interest in design for people affected by the condition. This is generating a more nuanced understanding of user needs and contexts, and an interest in looking into the support of prospective memory. Prospective memory allows us to follow through on a future intention; examples include remembering to attend an appointment, take medication at a particular time or buy milk on the way home. For people with dementia, progressive loss of prospective memory function hinders their ability to follow through with everyday tasks. This, in turn, erodes functional independence and results in increased reliance on caregivers or technological aids. Losing the ability to remember following through on some tasks can pose potential risks to their health, safety and well-being. For informal caregivers, juggling additional tasks can contribute to the daily stressors that drive caregiver burden. Loss of memory and autonomy and the transition to

L. Ramos (✉)
School of Computer Science, Faculty of Engineering and Information Technology, University of Technology Sydney, Ultimo, Australia
e-mail: Laura.L.Ramos@student.uts.edu.au

L. Miller
Neuropsychology Unit, Royal Prince Alfred Hospital and University of Sydney, Camperdown, Australia
e-mail: Laurie.Miller@sydney.edu.au

E. van den Hoven
School of Computer Science, Faculty of Engineering and Information Technology, University of Technology Sydney, Ultimo, Australia
e-mail: Elise.VandenHoven@uts.edu.au

Department of Industrial Design, Eindhoven University of Technology, Eindhoven, The Netherlands

Duncan of Jordanstone College of Art and Design, University of Dundee, Dundee, UK

© Springer Nature Switzerland AG 2020

R. Brankaert and G. Kenning (eds.), *HCI and Design in the Context of Dementia*, Human–Computer Interaction Series,
https://doi.org/10.1007/978-3-030-32835-1_9

dependency in relationships can have further emotional impacts on caregivers and people with dementia.

Therefore, we need to find better ways to support prospective memory among people with dementia. The effectiveness of such support may depend on a wide range of factors including relevance, timeliness, ability to attract attention and suitability to context, as well as individual preferences and control. Although research on design to support dementia is expanding rapidly, specific research on design relating to prospective memory is still relatively new.

This chapter provides an overview of the growing body of research on the design of systems to support prospective memory for people with dementia and their caregivers. It begins with a brief overview of prospective memory function, as well as impacts in older age and among people with cognitive impairment and their caregivers. There are multiple technical and non-technical interventions to support prospective memory; of these, assistive technologies to provide reminders for daily activities have been surveyed in multiple reviews (Ienca et al. 2017; Jamieson et al. 2014; Lorenz et al. 2019; Tulving 2007). In this chapter, three systems that focus specifically on supporting prospective memory for people with dementia (*COGKNOW* (Boer 2010; Davies et al. 2009; Mulvenna et al. 2010), *Robin* (Carroll et al. 2017) and *Living Well with Anne* (de Jong et al. 2018) have been identified; in addition, the *Multi-MemoHome* project (McGee-Lennon et al. 2011, 2012) has focused on the design of a home-based reminder system for a wide range of users, including people with disability, older people and caregivers of people with dementia. A brief exploration of research on support for caregivers has highlighted that reminder systems should coordinate the dual needs of those receiving and providing care adaptive to various situations. Flexibility in how reminders are entered, integrated with other activities and presented is particularly relevant for people affected by dementia. This is due to the progressive nature of the condition, with needs changing over time. Findings point to future directions for research to support people with dementia and their caregivers with prospective memory in everyday living.

## 9.2 Prospective Memory and Its Impact on People

Multiple aspects of human memory function have been mapped in memory research (Tulving 2007); one type of memory—prospective memory (PM)—is required to remember to take action in the future. PM is often described as remembering of future intentions or delayed intentions (Kvavilashvili and Ellis 1996). Following through with an intention in the future requires remembering events experienced or information learned in the past; the ability to remember things learned in the past is referred to as retrospective memory. PM incorporates retrospective memory, in that one needs to be able to remember what was learned in the past to carry out an intended future action.

PM is critical in everyday living. It is required to perform a wide range of tasks. PM includes both one-off and habitual tasks and plans that are meant to be carried out around a specific event (event-based) or at a specific time (time-based) (McDaniel and Einstein 2007). Remembering to buy a present for a loved one after going to the hairdresser is an example of an event-based PM; taking medication at a specific hour or paying a bill on time are examples of time-based PM. A meta-analysis of literature on PM among people with mild cognitive impairment and dementia (van den Hoven 2014) confirmed a clear degradation in their ability to carry out both event-based and time-based PM tasks. Reminders to take action may be useful for both event-based and time-based PM, but the nature of that prompt (e.g. a to-do list, a post-it note, an alternative physical reminder or an alarm) is likely to differ depending on whether the action is to be carried out in association with an event or at a certain time. Hence, there may be a need to adapt aspects of different solutions to meet different situations.

Ageing is not always associated with a decline in PM. The evidence on the extent to which PM is impacted by age is mixed, as some older adults have developed excellent strategies and routines to support PM in everyday living (McDaniel and Einstein 2007; Radford et al. 2011). However, memory complaints (including those related to PM) in older people have been associated with lower perceived quality of life and impaired ability to conduct activities of daily living (Montejo et al. 2012).

Research focusing on everyday memory failures (Kliegel and Martin 2003; Ramos et al. 2016; Terry 1988) has found that PM failures are the most frequent type of memory complaint across age groups. Whilst there is only limited research on the affective impacts of declining function in PM, there is some evidence in the literature. First, a study exploring how older people perceive everyday forgetting (Ramos et al. 2016) found that they tended to perceive these failings negatively, but sometimes responded with humour, suggesting their use of humour as a coping mechanism. Second, Lorenz et al. (2019) include a blog post by a person with dementia expressing frustration about alarm noises in her home that might have once been useful; this is because she could no longer associate the noise with the action that it was meant to prompt. The actual blog post includes some additional experiences and ends with the words 'LOL What a day !!! [sic]' (Truthful Loving Kindness 2015).

People with mild cognitive impairment and early dementia experience a clear degradation in PM function, compared to people with no diagnosed memory impairment. This extends to both event-based and time-based PM across multiple studies on PM (van den Berg et al. 2012). In addition to deterioration in memory function, people with dementia commonly experience difficulties with vision and hearing (Cronin-Golomb 2004; Wayne and Johnsrude 2015), which can result in environmental cues being missed or misinterpreted.

PM errors were found to be more frequent than retrospective memory errors among people with dementia (Smith et al. 2000). It also found that carers of people with dementia were more frustrated by PM failings of care recipients than other types of memory lapses, indicating how PM failures might contribute to stress for caregivers. Although a range of factors can impact caregiver burden in the context of dementia, burden could be reduced through tactics and tools to manage forgetting for the person with memory impairment (Miller et al. 2013).

Declining PM function in people with dementia impairs their ability to live independently, sustain health and maintain social connections. Between 70 and 80% of people with dementia in the United States live in the community (Brodaty and Donkin 2009). As a result, most people supporting someone with dementia are informal caregivers, often spouses, partners, family members and friends who juggle caregiving with other responsibilities. Although there are positive aspects in providing care, the strain of physical, psychological, social and financial impacts of caregiving are well documented. The prevalence and contexts of care and support for people with dementia highlight the need to find better ways to manage and support PM.

## 9.3 Technical and Non-technical Interventions for PM Support

Along with the growing awareness about the impact of dementia on individuals and their communities, the range of interventions to support cognitive abilities has also increased. These include drug treatments and cognitive-training interventions. However, recent reviews (Bahar-Fuchs et al. 2019; Fink et al. 2018; García-Casal et al. 2017) found limited evidence of positive effects from these approaches on cognitive function in people with dementia.

Interventions to support memory function have focused on retrospective memory, such as systems and therapies to assist people with dementia in reminiscing (De Vreese et al. 2001; Huber et al. 2019). Memory support for wider audiences has included design for *augmented memory systems* (van den Berg et al. 2012). Although these have yielded some positive outcomes, the interventions mentioned in those studies do not specifically address PM.

One study focused on *implementation intention* strategies to support PM for older people with and without mild cognitive impairment (MCI) (Shelton et al. 2016). This consisted of learning to associate a cue with an intended action by verbalising it (e.g. saying that 'if I *see* that it's 4 pm, then I will take my medication'). The study found positive results of the strategy in a laboratory setting where older people with and without MCI went through the Virtual Week task. Whilst researchers acknowledged the importance of PM function in real-world settings, the study had some limitations relating to its relevance outside the lab. In particular, participants were assessed on tasks that might not reflect how they manage PM in their day-to-day lives.

When it comes to PM function, most solutions for people with memory impairment rely on external memory aids rather than mnemonic strategies like implementation intention. The most easily available memory aids are paper-based tools, including notebooks, diaries and calendars. Their use is noted in multiple studies (McGee-Lennon et al. 2011; Ramos et al. 2016). Memory aids designed for people with memory impairment are increasingly relying on digital technology and systems. Some people with cognitive impairment can still learn how to use commercially available memory aids such as calendars and reminders on mobile handheld devices; however, this may not be possible for people with more severe impairment. The MEMOS system (Thöne-Otto and Walther 2003) was designed to support people with severe head injury and their caregivers to manage PM tasks. The system proved slightly more effective than commercially available systems in a small trial; this was attributed to greater flexibility in handling tasks and a requirement to confirm task completion (Walthe et al. 2004).

The number of published studies focusing on assistive technologies to support PM among people with dementia has grown significantly since the early 2000s (Ienca et al. 2017). One study (Oriani et al. 2003) found that, among people with mild to moderate Alzheimer's disease, using an electronic memory aid was more effective for helping them to remember to perform a series of tasks than using a written list of the tasks to be performed. That system allowed users to voice record a task reminder and associate the task with a particular time; it then generated an audio prompt at the assigned time. Still, the system was limited to time-based reminders and was evaluated only within a laboratory environment.

Researchers working on robotics to assist older people in an institutional care setting have developed software to handle scheduling and follow through of daily tasks (Pineau et al. 2003). As part of this work, the *Autominder* software was integrated in a trial robot to provide reminders and increase awareness of scheduled tasks to minimise growing dependency on nursing home staff (Pollack et al. 2003). This work was designed to provide cognitive support for older people and their formal carers in a nursing home setting. *Autominder* is one example of a broader range of cognitive assistant systems that provide assurance, guidance and assessment of tasks in care (Pollack 2005).

More recent research has honed in on more granular features. A systematic review of literature on *cognitive prosthetic technology* for people with memory impairment (Jamieson et al. 2014) noted the emergence of micro-prompting devices. This refers to systems that position prompting on a specific action and place. An example of this is the *COACH* system to remind people to wash hands in the bathroom (Mihailidis et al. 2008). The increased availability of wearable technologies and electronic sensors creates opportunities for new ways of imagining micro-prompting systems. Resulting applications of these technologies might take the form of a jacket that provides navigational directions that the user would sense whilst wearing it or a doormat that receives weather information and issues a reminder to household residents to take an umbrella, because it is going to rain (Uhlig et al. 2018). Systems can also track activity that could be integrated into other reminder systems. One example of this is a wearable device that can sense whether the user had brushed their teeth adequately to encourage better dental care among older persons (Cherian et al. 2017).

### *9.3.1 Home-Based Systems for People with Dementia*

There is a clear opportunity to apply new technologies to serve people with dementia, so that they can maintain well-being and independence whilst living at home. The *COGKNOW*, *Robin*, *Living Well with Anne* and *MultiMemoHome* projects support PM for that purpose.

The *COGKNOW* project built on prior research on cognitive prosthetics and electronic memory aids to support PM in people with cognitive impairment (Mulvenna et al. 2010). The project team focused on four key areas to improve quality of life for people living with dementia—remembering tasks, facilitating social contact, engaging in enjoyable activities and safety. The researchers applied participatory design methods in group workshops in Amsterdam, Ireland and Sweden. In each workshop, 5 or 6 older people with mild to moderate cognitive impairment due to dementia discussed how a new system could help them to improve autonomy and quality of life. The ideas generated in the workshops were synthesised ideas into a series of functional requirements. The resulting *COGKNOW Day Navigator* system consisted of a stationary 17-in. touch screen device connected to a desktop computer and a handheld portable device with a 2.8-in. screen. The system included a door sensor in the participant's home and a server that allowed caregivers to enter schedules and reminders for participants remotely. System components were connected via home-based and mobile networks. The system was tested in field trials in the homes of 16 participants (Davies et al. 2009). Video of the *Day Navigator* showed how a user engaged with the touch-screen device to receive reminders inside the home and with the handheld portable device to help her navigate outdoors (Boer 2010). Project researchers evaluated the user-friendliness and usefulness of the *COGKNOW* Day Navigator, as well as the product's effectiveness in supporting memory, increasing social contact and safety, and the evaluation yielded mixed results (Meiland et al. 2012). Although people with dementia reported that the product was easy to use and easy to learn, researchers noted that users with dementia had to be reminded how to use the system repeatedly, and that around half of the reminders were ignored when there was no researcher present. Users reported minimal difference in their perceived quality of life, sense of autonomy and ability to cope with their dementia after trialling the system (Meiland et al. 2012). Hence, results from this research suggest that the system may not be effective in terms of fully compensating for declining PM. However, the system can be useful to support well-being by reminding people with dementia to engage in enjoyable activities and social contact; it can also provide some relief for caregivers. In addition, more time for teaching the use of the device might be necessary. Given that alarm cues were found to be often ignored, exploring how to make these more attention-grabbing or more information-rich might be useful.

The *Robin* system (Carroll et al. 2017) used existing technology to support people with mild to moderate dementia. Based on feedback from experts and carers three use cases were identified for PM support by *Robin*—where an intervention is necessary (e.g. medication reminder), when guidance is required so a user can complete a task, and where quality of life for the person with dementia could be improved (e.g. suggesting an enjoyable activity). The designers created new functions on a commercially available voice-controlled assistant (Amazon Alexa), so that users could receive appropriate reminders. Whilst this is a novel use of a more recent and relatively low-cost commercial technology, the lack of involvement of people with dementia in the design process and limited evaluation data cast doubt on the potential effectiveness of the system in assisting with PM.

More recently, the *Living Well with Anne* project (http://livingwellwithanne.eu) has been developing a system to support both people with dementia and their caregivers using a virtual agent and machine learning algorithms on a tablet device. The system also relies on sensors around the home of the person with dementia. The system features easy-to-read daily schedules, supported by a virtual agent with a conversational interface. The system provides several advantages to paper-based calendars by incorporating reminder prompts and feedback mechanisms, as well as the voice-activated assistant to support system usage. Similar to the *Robin* project, the design was informed by engaging professional and informal carers; however, research participants have raised the need to adapt the system to maintain usability during different stages of dementia. In this way, the project is significant in that it considers how the system can remain accessible to people with dementia as their needs and abilities change over time (de Jong et al. 2018). As the product is in the early stages of development, there is limited evidence of potential effectiveness.

Whilst these studies are deliberately oriented to supporting PM needs of people with dementia, the *MultiMemoHome* (*MMH*) project demonstrates the complexities of meeting user needs in a real-world setting. Researchers used mixed methods (questionnaire, focus groups, and home tour interviews) to explore over a year the development of a multimodal reminder system for at home (McGee-Lennon et al. 2012). The system was designed for multiple age groups and people of different abilities, for caregivers as well as people receiving care. Although there were no participants in the *MMH* project with major cognitive impairment, the research included a broad range of older participants, some of which had memory problems. The researchers considered the needs of informal caregivers and acknowledged the potential for user needs changing in response to declining cognitive ability (McGee-Lennon et al. 2011).

By focusing on the home setting, researchers on the *MMH* project explored the importance of place and physical characteristics of memory aids that participants used in everyday life. Researchers identified what types of activities participants needed reminding about, what memory aids they employed to help them remember, and different user preferences for and expectations about reminder systems (McGee-Lennon et al. 2011). They found that the memory aids could be grouped into five categories: (1) Paper artefacts, such as diaries or calendars; (2) technology or manufactured items, such as digital calendars or alarms; (3) integrated into daily routines or an external schedules, such as using the timing of a radio programme to follow through on a separate action; (4) interactions with other people, thereby relying on others to provide a reminder and (5) physical placement of objects around the home, for example, placing an item by the door to remind the person to take action related to the item.

Whilst users reported different preferences to the modality of the reminder (e.g. visual or audible prompts), the majority of users (83%) reported that they would prefer receiving reminders from multiple devices throughout the home (e.g. on their mobile phones, desktop computer and on screens placed in the hallway or kitchen). The research identified user expectations of an effective reminder system, including adaptability, ability to personalise and the need for reminders to be discrete in the household. It also illustrated the challenges of balancing competing demands to address user diversity, context, task urgency, autonomy, shared spaces and optimal care (McGee-Lennon et al. 2011). Later work in the *MMH* project focused on whether synthetic speech could provide reminders that could be easily understood by older people who might have age-related hearing impairment that could impact comprehension (Wolters et al. 2014). Whilst this is a very specific aspect of usability, it shows the extent to which designers need to carefully consider how users engage with a system.

The *COGKNOW*, *Robin*, *Living Well with Anne* and *MMH* systems are examples of PM support within the home and in independent-living settings. The systems are not for the exclusive use of people with cognitive impairment; multiple parties may need to be involved with the creation of and follow through with reminders. As a result, these systems aim to cater for a very wide range of abilities, needs and expectations. It is worth noting, however, that these systems are often not relevant for people in more advanced stages of cognitive impairment who require ongoing assistance from caregivers for daily activities.

### *9.3.2 Systems to Support Caregivers with Everyday PM Support*

Researchers exploring design for caregivers are also finding opportunities to support PM. Two studies focusing on caregiver needs highlight memory support as a shared function between caregivers and care recipients. This places increased strain on the caregiver and creates new design challenges.

Research exploring the needs of caregivers (Chen et al. 2013) used semi-structured interviews with carers to understand their experiences in caregiving. They found that as caregivers spend more time attending to tasks to support the person who needs care, balancing tasks related to their own lives created increasing stress for the caregiver. The researchers identified a need to cater for personal as well as caregiving activities. An integrated care system could include prompts to remind caregivers to take time for self-care activities or to seek other supports to manage stress related to caregiving. By suggesting integrated management of everyday personal and caregiving tasks with reminders to practice self-care, Chen et al. (2013) opened an innovative approach to design for PM among caregivers.

In Europe, a case study of the TOPIC (The Online Platform for Informal Caregivers) project highlighted the use of ethnographic methods to generate a nuanced understanding of the information and communication needs of informal caregivers (Schinkinger and Tellioğlu 2014). The authors noted how non-technological tools, such as paper-based calendars and whiteboards, were used frequently for task coordination between caregivers and care recipients in home settings. They used culture probes to surface a wide range of technologies that caregivers relied upon to provide informal care tasks, including smart watches, healthcare recording and distributed scheduling systems. The researchers identified the need to integrate data from these various systems in a common platform that would be available to informal and formal caregivers. The need for coordination of caregiving tasks among family members as dementia progresses has also been noted in a recent review of multiple technologies to support people with dementia and their carers (Lorenz et al. 2019). The TOPIC case study further found that an integrated platform for caregivers would need to be easily accessible in the home setting, support multimodal interactions (e.g. voice, text and touch) and would also need to respect privacy.

Although these studies did not focus exclusively on caregivers of people with dementia, they are very relevant for that context in two ways. First, most people with dementia live at home and will require increasing levels of care over time from informal caregivers (Brodaty and Donkin 2009). As part of this, caregivers will manage more tasks for and on behalf of the care recipient. Transitioning that responsibility to caregivers would require shared and visible access to reminders, whilst somehow giving the care recipient a sense of privacy and control (Schinkinger and Tellioğlu 2014). In addition, whilst caring for a person with dementia contributes to higher levels of stress for the caregiver (Chiao et al. 2015), systems that support caregivers should acknowledge the complexities and context of providing care. This might require helping the caregiver schedule and manage personal tasks, including self-care, more easily and intuitively (Chen et al. 2013).

## 9.4 Involving People with Dementia in Design Practice

Researchers have been applying a range of methods and practices to engage with people with dementia, as well as with their formal and informal carers, throughout the design process. Participatory design and co-design practices have been used widely to learn and share expertise about what should be included in design (Vines et al. 2013). Understanding user needs and developing solutions for them has been done through various formats (interviews, focus groups, group workshops and home tours) (Bourazeri and Stumpf 2018; Chen et al. 2013; McGee-Lennon et al. 2012; Schinkinger and Tellioğlu 2014). In addition, researchers have co-designed personas with people with dementia and Parkinson's disease to explore technology choices and evaluate prototypes (Bourazeri and Stumpf 2018). Research to develop an assistant for people with dementia that leveraged mobile phone technology (Mayer and Zach 2013) has found that personas can be useful to encourage people with dementia to express concerns that they may be reluctant to mention if they were speaking about themselves.

The design of systems to support people with dementia is relatively new. As a result, there is still limited research on how to involve people with dementia in design and research practices to understand whether their needs are being met. Research from Gibson et al. (2016) specifically focused on identifying which established usability testing methods (questionnaires, *think aloud* protocol and observation) provided the greatest amount of user feedback to support system evaluation. They found that observation of task completion (including completion rate and time spent on task) was a more reliable measure of effectiveness than questionnaires or relying on the *think aloud* protocol. People with dementia might have difficulty understanding questions and verbalising their thoughts; however, they can still engage with new systems with adequate support and their behaviour can be observed and assessed. Further research to develop methods to assess emotional impacts of system use is required.

A common concern across these studies is how to involve individuals with dementia in a meaningful and respectful way throughout the design process, whilst working within constraints imposed by cognitive impairment and the increased reliance on caregivers. Researchers will need to continue adapting design practices to the specific context and need of the research. A sensitive and tailored approach to design practice will be essential when working with both people with dementia and their carers (Hendriks et al. 2014; Lazar et al. 2017; Lindsay et al. 2012)

Another critical perspective on designing for people with dementia (Madjaroff and Mentis 2017) challenges the notion of memory impairment as a problem to be fixed with technology. This is because the use of technology among people with cognitive impairment could be impacted by the relationship with caregivers, as well as physical context and individual preferences. One of the researchers who worked on the *MMH* project (Wolters 2014) reflected that people make active choices and combine multiple strategies to remember; these strategies build in physical, sensory, digital and non-digital cues to prompt PM. As they do this, they also factor in other people within their environment—and possibly the strategies that these other individuals use. In trying to create a supportive system, designers may be layering complexity on an already complicated environment.

The notion that PM challenges can be solved with technology points to an underlying tension in the research in this area. Much of the research reviewed here that new technology-based systems and interventions can provide a better substitute to the existing analogue or offline solutions, as well as existing digital systems for mass market audiences. Critically assessing this assumption is not without merit: there is ample evidence that traditional reminder systems can fail and cause frustration (McGee-Lennon et al. 2011, 2012; Ramos et al. 2016; Truthful Loving Kindness 2015). To date, however, new systems in this area (Carroll et al. 2017; Davies et al. 2009; García-Casal et al. 2017; Jamieson et al. 2014; Mulvenna et al. 2010; Oriani et al. 2003) have produced relatively limited benefits for users in memory function or overall well-being and quality of life. The challenges of engaging with people with dementia in research to understand their perceptions in relation to new systems have also been noted (Gibson et al. 2016; Hendriks et al. 2014). This might prompt questioning the value of researching and designing new solutions to support PM. However, growing numbers of people and communities require better options to enjoy life with the day-to-day realities of dementia. This already involves a range of technologies to support reminding, prompting and overall PM. And continuing this line of work to make these more accessible, useful and relevant, and finding new angles of support through research and design is therefore necessary.

## 9.5 Conclusion: Lessons Learned for Future Design Research

There are at least two reasons to continue our effort in design to support PM in everyday life for people with dementia and their caregivers. First, there is a growing body of research with increasing relevance to this area, evidenced by reviews on electronic memory aids (King and Dwan 2017), intelligent assistive technology (Ienca et al. 2017) and technologies that map the dementia care pathway (Lorenz et al. 2019). Second, there is a continued willingness to engage with people with dementia and with their caregivers throughout the design and delivery process—and to share learnings to support further work (Bourazeri and Stumpf 2018; Hendriks et al. 2014; Lindsay et al. 2012; Madjaroff and Mentis 2017; Mayer and Zach 2013). Increasing maturity in methods to engage users across the design, development and evaluation cycle will result in a better understanding of the diversity of user needs and contexts, including the complexities of designing for changes in cognitive ability and increased dependency on caregivers over time.

Overall, it is early days for research to design technology to support PM for people with dementia and their caregivers. A review of research on electronic memory aids to support PM in people with dementia (King and Dwan 2017) found that many studies featured technology solutions that were in an early stage of development, and that this posed issues for evaluating those systems. This also extends to a lack of research on designs that adapt to changes in perception and cognition of people with dementia. The same review also found limited evidence of improved outcomes for users, such as improvements in quality of life or in the ability to carry out activities of daily living. Furthermore, a separate review (Lorenz et al. 2019) noted that technologies to support memory have been primarily developed for people with mild cognitive impairment and early dementia and that their use was intended in the home, rather than residential care environments.

Future research will need to address the progressive and degenerative nature of dementia and increasing caregiver responsibilities over time (King and Dwan 2017). More exploration of changes in the motivations, needs and expectations of people with dementia and their caregivers as cognitive function degrades is critically needed. This will also require further iteration of design over longer timeframes, design of more mature systems, management of increased technical complexity, and establishing the boundaries of where technology can support in this context. This points to four opportunity areas for future research on design for PM and dementia.

First, changes in cognitive ability and perception that people with dementia experience (Chiao et al. 2015; Smith et al. 2000; Wayne and Johnsrude 2015) deserve further research. Following through on an intended action requires scheduling or sequencing an action, prompting at the right moment and supporting in the execution of that action (Pollack et al. 2003; Pollack 2005). However, people with dementia do not always respond or understand prompts (Lorenz et al. 2019; Meiland et al. 2012). Scheduling, sequencing, prompting and supporting functions could be tailored to the changes in individual ability and perception. This might mean personalization of alarm formats to suit changes in visual and auditory perception, increased guidance on the steps required to complete an action and reassurance on the execution of the intended task. However, not all of these may be required; the user should have the option to choose how much support is needed. Future work should also consider monitoring effectiveness of more personalized reminders.

Second, future research should consider the shifting of responsibilities between people with dementia and their caregivers as the disease progresses. As people with dementia face declining PM function (Smith et al. 2000), informal carers will be increasingly responsible for task scheduling and follow through (Lorenz et al. 2019); formal, paid caregivers may also play a part in this (Schinkinger and Tellioğlu 2014). This results in various opportunities to design reminder systems that support collaboration among people with dementia and informal and formal caregivers. The idea of distributed remembering among couples has been noted in prior research (Harris et al. 2014); this could be extended to a shared PM function. This would require flexible access and privacy controls so that the person with dementia could share and transition scheduling management to a caregiver or other support person. It could also provide better ways for caregivers to manage increasing workloads over time—a requirement previously noted (Chen et al. 2013). Prior research (King and Dwan 2017; Lorenz et al. 2019) has noted the need for design that adapt to the progression of dementia. Longitudinal research is needed to assess changing user needs and the effectiveness of technology solutions over time.

Third, reminder management will require balancing of complex user requirements and interconnected technologies with the need for simple and practical solutions for PM support in the real world. The need for reminders manifests in different places and contexts. This may include interfaces and connectivity across devices and integration into other systems to cater to the different contexts, as well as increasing use of sensors to track actions that prompt a reminder or the execution of an intended action. This is in line with a view of future assistive technologies to support people with dementia in the home that calls out use of assistive robots, biometric sensors, multimodal interactions, augmented reality and intelligent smart home technology (Zanwar et al. 2018). However, the feasibility and viability of technological solutions are critical. For example, the *Autominder* project (Pineau et al. 2003) featured robotics and sensor technologies that supported the scheduling management software; the complexity and expense of the system put it outside of the reach of everyday users. In contrast, the *Robin* project (Carroll et al. 2017) focused on low-cost, commercially available voice-activated technology. Handling increasing technical complexity whilst maintaining ease of use, providing users with a sense of control, ensuring security and managing obsolete system components will be an ongoing topic of research. Furthermore, research should include more evaluation of these technologies as they mature into more robust solutions.

Lastly, there is an opportunity to explore the limits of technology in addressing the needs of persons dealing with declining PM function due to dementia, either as caregivers or recipients of care. Commenting on medication adherence, past research (Wolters 2014) has noted that reminder systems can bring an undesirable level of complexity, because people already rely on multiple mechanisms to support remembering in everyday life; the best option for them may be to receive a *minimal dose* of technology support. This seems particularly relevant to people with dementia and their carers, who may already be dealing with overwhelming change. Clearly, further work is needed to design more appropriate solutions to help individuals adapt to declining PM function and maintain well-being when it is no longer possible to remember to follow through with an intended action unaided.

## References

Bahar-Fuchs A, Martyr A, Goh AM, Sabates J, Clare L (2019) Cognitive training for people with mild to moderate dementia. Cochrane Database Syst Rev (3)

Boer J (2010) Cogknow day navigator: the system in daily life. In: Extended abstracts on human factors in computing systems, CHI'10. ACM, pp 4755–4758

Bourazeri A, Stumpf S (2018) Co-designing smart home technology with people with dementia or Parkinson's disease. In: Proceedings of the 10th Nordic conference on human-computer interaction. ACM, pp 609–621

Brodaty H, Donkin M (2009) Family caregivers of people with dementia. Dialogues Clin Neurosci 11(2):217

Carroll C, Chiodo C, Lin AX, Nidever M, Prathipati J (2017) Robin: enabling independence for individuals with cognitive disabilities using voice assistive technology. In: Proceedings of the 2017 CHI conference extended abstracts on human factors in computing systems. ACM, pp 46–53

Chen Y, Ngo V, Park SY (2013) Caring for caregivers: designing for integrality. In: Proceedings of the 2013 conference on computer supported cooperative work. ACM, pp 91–102

Cherian J, Rajanna V, Goldberg D, Hammond T (2017) Did you remember to brush?: a noninvasive wearable approach to recognizing brushing teeth for elderly care. In: Proceedings of the 11th EAI international conference on pervasive computing technologies for healthcare. ACM, pp 48–57

Chiao CY, Wu HS, Hsiao CY (2015) Caregiver burden for informal caregivers of patients with dementia: a systematic review. Int Nurs Rev 62(3):340–350

Cronin-Golomb A (2004) Heterogeneity of visual presentation in Alzheimer's disease. Vis Alzheimer's Dis 34:96

Davies RJ, Nugent CD, Donnelly MP, Hettinga M, Meiland FJ, Moelaert F, Mulvenna MD, Bengtsson JE, Craig D, Dröes R-M (2009) A user driven approach to develop a cognitive prosthetic to address the unmet needs of people with mild dementia. Pervasive Mob Comput 5(3):253–267

de Jong M, Stara V, von Döllen V, Bolliger D, Heerink M, Evers V (2018) Users requirements in the design of a virtual agent for patients with dementia and their caregivers. In: Proceedings of the 4th EAI international conference on smart objects and technologies for social good. ACM, pp 136–141

De Vreese LP, Neri M, Fioravanti M, Belloi L, Zanetti O (2001) Memory rehabilitation in Alzheimer's disease: a review of progress. Int J Geriatr Psychiatry 16(8):794–809

Fink HA, Jutkowitz E, McCarten JR, Hemmy LS, Butler M, Davila H, Ratner E, Calvert C, Barclay TR, Brasure M (2018) Pharmacologic interventions to prevent cognitive decline, mild cognitive impairment, and clinical Alzheimer-type dementia: a systematic review. Ann Intern Med 168(1):39–51

García-Casal JA, Loizeau A, Csipke E, Franco-Martín M, Perea-Bartolomé MV, Orrell M (2017) Computer-based cognitive interventions for people living with dementia: a systematic literature review and meta-analysis. Aging Ment Health 21(5):454–467

Gibson A, McCauley C, Mulvenna M, Ryan A, Laird L, Curran K, Bunting B, Ferry F, Bond R (2016) Assessing usability testing for people living with dementia. In: Proceedings of the 4th workshop on ICTs for improving patients rehabilitation research techniques. ACM, pp 25–31

Harris CB, Barnier AJ, Sutton J, Keil PG (2014) Couples as socially distributed cognitive systems: remembering in everyday social and material contexts. Mem Stud 7(3):285–297

Hendriks N, Huybrechts L, Wilkinson A, Slegers K (2014) Challenges in doing participatory design with people with dementia. In: Proceedings of the 13th participatory design conference: short papers, industry cases, workshop descriptions, doctoral consortium papers, and keynote abstracts—volume 2. ACM, pp 33–36

Huber S, Berner R, Uhlig M, Klein P, Hurtienne J (2019) Tangible objects for reminiscing in dementia care. In: Proceedings of the thirteenth international conference on tangible, embedded, and embodied interaction. ACM, pp 15–24

Ienca M, Fabrice J, Elger B, Caon M, Pappagallo AS, Kressig RW, Wangmo T (2017) Intelligent assistive technology for Alzheimer's disease and other dementias: a systematic review. J Alzheimers Dis 56(4):1301–1340

Jamieson M, Cullen B, McGee-Lennon M, Brewster S, Evans JJ (2014) The efficacy of cognitive prosthetic technology for people with memory impairments: a systematic review and meta-analysis. Neuropsychol Rehabil 24(3–4):419–444

King AC, Dwan C (2017) Electronic memory aids for people with dementia experiencing prospective memory loss: a review of empirical studies. Dementia. https://doi.org/10.1177/1471301217735180

Kliegel M, Martin M (2003) Prospective memory research: why is it relevant? Int J Psychol 38(4):193–194

Kvavilashvili L, Ellis J (1996) Varieties of intention: some distinctions and classifications. Prospect Mem Theory Appl 6:183–207

Lazar A, Edasis C, Piper AM (2017) A critical lens on dementia and design in HCI. In: CHI, pp 2175–2188

Lindsay S, Brittain K, Jackson D, Ladha C, Ladha K, Olivier P (2012) Empathy, participatory design and people with dementia. In: Proceedings of the SIGCHI conference on human factors in computing systems. ACM, pp 521–530

Lorenz K, Freddolino PP, Comas-Herrera A, Knapp M, Damant J (2019) Technology-based tools and services for people with dementia and carers: mapping technology onto the dementia care pathway. Dementia 18(2):725–741

Madjaroff G, Mentis H (2017) Narratives of older adults with mild cognitive impairment and their caregivers. In: Proceedings of the 19th international ACM SIGACCESS conference on computers and accessibility. ACM, pp 140–149

Mayer JM, Zach J (2013) Lessons learned from participatory design with and for people with dementia. In: Proceedings of the 15th international conference on human-computer interaction with mobile devices and services. ACM, pp 540–545

McDaniel MA, Einstein GO (2007) Prospective memory: an overview and synthesis of an emerging field. Sage Publications

McGee-Lennon M, Smeaton A, Brewster S (2012) Designing home care reminder systems: lessons learned through co-design with older users. In: 2012 6th international conference on pervasive computing technologies for healthcare (PervasiveHealth) and workshops. IEEE, pp 49–56

McGee-Lennon MR, Wolters MK, Brewster S (2011) User-centred multimodal reminders for assistive living. In: Proceedings of the SIGCHI conference on human factors in computing systems. ACM, pp 2105–2114

Meiland FJ, Bouman AI, Sävenstedt S, Bentvelzen S, Davies RJ, Mulvenna MD, Nugent CD, Moelaert F, Hettinga ME, Bengtsson JE (2012) Usability of a new electronic assistive device for community-dwelling persons with mild dementia. Aging Ment Health 16(5):584–591

Mihailidis A, Boger JN, Craig T, Hoey J (2008) The COACH prompting system to assist older adults with dementia through handwashing: an efficacy study. BMC Geriatr 8(1):28

Miller LA, Mioshi E, Savage S, Lah S, Hodges JR, Piguet O (2013) Identifying cognitive and demographic variables that contribute to carer burden in dementia. Dement Geriatr Cogn Disord 36(1–2):43–49

Montejo P, Montenegro M, Fernandez MA, Maestu F (2012) Memory complaints in the elderly: quality of life and daily living activities. A population based study. Arch Gerontol Geriatr 54(2):298–304

Mulvenna M, Martin S, Sävenstedt S, Bengtsson J, Meiland F, Dröes RM, Hettinga M, Moelaert F, Craig D (2010) Designing & evaluating a cognitive prosthetic for people with mild dementia. In: Proceedings of the 28th annual European conference on cognitive ergonomics. ACM, pp 11–18

Oriani M, Moniz-Cook E, Binetti G, Zanieri G, Frisoni G, Geroldi C, De Vreese L, Zanetti O (2003) An electronic memory aid to support prospective memory in patients in the early stages of Alzheimer's disease: a pilot study. Aging Ment Health 7(1):22–27

Pineau J, Montemerlo M, Pollack M, Roy N, Thrun S (2003) Towards robotic assistants in nursing homes: challenges and results. Robot Auton Syst 42(3–4):271–281

Pollack ME, Brown L, Colbry D, McCarthy CE, Orosz C, Peintner B, Ramakrishnan S, Tsamardinos I (2003) Autominder: an intelligent cognitive orthotic system for people with memory impairment. Robot Auton Syst 44(3–4):273–282

Pollack ME (2005) Intelligent technology for an aging population: the use of AI to assist elders with cognitive impairment. AI Mag 26(2):9–9

Radford KA, Lah S, Say MJ, Miller LA (2011) Validation of a new measure of prospective memory: the Royal Prince Alfred Prospective Memory Test. Clin Neuropsychol 25(1):127–140

Ramos L, van den Hoven E, Miller L (2016) Designing for the other 'hereafter': when older adults remember about forgetting. In: Proceedings of the 2016 CHI conference on human factors in computing systems. ACM, pp 721–732

Schinkinger S, Tellioğlu H (2014) Design implications to systems supporting informal caregivers' daily life. In: International conference on human-computer interaction. Springer, pp 341–350

Shelton JT, Lee JH, Scullin MK, Rose NS, Rendell PG, McDaniel MA (2016) Improving prospective memory in healthy older adults and individuals with very mild Alzheimer's disease. J Am Geriatr Soc 64(6):1307–1312

Smith G, Del Sala S, Logie RH, Maylor EA (2000) Prospective and retrospective memory in normal ageing and dementia: a questionnaire study. Memory 8(5):311–321

Terry WS (1988) Everyday forgetting: data from a diary study. Psychol Rep 62(1):299–303

Thöne-Otto AI, Walther K (2003) How to design an electronic memory aid for brain-injured patients: considerations on the basis of a model of prospective memory. Int J Psychol 38(4):236–244

Truthful Loving Kindness (2015) Sound disorientation as dementia symptom. In: Truthful loving kindness: person with dementia symptoms, published 11 Aug 2015. https://truthfulkindness.com/2015/08/11/sound-disorientation-dementia-symptom/. Accessed 1 Nov 2019

Tulving E (2007) Are there 256 different kinds of memory. In: The foundations of remembering: essays in honor of Henry L Roediger, vol 3, pp 39–52

Uhlig M, Rieß H, Klein P (2018) Reminder objects in the connected home of the future and beyond. Technologies 6(1):1

van den Berg E, Kant N, Postma A (2012) Remember to buy milk on the way home! A meta-analytic review of prospective memory in mild cognitive impairment and dementia. J Int Neuropsychol Soc 18(4):706–716

van den Hoven E (2014) A future-proof past: designing for remembering experiences. Mem Stud 7(3):370–384

Vines J, Clarke R, Wright P, McCarthy J, Olivier P (2013) Configuring participation: on how we involve people in design. In: Proceedings of the SIGCHI conference on human factors in computing systems. ACM, pp 429–438

Walther K, Schulze H, Thoene-Otto A (2004) An interactive memory aid designed for patients with head injury: comparing MEMOS with two commercially available electronic memory aids

Wayne RV, Johnsrude IS (2015) A review of causal mechanisms underlying the link between age-related hearing loss and cognitive decline. Ageing Res Rev 23:154–166

Wolters MK (2014) The minimal effective dose of reminder technology. In: Extended abstracts on human factors in computing systems, CHI'14. ACM, pp 771–780

Wolters MK, Johnson C, Campbell PE, DePlacido CG, McKinstry B (2014) Can older people remember medication reminders presented using synthetic speech? J Am Med Inform Assoc 22(1):35–42

Zanwar P, Heyn PC, McGrew G, Raji M (2018) Assistive technology megatrends to support persons with Alzheimer's disease and related dementias age in habitat: challenges for usability, engineering and public policy. In: Proceedings of the workshop on human-habitat for health (H3): human-habitat multimodal interaction for promoting health and well-being in the internet of things era. ACM, p 1

# Chapter 10
# Intuitive Interaction Framework in User-Product Interaction for People Living with Dementia

**Alethea Blackler, Li-Hao Chen, Shital Desai, and Arlene Astell**

This chapter is focused on intuitive interaction with various interfaces for people living with dementia. First, we describe the enhanced intuitive interaction framework, which contains a continuum suggesting various pathways to intuitive use that can be included in the design of interfaces. We discuss how it relates to users, and specifically how it may assist users living with dementia. Then three empirical studies conducted over two continents are discussed. Each involved participants living with dementia using interfaces in a lab. Data were analyzed for task completion, reaction times and completion times (Studies 1 and 2), and presence and effectiveness of physical and perceived affordances (two of the proposed pathways to intuitive use on the EFII continuum). These data were then compared according to the enhanced intuitive interaction framework, and the findings suggested that employing interface features that are more familiar and more ubiquitous for the target population would likely make the interfaces more intuitive for people living with dementia to use. The

A. Blackler (✉)
QUT Design Lab, Queensland University of Technology, Brisbane, Australia
e-mail: A.Blackler@qut.edu.au

L.-H. Chen
Department of Applied Arts, Fu Jen Catholic University, Taipei, Taiwan
e-mail: Ahao55@gmail.com

S. Desai
Department of Design, School of Arts, Media, Performance and Design (AMPD), York University, Toronto, Canada
e-mail: Desais@yorku.ca

A. Astell
Department of Occupational Sciences and Occupational Therapy and Department of Psychiatry, University of Toronto, Toronto, Canada
e-mail: Arlene.Astell@utoronto.ca

School of Psychology and Clinical Language Sciences, University of Reading, Reading, UK

Toronto Rehabilitation Institute, Toronto, Canada

© Springer Nature Switzerland AG 2020

R. Brankaert and G. Kenning (eds.), *HCI and Design in the Context of Dementia*, Human–Computer Interaction Series,
https://doi.org/10.1007/978-3-030-32835-1_10

implications of these finders for users living with dementia and those designing for them are discussed.

## 10.1 Introduction

Intuitive interaction research has become firmly established in design and HCI over the past 20 years. As Blackler et al. (2010a, b) noted, intuitive interaction is defined as fast, somewhat non-conscious, and generally accurate interaction with an interface that is informed by past experience or technology familiarity. However, although several studies in intuitive interaction have been focused on designing for older people (e.g. Blackler et al. 2012; Gudur et al. 2013; Hurtienne et al. 2015a, b; Lawry et al. 2011; O'Brien 2019; O'Brien et al. 2011), only a very small amount of work has looked at its potential to help people living with dementia (e.g. Desai et al. 2019), much of it focused on the concept of affordances only (Chen and Liu 2018; Chen et al. 2018). This chapter will use the enhanced framework for intuitive interaction (EFII) (Blackler et al. 2019) to explore results from various empirical studies performed around the world with people living with dementia. Classifying interface features used in the studies according to the EFII framework allows us to understand how accessible they might be to people living with dementia.

## 10.2 The Enhanced Framework for Intuitive Interaction (EFII)

Blackler et al. (2019) proposed an enhanced framework for intuitive interaction to describe how to make product interfaces both engaging and intuitive. The framework illustrates the parallels and connections between the different dimensions of intuitive interaction. Figure 10.1 illustrates the part of the enhanced framework which indicates the pathways to intuitive use; this is a continuum based on a previous continuum developed by Blackler (2008a) and Blackler and Popovic (2016), which forms the heart of the EFII.

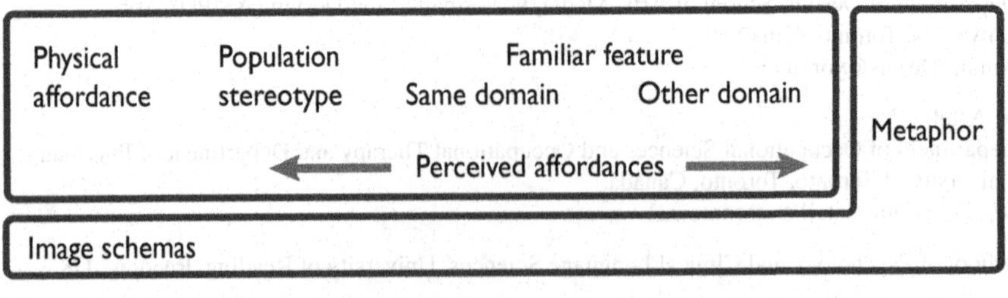


**Fig. 10.1** Continuum of pathways to intuitive interaction (derived from Blackler and Popovic 2016)

The continuum of pathways to intuitive interaction is based on sources of previous knowledge or technology familiarity (TF) that users can access. The most ubiquitous types of pathways (on the left-hand side in Fig. 10.1) are learned in childhood, used throughout the lifespan, and broadly applied in many areas of life. Ubiquity of previous experience and therefore potential for more people to be able to intuitively use a feature is highest at the lower end of the continuum and theoretically decreases from left to right. As explained in Blackler et al. (2019), this assumption is based on the fact that these pathways are based on sensorimotor and cultural knowledge held by many people. Pathways at the other end (right-hand side in Fig. 10.1) rely more on complex and specialist knowledge, particular interface experience, or tool expertise held by individuals. People living with dementia may benefit from interface features that are based on the most ubiquitous and longest understood pathways.

Blackler et al. (2019) claim that ubiquity (or near ubiquity) can be achieved by applying the appropriate interface features which relate to the lower (left hand) end of the pathways of intuitive use continuum, to ensure that features are known to everyone or almost everyone in a target population. Features based on physical affordances, image schemas, and population stereotypes will therefore be more intuitive to use for more people. These are the things that are so familiar that they become transparent until they break down or are designed away from their origins and break the mold; that is, these are re-designed so much that they no longer fit the stereotype or possess the affordance (Fischer 2019).

For example, physical affordances (e.g. a door knob that can be grasped and turned by hand) represent those possibilities for action that an environment offers in terms of its properties, mediums, and compositions (Gibson 1979). Physical affordances thus represent prompts derived from physical and material properties of elements in the environment. Perceived affordances are learned conventions (Norman 2013) derived from prior experience with similar interfaces (Blackler et al. 2010a, b). The concept of the perceived affordance refers to users' learned knowledge and culture, and so is equated with population stereotypes or familiar features in Fig. 10.1. Population stereotypes are interactions and icons endemic to a whole society or group.

Image schemas are metaphorical extensions of cognitive concepts which are based on experiences of interaction with the physical world. For example, the up-down image schema is established by experience of verticality, and is applied to our understanding of a range of other concepts like quantity (Blackler et al. 2019). Image schemas can be applied to interface design, and because they are based on past experience, and so well-known and so universal that they become unconscious, image schemas can be defined as intuitive (Hurtienne 2009). Hurtienne et al. (2015a, b) showed that image schemas (which are metaphors) can be ubiquitous (or known to most people in a society), and hence intuitive and inclusive, belonging to the left side of the framework with higher ubiquity rather than on the right with more traditional metaphors.

However, it should be recognized that it is not possible to stay purely at the left-hand side of the diagram (Fig. 10.1). Interface types that are more physical mostly rely on physical affordances (such as grasping, holding and sliding physical objects). Interfaces can, however, also leverage population stereotypes (or cultural conventions), interface features learned when using similar and dissimilar products, and metaphors (turning a wheel, how to use a racket to play tennis, balancing blocks one above the other to create a stack). In this framework (Blackler et al. 2019, Fig. 10.1), metaphor has been detached from the other parts of Blackler's (2008b) original continuum because it became clear that metaphor is not always a simple continuation from the other concepts and in fact could be applied in other ways than originally assumed. The extension of the metaphor block beneath the continuum is intended to demonstrate that metaphor can in fact be applied through any of the other pathways to intuitive use (e.g. physical affordances, familiar features, etc.), and that image schemas, despite being metaphors, are very ubiquitous.

## 10.3 Intuitive Interfaces for Users with Dementia

We have theorized that the pathways on the left-hand side of the continuum should be more ubiquitous (and hence more accessible to more people in the general population), and that potentially these pathways offer a way for users with dementia to more easily use designed features as these should be things so familiar to them that they are retained in memory after other things may be lost. The work on the reminiscence bump (Astell 2009; Hallberg et al. 2009; Sarne-Fleischmann et al. 2009; Wang 2009) offers some evidence that this may be the case.

Ubiquity is important in the application of intuitive interaction as there are many interfaces that are intended to be used by almost anyone, for example, ticket vending machines, point of sale systems, ATMs, websites of various types such as banking, patient records, government information, as well as operating systems for phones, tablets, and computers. Using many of these interfaces has become less of a choice and more of a necessity in recent years, as everyone is expected to be able to access and manipulate their money and information online and people need to be able to communicate using tools such as email, social media, and text if they are to stay connected with the rest of society. For users with dementia, being able to use these types of tools and interfaces for as long as possible is one of the keys to allowing extended independent living (Astell et al. 2018, 2019; Braley et al. 2018; Gibson et al. 2018; Joddrell and Astell 2019; Kim et al. 2019; Lorenz et al. 2019). This research used interface examples from empirical studies with users living with dementia from two continents to explore whether the design pathways in the EFII can be useful to inform the design of products and interfaces for people living with dementia.

## 10.4 Studies 1 and 2: People Living with Dementia in Taiwan

The two empirical studies carried out in Taiwan mainly focus on investigations for users with mild dementia interacting with different types of microwave oven interfaces. The definition of mild dementia was based on a score of 0.5 or 1 in the clinical dementia rating (CDR) scale which is often used by neurologists in hospitals in Taiwan. Regarding cognitive skill assessments, participants who scored moderately low in short-term memory function, long-term memory function, and hand–eye coordination were chosen as the participants. In the two studies, the test interfaces involved a custom program that recorded at two different times. First, the time elapsed before a participant touched the screen on the first attempt (i.e. the initial reaction time) was recorded. This can be equated to the latency criterion used to indicate intuitive uses by Blackler et al. (2010a, b). Second, the task completion time was recorded to analyze the overall usability of the test interface. Also, we observed and recorded whether the participants correctly completed tasks and any problems experienced in operating the user interfaces.

### *10.4.1 Study 1*

Seven common types of user interface for setting heating time periods on microwave ovens were collected as the test interfaces, and the corresponding feature types based on the pathways to intuitive use of EFII are shown in Fig. 10.2. To prevent factors such as color and material from influencing the participants, the outlines of the buttons were redrawn using graphics software. During the experiment, testing samples were presented as a white background and black lines and displayed on a tablet computer with a 10-inch touch screen.

A total of 20 participants (mean age = 79.6 years; SD = 10.1) with mild dementia and without major difficulties in verbal communication were invited for the study. The participants were asked to set a specific heating time period and initiate the heating process on the microwave interface. At the beginning of the tests, the participants were required to read the task instructions on a tablet computer. They were orally informed of the task content if they were unable to understand the instructions. After one task was completed, the screen displayed the instructions for the task of the next testing interface, and each testing interface was randomly selected and displayed in a single image.

In Table 10.1, the interfaces with shorter mean reaction times and shorter mean completion times are indicated with *. The one-way ANOVA[1] results show that the average initial reaction times among the seven test interfaces differed significantly ($p < 0.05$). As shown in Table 10.2, the post-hoc ANOVA results showed that B1, C1, D1,

[1]The one-way analysis of variance (ANOVA) is used to determine whether there are any statistically significant differences between the means of three or more independent (unrelated) groups.

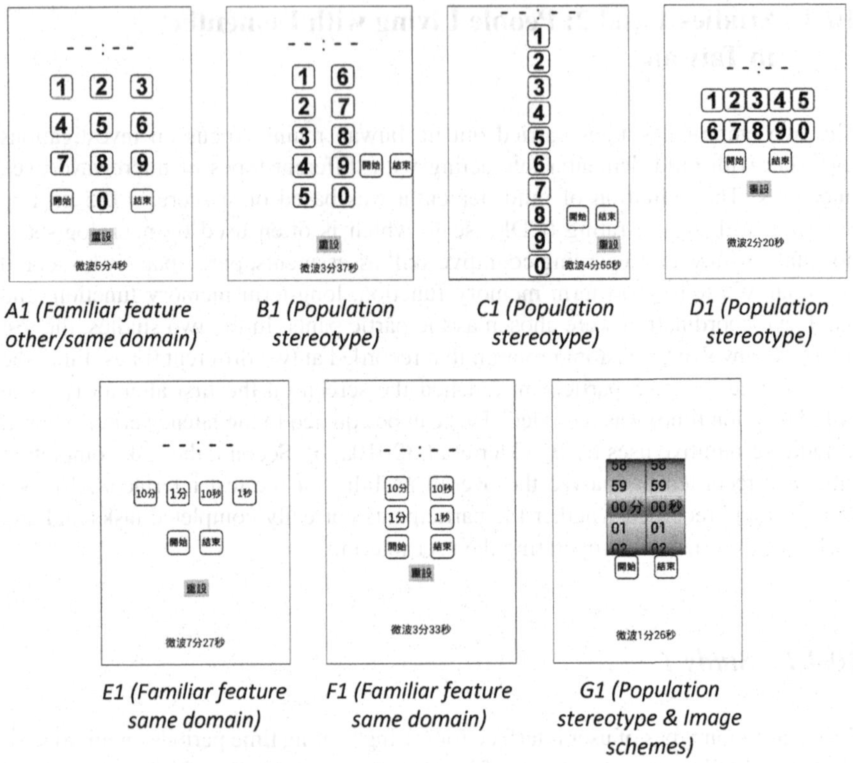


**Fig. 10.2** Test interfaces (setting heating time)

and G1 yielded shorter mean reaction times, whereas A1, E1, and F1 demonstrated relatively longer mean reaction times. For completion time, post-hoc ANOVA results showed that average completion times for A1, B1, C1, and D1 are shorter and differ significantly from E1, F1, and G1 (Table 10.3).

The major problems that participants experienced during task operation can be seen in Table 10.4. The results indicated that among the participants who did not complete the tasks, most failed because of entering incorrect numbers or not understanding how to enter heating time periods. The most common method of setting heating time periods on the microwave ovens was to enter time directly. For example, to enter 5 min and 23 s, users needed only to press the numeric keys 5, 2, and 3 sequentially. Several of the participants did not understand this method, which resulted in long periods of operating time and entering incorrect information.

**Table 10.1** Results of Study 1

| Interface | Feature type | Feature image | Average initial reaction time | Average completion time | Participants who did not correctly complete the task |
|---|---|---|---|---|---|
| A1 | Familiar feature other/same domain |  | 14.7 | 28.2* | 10<br>50% |
| B1 | Population stereotype |  | 10.5* | 23.9* | 5<br>25% |
| C1 | Population stereotype | 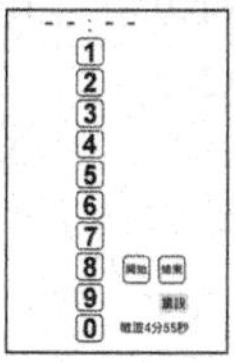 | 5.8* | 21.7* | 6<br>30% |
| D1 | Population stereotype |  | 9.5* | 25.4* | 4<br>20% |
| E1 | Familiar feature same domain | 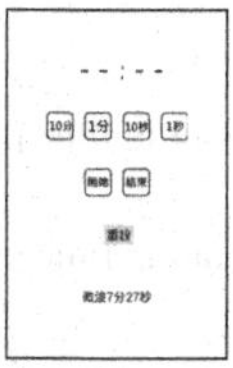 | 14.2 | 57.5 | 5<br>25% |
| F1 | Familiar feature same domain | 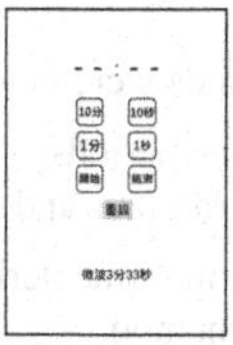 | 13.1 | 48.4 | 9<br>45% |
| G1 | Population stereotype Image schemes | 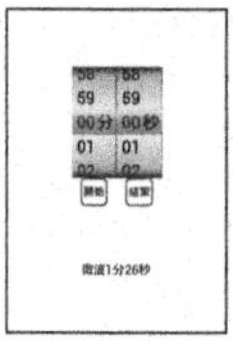 | 3.2* | 69.3 | 4<br>20% |

Table 10.2 Post-hoc $p$ values for initial reaction times in Study 1

| Interface | A1 | B1 | C1 | D1 | E1 | F1 | G1 |
|---|---|---|---|---|---|---|---|
| A1 | | 0.054 | 0.002 | 0.091 | 0.891 | 0.613 | 0.000 |
| B1 | | | 0.012 | 0.708 | 0.099 | 0.276 | 0.001 |
| C1 | | | | 0.120 | 0.000 | 0.000 | 0.064 |
| D1 | | | | | 0.005 | 0.228 | 0.011 |
| E1 | | | | | | 0.687 | 0.000 |
| F1 | | | | | | | 0.000 |
| G1 | | | | | | | |

Table 10.3 Post-hoc $p$ values for completion times in Study 1

| Interface | A1 | B1 | C1 | D1 | E1 | F1 | G1 |
|---|---|---|---|---|---|---|---|
| A1 | | 0.136 | 0.130 | 0.218 | 0.001 | 0.001 | 0.003 |
| B1 | | | 0.519 | 0.499 | 0.001 | 0.000 | 0.001 |
| C1 | | | | 0.282 | 0.001 | 0.000 | 0.001 |
| D1 | | | | | 0.000 | 0.000 | 0.001 |
| E1 | | | | | | 0.236 | 0.360 |
| F1 | | | | | | | 0.107 |
| G1 | | | | | | | |

Table 10.4 Observation records of setting heating time task in Study 1

| Test interface | Observation<br>Reason |
|---|---|
| A1 | Not understanding how to enter heating time periods<br>Entering incorrect numbers |
| B1 | Entering incorrect numbers |
| C1 | Not understanding how to enter heating time periods<br>Entering incorrect numbers |
| D1 | Not understanding how to enter heating time periods<br>Entering incorrect numbers |
| E1 | Spending relatively longer time on understanding how to enter heating time periods<br>Failure to complete the task (seconds were not set after minutes were set) |
| F1 | Failure to enter correct heating time periods<br>Failure to complete the setting of minutes and seconds |
| G1 | Not understanding how to set heating time periods<br>Not understanding the operating method |

### 10.4.2 Study 2

Six different types of interface for adjusting cooking power were used as the test interfaces, and the features as they correspond to the pathways are shown in Fig. 10.3. As in Study 1, graphics software was used to redraw the interfaces. The participants were asked to adjust the cooking power to medium-high (available levels include slow, low, thawing, middle, medium high, and high). Three of the interfaces (A2, B2, and F2) were operated by pressing buttons at the bottom to cycle through the available power settings. C2 was operated by directly pressing the buttons labeled with the

**Table 10.5** Results of Study 2

| Interface | Feature type | Feature image | Average initial reaction time | Average completion time | Participants who did not correctly complete the task |
|---|---|---|---|---|---|
| A2 | Familiar feature same domain | 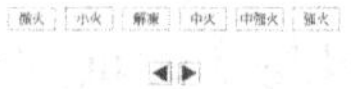  | 14.2 | 34.7 | 1<br>4% |
| B2 | Familiar feature same domain |   | 13.4 | 32.2 | 2<br>8% |
| C2 | Physical affordance Familiar feature same domain |  | 13.9 | 18.8* | 0<br>0% |
| D2 | Familiar feature same domain |  | 14.9 | 22.3* | 0<br>0% |
| E2 | Population stereotype |  | 10.5* | 32.7 | 3<br>12% |
| F2 | Familiar feature same domain | 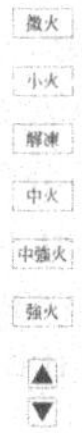  | 15.2 | 34.5 | 0<br>0% |

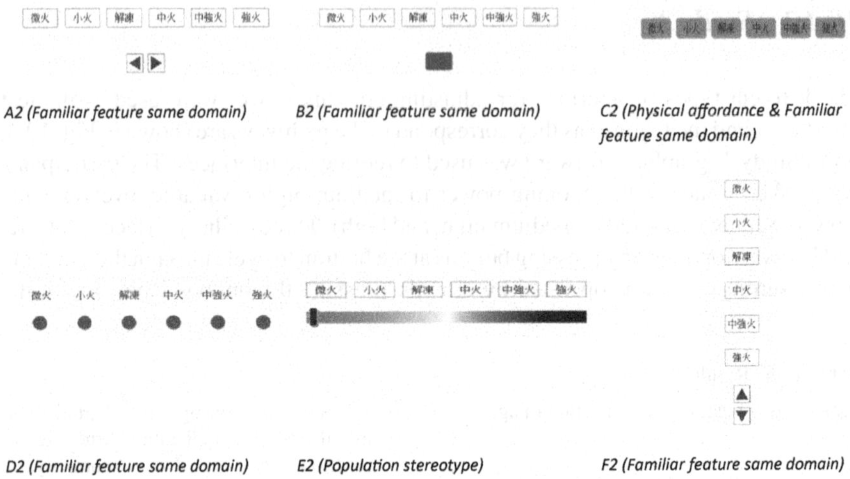


**Fig. 10.3** Test interfaces (adjusting cooking power)

different power settings. D2 was operated by pressing the round buttons directly underneath the power setting labels. E2 was operated by sliding a bar underneath the power setting labels.

The test interfaces were displayed on a tablet computer with a 10-inch touch screen, randomly one at a time. The participants each sat in front of the tablet and read the task instructions displayed on the screen. If they did not understand the written instructions, verbal explanations of the task were provided. No time limit was set for completing the task. Hospital neurologists nominated 25 participants who had mild dementia, demonstrated acceptable communicative and cognitive functions, and were experienced in using home appliances. The participants averaged 81.8 years of age (SD = 7.2).

In Table 10.5, shorter mean reaction times and shorter mean completion times are marked with *. The average initial reaction times for interfaces A2, D2, and F2 were relatively slow, with E2 attaining the shortest average initial reaction time. The post-hoc ANOVA results showed statistically significant differences between mean initial reaction times on E2 and F2, indicating that the slider interface was more likely to be intuitive for the participants in their initial encounters with the interface (Table 10.6). The one-way ANOVA results show that the average completion times among the six test interfaces reach a significant standard ($p < 0.05$). As shown in Table 10.7, C2 and D2 enabled relatively short mean times, which were statistically different from the completion times attained through A2, B2, E2, and F2.

Table 10.8 displays the reasons for participants' mistakes. The primary reason for failing to complete the task was that the participants pressed the incorrect buttons. For example, on B2 and E2, some participants did not realize that the buttons at the bottom of the interface could be manipulated to adjust the cooking power settings.

**Table 10.6** Post-hoc $p$ values for initial reaction time of study 3

| Interface | A2 | B2 | C2 | D2 | E2 | F2 |
|---|---|---|---|---|---|---|
| A2 | | 0.509 | 0.904 | 0.747 | 0.094 | 0.556 |
| B2 | | | 0.808 | 0.477 | 0.133 | 0.177 |
| C2 | | | | 0.621 | 0.052 | 0.524 |
| D2 | | | | | 0.065 | 0.897 |
| E2 | | | | | | 0.028 |
| F2 | | | | | | |

**Table 10.7** Post-hoc $p$ values for completion time of study 3

| Interface | A2 | B2 | C2 | D2 | E2 | F2 |
|---|---|---|---|---|---|---|
| A2 | | 0.251 | 0.001 | 0.005 | 0.681 | 0.962 |
| B2 | | | 0.001 | 0.015 | 0.917 | 0.493 |
| C2 | | | | 0.177 | 0.000 | 0.000 |
| D2 | | | | | 0.003 | 0.001 |
| E2 | | | | | | 0.621 |
| F2 | | | | | | |

**Table 10.8** Observation records of the cooking power task

| Test interface | Observation |
|---|---|
| | Reasons |
| A2 | Did not understand the task and chose the wrong cooking power |
| B2 | Did not understand the task and chose the wrong cooking power<br>Did not understand that the buttons underneath the labels could be pressed to adjust cooking power and chose the wrong cooking power |
| C2 | |
| D2 | |
| E2 | Did not understand that the slider could be moved<br>Inadvertently chose the wrong cooking power |
| F2 | |

### *10.4.3 Discussion*

Interfaces with good intuitive interaction for initial operation do not necessarily have equally good usability for users with mild dementia. For example, G1 in Study 2 could effectively guide the subjects' initial operation, but the participants needed more time to complete the task with it. The interface features of the two empirical studies can be classified according to the pathways to intuitive use (Fig. 10.1, Tables 10.3 and 10.5). Some of the interfaces (such as A1, C2, and G1) are hard to simply classify into only one design pathway. For example, the layout of interface A1 might be familiar from users' experiences in using the same product (microwave) or other relevant products (telephone). For initial reaction time, the interfaces with population stereotypes and image schemes present better performance in eliciting users' intuitive initial operations than others. The interfaces with better average completion times are spread between the three pathways: physical affordance, population stereotype, and familiar features. These tended to be toward the left-hand side of the continuum, bearing in mind that there were minimal physical affordances due to the nature of these interfaces. There were no interfaces in Studies 1 or 2 which had significantly shorter reaction time or completion time and are familiar features from other domains (although one was familiar from both other and same domains), and none that were metaphors. This supports our view that interface features that are more ubiquitous could be more intuitive for people living with dementia to use.

## 10.5 Study 3: Mixed Reality Technologies to Support People Living with Dementia (Canada)

People with dementia struggle to participate in everyday activities such as cooking and laundry as they have difficulty in sequencing tasks in an activity. Technology-based prompting can support people with dementia through the sequences required to complete activities (Mihailidis et al. 2008; Pigot et al. 2003). Mixed reality technologies (MRTs) could offer scalable and adaptable solutions that can be easily deployed. On a continuum of physical–virtual devices, MRTs are anything in between (Desai et al. 2016). Augmented systems can either consist of augmenting the real physical world with virtual objects, as in augmented reality (Azuma et al. 2001) or the virtual world augmented with real physical objects, as in augmented virtuality (Regenbrecht et al. 2004). Prompts can be generated in response to people's actions and behavior (Desai et al. 2019). However, the design and development of MRTs for generating prompts for people with dementia first requires an understanding of how people with dementia interact with MRTs. This study thus investigated interactions and prompts that might be intuitive for people with dementia interacting with MRTs. The aim of this research was to identify factors that contribute to a feeling of being part of the real world with mediated elements, in the context of mixed reality environments. For this to be possible, the interactions with the technology should be natural to the user, such that the cyclic perception action process is invisible to the user. Intuitive interaction in MRTs thus involves non-conscious interactions such that people are unable to explain how and why they made decisions during the interaction, with the presence of mediating virtual technology being transparent to the user, and people experiencing *being there* in the physical real world.

### *10.5.1 Research Design*

Participants were recruited from Alzheimer's Society York Region and Memory and Company, a memory health club in Toronto, Canada, for people living with dementia. An observational study was carried out in participants' homes and at Memory and Company. Nine people with dementia (MoCA = 19–24, mean MoCA = 21.89, age = 63–90 years, mean age = 76.89[2]) were observed playing a game of Tangram on Osmo, an augmented virtuality MRT, and a game of Young Conker on HoloLens, an augmented reality MRT (Fig. 10.4).

Osmo from Tangible Play is an augmented virtuality MRT with distinct physical and virtual environments for people to interact with separately. The participants interacted with Tangram puzzle pieces in the physical environment to complete the puzzle presented in the virtual environment (tablet). The tablet camera tracks the progress of the participant solving the puzzle in the physical environment and updates the progress in the virtual environment. The virtual environment generates prompts for the participants to solve the puzzle.

HoloLens from Microsoft is an augmented reality technology with overlapped physical and virtual environments. It uses the real physical world of the user to overlay virtual elements (holograms) for the user (who wears the headset) to interact with, see, and hear within their environment (such as workspace and living room). The Young Conker game developed by Microsoft Studio for HoloLens directs the player through various levels in the game where a player is expected to guide a holographic squirrel named Conker through gaze movements, to solve a mystery by performing tasks such as collecting coins, plugging a cable into a socket, and turning on a switch. Conker

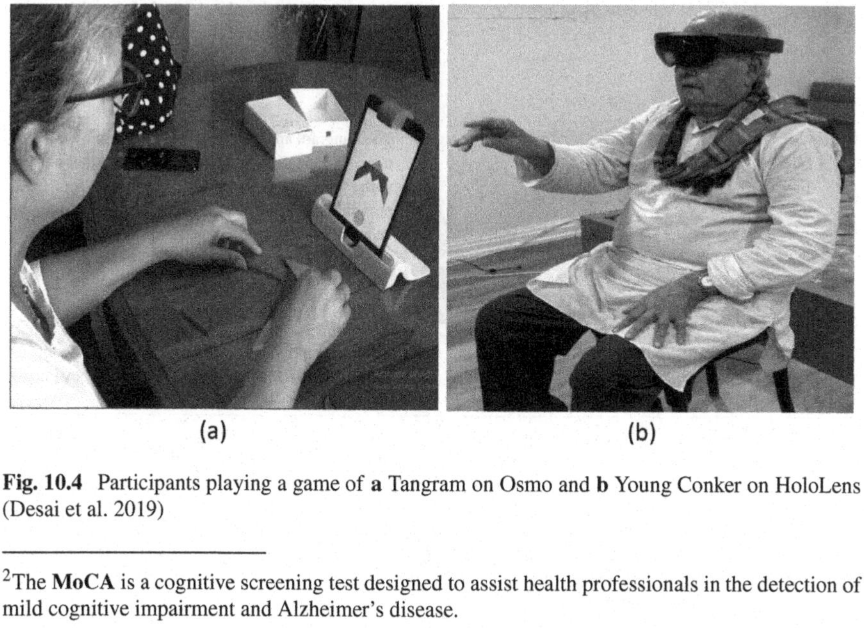

(a) (b)

**Fig. 10.4** Participants playing a game of **a** Tangram on Osmo and **b** Young Conker on HoloLens (Desai et al. 2019)

[2]The **MoCA** is a cognitive screening test designed to assist health professionals in the detection of mild cognitive impairment and Alzheimer's disease.

**Table 10.9** Features in Osmo and HoloLens related to EFII

| Themes identified | MRT type | Interaction | Description |
|---|---|---|---|
| Physical affordance | Osmo | 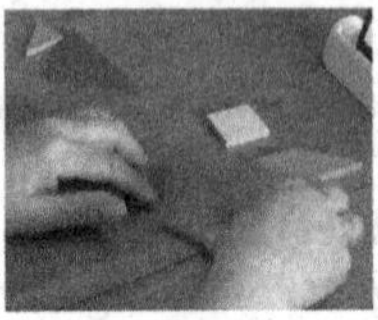 | Shape, size, and color used to put the pieces together in a puzzle |
| Perceived affordance | Osmo |  (a)   (b) | Every time players are successful in completing a puzzle, they earn *gems* (see (a)) which they could use to see prompts while solving a puzzle (see (b)) Players are prompted to use gems to reveal a prompt through an owl speaking in a female voice, a text in a speech bubble, (a) shows gems collected at the end of the puzzle, (b) shows the owl prompting the player to use the gems to receive a prompt. The gem has a number that indicates number of gems available to the player. The circle has a text "Use Gems Cost #", where # is the number of gems required to generate a prompt for the puzzle |
| Perceived affordances | Osmo | 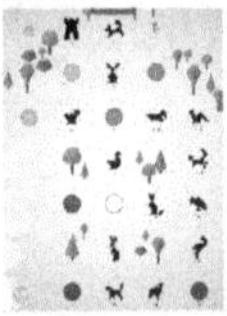 | Yellow, orange, and red ellipses representing easy, medium, and hard levels, respectively. Purple represents the highest level, which the participants did not play in the study |
| Perceived affordances | Osmo | 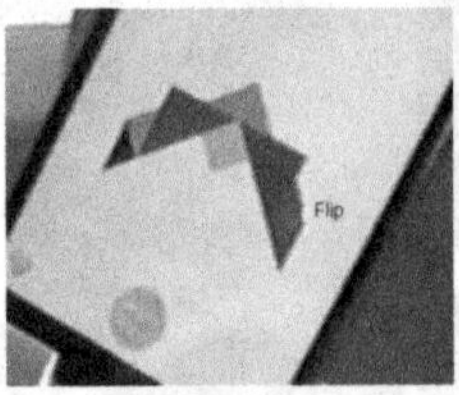  | The Tangram app prompts players to turn over the physical orange Tangram piece when it is not placed with the correct side upwards. The prompt is provided through a text "Flip" on the touch screen near the orange Tangram piece which is still black in the app as the physical piece has not been placed correctly |
| Perceived affordances | Osmo | Music | Music tone provides feedback to the player about the progress of the puzzle solving task as they put the pieces together |

(continued)

**Table 10.9** (continued)

| Themes identified | MRT type | Interaction | Description |
|---|---|---|---|
| Perceived affordances | Osmo | <br>(a)<br><br>(b) | Flickering between red and blue prompting the participants to use either of the two shapes in that position |
| Perceived affordances | HoloLens |  | Tap icon prompting participants to air tap. This is in line with a tap on a mouse to select |
| Perceived affordances | HoloLens |  | Air tap to select |
| Perceived affordances | HoloLens | <br>*Step 1*<br>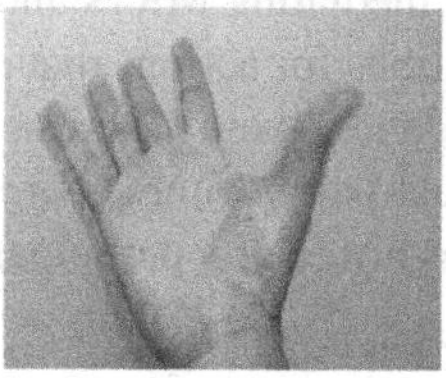<br>*Step 2* | A bloom gesture to reset HoloLens to Home screen |

communicates with the player through speech and gestures/animations. Prompts in the form of text, graphics, and animations are presented to the player to accomplish a set mission in the game.

Four types of prompts were presented by the technologies during game play; textual, graphical, animated, and speech. People interact with the two technologies (Osmo and HoloLens) in the following three ways—gaze (interaction through eye movements), speech, and gestural interactions which included tapping on the touch screen, object manipulations, and hand gestures (air tap and bloom). Table 10.9 shows the features of both Osmo and HoloLens and how they relate to the continuum in Fig. 10.1.

The game play of the participants was video recorded for analysis. Qualitative analysis of the video data was carried out in NVivo™ plus 12.0[3] to identify themes that corresponded to people interacting with the physical and virtual worlds through perception-action sequences without noticing the presence of mediating technology. The ability of MRTs to sustain continuous uninterrupted perception-action loops in an interaction (Hinton 2014), and the extent to which the presence of mediating technologies are familiar to the user, determines the intuitiveness of the interfaces and the interactions. For this to happen, people living with dementia should be able to perceive the prompts presented to them (Desai et al. 2016), and respond to the prompts with correct, often unconscious, actions (Blackler et al. 2010a, b).

The type of MRT—HoloLens and Osmo—was the categorical independent variable. The perception of the prompts and the actions performed by people with dementia in the video data were coded to differentiate when or whether the mediating technology was transparent to people with dementia while they were carrying out the intended task. Distractions caused due to physical/virtual couplings, ergonomics of the mediating technology, prompts that could not be understood by the participants or were understood incorrectly, and incorrect actions performed by the participants were the heuristics used to code the interactions with the MRT.

### *10.5.2 Results*

Two major themes emerged from the analysis of the video recordings of the game play—physical affordances and perceived affordances. The number of occurrences of interactions using physical and perceived affordances is presented in Fig. 10.5. The physical and virtual elements in the mediating MRTs and the games provided clues to people with dementia on possibilities for actions that could be performed.

The results indicate that physical affordances were the prime factor for interacting with Osmo, both with physical and virtual parts of the environment, such that the presence of the mediating technology was not felt by participants. In the absence of

[3]**NVivo** is a qualitative data analysis (QDA) computer software package produced by QSR International.

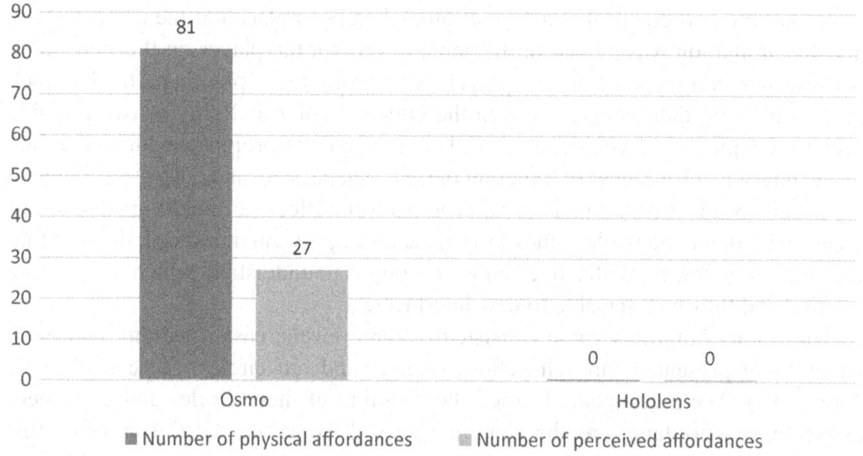


**Fig. 10.5** Number of uses of affordances in mixed reality technologies, Osmo and HoloLens

physical affordances, participants used perceived affordances to interact with Osmo. Examples of affordances for both the MRTs are shown in Table 10.9.

Participants found HoloLens difficult to use, both in terms of interactions as well as in terms of understanding the prompts from the technology:

'What is he [Conker] saying?' P1_2001

'Where do I go? What do I do now? I can't find anything?' P8_2008

'It [HoloLens] is very heavy, my head hurts' P4_2004

The affordances in HoloLens and the Young Conker game could not be deciphered by the participants to decide on the actions to be performed in the game. This was due to gestures and interactions with the technology not being familiar; people with dementia found the prompts from the technology difficult to understand and the headset caused distraction and clearly left a red mark on the participants' noses. These issues resulted in the mediating technology not being intuitive to the user.

### *10.5.3 Discussion*

HoloLens and Young Conker did not present any physical affordances to the participants. Although the game app presented perceived affordances in the form of visual images, texts, and animations, people living with dementia were unable to perceive the meaning of these prompts and therefore there were no successful uses of affordances in HoloLens. However, in the case of Osmo and Tangram, the puzzle pieces offered appropriate physical affordances which allowed participants to perform effective actions in the game play. The Osmo game offered the following prompts to enable people with dementia to make correct decisions (Table 10.9); a music tone was played to prompt the participant that a correct block had been placed at the correct place, a visual animation was played in the game to prompt the player on the steps to be performed to complete the puzzle, players were prompted to place a particular block in a position by flickering it between the intended color and gray or two possible options. People living with dementia did not notice these prompts and mostly relied on the physical affordances of Tangram pieces—shape, size, and color—to complete the puzzle. Study 3 found that verbal prompts were effective in getting attention of people with dementia while some of the visual prompts went unnoticed, highlighting how important testing with a relevant user group is to understand which features are familiar and thus transferrable to new interfaces.

The Osmo Tangrams game consisted of three levels; easy, medium, and hard, which were presented through yellow, orange, and red circles, respectively (see Table 10.7). The participants learned the meaning of these circles and used them as perceived affordances as the game progressed. However, these were often forgotten at some stage of the game play, so participants had to be prompted by the researcher verbally and the meaning of the colored circles had to be relearnt. A similar pattern was observed in the use of *gems* to generate *paid* prompts to start a medium or high-level puzzle. An owl emerges on the screen and prompts the player to use gems. However, people living with dementia did not initially understand the concept of the use of gems. They learnt this as the game progressed, but they often had to relearn at some stage of the game as they forgot the meaning. Thus, participants mostly used physical affordances rather than perceived affordances in their interactions with Osmo.

Study 3 found that people living with dementia respond through embodied activities and gestures (physical affordances) more effectively than other interaction modalities. They were able to use the physical affordances of the Tangram pieces to determine the next course of actions to be performed, so the physical affordances in the form of object manipulations offered intuitive interactions in Osmo.

Perceived affordances, as they are learned conventions, require people living with dementia to access population stereotypes, idioms, and metaphors from their long-term memory. Learning new population stereotypes and metaphors requires access to working memory to retain learned conventions. Participants in Study 3 found it difficult to learn and/or remember the new conventions, which explain the increased use of physical affordances over perceived affordances. Thus, mediating technologies that offer access to physical affordances to interact with the technologies are more intuitive to interact with, as in the case of Osmo.

Dementia can affect parts of the brain that control language (Bayles 1982), which helps to explain the effectiveness of non-verbal forms of responses to the prompts such as gestures over speech or language-based interactions. Gestures such as object manipulation and touch screen interactions came naturally to the participants, due to familiarity with other object manipulations (Astell et al. 2016). Gestural interactions such as hand gestures, for example bloom and air tap (Table 10.9), were also effective but only when the participants were prompted by the researcher either verbally or through a hand gesture prompt; the participants found it difficult to remember the gestures as they were unfamiliar with these interactions.

## 10.6 Overall Discussion

The findings of these three studies suggest that using a framework such as the EFII could help designers to make interfaces more intuitive for people living with dementia, which could help them to live independently for longer, especially if applied to self-care products and services such as in home alarms, fall alarms, and communications technologies, for example. Those features based on the simplest and most ubiquitous pathways such as physical affordances and population stereotypes generally show, in the experiments reported here, better reaction times and lower times on task for people living with dementia than features toward the other end of the continuum, such as features from other domains. Participants living with dementia were found to predominantly use physical affordances when they were available in their interactions with interfaces, and it appears that natural physical and material properties of objects are important drivers of intuitive interactions in people living with dementia.

The affordance is the intrinsic relationship between users and objects, and is theorized as perceptually obvious to any person with the physical capability to use it (Norman 1988; You and Chen 2007). For example, a handle implies grasping. This is why physical affordances are at the lowest end of the continuum, as any physically able person should be able to understand and use them. In Study 3, where physical affordances were available in the test interfaces, people with dementia primarily relied on direct interactions with them. However, the anterolateral entorhinal cortex part of the brain which is responsible for processing spatial information is first affected by Alzheimer's disease (Olsen et al. 2017). Thus, people with dementia due to Alzheimer's disease may not be able to use physical affordances which require them to use spatial knowledge, and physical affordances should be complemented with perceived affordances such as population stereotypes, so that people are able to use their past experience and familiarity to interact with the interfaces intuitively.

Our studies did not directly measure familiarity as information about participants' past experience with technology was not available. However, the results based on coding of participants' behavior with the technology suggest that lack of familiarity with contemporary interaction styles such as the bloom and air tap gestures, or with some of the less common features in the microwave interfaces, presented enormous challenges to people living with dementia. They were also unable to retain information that they learned during the sessions (e.g. the color coding), so it is important for designers to draw on the previous experience of users living with dementia rather than expecting them to learn new interaction modalities.

As Silver (2005) notes, people have learned many conventions: buttons are for pushing, knobs are for turning, switches are for flicking (although direction of on and off varies by country), strings are for pulling, red is for stop, turning a knob on a device in a clockwise direction means to increase and counterclockwise direction means to decrease. Population stereotypes are on the lower side of the continuum because they are common to a whole community and can effectively facilitate users to interact with a product interface intuitively. Interfaces with population stereotypes such as B1, C1, D1, G1 in Study 1 and E2 in Study 2 were familiar for people and allowed participants to use them non-consciously and rapidly at first operation. Participants in Study 3 found it difficult to learn the visual representations of easy, medium, and high levels of the Osmo game as the color codes used were not based on population stereotypes prevalent in North America (red for hard, green or white for easy). However, they were familiar with the stereotypes associated with touch screen interactions such as tapping on buttons or swiping on the screen.

People have an increased tendency to recollect events and memories from the age of 10–30 years (Glück and Bluck 2007), most prominently from the late teens and early twenties. This is referred to as the reminiscence bump. These memories and recollections remain strong for people with dementia until their illness enters an advanced stage (Fromholt and Larsen 1992). Utilizing physical affordances complemented with population stereotypes and familiar interfaces and features (perceived affordances) derived from users' experiences with interfaces and technologies from earlier in their lives may be beneficial for people with dementia. Our findings emphasize the importance of thinking carefully about the familiarity and experience of people living with dementia with the technologies and interfaces they have used in the past. The more familiar the features are and the more ubiquitous they are (i.e. the lower on the continuum they are), the longer they may remain familiar to users living with dementia. We posit that these ubiquitous features which have been long engrained (such as physical affordances and population stereotypes learned in childhood and early adulthood) may remain the longest in memory.

Familiar features in the EFII are connected to users' prior experiences in using similar product interfaces as well as those that may be quite different (e.g. transferred from other domains). In Studies 1 and 2, some of the interfaces with familiar features (A1, C2, and D2) showed better performance than others with familiar features (such as E1, F1, A2, B2, E2, and F2). The domain transfer distance is the distance between the application domain and the source domain of transferred prior knowledge (Diefenbach and Ullrich 2015). As transfer distance increases, people find it increasingly difficult to interpret the features. Domain transfer distance generally increases as you move to the right of the continuum, from similar domains to those that can be far removed from the task at hand (Blackler et al. 2019). For example, in Study 3, participants could not understand the metaphorical text "flip" derived from the metaphorical action of "flipping pancakes" to flip an orange block in the Tangram puzzle. Researchers had to provide a correction to the participants to *turn over* the block, which they were able to understand straightaway.

By seeking to ensure that features are as ubiquitous as possible for this user group (by encouraging use of those from the lower side of the continuum), we hope to assist a wider range of people in accessing their long-term familiarity and experience to use an interface intuitively and for longer.

## 10.7 Conclusion and Future Work

This work suggests that designers who apply the EFII and create features on the left-hand side of the continuum as far as possible will enable more users to intuitively access their interfaces. Exactly how the pathways to intuitive use in EFII facilitate users with dementia to intuitively interact with product interfaces in the whole process of user-product interaction is worthy of further study. For example, Chen is investigating the influences of characteristics of products' functional images (e.g. metaphors) on intuitive use for users living with dementia. Desai and Astell are further studying prompts with various combinations of sensory modalities that are successful in eliciting correct actions from people living with dementia and the kinds of gestures that are intuitive to use across various stages of cognitive impairment. Blackler is investigating ways to design with and for people living with dementia.

**Acknowledgments** The Taiwanese researchers would like to extend their gratitude to the Department of Neurology, Cardinal Tien Hospital, as well as to all the participants that made this study possible. The research was supported by the grant from the Ministry of Science and Technology, Taiwan, Grant 107-2410-H-030-059-MY2.

The Canadian researchers are thankful to all the participants and the staff at Alzheimer's Society of Durham and Memory and Company for facilitating recruitment of participants and data collection. The authors gratefully acknowledge the grant from AGE-WELL.

## References

Astell AJ (2009) REAFF—a framework for developing technology to address the needs of people with dementia. In: CEUR Workshop Proceedings, vol 499, pp 5–10

Astell AJ (2019) Creating technology with people who have dementia. In: Sayago S (ed) Perspectives on human-computer interaction research with older people. Springer, New York

Astell AJ, Joddrell P, Groenewoud H, de Lange J, Goumans M, Cordia A, Schikhof Y (2016) Does familiarity affect the enjoyment of touchscreen games for people with dementia? Int J Med Inform. https://doi.org/10.1016/j.ijmedinf.2016.02.001

Astell A, Smith S, Joddrell P (2019) Using technology in dementia care: a guide to technology solutions for everyday living. Jessica Kingsley Publishers

Astell A, Williams E, Hwang F, Brown L, Cooper S, Timon C, Khadra H (2018) NANA: a tale of ageing and technology. The New Dyn Ageing 2:157

Azuma R, Baillot Y, Behringer R, Feiner S, Julier S, MacIntyre B (2001) Recent advances in augmented reality. IEEE Comput Graph Appl 21(6):34–47. https://doi.org/10.1109/38.963459

Bayles KA (1982) Language function in senile dementia. Brain Lang 16(2):265–280

Blackler A (2008a) Intuitive interaction with complex artefacts: empirically-based research. VDM Verlag, Saarbrücken, Germany

Blackler A (2008b) Applications of high and low fidelity prototypes in researching intuitive interaction. Paper presented at the Undisciplined! Design Research Society 2008 Conference, Sheffield, UK. http://www3.shu.ac.uk/Conferences/DRS/Proceedings/Proceedings.htm

Blackler A, Desai S, McEwan M, Popovic V, Diefenbach S (2019) Perspectives on the nature of intuitive interaction. In: Blackler A (ed) Intuitive interaction: research and application. CRC Press, Boca Raton, L, pp 19–39

Blackler A, Mahar D, Popovic V (2010) Older adults, interface experience and cognitive decline. Paper presented at the OZCHI The 22nd annual conference on the Australian computer-human interaction special interest group: design—interaction—participation, Brisbane

Blackler A, Popovic V (2016) Intuitive interaction research—new directions and possible responses. Paper presented at the DRS2016: design + research + society—future-focused thinking, Brighton, UK

Blackler A, Popovic V, Mahar D (2010b) Investigating users' intuitive interaction with complex artefacts. Appl Ergon 41(1):72–92. https://doi.org/10.1016/j.apergo.2009.04.010

Blackler A, Popovic V, Mahar D, Reddy RG, Lawry S (2012) Intuitive interaction and older people. Paper presented at the DRS 2012 Bangkok—Research: uncertainty, contradiction and value, Bangkok

Braley R, Fritz R, Van Son CR, Schmitter-Edgecombe M (2018) Prompting technology and persons with dementia: the significance of context and communication. The Gerontologist 59(1):101–111

Chen LH, Liu YC (2018) Affordance design requirements to promote intuitive user-product interaction for elderly users with dementia (I). J Sci Des 2(2):53–62. https://doi.org/10.11247/jsd.2.2_2_53

Chen LH, Liu YC, Cheng PJ (2018) Perceived affordances in older people with dementia: designing intuitive product interfaces. Paper presented at the 2018 3rd international conference on design and manufacturing engineering, Melbourne, Australia

Desai S, Blackler A, Popovic V (2016) Intuitive interaction in a mixed reality system. In: Design research society, p 16

Desai S, Fels D, Astell A (2019) Investigating factors that contribute to presence in mixed reality technologies for people with dementia. In: Proceedings of the 21th international ACM SIGACCESS conference on computers and accessibility

Diefenbach S, Ullrich D (2015) An experience perspective on intuitive interaction: central components and the special effect of domain transfer distance. Interact Comput 27(3):210–234. https://doi.org/10.1093/iwc/iwv001

Fischer S (2019) Desiging intuitive products in an agile world. In: Blackler A (ed) Intuitive interaction: research and application. CRC Press, Boca Raton, FL, pp 195–212

Fromholt P, Larsen SF (1992) Autobiographical memory and life-history narratives in aging and dementia (Alzheimer type). In: Theoretical perspectives on autobiographical memory. Springer, pp 413–426

Gibson (1979) The theory of affordances in the ecological approach to visual perceptual. Houghton Mifflin

Gibson G, Dickinson C, Brittain K, Robinson L (2018) Personalisation, customisation and bricolage: how people with dementia and their families make assistive technology work for them. Ageing Soc 1–18

Glück J, Bluck S (2007) Looking back across the life span: a life story account of the reminiscence bump. Mem Cogn 35:1928–1939. https://doi.org/10.3758/BF03192926

Gudur RR, Blackler AL, Popovic V, Mahar D (2013) Ageing, technology anxiety and intuitive use of complex interfaces. Lect Notes Comput Sci: Hum-Comput Interact—INTERACT 2013(8119):564–581

Hallberg J, Kikhia B, Bengtsson JE, Sävenstedt S, Synnes K (2009) Reminiscence processes using life-log entities for persons with mild dementia. In: CEUR workshop proceedings, vol 499, pp 16–21

Hinton A (2014) Perception, cognition, and affordance. In: Understanding context: environment, language, and information architecture. O'Reilly Media, Inc.

Hurtienne J, Klöckner K, Diefenbach S, Nass C, Maier A (2015a) Designing with image schemas: resolving the tension between innovation, inclusion and intuitive use. Interact Comput 27(3):235–255

Hurtienne J, Klöckner K, Diefenbach S, Nass C, Maier A (2015b) Designing with image schemas: resolving the tension between innovation, inclusion and intuitive use. Interact Comput 27:235–255. https://doi.org/10.1093/iwc/iwu049

Joddrell P, Astell AJ (2019) Implementing accessibility settings in touchscreen apps for people living with dementia. Gerontology 1–11

Kim S, Shaw C, Williams KN, Hein M (2019) Typology of technology-supported dementia care interventions from an in-home telehealth trial. West J Nurs Res 193945919825861

Lawry S, Popovic V, Blackler A (2011) Diversity in product familiarity across younger and older adults. Paper presented at the IASDR2011, the 4th world conference on design research, Delft

Lorenz K, Freddolino PP, Comas-Herrera A, Knapp M, Damant J (2019) Technology-based tools and services for people with dementia and carers: mapping technology onto the dementia care pathway. Dementia 18(2):725–741

Mihailidis A, Boger JN, Craig T, Hoey J (2008) The COACH prompting system to assist older adults with dementia through handwashing: an efficacy study. BMC Geriatr 8(1):28

Norman D (1988) The psychology of everyday things. Basic books

Norman D (2013) The design of everyday things: revised and expanded edition. Basic books

O'Brien M (2019) Lessons on intuitive usage from everyday technology interactions among younger and older people. In: Blackler A (ed) Intuitive interaction: research and application. CRC Press, Boca Raton, FL, pp 89–111

O'Brien M, Weger K, DeFour ME, Reeves SM (2011) Examining age and experience differences in use of knowledge in the world in everyday technology interactions. Paper presented at the human factors and ergonomics society annual meeting

Olsen RK, Yeung L-K, Noly-Gandon A, D'Angelo MC, Kacollja A, Smith VM, Ryan JD, Barense MD (2017) Human anterolateral entorhinal cortex volumes are associated with cognitive decline in aging prior to clinical diagnosis. Neurobiol Aging 57:195–205. https://doi.org/10.1016/j.neurobiolaging.2017.04.025

Pigot H, Mayers A, Giroux S (2003) The intelligent habitat and everyday life activity support. In: Proceedings of the 5th international conference on simulations in biomedicine, pp 2–4

Regenbrecht H, Lum T, Kohler P, Ott C, Wagner M, Wilke W, Mueller E (2004) Using augmented virtuality for remote collaboration. Presence: Teleoperators Virtual Environ 13(3):338–354

Sarne-Fleischmann V, Tractinsky N, Dwolatzky T (2009) Computerized personal intervention of reminiscence therapy for Alzheimer's patients. In: CEUR workshop proceedings, vol 499, pp 11–15

Silver M (2005) Exploring interface design. Thomson Reuters, New York

Wang JJ (2009) Group reminiscence intervention for institutionalized demented elders in Taiwan. In: CEUR workshop proceedings, vol 499, pp 43–44

You H, Chen K (2007) Application of affordance and semantics in product design. Des Stud 28(1):22–38

# Chapter 11
# Using the TUNGSTEN Approach to Co-design DataDay: A Self-management App for Dementia

**Arlene Astell, Erica Dove, Chris Morland, and Steve Donovan**

## 11.1 Introduction

User expertise illuminates people's motivations for using technology (Hassenzahl 2011), including the reasons that they do or do not use applications, devices and services. Identifying user's priorities aligns with the current or 'third wave' of HCI, which embraces the experience and meaning-making of the technology user(s) (Bødker 2015). When working with people living with dementia, expertise from families can also deepen one's understanding of potential users' motivations for and challenges experienced when using new technologies, particularly at home (Astell et al. 2009). In healthcare settings, frontline staff are also experts in understanding the technologies they both use and support, as well as the challenges to innovation and implementation within their services (Astell and Fels In Press).

At the present time there are no disease-modifying therapies for dementia (Bennett 2018; Mehta et al. 2017), but current and future technologies could provide practical, affordable and scalable solutions (Astell 2019). Globally, the majority of people live with dementia at home, supported by family, friends and the wider community (Prince et al. 2015). Thus, what is needed are accessible and affordable digital solutions that

A. Astell (✉) · E. Dove
KITE, University Health Network, Toronto, Canada
e-mail: Arlene.Astell@utoronto.ca

A. Astell
Department of Occupational Sciences & Occupational Therapy and Department of Psychiatry, University of Toronto, Toronto, Canada

A. Astell · E. Dove
School of Psychology & Clinical Language Sciences, University of Reading, Reading, UK

Rehabilitation Sciences Institute, University of Toronto, Toronto, Canada

C. Morland · S. Donovan
Citrus Suite, Liverpool, UK

© Springer Nature Switzerland AG 2020

R. Brankaert and G. Kenning (eds.), *HCI and Design in the Context of Dementia*, Human–Computer Interaction Series,
https://doi.org/10.1007/978-3-030-32835-1_11

empower people with dementia to live as well as possible at home (Astell and Semple 2019). This requires partnership with people who have dementia in order to identify their priorities, needs and aspirations and to co-design new digital solutions targeting these.

TUNGSTEN or 'Tools for User Needs Gathering to Support Technology Engagement' (Astell et al. 2018a) is an approach to technology design and development that views the intended users of new applications, services and devices as 'experts' (Astell and Fels In Press). As a core project of AGE-WELL, Canada's Network of Centres of Excellence on ageing and technology (AGE-WELL 2019), TUNGSTEN is partnering with older adults to co-design technologies that people want in their lives. We do this by bringing together older adults, formal and informal caregivers, clinicians, policymakers and technology developers in facilitated workshops comprising hands-on activities related to technology adoption and service development. The TUNGSTEN tools are generic and can be applied to any technology topic with any population.

This chapter describes the use of TUNGSTEN tools in a recent co-design project with people living with dementia, family caregivers and clinical teams. This chapter focuses on the co-design sessions with people living with dementia and family caregivers and illustrates the benefits of the TUNGSTEN approach for co-designing with this population.

## 11.2 Co-designing with People Who Have Dementia

Co-design is broadly defined as the process of designers and people untrained in design working together in the design and development process (Tsekleves et al. 2018). Co-design encourages a wide range of people to contribute to the formulation of a problem as well as its solution. This involves including end users as experts regarding their own needs and experiences, and how these relate to the design of a solution (Ibid). When using a co-design approach, the researcher or designer's role shifts from translating user needs to facilitating conversations with users that encourage people to engage with one another and test out new ideas (Ibid).

Until recently people living with dementia were largely excluded from the co-design process due to negative perceptions and low expectations about their abilities (Astell 2019). However, a growing body of examples of co-design with people living with dementia including Favilla and Pedell's (2014) collaborative music, Lazar et al's. (2016) Creating and Sharing art and Rodgers (2018) 'dementia tartan' are challenging this. DataDay came from several previous technology projects and interactive workshops with people living with dementia. Some of these early projects were also instrumental in developing what has become the TUNGSTEN approach. For example, the Computer Interactive Reminiscence and Conversation Aid (CIRCA: Alm et al. 2004) project identified the need for creative ways to elicit the views of people living with dementia and keep them at the forefront of innovation (Astell et al. 2009). Using an iterative development and test design process over 12 months, a multidisciplinary team co-designed CIRCA with people living with dementia and

**Fig. 11.1** Iteratively developing CIRCA interface

caregivers to produce an intuitive interface that people with dementia can use to select conversation topics (Gowans et al. 2007; Fig. 1.)

The success of the co-design approach can be seen in the benefits of CIRCA, which acts as a 'cognitive prosthetic device' for people living with dementia by mitigating their working memory difficulties in conversation, rendering them equal partners in communication (Astell et al. 2008). Using CIRCA positively changes professional caregivers' perceptions of the people they care for (Astell et al. 2009b), and impacts their caregiving relationships (Astell et al. 2010). CIRCA has been further developed to accommodate diversity (Purves et al. 2014), and an eight-week group intervention using CIRCA in long-term care significantly improved cognition and quality of life of people living with dementia (Astell et al. 2018b).

Building on this co-design success, the same team who developed CIRCA went on to partner with people living with dementia to develop interactive digital games (Living in the Moment: LIM). This partnership saw iterative development and testing of 30 novel activities over three years (Astell et al. 2014a). Video recording was used to capture interactions with physical artefacts and touchscreens, from which LIM identified the types of prompts people with dementia need to play digital games independently. For example, the LIM studies highlighted the importance of immediate feedback when a person with dementia touches the screen (Astell et al. 2014b). The LIM findings led to the AcToDementia project (www.actodementia.com) and consolidation of accessibility settings in digital applications specifically for dementia (Joddrell and Astell 2019).

A further co-design project with community-living older adults developed the Novel Assessment of Nutrition and Ageing (NANA: Astell et al. 2014b) toolkit to support self-management of their health and well-being. Nutrition is particularly important in later life but avoiding late-life malnutrition is dependent on a number of factors including physical, mental and cognitive health (Astell et al. 2018a). NANA was co-designed with older adults as a self-report tool that they could use every day to keep track of what they eat and drink, as well as their mood, cognition and physical activity.

As with CIRCA and LIM, each component of the NANA toolkit was iteratively developed with older adults as experts (Astell et al. 2018c). Over the course of 42 sub-projects, more than 530 older adults (aged between 65–91 years of age), 53 nutritionists, 15 health professionals and 90 working age adults co-designed all aspects of the toolkit, such as developing the food tree for meal selections and selecting camera function, which is required when taking photographs of meals. This iterative approach to co-design confirmed the essential need to make all design decisions, from large (e.g. concept, content) to small (e.g. fonts, colours, layouts), in partnership with the users (Astell et al. 2018).

Co-designing over four years with hundreds of older adults also confirmed their willingness to use new technologies in their homes, as well as their comfort with recording and completing nutrition, mood, physical activity and cognitive measures on a daily basis (Astell et al. In Press). The four NANA modules were validated against currently available gold-standard measures for nutrition (Timon et al. 2015), cognition (Brown et al. 2016), mood (Brown et al. 2018) and physical activity (Astell et al. 2014b) and have been shown to be predictive of future depression (Andrews et al. 2017). These findings demonstrate the accessibility and acceptability of NANA as an everyday technology for older adults, as well as the feasibility of collecting reliable data from older adults within their own homes (Astell et al. 2018a).

## 11.3 TUNSGTEN Tools

The experiences of co-designing CIRCA, LIM and NANA were gathered together in TUNGSTEN to provide a framework and practical tools for technology innovators to work with older adults as experts (http://tungsten-training.com). The TUNGSTEN Tools were developed as a resource for the AGE-WELL network to foster involvement of older adults at all stages of the technology development process. The aim was to encourage all technology innovators to partner with older adults right from the start of their projects by providing a range of easily adoptable techniques supported by use cases.

To get people started with this approach, we provide step by step guidance for three TUNGSTEN activities: (i) Technology Interaction, (ii) Show and Tell and (iii) Scavenger Hunt (Astell et al. 2018b). Each of these activities has been developed to uncover different aspects of user needs in relation to technology. Each activity can be offered as a standalone session or they can be combined into a longer workshop.

Fig. 11.2 Technology Interaction session

### 11.3.1 Technology Interaction

Technology Interaction involves providing participants with a 'mystery box' filled with an array of off-the-shelf devices in their original packaging (with batteries or access to power outlets; Fig. 1). Working in pairs, participants have ten minutes to get their chosen device(s) assembled and working. Each pair then provides feedback on their progress in the ten minutes, such as the positives and negatives of their chosen device. Technology Interaction is usually run as an ice breaker activity to empower all attendees to feel comfortable speaking about technology within a group setting. It also provides insights into what features influence people's immediate impressions of new technologies out of the box, and whether they will persevere with trying to get them working or quickly abandon them.

### 11.3.2 Show and Tell

Show and Tell involves attendees demonstrating one device of their own that they love and one they have abandoned, plus their reasons for making these decisions. 'Devices' can include hardware, software or other artifacts that people use in their daily lives (e.g. wall calendars). The information generated through Show and Tell provides insights into what factors influence people's adoption decisions, particularly in regard to self-purchases versus gifts or prescribed items.

Fig. 11.3 Individuals with dementia testing the NANA application

### 11.3.3 Scavenger Hunt

Scavenger Hunt requires workshop attendees to visit stations set up around the room, each showcasing an emerging or prototype technological innovation. Examples of emerging technologies at recent TUNGSTEN workshops include assistive robots, virtual reality cognitive exercises and smart home systems. Attendees are asked to engage with each emerging solution and provide feedback using device-specific evaluation forms, which contain questions about the usability and potential applications of the innovation. Scavenger Hunt provides attendees with opportunities to interact both with innovations at an early stage and with their inventors for mutually beneficial exchange of ideas.

TUNGSTEN is essentially a mindset for partnering with individuals who come from outside of research and development, the so-called 'people untrained in design' (Tsekleves et al. 2018) to provide their expertise on what is important to them. The TUNGSTEN approach evolved over a number of years as an alternative to focus groups. Using interactive methods that engage all participants in the sessions as equal contributors is both more successful at fostering co-design and also more rewarding for all parties involved (Astell et al. 2018a).

## 11.4 DataDay—A Self-management Application for People Living with Dementia

An example of the TUNGSTEN methods in action can be seen in the co-design of DataDay. DataDay is a self-management app created by combining the NANA modules with ReMind, a prototype scheduling and reminding app (Citrus Suite 2019). Given the success of using NANA on a large (tabletop) touchscreen monitor (Fig. 3), and the increasing popularity of portable mobile devices among older adults (Pew Research Center 2017), it was always intended that DataDay would be developed as a mobile application. This was informed by three earlier sessions with people living with dementia who tried out the original NANA application and provided feedback on what they would like to see in a revised version (unpublished data). This led to the conceptualisation of DataDay as a self-management application to support individuals with dementia from the point of diagnosis.

The DataDay co-design process with people living with dementia and family members caring for a person with dementia was facilitated through a series of workshops. That is, the TUNGSTEN framework and tools informed the development of each session to empower people living with dementia, family members and healthcare staff to co-design the app and portal, although it was not limited to the three TUNGSTEN tools listed above. Each attendee gave consent to be video recorded and their images to be used. Here we describe the app development steps of DataDay to illuminate the application of TUNGSTEN in practice.

**Workshop 1: Technology Adoption**

The first two interactive workshops were held in the community with people living with dementia, their family members, and health and social care providers to inform the initial design of the app's interface. The first technology adoption workshop (January 2018) focused specifically on participants' perceptions of different sized 'smart' devices, including tablets and smartphones. In addition to Show and Tell, Technology Interaction and Scavenger Hunt, participants were invited to identify what they did or did not like about each device, including tablets, e-readers and smartphones of different makes, models, shapes, screen sizes, interfaces and button layouts. Technology facilitators were identified: "*We liked the fact that it was easy to turn on and that it's small and really portabe.*" And also technology obstacles: "*… not intuitive to use. There's too many buttons—the average person with memory challenges would have difficulty to remember the steps required to run it.*"

Workshop attendees discussed the types of devices they currently used, as well as the ways in which they used these specific devices (e.g. communication, reminders, navigation, etc.). Several participants owned and used a smart device, while those who did not were familiar with and intrigued by the concept of adopting these devices. Several stated that they were interested in purchasing a smart device but did not know where to purchase one or which variety to buy, highlighting the need for guidance and support both before and after acquisition. This workshop identified key features within existing smart devices that are of importance to older adults, such as the size of the screen and the number and location of buttons. These initial discussions also provided important understanding of when and how people living with dementia are currently engaging with smart devices and why they use them. The workshop also confirmed the need to leverage the functionality and potential benefit of mainstream devices, given they are desirable, 'sexy' and increasingly accessible, without any of the stigma often associated with 'devices for old people' (Astell

**Fig. 11.4** Leisure apps

et al. 2019). In response to these discussions, it was decided that DataDay would be developed primarily as a tablet-based application, although smartphone use would also be possible.

**Workshop 2: Technology Use**

The second technology workshop (February 2018) with new participants, examined their current app use, focusing on health, wellbeing and self-management, in addition to what they liked and disliked about current apps. The three TUNGSTEN activities were again used to elicit people's experience and preferences for apps they currently used and their reactions to unfamiliar ones. Many participants reported using calendar apps to keep track of appointments and social events. Similarly, participants also reported using apps that supported communication with others, such as friends, family members and health and social care providers. Thirdly, apps that supported participation in leisure activities (e.g. playing games; Fig. 4) were also used by many of our workshop attendees as engaging pastimes. These discussions allowed us to gain an understanding of whether and how older adults, including people living with dementia, currently engage with apps. For example: "*The calendar for instance…I need my calendar to keep track of what's going on. A reminder list I use extensively on here…*"

A second focus of this workshop was to determine important features within existing apps, particularly ones that drive adoption or abandonment. Unsurprisingly, workshop attendees favoured apps they felt were beneficial (e.g. increasing independence, convenience) and easy to use. This echoes the long-established Technology Adoption Model (TAM: Davis 1989), which identified perceived usefulness and ease of use as significant predictors of technology adoption. The TAM was further developed into the Senior Technology Acceptance Model (STAM: Chen and Chan 2014) to capture additional predictors of technology adoption specifically relevant to older adults, such as age-related cognitive and physical changes and device self-efficacy. Additionally, maintaining or portraying a desired identity also plays a critical

**Fig. 11.5** Interacting with DataDay prototype

role in older adult's technology adoption decisions (Astell et al. 2019). This highlights the multidimensional and complex decision-making process that older users of technology undertake when choosing whether to adopt or reject technological devices.

For example, when looking at features within currently available apps and devices that influenced attendees to adopt or start using them, participants preferred apps with an easy setup process, one-time (or no) login, easy navigation, minimal text, limited methods of interaction (e.g. fewer types of touch—tap, swipe, drag, flick—required), adjustable accessibility (e.g. font size, background colours, etc.), limited icons and a clear objective with few steps required to meet the objective. In contrast, features that influenced users to abandon or stop using current apps included complex passwords, navigation difficulties, privacy concerns, complex mechanisms of interaction (i.e. not intuitive), a steep learning curve, cumbersome usage (e.g. too many steps involved in completing a task), lack of age-appropriateness, intrusive and annoying pop-up advertisements, lack of accessibility (e.g. no ability to increase font size or volume), and most importantly, lack of a clear purpose or implications for usefulness.

**Workshop 3: Co-designing DataDay Interfaces**

DataDay was conceptualised to empower people to self-manage their life with dementia by providing tools for them to keep track of how they are doing, support everyday activities and also detect signs of change. Self-management is an active process, which can be accomplished by equipping individuals with the knowledge, confidence and skills to manage their condition (Bodenheimer et al. 2002). Two further co-design sessions were held with people with dementia and family members (e.g. spouse, parent) of people with dementia to examine the usability, accessibility and functionality of the newly designed DataDay app. Additional co-design sessions of the app and portal were held with members of the local memory services, but these are not described here.

The third co-design session (March 2018) was held with a new group of people living with dementia plus people providing care for a family member with dementia at home. The session started with each participant independently exploring the DataDay prototype. Participants were given a brief overview of the DataDay prototype (Fig. 5) by a member of the design team, and invited to explore the app independently. We wanted to understand how they 'organically' interacted with both the app and the interface so no specific instructions regarding where to go or what activities to complete were provided. The goal was to see what features within the app were capturing participants' attention, as well as to identify areas where participants were experiencing navigation or interaction difficulties (e.g. where people became stuck or were unsure what to do).

Participants were video recorded over their shoulder to capture the screen and the mechanisms (e.g. touch—tapping, swiping, hesitation, etc.; Astell et al. 2016) with which they interacted with the app. Additionally, video-recorded data can be reviewed thoroughly and repeatedly to pinpoint design flaws (e.g. which button causes an issue), rather than going from memory or relying on field notes. Immediately following participants' individual interactions with the app, each participant was asked to complete the System Usability Scale (SUS; Brooke 1986) in order to measure their usability perceptions of the DataDay app.

Once all of the participants had interacted with the app independently and completed the SUS, they were invited to share their individual experience with the other attendees, to determine overarching 'themes' regarding what they liked and/or did not like about the app, the design of the app (colours, fonts, layouts, etc.), potential usefulness, and whether or not they would use the app in their everyday lives (i.e. what works, and what needs improvement). Participants were asked for feedback on the overall content within each of the four modules by displaying screenshots of each module on a large screen. Additionally, several tablets with the DataDay prototype were placed on the table for participants to pick up and use at any time to facilitate discussion and prompt recollection of their user experience.

After reviewing each module in turn, the discussion was broadened to capture additional feedback. This included the perceived relevance of the DataDay app for their everyday lives, whether they would use an app like this, or how they thought an app like this might be helpful to themselves or others. They were also asked whether there were other elements they would like to see in DataDay. In response to this, the attendees expressed a strong desire for receiving regular feedback regarding the information they entered in the app, such as their scores on the cognition games, to see how they are doing.

**Workshop 4. Finalising the Interface**

The fourth and final co-design session (July 2018) focused on specific concepts including granular usability, the number and complexity of steps involved in each data entry activity (e.g. completing the cognition games, entering a meal, etc.), the onboarding process (e.g. setting up an account), and the way in which the requested user feedback was provided through the app (e.g. statistical and graphical feedback). Some of the participants had attended the first co-design session and provided feedback on the initial app prototype, while others were new to DataDay. Blending new with previous participants was helpful for gaining additional insights regarding the app as a whole, as well as assessing how successfully the participant's feedback had been incorporated into the revised design of DataDay.

As in Workshops 1 and 2, the co-design participants completed the Technology Interaction step first to stimulate group discussions regarding the reasons why they do or do not adopt specific technologies, services or products. Also similar to the Workshop 3, attendees were excused one by one during the group activity and invited to interact independently with the revised DataDay app in a separate area of the room. This time around we asked our co-design partners to complete a list of standardised tasks (e.g. complete the cognition games, enter a meal) found within the DataDay app, rather than exploring the app organically. The goal of this structured interaction was to evaluate how different individuals interacted with the same components of the app (e.g. how many steps it took on average to complete a task; Fig. 5). As before these interactions were video recorded over their shoulder to capture accessibility and usability issues.

In the subsequent group discussion many attendees reported that they found all modules easy to use except for the nutrition module, given that it contained more steps to complete (i.e. enter a meal) than the other three modules. After reviewing each of the screens and steps within the DataDay app, the discussion was broadened for further feedback unrelated to the specific tasks. For example, attendees were asked about the aesthetics of the app (e.g. colours, fonts, layouts, etc.), as well as the way feedback was provided (e.g. bar graphs), the onboarding process (e.g. signing up and creating an account), and whether there were other elements missing from the revised design. The discussion, feedback and videos were used to further iteratively revise DataDay into a version deemed suitable for pilot testing with people living with dementia in the community.

**Feasibility Testing DataDay**

DataDay is similar to the NANA toolkit in featuring four core modules—cognition, nutrition, activity, and mood—which users complete each day. Information can be easily and instantly logged when users play cognition games, enter meals, and answer questions about their mood and physical activity. The aim is to empower people to stay informed about their well-being by providing scores and feedback about their performance in each of the modules, as well as keeping reminders about daily activities. DataDay can be used independently or connected to health and social care providers through a corresponding memory services portal co-designed with members of local memory clinic teams.

DataDay is currently being tested 'in the wild' by individuals living with dementia. The purpose is to test the feasibility of people living with dementia adopting DataDay and incorporating it into their everyday lives to support self-management. The hope is for DataDay to be offered to individuals receiving a diagnosis of dementia from a memory clinic, in order to provide them with additional support between follow-up appointments, and the ability to self-manage their condition.

## 11.5 Conclusions: Co-designing Future Direction with People Living with Dementia

This chapter focused on the experience of co-designing DataDay, a self-management application, with people living with dementia and family caregivers. In considering what worked well, the interactive workshop format provided a supportive environment for everyone's voice to be heard. This is especially important for people living with dementia who have traditionally been excluded from the co-design process, with caregivers being used—mistakenly—as proxies (Astell 2006). In DataDay, people living with dementia were full participants at all stages of development and informed all interface and interaction decisions. This is an extremely important message firstly for innovators seeking to work in this space who may have little or no experience of people who have dementia. Secondly, this finding adds to the growing examples of co-design with people living with dementia on a wide range of topics (e.g. Favilla and Pedell 2014; Lazar et al 2016; Rodgers 2018). This evidence is crucial for challenging the negative perceptions and low expectations people living with dementia constantly face (Astell 2019) and ensure they are involved as full partners in all projects and decision making.

Whilst the TUNGSTEN tools were successful in fully engaging people living with dementia in the DataDay project, timing can be a challenge with interactive activities—once the sharing begins, everyone must be given time and space to have their say—which means building flexibility into the schedule. It is also extremely important that the individuals living with dementia set the pace of the sessions so that everything they want to cover is given adequate time and space. Successful participation may also require accommodation of additional needs, such as hearing or mobility challenges.

Organising successful co-design projects with people living with dementia is both rewarding and vitally important. A few simple steps can help to ensure maximum benefit to everyone. First is to consider the environment where the sessions will be held to ensure that seating and movement in the space are optimal. Second is to establish house rules for co-design sessions relating to respect, confidentiality and valuing everyone's contribution. Third is to clarify what you aim to achieve in each session. Fourth is to identify the activities that you will use during each session to achieve this and prepare any necessary materials. Estimate how much time each activity will take, bearing in mind the number of attendees, and also consider how demanding or tiring each activity can be. Try to balance high-demand activities with resting or more relaxing activities to allow people to recharge. Finally, don't forget to have fun.

**Acknowledgments** This work was supported by an RCPP grant from the Centre for Aging and Brain Health Innovation (CABHI) and award AW CRP 2015-WP1.2 from AGE-WELL to the first author. The work reported here was undertaken as part of the first author's tenure as Ontario Shores Research Chair for Dementia Wellbeing sponsored by Ontario Shores Centre for Mental Health Sciences, Ontario Shores Foundation and University of Toronto between August 2013 and March 2019. We are eternally grateful to all of the people who generously gave up their time to co-design DataDay, including our partners at Alzheimer's Society Durham Region and Central East LHIN Primary Care Collaborative Memory Services.

## References

AGE-WELL NCE (2019) Core research projects. Retrieved April 17, 2019 from http://agewell-nce.ca/age-well-core-research-projects

Alm N, Astell A, Ellis M, Dye R, Gowans G, Campbell J (2004) A cognitive prosthesis and communication support for people living with dementia. Neuropsychol Rehabil 14(1–2):117–134. https://doi.org/10.1080/09602010343000147

Andrews JA, Harrison RF, Brown LJE, MacLean LM, Hwang F, Smith T et al (2017) Using the NANA toolkit at home to predict older adults' future depression. J Affect Disord 213:187–190. https://doi.org/10.1016/j.jad.2017.02.019

Astell AJ (2006) Technology and personhood in dementia. Quality in Ageing and Older Adults 7(1):15–25

Astell A (2019) Creating technologies with people who have dementia. In: Sayago S (ed) Perspectives on human-computer interaction research with older people. Springer International Publishing, Berlin, pp 21–36

Astell AJ, Fels D (In Press) Co-production methods in health research. In: Sixsmith A, Mihailidis A, Sixsmith J, Fang M-L (eds) Knowledge, innovation and impact—a guidebook for the engaged health researcher. Springer, New York

Astell AJ, Semple J (2019) Can robots, apps and other technologies meet the future global demands of dementia? In: Elger B, Jotterand P, Wangmo T, Ienca M (eds) Assistive technologies for dementia care. Oxford University Press, Oxford, UK

Astell AJ, Alm N, Gowans G, Ellis M, Dye R, Campbell J (2008) CIRCA: a communication prosthesis for dementia. Assis Technol Res Series 21:67–76

Astell AJ, Alm N, Gowans G, Ellis M, Dye R, Campbell J (2009a) Developing technology to meet psychosocial needs. J Dementia Care 17(6):36–39

Astell AJ, Alm N, Gowans G, Ellis M, Dye R, Vaughan P (2009b) Involving older people living with dementia and their carers in designing computer-based support systems: some methodological considerations. Uni Access Inf Soc 8(1):49–59. https://doi.org/10.1007/s10209-008-0129-9

Astell AJ, Ellis MP, Bernardi L, Alm N, Dye R, Gowans G et al (2010) Using a touch screen computer to support relationships between people living with dementia and caregivers. Int Comp 22(2010):267–275. https://doi.org/10.1016/j.intcom.2010.03.003

Astell A, Alm N, Dye R, Gowans G, Vaughan P, Ellis M (2014a) Digital video games for older adults with cognitive impairment. In: Miesenberger K, Fels D, Archambault D (eds) Computers helping people living with special needs. Springer International Publishing, Berlin, pp 264–271

Astell AJ, Hwang F, Brown LJE, Timon C, Maclean LM, Smith T et al (2014b) Validation of the NANA (Novel Assessment of Nutrition and Ageing) touch screen system for use at home by older adults. Exp Gerontol 60(2014):100–107. https://doi.org/10.1016/j.exger.2014.10.008

Astell AJ, Joddrell P, Groenewoud H, de Lange J, Goumans M, Cordia A, Schikhof Y (2016) Does familiarity affect the enjoyment of touchscreen games for people with dementia? Int J Med Inf 91:e1–e8. https://doi.org/10.1016/j.ijmedinf.2016.02.001

Astell AJ, Andrews J, Bennion M, Clayton D, Dove E, Ellis MP, Hwang F, McGrath C, Williams EA (2018a) COBALT, TUNGSTEN, and THAW: New tools for engaging older adults as technology experts. Gerontechnology 17(s):76

Astell AJ, Smith SK, Potter S, Preston-Jones E (2018b) Computer interactive reminiscence and conversation aid groups—delivering cognitive stimulation with technology. Alzheimer's Dementia Trans Res Clin Int 4(2018):481–487. https://doi.org/10.1016/j.trci.2018.08.003

Astell A, Williams E, Hwang F, Brown L, Cooper S, Timon C et al (2018c) NANA: A tale of ageing and technology. In: Walker A (ed) The new dynamics of aging. Policy Press, Bristol, UK, pp 157–175

Astell A, McGrath C, Dove E (2019) That's for old so and so's!: the role of identity in older adults' technology adoption decisions. Ageing Soc 40:1–27. https://doi.org/10.1017/s0144686x19000230

Astell AJ, Adlam T, Hwang T, Williams EA. Co-creating NANA (Novel Assessment of Nutrition and Ageing) with older adults living at home. In: Sixsmith A, Mihailidis A, Sixsmith J, Fang M-L (eds) Knowledge, innovation and impact—a guidebook for the engaged health researcher. Springer, New York

Bennet DM (2018) Lack of benefit with idalopirdine for Alzheimer disease. J Am Med Ass (JAMA) 319(2):123–125. https://doi.org/10.1001/jama.2017.19700

Bodenheimer T, Lorig K, Holman H, Grumbach K (2002) Patient self-management of chronic disease in primary care. J Am Med Ass (JAMA) 288(19):2469–2475. https://doi.org/10.1001/jama.288.19.2469

Bødker S (2015) Third-Wave HCI, 10 years later—participation and sharing. Interactions 22:24–31

Brooke J (1986) SUS—A quick and dirty usability scale. Redhatch Consulting Ltd, Earley, Reading, UK. Retrieved April 14, 2019 from http://dag.idi.ntnu.no/IT3402_2009/sus_background.pdf

Brown LJ, Adlam T, Hwang F, Khadra H, Maclean L, Rudd B, Smith T, Timon C, Williams EA, Astell AJ (2016) Computer-based tools for assessing micro-longitudinal patterns of cognitive function in older adults. Age 38(4):335–350

Brown LJ, Adlam T, Hwang F, Khadra H, Maclean L, Rudd B, Smith T, Timon C, Williams EA, Astell AJ (2018) Computerized self-administered measures of mood and appetite for older adults: the Novel Assessment of Nutrition and Ageing (NANA) toolkit. J App Gerontol 37(2):157–176

Chen K, Cha AHS (2014) Gerontechnology acceptance by elderly Hong Kong Chinese: a Senior Technology Acceptance Model (STAM). Ergonomics 57:635–652. https://doi.org/10.1080/00140139.2014.895855

Citrus Suite (2019) Mobile apps, web design & enterprise software system development. Retrieved April 23, 2019 from http://www.citrussuite.com/

Davis FD (1989) Perceived usefulness, perceived ease of use, and user acceptance of information technology. MIS Q 13:319–340

Gowans G, Dye R, Alm N, Vaughan P, Astell A, Ellis M (2007) Designing the interface between dementia patients, caregivers and computer-based intervention. Des J 10(1):12–23

Hassenzahl M (2011) User experience and experience design. Encycloped Human-Comput Interact 2:1–35

Joddrell PM, Astell AJ (2019) Implementing accessibility settings for people living with dementia in touchscreen apps. Gerontology 65:560–570

Lazar A, Cornejo R, Edasis C, Piper AM (2016) Designing for the third hand: empowering older adults with cognitive impairments through creating and sharing. In: DIS 2016, Proceedings of the 2016 ACM conference on designing interactive systems. Association for Computing Machinery, New York, NY, pp 1047–1058

Mehta D, Jackson R, Paul G, Shi J, Sabbagh S (2017) Why do trials for Alzheimer's disease drugs keep failing? A discontinued drug perspective for 2010–2015. Exp Opin Inv Drugs 26(2):735–739. https://doi.org/10.1080/13543784.2017.1323868

Favilla S, Pedell, S (2014) Touchscreen collaborative music: designing NIME for older people with dementia. In: Proceedings of the International Conference on New Interfaces for Musical Expression, June 30-July 4th London, UK, pp 35–39

Pew Research Center (2017) Technology use among seniors. Retrieved April 24, 2019 from https://www.pewinternet.org/2017/05/17/technology-use-among-seniors/

Prince M, Wimo A, Guerchet M, Ali G-C, Wu Y-T, Prina M (2015) World Alzheimer's report 2015: the global impact of dementia. Alzheimer's Disease International (ADI), London, UK

Purves B, Hulko W, Phinney A, Puurveen G, Astell AJ (2014) Developing CIRCA-BC and exploring the role of the computer as a third participant in conversation. Am J Alzheimer's Dis Dementias 30(1):101–107

Rodgers PA (2018) Co-designing with people living with dementia. Co Design Int J CoCreation Des Arts 14(3):188–202

Timon CM, Astell AJ, Hwang F, Adlam TD, Smith T, Maclean L et al (2015) The validation of a computer-based food record for older adults: The Novel Assessment of Nutrition and Ageing (NANA) method. British J Nut 113:654–664. https://doi.org/10.1017/S0007114514003808

# Part III
# Design and Experience: In the Context of Dementia

# Chapter 12
# Assistive Media for Well-being

**David M. Frohlich, Emily Corrigan-Kavanagh, Sarah Campbell, Theopisti Chrysanthaki, Paula Castro, Isabela Zaine, and Maria da Graça Campos Pimentel**

## 12.1 Introduction

In this chapter, we attempt to define, characterise and illustrate a new category of assistive technologies that we believe could be beneficial for people with dementia and their carers. These might be called *assistive media systems*, because they involve the use of personal digital media to bring about therapeutic benefits for positive mental health and wellbeing.[1]

We approach this area from a number of disciplinary perspectives, including HCI (Frohlich and Pimentel), Psychology (Chrysanthaki, Zaine and Campbell), Gerontology (Castro) and Design for Well-being (Corrigan-Kavanagh). Our experience is based primarily on a 2-year UK–Brazil network on 'Assistive media for health and well-being in ageing' in which we have been exploring a range of new media experiences with the older population in Brazil and the UK.

The area we want to define appears to be growing out of a convergence between the fields of assistive technology within the healthcare sector, and that of personal media systems within the consumer product sector (see Fig. 12.1). Assistive technology has traditionally been defined from a rehabilitation perspective as that which

[1]We distinguish this definition from two previous uses of the term 'assistive media' to refer to a particular internet-based audio reading service and a German research project on assistance within human-computer interaction: https://www.assistivemedia.org/Assistive_Media/Welcome.html, https://www.leuphana.de/en/research-centers/cdc/research/assistive-media.html.

D. M. Frohlich (✉) · E. Corrigan-Kavanagh · S. Campbell · T. Chrysanthaki · I. Zaine
Digital World Research Centre, University of Surrey, Guildford, UK
e-mail: D.Frohlich@surrey.ac.uk

D. M. Frohlich · P. Castro
Federal University of São Carlos, São Carlos, Brazil

I. Zaine · M. da Graça Campos Pimentel
University of São Paulo, São Paulo, Brazil

© Springer Nature Switzerland AG 2020

R. Brankaert and G. Kenning (eds.), *HCI and Design in the Context of Dementia*, Human–Computer Interaction Series,
https://doi.org/10.1007/978-3-030-32835-1_12

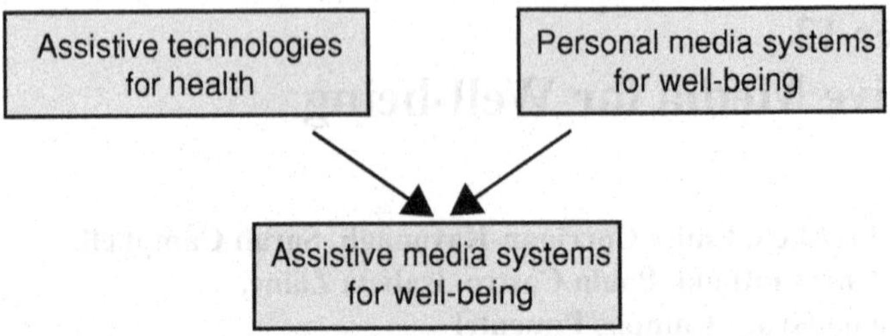


**Fig. 12.1** The convergence of assistive and media technologies in assistive media

restores or aids a physical or psychological function to individuals with disabilities or suffering from impairment of some kind (e.g. US Disabilities Act 1988, renewed 1998). Typical examples are limb prostheses to restore mobility, or low vision aids to maximise residual eyesight. In recent years with the advent of digital technology, assistive technology has expanded to support prevention and monitoring as well as rehabilitation, for example, through health monitoring with wearable devices and exercise apps to encourage healthier lifestyles. A further expansion has been to support mental as well as physical health, for example, through systems which keep people better connected to remote carers. Note that all these approaches do not cure disabilities as such but help people to live with them while enjoying a better quality of life.

Personal media systems, on the other hand, might be defined as those for the capture and communication of self-made or self-appropriated media such as photos, text, video and music. Examples include cameras and cameraphones, MP3 players and smart TVs, social media systems and photo printing services. They have typically been designed for 'consumers', especially the youth market and families with children, and tend to promote psychological benefits for remembering, communicating and managing identity (e.g. Van Dijck 2008). These are also highly social technologies supporting multiple ways of sharing media in co-present and remote settings, such as through photo sharing or social media systems (e.g. Frohlich et al. 2002). Growing attention to the ageing population by researchers in this area, including ourselves, has resulted in simplified or adapted systems for media capture and sharing, such as augmented paper photograph albums, communicating photo displays and novel social media systems (Piper et al. 2013; Waycott et al. 2013; Zaine et al. 2019). The increased attention of assistive technology for well-being, combined with the adaptation of personal media systems to meet the needs of the older population, is leading to a new field of assistive media systems for well-being. By definition, these involve the creation and/or consumption of digital media having beneficial effects on well-being.

Numerous assistive media systems are already on the market for dementia care. Some of these are sold to care homes such as the *Tovertafel*[2] (Magic Table) for

[2]https://tovertafel.co.uk.

playing interactive games or the *RemindMe Care*[3] reminiscence system. Others are consumer products sold to informal carers, such as the *Unforgettable music player*,[4] the *InteractiveMe*[5] online memory box service or the *LookBack*[6] virtual reality experience for reminiscing. Another category are research prototypes which have not yet made it to market, but indicate the future possibilities of assistive media. These include the *Vita music pillow* for playing music and sound (Houben et al. 2020), the *Hug* wearable audio-doll for comforting those in the later stages of dementia (Treadaway et al. 2018) and the *Moments* interactive picture frame for capturing and sharing physical artwork (Lazar et al. 2017a). All of these systems claim some kind of therapeutic benefit for people with dementia, although few provide the kind of quantitative evidence from randomised controlled trials that would usually be expected for health interventions. The plasticity of any technological intervention lends itself to a more iterative approach to design and testing, in which products are evolved within and between trials to optimise their effects on well-being. Here, well-being might be equated with quality of life, and improved as much through personal growth and agency as through compensation of function. Therefore, assistive media systems are best viewed as part of a *critical dementia* movement in HCI and design which respects the agency of people with dementia and amplifies what they *can* do rather than what they cannot (Lazar et al. 2017b). Given the diversity of these systems and the difficulty of evaluating them, how can we go about understanding exactly how they work and what kinds of benefits they deliver through media content and experiences?

In the rest of the chapter, we address this question by proposing a framework for assistive media systems and their effect on wellbeing. This is based on a brief review of three established media-based therapies for which there is a body of evidence and understanding. These are not all exclusive to dementia care, but nevertheless teach us about the influence and dynamics of media content in therapeutic contexts. The resulting framework will then be illustrated by its application to an assistive media intervention we conducted in a Brazilian care home, before discussing some general principles and recommendations for the field of HCI and design.

## 12.2 Three Media-Based Therapies

### *12.2.1 Art Therapy*

Art therapy is a type of psychotherapy that combines visual art, such as painting and sketching, with counselling psychology (Malchiodi 2007). The therapeutic benefits

[3]https://www.remindmecare.com.

[4]https://www.unforgettable.org/.

[5]http://www.interactiveme.org.uk.

[6]https://www.virtue.io/lookback/.

of art creation are used within this field to treat physiological and mental disorders or to aid in self-development (Malchiodi 2003). Unlike traditional fine art classes, where artwork is created from one's imagination or objects on display: art creation within art therapy emphasises the depiction of one's pre-existing feelings and thoughts in resulting compositions. Making art therapy artwork therefore involves the participant connecting with and visualising internal images through artistic self-expression and reflection, and this process is facilitated by the art therapist using specific art therapy techniques (Malchiodi 2007). In fact, art making that is focused on positive themes can encourage pleasant feelings by making users aware of and focus on the good things in their life and find life meaning through their artistic depiction (Wilkinson and Chilton 2013).

Parallels can be drawn here between Seligman's (2002) Authentic Happiness theory for long-term happiness, which postulates that in order to experience deep contentment in one's life it is necessary to have experiences of: *pleasure* (immediate emotional joy), *engagement* (immersion in an enjoyable task) and *meaning* (feeling part of something bigger than yourself) that tend to occur sequentially with greater happiness effects. This experiential journey can be facilitated through art therapy, where users can feel spontaneous joy (pleasure) from the therapeutic/relaxing effects of art making, become immersed in the process (engagement) and be encouraged to reflect on and be thankful for the positive aspects in their life by depicting these (meaning). Seligman's Authentic Happiness theory belongs to a field of psychology known as Positive Psychology, which focuses on supporting emotional well-being or human flourishing as opposed to treating mental ailments (Seligman 2011). Wilkinson and Chilton (2013) propose the term 'Positive Art Therapy' to represent the intersection between art therapy and positive psychology.

Some specific art therapy techniques include silent and spontaneous image making, followed by open reflection. Silverstone (2009) argues that 'talking can shatter the image' when referring to internal images of the imagination. Some art making is therefore carried out in complete silence to help participants' focus and enable more authentic visualising of personal mental imagery (Regev et al. 2016). Spontaneous art making utilised in Art Therapy is based on the concept of transference in which individuals project their unconscious feelings, perceptions and ideas onto the therapist or artefact leading to negative or positive responses (Hogan 2009). Through spontaneous art expression, individuals can be encouraged to freely associate these feelings to allow them to realise and understand their unconscious projections (Malchiodi 2003). Finally, most art therapists assert that it is necessary for an individual to verbally share their reflections about an artwork to comprehend its meaning (Malchiodi 2007). Therefore, participants are encouraged to describe their art making process, including the feelings they experienced, to a therapist or a group who listen and respond (Wilkinson and Chilton 2013).

Although Art Therapy is generally performed using traditional art approaches alone, such as painting and drawing, as opposed to digital technologies, it is demonstrative of the power of creating personally made media and explaining it to others for emotional wellbeing. Furthermore, digital augmentations where an artwork, such as a painting or drawing, is connected to a related video, audio, weblink or additional digital images, could be used to add supplementary layers of complexity and meaning to Art Therapy-based processes through a tailored assistive media system. In this manner, assistive media systems could extend traditional methods of Art Therapy beyond their basic physicality, and facilitate extended meaning making to the virtual world. Similarly, art therapy techniques, such as silent and spontaneous art making, could be incorporated into the creation of digital media artefacts to increase their positive emotional impact on the viewer and creator.

### *12.2.2 Reminiscence Therapy*

One of the most popular and promising non-pharmacological interventions used for supporting people with varying levels of cognitive impairment and dementia is reminiscence therapy (RT). Offered either on an individual or a group level, reminiscence therapy refers to the act or process of recalling and prompting conversations about life events, past experiences and long-term memories using videos, photos, music, life story books and other personal objects (Butler 1963). The definition of Butler and others suggests that this process of recall is prompted and structured in stages triggered by objects familiar to the individual (Merriman 1989; Gibson 2004; Woods et al. 2005). The initial stage involves the selection of a personal or group memory followed by the immersion in that memory (middle point). The gradual return of the individual or group to the present reality is the end point of this process. During these sessions, people tap into their long-term memory and interact with others (nurse, caregiver, reminiscence group) to review, relive and revalidate past life events and emotions. Research has indicated that such activities may help them sustain or even boost their psychological well-being, alleviate depressive symptoms, connect with others and reduce social isolation (Brooker and Duce 2000; Wang 2007; Yamagami et al. 2007; Zhou et al. 2012). There is also evidence that RT can trigger sad memories and negative emotions which may in turn be associated with a greater sense of social isolation (Henkel et al. 2016). Some of these effects are small or inconclusive, so the quantitative evidence of RT benefits on quality of life, cognition, mood and communication is weak or ambivalent (Woods et al. 2018).

Critiques of traditional methods for delivering reminiscence sessions have suggested that they are time and resource intensive as their delivery usually requires the physical presence of a trained formal and/or informal caregiver (Gowans et al. 2004). The use of Information and communication technology (ICT) multimedia systems can not only stimulate the process of RT (sharing the evoked memories as a group activity) but also aid its delivery using multisensory and personalised triggers (e.g. Astell et al. 2018). For example, in the commercial *InteractiveMe* system, care home staff, family and friends are expected to input data (generic and/or personal) in collaboration with residents, who can then access and use the materials alone or with others. A review published in 2014 assessed the state of evidence regarding the level and the type of ICT technologies used for facilitating RT for people with dementia (Lazar et al. 2014). The findings indicated that there were a number of benefits in using technologically supported RT interventions. The use of technology could provide opportunities for both individualised and group-based RT activities with multiple users, reduce therapists' preparation time and effort and make the RT sessions and material remotely accessible to all users. There was a great diversity of technologies used in the studies reported in the review ranging from accommodating for deficits (motor, sensory, memory) to using technologies to harness abilities, ease the burden of RT delivery and evaluating progress of users and system performance. In addition, the most prominent media type across all the ICT projects was music.

### 12.2.3 Music Therapy

Music therapy is a broad term (Kemper and Danhauer 2005), encompassing any music-based intervention aimed at creating benefit. Music therapy broadly falls into two types: music making (also known in the literature as music production, interactive music therapy or active music therapy) and music listening (also called in the literature receptive music therapy or passive music therapy) (Wigram et al. 2013; Grocke and Wigram 2006). Interactive music therapy is the most common approach in the UK, although the burgeoning evidence base of the benefits of music listening is leading to increasing applications of receptive music listening, particularly in healthcare. Music making (including singing) is particularly beneficial for enhancing communication, social skills, confidence, emotional expression and subjective happiness and usually involves facilitation by a music therapist or professional musician (Elliott and Gardner 2018). The integration of music therapy with movement also has the capacity to enhance cognitive and motor skills. Therapeutic music listening is particularly useful for strengthening identity, reminiscing, memory-related interventions and emotion regulation (Leggieri et al. 2019). Therapeutic music listening is increasingly being used to manage anxiety, agitation, pain, depression and stress, by utilising music's capacity to lower physiological arousal to create a sedative effect, and to alter emotional state. One benefit of therapeutic music listening is it does not necessitate a music therapist or professional musician as facilitator, although usually is delivered by a trained therapist (Särkämö 2018).

When considering assistive media technologies, the therapeutic benefits of music listening (or sharing) are most pertinent, capitalising on music's emotive power. There is a large body of evidence demonstrating what compositional aspects of music itself elicit different emotions, although work in this area often conflates emotions perceived in the music with actual felt emotional response, and similar single compositional techniques can elicit different emotions in different listeners (Gabrielsson 2002). Work looking beyond the compositional aspects of the music itself has identified music that is highly familiar, from a preferred genre and associated with strong personal memories elicits the strongest responses, with preferences seemingly more important compared to specific properties of the music. This is because the emotional power of music results from an interplay between the music, the listener and the context (Juslin and Västfjäll 2008). The emotion people experience from music is not necessarily based on the music alone, but rather an interaction of this with the emotional content of people's personal experiences, preferences and memories triggered by the music.

One proposed mechanism of how music elicits emotions is through setting up expectations based on musical cultural rules, violating these expectations, then resolving the violation (Huron 2006). Our brains experience this expectancy process as highly rewarding, eliciting a strong pleasurable response. This explains why music generally elicits positive emotions in the listener, including sad music that has been shown to elicit positive emotions, as well as sadness (Garrido 2017). This explains the value of music in enhancing well-being. One way the listener is thought to make meaning of the music is via emotional contagion, where the emotion expressed in the music is "caught" by the listener (Juslin and Västfjäll 2008). Emotions are highly contagious among people, such as if one person smiles, the observer also smiles, and this action then alters emotional state of the observer (Hatfield et al. 1993). Music-evoked emotions are particularly strong in a group setting, with the strongest emotional experiences to music experienced in group listening contexts (Gabrielsson 2010). This is one explanation for the success of group music listening exercises in a therapeutic context, where music listening extends beyond the positive impact on emotion regulation to also include a sense of connection and bonding in a shared emotional experience. However, the benefit of individual listening means the experience can be more personalised, and emotions can be accessed that an individual may not feel comfortable experiencing in a group context. In music sharing, there is a sense of connection and bonding, as sharing music is often a form of expressing and sharing personal identity, which is strengthened and affirmed when positively received and acknowledged. When designing assistive media systems, consideration of these different aspects of music listening and the emotional effects would be important.

## 12.3 A Framework for Assistive Media

Having looked briefly at three media-based therapies and ideas about how they work, we can now consider what properties they have in common for making media assistive. Art and music therapy both involve the creation of visual or sonic media in the form of painting, drawing and playing music instruments. These activities are said to be therapeutic in their own right, as non-verbal forms of self-expression and creativity. Reminiscence therapy in contrast does not usually involve creating the materials acting as memory triggers, but rather looking and listening to them as given, in the context of a group discussion. Some forms of music therapy also involve passive listening to live or recorded music played by others. Finally, all three forms of media therapies involve discussion of media items with others. This can be with trained therapists or counsellors who intentionally help their clients reflect on the meaning of what they have created, or it can be with untrained peers who share their reflections with each other.

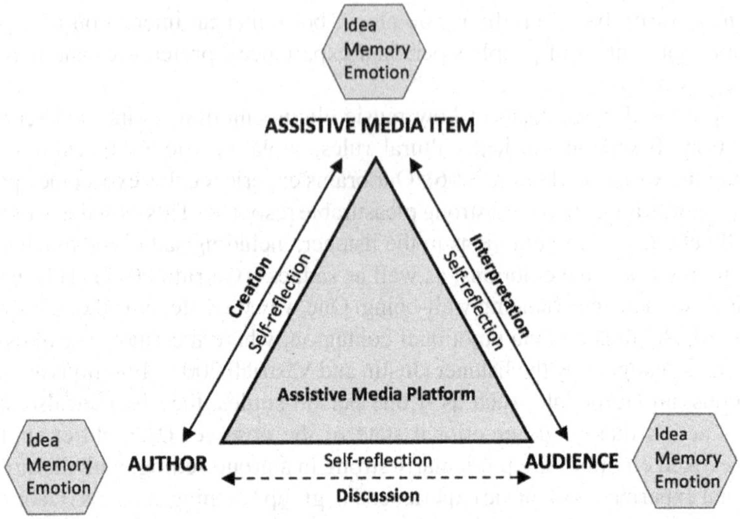


**Fig. 12.2** The triangle framework for the dynamics of assistive media use

Hence, three core interactions are illustrated in the triangle of Fig. 12.2. A creative interaction takes place between author and media item. An interpretive interaction takes place between media item and audience. And a conversation about the media item takes place between author and audience. These interactions lie between the three primary 'actors' in assistive media systems, including assistive media items which have a kind of agency of their own. This framework is inspired by the first author's diamond framework for domestic photography (Frohlich 2004). In what might be called **creative assistive media systems**, the *authors* are the main beneficiaries through direct interaction with the media and an audience, who may include a professional therapist (e.g. art and music therapy). However, in **consumptive assistive media systems**, members of the audience are the main beneficiaries through direct interaction with the media and each other (e.g. reminiscence therapy). Here there may be no direct interaction between the author and audience, as in music listening therapy. The dotted line between these actors in the diagram indicates the possible presence or absence of interaction across contexts. In both cases there may be more than one author and/or audience member. Authors may become audiences for their own creations over time. Creation, interpretation and discussion appear to be critical activities in these interactions, together with a self-reflection that each seems to encourage. Ideas, memories and emotions are said to be triggered by media items in the participants during all these therapies, and these can travel between them and the media items themselves. Clearly, media items cannot experience ideas, memories and emotions, but these may be transferred to and from the items by the human actors.

In addition to these interactions between the actors in assistive media systems, there are other important properties which characterise them. As with any media system, it may be characterised by the combination of platform, content and experience involved (e.g. Weill and Woerner 2013). We also agree with Kenning and Brankaert (2020) in Chap. 1 of this volume, that the context for which a system is designed and used is key to its characterisation. This can be defined in a number of ways but should include at least reference to the user population together with the rules and setting of use. For example, in systems intended for dementia care, it is important to specify whether people with dementia are themselves the target users, and the role of both formal and informal carers as additional or even primary users.

A final consideration for assistive media systems is the range of therapeutic outcomes that are claimed for them. These are not always clearly articulated, and there is an active debate in well-being science about how to define and measure well-being outcomes (e.g. Huppert 2014). However, the literatures in art, reminiscence and music therapy mention multiple media-related outcomes, such as the deepening of **R**elationships, the stimulation of **E**motions, the triggering of **M**emories, the facilitation of **C**ommunication, and strengthening of **I**dentity through forms of personal development. We suggest the acronym **REMCI** to refer to these outcome categories for media systems, and advocate future research to refine these and relate them to other measures of well-being, such as life satisfaction or happiness.

## 12.4 Designing a Digital Story Therapy

Having pointed to some characteristics of assistive media through the framework above, we now want to illustrate these in a case study of technology use carried out in a Brazilian care home. The case study has been published elsewhere (Abrahão et al. 2018), but we report a new analysis of its findings in relation to the framework to show how assistive media can work in practice to help people with dementia and their carers. Furthermore, the case study utilises a classic HCI method of trialling a technology probe (Hutchinson et al. 2003). It does this to uncover the potential of a new technology in a particular context and gather requirements for its re-design. In this respect, it was generative and oriented to creating a *new* assistive media system or therapy for this population. By choosing it as our example, we want to show how HCI can be used to create new kinds of assistive media therapies by understanding how digital media work within therapeutic contexts.

The starting point for the study was the observation that reminiscence therapy is largely passive as described above and might benefit from more active creation of memory triggers and their social sharing. Indeed, there is recent evidence that deliberate creation of 'digital stories' in group settings, in the form of short personal films, is beneficial for older people for reflecting on life, reminiscing, feeling social connected and creating a legacy (Hausknecht et al. 2018). The conventional approach to this is to learn and practice story creation and digital production techniques in community workshops over several days or weeks (e.g. Lambert 2013). However, in our own work we have been exploring forms of 'mobile digital storytelling' in which a storyboard of images are set to text, voiceover, music or sound effects on a tablet or smartphone in a single session (Frohlich 2015; Frohlich et al. 2012). This seemed relevant to supporting reminiscing and communication by people with dementia and their carers, especially in care home contexts where stories could perhaps be used for conveying practical as well as sentimental information (such as health reports or reminders).

To explore some of the latent values of mobile digital storytelling in this context, we conducted a case study focused on one 60-year-old woman with moderate dementia living in a residential care home in Brazil, together with her formal and informal carers. The carers included her sister and brother-in-law and the care home manager and a nutritionist. The resident had cognitive impairment but communication skills intact, scoring 10 on the Mini Mental State Examination. A Portuguese language version of our own *Com-Phone*[7] story creator app was deployed for 4 weeks in a field trial by these participants, after demonstration and installation on a dedicated tablet and various personal smartphones. Figure 12.3 shows the home screen interface to the Portuguese version of Com-Phone app, and the way you add image, sound or text to each new story frame. Here the creation of story 2 is being shown, with the second two panels indicating the way in which these three media types can be added to each frame. Up to three sound files can be added to each frame and will be played back simultaneously. Although not designed for this context, the app served as a technology probe to uncover attitudes, values and behaviours towards this technology

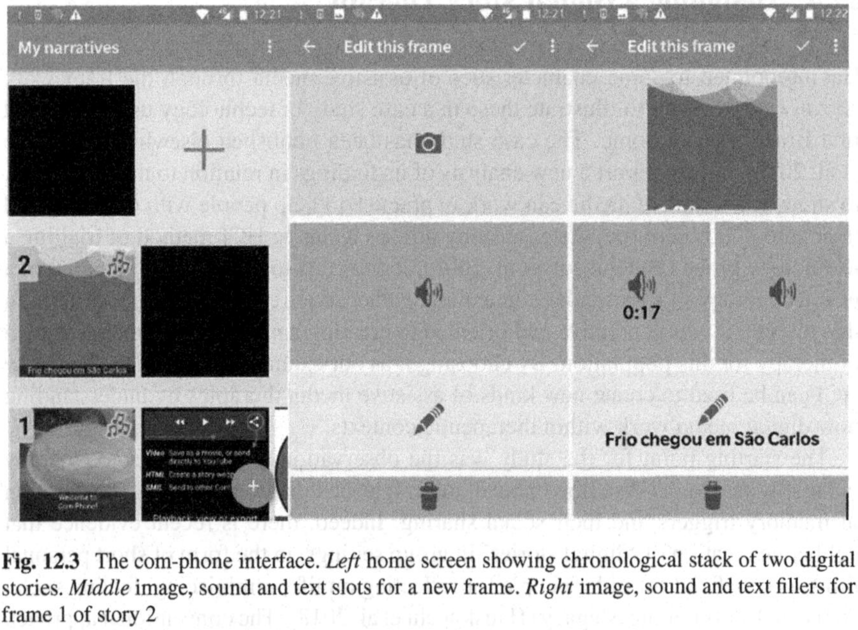


**Fig. 12.3** The com-phone interface. *Left* home screen showing chronological stack of two digital stories. *Middle* image, sound and text slots for a new frame. *Right* image, sound and text fillers for frame 1 of story 2

[7] http://digitaleconomytoolkit.org/com-phone/.

and requirements for its modification and use. For example, we were interested in whether the app could be used directly by the person with dementia or not, and what different values it might have for communication by that person compared with their formal and informal carers. The design of the trial was deliberately open-ended and unstructured compared with the introduction of a known therapeutic procedure, and its outcomes were measured qualitatively in terms of the stories made by different participants and what they said about them.

A typical story is shown in Fig. 12.4. It comprises five frames, each with a separate photo and accompanying music or voiceover shown by musical note or 'sound' icons. The total duration was 1 min 45 s and the story was assembled collaboratively on a visit of the sister and brother-in-law to the resident by two researchers (see last frame). It is not very story-like, since it simply documents aspects of the visit, with a recorded conversation about how many winter clothes the resident is wearing indoors, a photo of a prescription handed to the sister, and a group shot set to music. Despite its simplicity, we found assembly of these stories triggered additional conversation about the materials and conveyed something of the warmth of the encounter and the

**Fig. 12.4** A typical digital story

personality of the resident. Here, for example, she is pictured drawing in four of the five frames, which was her favourite activity. Another story documented a series of drawings themselves with some textual labels. The resident and family were delighted to see these play on a tablet as video sequences afterwards, and the family members described them as valuable mementoes of their time with the resident for future reminiscing.

The system and our findings can be summarised with respect to the framework above. The system comprises two kinds of devices (tablet and smartphone) that were used to create digital narratives out of photos, text and sound recordings of various types. In the context of the care home, three classes of participants could potentially use the system to create or view stories, although in practice the care home staff largely rejected the system due to pressure of work and lack of management support. Their main reported focus was on the day-to-day physical care of the resident and they could see no value in the technology for supporting that. The person with dementia was not able to use the system unaided but she was able to use it under supervision by her informal carers, particularly her sister, and one or more of the researchers who stood in for the formal carers on regular visits. The sister and her husband also used the app on their smartphones from home to record family events and activities to show the resident on face-to-face visits. Stories could technically be shared remotely via YouTube but the resident had no personal access to this from the care home making it pointless for the family to upload. For the same reason, the resident couldn't easily share stories made in the home with remote family and friends, despite a desire to do so.

The dynamics of the activity can be illustrated with respect to a variation of the triangle framework shown in Fig. 12.5. Authorship of stories moved variously between

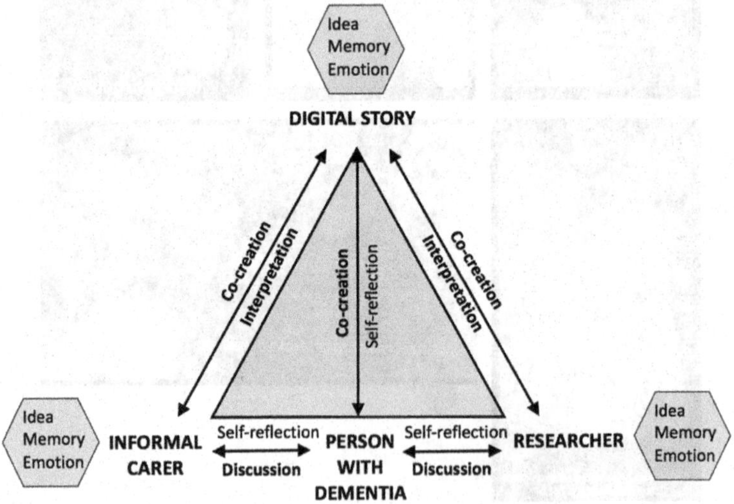


**Fig. 12.5** The triangle framework illustrating the dynamics of digital story creation and sharing

resident, informal carer and researcher, with most stories being made collaboratively by two or three of these people. Similarly, audience status varied between groups with stories reviewed by the authors themselves as well as being shown to others later on. Common stories were **Visit conversations** documenting topics of discussion with pictures of the visit, and **Social event**s captured in pictures and sound, in or out of the home. These were usually made with the participation of the resident who was typically photographed and interviewed for her comments by an informal carer or researcher. These would be shown to other visitors or residents, and viewed repeatedly by the resident as they built up on the tablet in the home. This kind of complexity is hard to represent in the framework and shows that authors are themselves audiences for their own creations at different points in time, and audiences may *become* authors through facilitating joint authorship. The fact that authorship was inherently collaborative in this study and focused on the *current* life of the person with dementia, was a major finding. Many of the values of the technology appeared to be in stimulating joint creativity and enriching the conversation between the person with dementia and their informal carers. This happened both at the time of media creation and afterwards in its review. In contrast to reminiscence therapy which is about remembering the past together, this activity was about creating or capturing a current memory together and being able to look back on it later. Indeed, the family members in the trial were aware of the reminiscing value of the stories to them in the future, when their relative was no longer with them.

These findings can be summarised in terms of the **REMCI** categories above. Mobile digital storytelling appeared to have benefits in terms of strengthening the **R**elationship between the person with dementia and their informal carers, stimulating **E**motions tied to the content of media being assembled, triggering **M**emories *after* media creation on subsequent review of the stories, facilitating richer **C**ommunication between the person with dementia, their informal carers and our own research team, and strengthening the **I**dentity of the person with dementia by laying down personal records of daily life but also of the informal carers in visibly caring for the well-being of their relative or friend through random acts of media co-creation.

## 12.5 Discussion

The purpose of this paper has been to acknowledge and explore the properties of an emerging class of what we call assistive media systems, directed broadly to an ageing population including people with dementia. We presented a framework for understanding these systems inspired by the literatures on art, music and reminiscence therapies, and then described an example drawn from our own work involving the creation of mobile digital stories by a person with dementia and her informal carers. Here, we reflect on the lessons of this exercise and implications for the conceptualisation and design of such systems in the future.

An immediate lesson from the literature review was that media can undoubtedly have therapeutic benefits for well-being through influencing mood, triggering memories and stimulating ideas through processes of personal reflection and creativity. They also seem to stimulate new kinds of conversation and interaction between authors and audiences, around media. These insights were central to our framework with involves a triangle of participant and media interactions, together with a description of system properties and their effects on a range of outcomes. While these may prove to be insufficiently nuanced to capture the range and variety of systems, interactions and benefits of assistive media, we believe they point to three important dimensions for their characterisation and understanding: interaction dynamics, system properties and outcomes.

Another lesson which emerged from the framework itself was to call attention to authorship of media. Some (creative) assistive media systems and benefits seem to be founded on active creation of media by the target beneficiaries, while others (consumptive systems) do not. These are represented roughly by art therapies and reminiscence therapies, respectively, with music therapies falling into two kinds based on this distinction (i.e. performance and listening). This suggests at least that creation of media is not necessary in order to experience *some* of the benefits of media content, but that *additional* benefits result from creation itself. We saw this in our case study for family members who viewed stories created by the resident and a researcher, and were given insight into the life of the resident in their absence. In contrast, the person with dementia experienced the additional benefit of creative expression in making stories collaboratively with a researcher or family member. Collaborative authorship is not fully represented in the simple triangle of Fig. 12.2, and requires redrawing in particular instances to capture the participant roles and interactions in various contexts (see again Fig. 12.4).

The implication for conceptualising assistive media systems is that our framework is only a starting point for researchers to edit in representing their own systems. We encourage creativity in revising the framework rather than seeking to mandate application in its original form. In particular, our own case study has shown limitations in the representation of different roles for human participants in the media creation and sharing process, and a difficulty in representing changes in roles and media over time. Frohlich (2004) found the same difficulty with his diamond framework for photography. He suggested the notion of 'photo outings' to represent the reconfiguration of participants and media on each separate occasion on which photographs are shared, leading to a *series* of interactive configurations over time. The same properties seem to apply in the case study here, for example, after an initial story is created, and then shared with different participants such as care home staff or other family and friends. In general, the careful representation of people, media items and interactions between them for a range of systems and situations will illuminate the complex psychosocial effects of media, rather than treating them as a single 'intervention' and looking for general effects.

Finally, we observe that contemporary HCI approaches to design in this context are well equipped to do this in the process of developing new assistive media systems for people with dementia. Our example of introducing simple creative technology probes speculatively as a vehicle for understanding the dynamics and requirements of use, demonstrates a complementary approach to randomised controlled trials focused on demonstrating the benefits of a single intervention. In our context, failure is as important as success for future design, as with the inability of the *Com-Phone* app to support full collaborative story creation and remote sharing. This will help us to create a better designed system in the future, customised to the demands of the situation, the nature of the participants and the properties of the media being created or consumed. Lazar et al. (2017a) report a similar example in which they used paper prototypes to understand the dynamics and benefits of sharing artwork before designing and testing the *Moments* system. Iterative small-scale design and co-design with people with dementia and their carers is more likely to lead to greater understanding of the complexities of assistive media and how to support them, than large-scale studies assessing the effects of relatively fixed technologies. We also recommend unpacking the term 'therapeutic' in these studies, to reflect the diversity of positive outcomes affecting wellbeing in different ways over the short and long term.

**Acknowledgements** This work was funded by two FAPESP visiting scholarships to Paula Castro (2016/10982-3) and Isabela Zaine (2017/09549-6), and by the University of Surrey and FAPESP through a UK-Brazil SPRINT network grant on *Assistive Media for Health and Wellbeing in Ageing* (2016/50489-4). We also thank participants in the Brazilian case study for their time, activity and insights into mobile digital storytelling, and Rens Brankaert, Gail Jennings, Amanda Lazar and Anne Marie Piper for discussions of their related work.

## References

Abrahão AR, da Silva PFC, Frohlich DM, Chrysanthaki T, Gratão A, Castro P (2018, July) Mobile digital storytelling in a Brazilian care home. In: International conference on human aspects of IT for the aged population. Cham, Springer, pp 403–421

Astell AJ, Smith SK, Potter S, Preston-Jones E (2018) Computer interactive reminiscence and conversation aid groups—delivering cognitive stimulation with technology. Alzheimer's Dement Transl Res Clin Int 4:481–487

Brooker D, Duce L (2000) Wellbeing and activity in dementia: a comparison of group reminiscence therapy, structured goal-directed group activity and unstructured time. Age Ment Health 4(4):354–358

Butler RN (1963) The life review: an interpretation of reminiscence in the aged. Psychiatry 26(1):65–76

Elliott M, Gardner P (2018) The role of music in the lives of older adults with dementia ageing in place: a scoping review. Dementia 17(2):199–213

Frohlich DM (2015) Fast design, slow innovation: audiophotography ten years on. Springer, London

Frohlich DM (2004) Audiophotography: Bringing photos to life with sounds (vol 3). Springer Science & Business Media, Berlin

Frohlich D, Kuchinsky A, Pering C, Don A, Ariss S (November, 2002). Requirements for photoware. In: Proceedings of the 2002 ACM conference on Computer supported cooperative work. Association for Computing Machinery, New York, NY, pp 166–175

Frohlich D, Robinson S, Eglinton K, Jones M, Vartiainen E (2012) Creative cameraphone use in rural developing regions. In: Proceedings of the 14th international conference on Human-computer interaction with mobile devices and services. ACM, pp 181–190

Gabrielsson A (2010) Strong experiences with music. In: Juslin PN, Sloboda JA (eds) Handbook of music and emotion: theory, research, applications. Oxford University Press, Oxford, pp 547–574

Gabrielsson A (2002) Perceived emotion and felt emotion: same or different? Musicae Sci 6:123–148

Garrido S (2017) Why are we attracted to sad music? Palgrave Macmillan, Cham

Gibson F (2004) The past in the present; using reminiscence in health and social care. Health Professions Press, Baltimore, MD

Gowans G, Campbell J, Alm N, Dye R, Astell A, Ellis M (2004, April) Designing a multimedia conversation aid for reminiscence therapy in dementia care environments. In: CHI'04 extended abstracts on human factors in computing systems. ACM, pp 825–836

Grocke D, Wigram T (2006) Receptive methods in music therapy: techniques and clinical applications for music therapy clinicians, educators and students. Jessica Kingsley Publishers, London

Hatfield E, Cacioppo JT, Rapson RL (1993) Emotional contagion. Current Direct Psychol Sci 2(3):96–100

Hausknecht S, Vanchu-Orosco M, Kaufman D (2018) Digitising the wisdom of our elders: connectedness through digital storytelling. Ageing Soc 39:1–21

Henkel LA, Kris A, Birney S, Krauss K (2016) The functions and value of reminiscence for older adults in long-term residential care facilities. Memory 25(3):1–11

Hogan S (2009) The art therapy continuum: a useful tool for envisaging the diversity of practice in British art therapy. Int J Art Ther 14(1):29–37. https://doi.org/10.1080/17454830903006331

Houben M, Brankaert R, Bakker S, Kenning G, Bongers I, Eggen B. (2020, April). The role of everyday sounds in advanced dementia care. In: 2020 CHI Conference on Human Factors in Computing Systems. ACM Press, p. 450

Huppert FA (2014) The state of wellbeing science: concepts, measures, interventions, and policies. Wellbeing Compl Refer Guide 6:1–49

Huron D (2006) Sweet anticipation: music and the psychology of expectation. A Bradford Book, Cambridge, MA

Hutchinson H, Mackay W, Westerlund B, Bederson BB, Druin A, Plaisant C, … Roussel N (2003, April) Technology probes: inspiring design for and with families. In Proceedings of the SIGCHI conference on human factors in computing systems. ACM Press, New York, pp 17–24

Juslin PN, Västfjäll D (2008) Emotional responses to music: the need to consider underlying mechanisms. Behav Brain Sci 31:559–621

Kemper KJ, Danhauer SC (2005) Music as therapy. South Med J 98(3):282–288

Kenning G, Brankaert J (2020) Introduction: framing in context. Chapter 1, In: Kenning G, Brankaert J (eds) HCI and design in the context of dementia. Springer, New York

Lambert J (2013) Seven stages: story and the human experience. Digital Diner Press, Berkeley, CA

Lazar A, Edasis C, Piper AM (2017a) Supporting people with dementia in digital social sharing. In: Proceedings of the 2017 CHI conference on human factors in computing systems. ACM Press, New York, pp 2149–2162

Lazar A, Edasis C, Piper AM (2017b) A critical lens on dementia and design in HCI. In: Proceedings of the SIGCHI conference on human factors in computing systems. ACM Press, New York, pp 2175–2188

Lazar A, Thompson H, Demiris G (2014) A systematic review of the use of technology for reminiscence therapy. Health Educ Behav 41(1 Suppl):51S–61S

Leggieri M, Thaut MH, Fornazzari L, Schweizer TA, Barfett J, Munoz DG, Fischer CE (2019) Music intervention approaches for Alzheimer's disease: a review of the literature. Frontiers Neurosci 13:132

Malchiodi CA (2003) Handbook of art therapy, psychiatric services. The Guilford Press, New York. https://doi.org/10.1176/appi.ps.54.9.1294-a

Malchiodi CA (2007) The art therapy sourcebook, 2nd edn. Bruner-Routledge, Hove, New York

Merriman S (1989) The structure of simple reminiscence. Gerontologist 29(6):761–771

Piper AM, Weibel N, Hollan J (2013, February) Audio-enhanced paper photos: encouraging social interaction at age 105. In: Proceedings of the 2013 conference on computer supported cooperative work. ACM, pp 215–224

Regev D, Chasday H, Snir S (2016) Silence during art therapy-the client's perspective. Arts Psychother 48:69–75. https://doi.org/10.1016/j.aip.2016.02.001

Särkämö T (2018) Music for the ageing brain: cognitive, emotional, social, and neural benefits of musical leisure activities in stroke and dementia. Dementia 17(6):670–685

Seligman MEP (2002) Authentic happiness. Atria Paperback, New York

Seligman MEP (2011) Flourish: a new understanding of happiness and well-being. Nicholas Brealey Publishing, Boston

Silverstone L (2009) Art therapy exercises: 'inspirational and practical ideas to stimulate the imagination. London: Jessica Kingsley Publishers.

Treadaway C, Taylor A, Fennell J (2018) Compassionate design for dementia care. Int J Des Creativity Innov 7:1–14

Van Dijck J (2008) Digital photography: communication, identity, memory. Vis Commun 7(1):57–76

Wang JJ (2007) Group reminiscence therapy for cognitive and affective function of demented elderly in Taiwan. Int J Geriatric Psychiatry 22(12):1235–1240

Waycott J, Vetere F, Pedell S, Kulik L, Ozanne E, Gruner A, Downs J (2013, April) Older adults as digital content producers. In: Proceedings of the SIGCHI conference on human factors in computing systems. ACM, pp 39–48

Weill P, Woerner SL (2013) Optimizing your digital business model. MIT Sloan Manage Rev 54(3):71

Wigram T, Saperston B, West R (eds) (2013) Art & science of music therapy: a handbook. Routledge, New York

Wilkinson RA, Chilton G (2013) Positive art therapy: linking positive psychology to art therapy theory, practice, and research. Art Therapy 30(1):4–11. https://doi.org/10.1080/07421656.2013.757513

Woods B, O'Philbin L, Farrell EM, Spector AE, Orrell M (2018) Reminiscence therapy for dementia. Cochrane Database Syst Rev 3:CD001120

Woods B, Spector AE, Jones CA, Orrell M, Davies SP (2005) Reminiscence therapy for dementia (Review). Cochrane Database Syst Rev 18(2):CD001120

Yamagami T, Oosawa M, Ito S, Yamaguchi H (2007) Effect of activity reminiscence therapy as brain-activating rehabilitation for elderly people with and without dementia. Psychogeriatrics 7(2):69–75

Zaine I, Frohlich D, Rodrigues KRH, Cunha BCR, Orlando AF, Scalco L, Pimentel MGP (2019) Promoting social connection and deeper relations in older people: design of media parcels for time-based media sharing. Manuscript under review

Zhou W, He G, Gao J, Yuan Q, Feng H, Zhang CK (2012) The effects of group reminiscence therapy on depression, self-esteem, and affect balance of Chinese community-dwelling elderly. Arch Gerontol Geriatr 54(3):e440–e447

# Chapter 13
# Exploring Everyday Sounds in Dementia: Practical Guidelines for Interactive Workshops

**Maarten Houben, Rens Brankaert, Saskia Bakker, Inge Bongers, and Berry Eggen**

## 13.1 Introduction

Researchers from fields such as behavioral sciences, human–computer interaction (HCI), and design have been exploring non-pharmacological approaches to improve the well-being of people with dementia (Olazarán et al. 2010). A large body of literature in this research context is reporting on the beneficial effects of music on people with dementia. For example, how actively participating in music therapy sessions by singing or playing instruments can positively influence mood and behavior (Raglio et al. 2014) and stimulate social interactions (Morrissey et al. 2016). Furthermore, it has been demonstrated how listening to music from the past can evoke meaningful memories (Baird and Samson 2009) and offer cues for recognizing and maintaining selfhood (Baird and Thompson 2018).

M. Houben (✉) · R. Brankaert · S. Bakker · B. Eggen
Department of Industrial Design, Eindhoven University of Technology, Eindhoven, The Netherlands
e-mail: M.Houben1@tue.nl

R. Brankaert
e-mail: R.G.A.Brankaert@tue.nl

S. Bakker
e-mail: S.Bakker@tue.nl

B. Eggen
e-mail: J.H.Eggen@tue.nl

M. Houben · I. Bongers
Tranzo, School of Social and Behavioral Sciences, Tilburg University, Tilburg, The Netherlands
e-mail: I.M.B.Bongers@tilburguniversity.edu

R. Brankaert
School of Allied Health Professions, Fontys University of Applied Sciences, Eindhoven, The Netherlands

© Springer Nature Switzerland AG 2020

R. Brankaert and G. Kenning (eds.), *HCI and Design in the Context of Dementia*, Human–Computer Interaction Series,
https://doi.org/10.1007/978-3-030-32835-1_13

In addition to music, we perceive a wide variety of nonmusical sounds in our everyday surroundings. These everyday sounds help to build an understanding of the environment and provide information on how we physically and socially negotiate it (Eggen 2016). After years of listening, people develop highly personal connections and associations with everyday sounds by assigning social and emotional values to specific sounds (Schine 2010; Truax 2001). For example, beach soundscapes can evoke positive emotional responses due to potential associations with past family holidays or favorite vacation spots (Campbell et al. 2019). Therefore, researchers have taken an interest in exploring the added value of re-experiencing everyday sounds in dementia care (Bulsara et al. 2016; Devos et al. 2018; van den Bosch et al. 2017).

In these first explorations on everyday sounds and dementia, researchers suggested how re-presenting everyday sounds as soundscapes in care environments can have beneficial effects for people with dementia as pleasant or recognizable sounds provide structure in day-to-day life (van den Bosch et al. 2016), facilitate social interactions (Teunissen et al. 2017), and reduce stress (Bulsara et al. 2016). However, the experience of dementia is different for every individual (Kitwood 1997), and people respond differently to sound and have vastly different personal preferences, values, and existing relationships. In that sense, an understanding is needed of how people with dementia personally respond to re-presentations of sounds from everyday life. How to identify what sounds have a meaningful impact on individuals with dementia is still under-researched. Therefore, inclusive approaches are needed to involve the perspective of people with dementia (Branco et al. 2017), and to enable designers and care practitioners (CPs) to identify what everyday sounds are affective for a specific person.

In this chapter, we provide a critical reflection on the research protocol of a series of interactive workshops that explored the personal responses elicited by everyday sounds of people in early to mid-stages of dementia. We adopted a design research approach by using the *dementia soundboard* (Houben et al. 2019) and everyday objects as tools for exploring the multilayered soundscapes, facilitating a meaningful and enjoyable activity for people with dementia while gaining crucial insights into their experience of everyday sounds. The primary aim of these workshops was to build a qualitative understanding of the individual responses to re-presented sounds from everyday life. These personal responses of the participants are reported and discussed in more detail in a previous publication (Houben et al. 2019). In this chapter, we will further discuss our research protocol by providing an outline of the setting, procedure, and props. Next, we critically reflect on our research protocol and formulate five practical guidelines for involving people in early stages of dementia in interactive workshops: 1. *enjoyable and safe atmosphere*; 2. *using familiar objects*; 3. *space for shared experiences*; 4. *gradual build-up and moments of rest*; and 5. *participation through interaction*. These guidelines offer guidance in the design of workshop sessions to identify personal sounds for people with dementia in a meaningful and engaging way.

## 13.2 Background

The workshops described in this chapter build further on existing research concerning *everyday sounds for dementia care* and *involving people with dementia in research* and are discussed in this section.

### *13.2.1 Everyday Sounds for Dementia Care*

In the fields of psychology and acoustics, there is a growing body of work investigating the effects of everyday sounds or soundscapes on people with dementia and their CPs (Bulsara et al. 2016; Devos et al. 2018; Hayne and Fleming 2014). In this respect, researchers have been exploring how re-presenting everyday sounds as soundscapes could serve as a stimulus to influence behavior (Devos et al. 2018), reduce agitation (Bulsara et al. 2016), and provide a sense of relief and rest (van den Bosch et al. 2017). Workshops and focus groups reported in related work (Devos et al. 2018; van den Bosch et al. 2016) have mainly involved stakeholders such as care staff or informal caregivers. For instance, CPs have stated how everyday sounds could provide a sense of safety and bring structure by cueing daily care activities and routines (van den Bosch et al. 2016). Furthermore, research involving informal caregivers has demonstrated the potential of using everyday sounds to facilitate collaborative reminiscence activities (Campbell et al. 2019). While providing valuable insights into the implementation of soundscapes in care practice, this still leaves a gap in literature on how to involve people with dementia in the process of selecting and curating affective soundscapes. We argue that for sound-related interventions to be successful, the personal experience of people with dementia also needs to be considered (Suijkerbuijk et al. 2015; Houben et al. 2020).

### *13.2.2 Involving People with Dementia in Research*

Participatory approaches are in nature challenging for people with dementia, as participants are required to work with abstract concepts and extensively communicate opinions and thoughts (Hendriks et al. 2013). Therefore, involving people with dementia in research can cause stress or confrontations with their disabilities (Hendriks et al. 2014), and so the experience of the participants during the research activity needs to be carefully considered. By adopting a *reciprocal approach* (Kenning 2018), designers can gain crucial insights into the experience of dementia while offering a pleasant and meaningful activity for the participants. This approach may involve, for example, setting up activities where people with dementia engage with everyday objects or interactive prototypes, as participants do not have to solely rely on cognitive skills such as making abstractions or communicating specific ideas and thoughts (Kenning 2017). Similarly, creative activities in care facilities, such as music sessions (Gold 2014) or art therapy (Chancellor et al. 2014) have provided insight into how to involve and engage people with dementia in participatory approaches (Lazar et al. 2016). For example, physical tools and materials such as brushes, paint, and cloth can enable self-expression that focusses on the abilities of the person rather than the deficits caused by dementia (Lazar et al. 2018). During music sessions, physical props serve as a stimulus for social interactions among people with dementia by facilitating collective movements, engaging people with dementia in interactions with music, as well as with each other (Morrissey et al. 2016). These examples illustrate how the use of props and high-quality materials are keys to involving people with dementia in activities or participatory approaches.

## 13.3 Interactive Workshops with the Dementia Soundboard

We conducted three workshops during which three to four participants in early to mid-stages of dementia explored and listened to re-presentations of everyday sounds (see Table 13.1). By interacting with the *dementia soundboard*, the participants explored soundscapes of everyday sounds while being encouraged to express their reactions, opinions, and feelings in a group setting.

### *13.3.1 Setting and Participants*

The workshops were facilitated by the principal researcher (F), accompanied by a research assistant (RA) who took field notes, and a CP who safeguarded the participants. The CP who attended the workshops also selected and recruited eligible participants if they:

1. were diagnosed with Alzheimer's disease;
2. were in early to mid-stages of dementia;
3. visited the day-care facility multiple times a week, but still lived at home;
4. were not hindered by severe visual or auditory processing disorders;

**Table 13.1** In total, we conducted 3 workshop sessions in which 11 participants in early to mid-stages of dementia participated

| | Workshop 1 | | | | Workshop 2 | | | | Workshop 3 | | |
|---|---|---|---|---|---|---|---|---|---|---|---|
| Participant# | P1 | P2 | P3 | P4 | P5 | P6 | P7 | P8 | P9 | P10 | P11 |
| Age | 77 | 73 | 66 | 64 | 69 | 67 | 86 | 72 | 81 | 87 | 87 |
| Male/Female | M | F | F | F | F | F | F | F | M | M | M |
| Dementia stage | early | early | early | early | early | early | early | early | mid | mid | mid |

**Fig. 13.1** Overview of the workshop setting in one of the activity rooms in the day-care center

5. had physical abilities to participate in the workshop;
6. were willing to participate in a group setting.

This research was granted approval by the Ethics Review Board of the Tilburg School of Social and Behavioral Sciences (EC-2018.70). The participants were clients of a day-care facility in the Netherlands, where they participated in activities that involved making art or music, group discussion sessions, and social events. All participants were able to give informed consent, and their informal caregivers were extensively informed about the research activity. To minimize the perceived time burden of the participants and the CP, the workshops were organized in the same timeframe that activities were usually scheduled for. The workshops took place in one of the activity rooms of the day-care facility with favorable acoustic properties and reduced sources of distraction (see Fig. 13.1). A CP familiar to all participants was present to maintain the duty of care of the participants.

### *13.3.2 Development of the Dementia Soundboard*

A review of existing research and design concerning sound and music has highlighted the importance of using high-quality props and materials to elicit responses from people with dementia. Therefore, to focus the participants' attention on the soundscapes and prevent forms of disengagement, we designed and built the *dementia soundboard* (see Fig. 13.2). This prototype was not designed as a final product in its own right, but as a physical means to facilitate sound exploration and encourage participant responses during the workshops. The goal of the soundboard was to offer a sense of agency or control to the participants by inviting them to trigger the soundscapes themselves, rather than sounds being played for them. An everyday object represented each soundscape, for example, a seashell represented a beach soundscape. The participants could then play the soundscapes by placing the object on the central circle of the soundboard. This action would *load* the layers of sound relevant to the

**Fig. 13.2** The dementia soundboard served as a tangible means for playing soundscapes by placing the corresponding objects on the central circle. By tapping the surrounding touchpads, the sound layers that make up the soundscape could be muted or unmuted

object, ready for the participants to choose and play. Using the touch pads surrounding the object, participants could mute or unmute each of the four different sound layers that made up the general soundscape. Blue LEDs illuminated the touchpads to provide visual feedback on the current state of each layer, making the interaction minimal and understandable. With this interactive feature, we aimed to actively engage the participants by facilitating autonomy in the exploration and personalization of the soundscapes. Furthermore, the soundboard was explicitly designed to facilitate social engagement in the workshop setting, as the round symmetrical shape affords interactions in a group setting. The soundboard provided access to four soundscapes: *beach, forest, city*, and *home* that could be, respectively, triggered by a *seashell, tree leaf, small bell*, and a *coffee mug*. These four soundscapes were chosen to represent different everyday sounds from both natural as human environments with which the participants would likely be familiar with. Each soundscape consisted of four different sound layers based upon different sources of sound and were categorized as follows: *human, animal, water*, and *background*. For instance, the soundscape *beach* consisted of *children playing, seagulls, waves*, and *wind*.

### 13.3.3 Workshop Procedure and Buildup

In order not to overwhelm the participants, we designed the workshop in consecutive steps, iterated for every soundscape: 1. *familiarizing*, 2. *listening*, and 3. *exploring*. It began with an easy and straightforward exercise immersing the participants gradually in the soundscapes during each step. During the first step *familiarizing*, each participant received and passed on one of the everyday objects (e.g., seashell). This step introduced the workshop format by including everyone in the group setting and starting a first group conversation. Secondly, the step *listening* involved one of the participants triggering the soundscape by placing the everyday object on the central circle of the *dementia soundboard*. The facilitator would ask the participants to close their eyes and listen to the soundscape. After several minutes the facilitator asked if participants were willing to share their reactions on the soundscapes verbally. Lastly, during the *exploring* step, the participants were invited to explore the different layers of the soundscape by using the illuminated touch pads of the *dementia soundboard*. Similarly to the previous steps, a discussion was initiated based on their reactions to the changes in the soundscape and the underlying sound layers. At the end of the workshop, the participants were informally asked about their experience of the research activity. For example, the facilitator asked if they enjoyed the experience and if they had learned something from it.

The workshops were audio and video recorded for analysis of both verbal and nonverbal expressions. The audio was transcribed verbatim, and the video footage was annotated with descriptions of bodily responses, such as making gestures or touching and expressing emotions such as laughing or yawning. We aggregated all the data and conducted a thematic analysis, using an inductive approach (Braun and Clarke 2006).

## 13.4 Reflection on Research Protocol

The thematic analysis revealed several themes that offered insight into the personal experience of everyday sounds by people in early to mid-stages of dementia, which are reported in more detail in an earlier publication (Houben et al. 2019). These outcomes illustrate the potential for everyday sounds to evoke meaningful associations and elicit emotional responses from people with dementia linked explicitly to sound. In this section, we focus on the outcomes that address the participants' experience of the workshop itself, providing insights into the effectiveness of the different workshop steps and how the use of the soundboard facilitated participation and engagement.

### *13.4.1 Enjoyable and Safe Atmosphere*

Prior to the formal start of the research activity, the facilitator and RA welcomed all participants in the workshop space by offering refreshments and engaging in informal *small talk*. The researchers introduced themselves to the participants during this brief chat and talked about general topics that were specifically unrelated to the research. As other participants entered the room, they also started to converse with each other, revealing that some participants already knew each other. These short introductory chats established social connectedness between the participants themselves and with the researchers before the start of the workshops. This informal setting provided a sociable and safe atmosphere (see Fig. 13.3), where thoughts, expressions, and bodily responses could be shared in group, without feeling pressured or forced:

**Fig. 13.3** Participants interacting in a safe and enjoyable group setting

P2: You can hear that right away; you are blown away by the wind!

P1: (at P2) Are you blown away? (Laughs)

P2: I'm blown away (laughs back) … and you?

P1: No, I'm a jack of all trades!

Furthermore, the group format reduced social awkwardness by not concentrating the focus on one single participant. For example, it was observed how during the workshops several participants [P2, P5, P8] were passive or stayed in the background, as they experienced difficulties in taking part in a specific conversation actively or just had no significant association with the sounds being played at the time. However, participants remained part of the project even when they were not actively participating and their behaviors contributed to the findings, because they watched or listened to others, and provided signs of acknowledgments such as reacting, laughing, or nodding along, as observed by the RA: 'P3 is reminded of her vacation, the others are nodding along.' [RA].

The CP who recruited the participants attended each workshop and continuously evaluated if it was still suitable for the participants to continue taking part (Dewing 2007). As she was familiar with most participants, she safeguarded the participants by intervening if the activity appeared to be becoming burdensome for some people. However, no intervention was needed during the workshops and all participants remained and seemingly enjoyed their participation. Her attendance as a familiar face contributed to the safe and secure atmosphere established during the workshop.

### 13.4.2 Using Familiar Objects

The handling of familiar everyday objects during *step 1: familiarizing* served as an easy group exercise to introduce the setting and to break the ice (see Fig. 13.4). Participating in this rather simple exercise allowed the participants to become more familiar with the setting and with each other. In addition, the facilitator asked simple questions about the objects which modeled the format of sharing their responses and helped the researcher to stress that there were no right or wrong answers and that even no answer was completely fine:

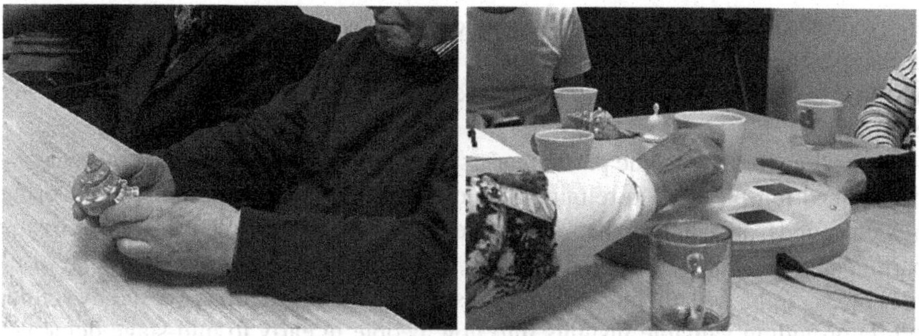

**Fig. 13.4** Participants handling the everyday objects during step (1) familiarizing to introduce the setting and format of the workshops (left); and triggering the soundscapes by placing the objects on the dementia soundboard during step (2) listening (right)

F: What does the leaf remind you (P9) of?' (P9 thinks for a moment)

P9: Yes this is a bit out of the blue for me, if you get one of those things… so then I have to give something back right away, in mind, but I don't know yet…

CP: But what do you think of when you see a leaf?

P9: Well… (pauses) Yes, then it is immediately you… (pauses) Nature!

CP: Yes, nature, being outside…

P9: Yes, that is the first thing that comes to mind, yes!

CP: Yes, we are asking about that, what you're thinking of, what your thoughts are.

During the second step *listening*, the participants triggered the soundscapes by placing the objects onto the soundboard. Immediately their attention shifted toward the sounds and away from the object they previously discussed. For example, P1 and P2 associated the *leaf* with *nature* and *trees,* but still associated the corresponding *forest* soundscape with a *beach.* Surprisingly, they did not appear to notice the object anymore, and there was no mention of the objects in the audio transcripts during the *listening* and *exploring* step. The CP also confirmed this during the exit interview: 'And I don't know if people then associated it with the object at any given time. Yes, at some point that also didn't matter anymore.' [CP] This was in contrast to our expectations, and may be attributed to the short-term memory loss of the participants. However, this was not of concern as the objects had served their purpose as an icebreaker, and the participants were at this point focusing on the soundscapes.

### *13.4.3 Space for Shared Experiences*

The everyday sounds assessed in the workshops elicited numerous participants' responses linked to past experiences (Houben et al. 2019). While sharing in a group setting, participants experienced a sense of self-fulfillment and enjoyment by recalling these moments and reliving them in the present. Participants also appreciated and enjoyed the esthetic qualities of the soundscapes by listening and being immersed in the everyday sounds. These responses ranged from P2 'getting the jitters from all those birds', or P7 leaning back with eyes closed while listening to a crackling campfire.

After the workshops, the participants suggested that they had enjoyed the activity and had felt pleasure in reliving memories, experiencing emotions, discovering hidden sounds, and sharing their experiences. The workshops were described by the participants as a *fun* [P9] or *pleasant* [P3] activity, as they 'enjoyed being part of it' [P1] by engaging with memories, emotions, and social interactions evoked by sound. While providing valuable insights into how people in early to mid-stage dementia individually engage with sound, the participants experienced the research activity as pleasant and not a burden or too time-consuming: 'Once again, it is something different… besides, I really enjoyed it' [P9].

However, recalling memories was confronting for two participants [P5, P9] during the workshops. Memories about going to the beach confronted P5 with her difficulty in walking and that she is now dependent on a walker:

CP: Have you never seen the sea then (P5)?

P5: Yes, if I went to the beach, but that was a long time ago […] I could walk back then, but now I can't…

CP: But you can do small distances, with the walker, that's still going well.

P5: Yes, small distances…

P9 elaborated multiple times on his period of working in a timber factory. However, he experienced this with mixed feelings as this also evoked a sense of sadness: 'in the atmosphere of his story, you notice that he is nostalgic for his story.' [CP] When dealing with memories and emotions, there is always the risk of confronting people with their dementia, despite all measures and intentions for providing enjoyable experiences. However, such responses are not necessarily harmful, as mixed feelings or sadness can also evoke nostalgia or reminiscing and should not necessarily be censored out or intentionally avoided.

## 13.4.4 Gradual Build-up and Moments of Rest

As the three steps were repeated for each soundscape, the recurring *familiarizing* phases involving the everyday objects acted as small pauses between the different soundscape themes. During the workshops, these moments of rest provided some relief as we observed how listening to soundscapes became tiring for some participants. Participants P1 and P7 expressed this in-between playing two soundscapes: 'Ha finally rest yes.' [P1] Furthermore, these in-between sessions of silence also worked as a reset or new start and demarcated the different soundscapes. The participant responses illustrated how short periods of rest and silence prevented listening to the soundscapes from becoming a burden, and allowed it to remain enjoyable.

The CP who attended the workshop noted that the activity in itself was accessible and easy to understand: 'The general impression was that it was a very relaxing activity without high expectations and that the atmosphere was great and accessible.' [CP] However, as reported in our previous publication (Houben et al. 2019), the soundscapes with all four sound layers played at once were perceived as too chaotic in all three soundscape explorations. For example, P5 was suddenly overwhelmed when the city soundscape was triggered: 'Ooh a lot of sounds!' The individual sound layers, on the other hand, evoked more meaningful responses:

> I think the babbling brook is lovely, but I find all sounds together a racket! […] That actually also applies to all 4 of them (soundscapes), the fuss just has to get out of it. It just has a lot of impact, I noticed, you get tired. [P4]

These findings suggest that starting with the individual sound layers and gradually building up to a composed soundscape could decrease the risk of overwhelming the participants.

### *13.4.5 Participation Through Interaction*

The post-event analysis of the video recordings gave insights into how the participants interacted very differently with the soundboard during the workshops. We identified three different forms of interaction: *initiate*, *discover*, and *observe*.

The dementia soundboard enabled the participants to *initiate* the listening sessions during the workshop. For each soundscape, the facilitator asked a different participant to place the object on the soundboard and initiate the corresponding soundscape (see Fig. 13.4). By doing so, the facilitator included all the participants in the setting and offered a sense of agency. Most participants [P1-8, P11] seemed to understand the interaction design of the soundboard and were able to link their actions to the perceived changes in the soundscapes. P9 and P10 confused the central place where the objects needed to be placed for the touchpads, because of the minimalistic appearance and abstract quality of the soundboard. Their interactions were often brief and in response to a request by the facilitator. Nevertheless, it kept the participants engaged in the workshop and aware of changes in the soundscapes. The CP compared this to a board game:

> Yes, it was a kind of game form, like moving a pawn, or tapping a light. [CP]

During the workshop, participants were invited by the facilitator to tap one of the touchpads on the soundboards. Participants P2 and P3, in particular, were devoted to *discovering* the soundboard by actively interacting with the touchpads in order to explore and understand how the soundscape would change (see Fig. 13.5). They described it as a 'game' [P4] and enjoyed naming the hidden sounds in each sound layer: 'I really enjoyed unraveling the sounds.' [P3] They also stated their fondness for guessing and recognizing all the different sounds of the soundscape, while sharing memories, stories, and emotions with the other participants.

**Fig. 13.5** Participants are exploring the sound layers with the *dementia soundboard* in group

While one of the participants was interacting with the soundboard, others could *observe* and passively engage, for example, by watching someone interact with the soundboard. The interactions with the soundboard served as cues to indicate a change in the soundscape played at that time. For example, at times when the participants did not interact with the soundboard, the facilitator or CP briefly interacted with it. The participants then watched and listened to the variations in the soundscapes. These forms of passive engagement offered some relief while still keeping everyone engaged. Therefore, despite interaction sometimes becoming sparse, the *dementia soundboard* was a useful tool for stimulating exploration and engagement, while including all the participants in the setting.

## 13.5 Conclusion: Practical Guidelines

Based on the reflection on our research protocol, we outline five practical guidelines on how to involve people in early to mid-stage of dementia in participatory approaches to identify personal experiences evoked by sound:

- By establishing an enjoyable and safe atmosphere, participants can share opinions and thoughts in a nonthreatening and sociable setting. By embedding research in a familiar context, the participants are safeguarded by a familiar CP in a secure environment where they feel at ease and comfortable.
- Introducing familiar objects as a first and straightforward exercise can help to introduce the setting and sound content that will be addressed, preventing potential forms of disengagement.
- Creating space for sharing of experiences provides opportunities for participants to seek and receive acknowledgment by engaging in each other's stories or responses within a group setting.
- Integrating moments of rest and relief within the workshop protocol can reduce the risk of overwhelming participants and provide opportunities to refocus for the next step in the research protocol.

- Encouraging participation through interaction with design artifacts offers a sense of agency and stimulates the participants in exploring their experiences and comparing it with others. Not only discovering and initiating sounds themselves but also observing others can cue changes being made to variables in sound.

The *dementia soundboard* facilitated the exploration of personal participant responses to the soundscapes of everyday sounds. These results are in line with existing literature demonstrating how interacting with design artifacts can elicit personal stories and associations that have emotional value for people with dementia (Wallace et al. 2013). In addition, the *dementia soundboard* was able to facilitate these responses in a small group setting where participants experienced how their responses were acknowledged and appreciated by others. These social interactions contributed to establishing an informal atmosphere, which made the research activity pleasant while offering insight into the participants' personal perspective (Suijkerbuijk et al. 2015).

There is a risk that participants can become disrespectful toward each other, resulting in negative feelings or uncomfortable situations during the activity (Bamford and Bruce 2001). To minimize these potentially negative effects, it is recommended that group activities are organized with people at similar stages of dementia (Hendriks et al. 2013). Our findings concur with this, and so participants in early and mid-stage of dementia participated in different workshops (see Table 13.1), and all participants could engage in the workshop at a similar level of involvement. In this project, we did not observe any exchange of disrespectful comments or behavior between the participants.

This research focused mainly on people in early to mid-stages of dementia. Therefore, further research is needed to increase the scope of these insights on how to involve people in the more advanced stages of dementia. The workshops were integrated within an existing care activity, but within a controlled setting as the workshops space was isolated from the common living spaces to prevent the participants from being distracted by other stimuli. This poses questions of how workshops can take into account the social dynamics of other spaces in care facilities, such as private rooms or common living spaces, where a range of different sounds and distractions are already present. Building on these findings, we will focus in future work on people in mid to late-stage dementia and explore the role of everyday sounds in residential care facilities to demonstrate the beneficial effects of sound in real-life care settings.

In conclusion, we have shared our experience of conducting interactive workshops with people in early to mid-stages of dementia. We used an interactive prototype and familiar everyday objects to elicit personal responses to sound content. By using the dementia soundboard, we were able to facilitate the workshops in a reciprocal and engaging way. Furthermore, we demonstrated how sharing these experiences in a group can provide a pleasant and meaningful activity for the involved participants. With this work, we aim to inspire future participatory approaches to involve the personal perspective of people with dementia in design.

**Acknowledgements** This research is part of the 'Everyday Sounds of Dementia' project funded by ZonMw in the Create Health program (grant number 40-44300-98-117). We want to thank Archipel care organization, Betty Jansen and Jolien ter Brugge for their assistance, and the participants for their involvement in the workshops.

## References

Baird A, Samson S (2009) Memory for music in Alzheimer's disease: unforgettable? Neuropsychol Revi 19(1):85–101. https://doi.org/10.1007/s11065-009-9085-2

Baird A, Thompson WF (2018) The impact of music on the self in dementia. J Alzheimer's Dis JAD 61(3):827–841. https://doi.org/10.3233/JAD-170737

Bamford C, Bruce E (2001) Successes and challenges in using focus groups with older people with dementia. In: The perspectives of people with dementia research methods and motivations. Jessica Kingsley, London, pp 139–164

Branco RM, Quental J, Ribeiro Ó (2017) Personalised participation: an approach to involve people with dementia and their families in a participatory design project. CoDesign 13(2):127–143. https://doi.org/10.1080/15710882.2017.1310903

Braun V, Clarke V (2006) Using thematic analysis in psychology. Qual Res Psychol 3(2):77–101. https://doi.org/10.1191/1478088706qp063oa

Bulsara C, Seaman K, Steuxner S (2016) Using sound therapy to ease agitation amongst persons with dementia: a pilot study. Aust Nurs Midwifery J 23(7):38–39

Campbell S, Frohlich D, Alm N, Vaughan A (2019) Sentimental audio memories: exploring the emotion and meaning of everyday sounds. In: Brankaert R, IJsselsteijn W (eds), Dementia lab 2019. Making design work: engaging with dementia in context. D-Lab 2019. Springer, Cham, pp 73–81. https://doi.org/10.1007/978-3-030-33540-3_7

Chancellor B, Duncan A, Chatterjee A (2014) Art therapy for Alzheimer's disease and other dementias. J Alzheimer's Dis 39(1):1–11. https://doi.org/10.3233/JAD-131295

Devos P, Aletta F, Thomas P, Filipan K, Petrovic M, Botteldooren D, … De Vriendt P (2018) Soundscape design for management of behavioral disorders: a pilot study among nursing home residents with dementia. In: Herrin D, Cuschieri J, Ebbitt G (eds) Impact of noise control engineering: proceedings of inter-noise 2018. Institute of Noise Control Engineering of the United States of America, p 8

Dewing J (2007) Participatory research: a method for process consent with persons who have dementia. Dementia 6(1):11–25. https://doi.org/10.1177/1471301207075625

Eggen B (2016) Interactive soundscapes of the future everyday life. In: Peripheral interaction: challenges and opportunities for HCI in the periphery of attention, pp 239–251. https://doi.org/10.1007/978-3-319-29523-7_11

Gold K (2014) But does it do any good? Measuring the impact of music therapy on people with advanced dementia: (Innovative practice). Dementia (London, England) 13(2):258–264. https://doi.org/10.1177/1471301213494512

Hayne MJ, Fleming R (2014) Acoustic design guidelines for dementia care facilities. In: Proceedings of 43rd international congress on noise control engineering: internoise 2014. Australian Acoustical Society, Australia, pp 1–10

Hendriks N, Huybrechts L, Wilkinson A, Slegers K (2014) Challenges in doing participatory design with people with dementia. In: Proceedings of the 13th participatory design conference on short papers, industry cases, workshop descriptions, doctoral consortium papers, and keynote abstracts—PDC '14, vol 2. ACM Press, New York, USA, pp 33–36. https://doi.org/10.1145/2662155.2662196

Hendriks N, Truyen F, Duval E (2013) Designing with dementia: guidelines for participatory design together with persons with dementia. In: IFIP conference on human-computer interaction. Springer, Berlin, Heidelberg, pp 649–666. https://doi.org/10.1007/978-3-642-40483-2_46

Houben M, Brankaert R, Bakker S, Kenning G, Bongers I, Eggen B (2019) Foregrounding everyday sounds in dementia. In: Proceedings of the 2019 on designing interactive systems conference—DIS '19. ACM Press, New York, USA, pp 71–83. https://doi.org/10.1145/3322276.3322287

Houben M, Brankaert R, Bakker S, Kenning G, Bongers I, Eggen B (2020) The role of everyday sounds in advanced dementia care. In: Proceedings of the 2020 CHI Conference on Human Factors in Computing Systems (CHI '20). ACM, pp 1–14

Kenning G (2017) Making it together: reciprocal design to promote positive Wellbeing for people living with dementia

Kenning G (2018) Reciprocal design: inclusive design approaches for people with late stage dementia. Design for Health 2(1):142–162. https://doi.org/10.1080/24735132.2018.1453638

Kitwood T (1997) The experience of dementia. Aging Ment Health 1(1):13–22. https://doi.org/10.1080/13607869757344

Lazar A, Cornejo R, Edasis C, Piper AM (2016) Designing for the third hand: empowering older adults with cognitive impairments through creating and sharing. In DIS 2016—proceedings of the (2016) ACM conference on designing interactive systems (pp 1047–1058). ACM Press, New York, USA. https://doi.org/10.1145/2901790.2901854

Lazar A, Feuston JL, Edasis C, Piper AM (2018) Making as expression: informing design with people with complex communication needs through art therapy. In: Proceedings of the 2018 CHI conference on human factors in computing systems—CHI '18. ACM Press, New York, USA, pp 351, 1–16. https://doi.org/10.1145/3173574.3173925

Morrissey K, Wood G, Green D, Pantidi N, McCarthy J (2016) 'I'm a rambler, I'm a gambler, I'm a long way from home': the place of props, music, and design in dementia care. In: Proceedings of the 2016 ACM Conference on designing interactive systems—DIS '16. ACM Press, New York, USA, pp 1008–1020. https://doi.org/10.1145/2901790.2901798

Olazarán J, Reisberg B, Clare L, Cruz I, Peña-Casanova J, del Ser T, … Muñiz R (2010) Nonpharmacological therapies in Alzheimer's disease: a systematic review of efficacy. Dementia Geriat Cognit Disord 30(2):161–178. https://doi.org/10.1159/000316119

Raglio A, Filippi S, Bellandi D, Stramba-Badiale M (2014) Global music approach to persons with dementia: evidence and practice. Clin Int Aging 9:1669–1676. https://doi.org/10.2147/CIA.S71388

Schine J (2010) Movement, memory & the senses in soundscape studies. Can Acoust 38(3):100–101

Suijkerbuijk S, Brankaert R, De Kort YAW, Snaphaan LJAE, Den Ouden E (2015, January 1) Seeing the first-person perspective in dementia: a qualitative personal evaluation game to evaluate assistive technology for people affected by dementia in the home context. Interacting with computers. Oxford University Press. https://doi.org/10.1093/iwc/iwu038

Teunissen L, Luyten T, de Witte L (2017) Reconnecting people with dementia by using the interactive instrument CRDL. Stud Health Technol Inf 242:9–15

Truax B (2001) Acoustic communication. Greenwood Publishing Group

van den Bosch KA, Andringa TC, Başkent D, Vlaskamp C (2016) The role of sound in residential facilities for people with profound intellectual and multiple disabilities. J Policy Pract Int Dis 13(1):61–68. https://doi.org/10.1111/jppi.12147

van den Bosch KA, Andringa TC, Peterson W, Ruijssenaars WAJJM, Vlaskamp C (2017) A comparison of natural and non-natural soundscapes on people with severe or profound intellectual and multiple disabilities. J Int Develop Dis 42(3):301–307. https://doi.org/10.3109/13668250.2016.1250251

Wallace J, Wright PC, McCarthy J, Green DP, Thomas J, Olivier P (2013) A design-led inquiry into personhood in dementia. In: Proceedings of the SIGCHI conference on human factors in computing systems—CHI '13. ACM Press, New York, USA, pp 2617–2626. https://doi.org/10.1145/2470654.2481363

# Chapter 14
# Color Design and Dementia: Harnessing HCI to Improve Environmental Visual Literacy

Zena O'Connor

## 14.1 Introduction

This chapter defines environmental visual literacy and the roles that color and contrast play in visual perception and color design strategies that enhance environmental visual literacy. In addition, techniques are described which highlight the ways in which color design strategies can be investigated, evaluated and effectively implemented for people living with dementia in human–computer interaction (HCI). Color is an under-researched area in the area of HCI and dementia. This chapter provides an overview of perspectives that contribute to visual and environmental literacy and how this is impacted by cognitive decline as occurs in aging and dementia. It provides insights into the rationale and guidelines for color use in care environments, and shows how this area requires a greater focus in HCI. This is necessary as designers and HCI researchers engage in the care space with the development of assistive technologies, intervene in the care environment with sensor driven technologies, or design screen-based interfaces for people living with dementia. The focus of this chapter is on the mechanics of how we see and understand spaces and environments in relation to color. While the focus is on physical spaces, contrast and color have implications in virtual spaces light design as well to support people living with dementia.

Z. O'Connor (✉)
Design Research Associates, Sydney, Australia
e-mail: Zena@zenaoconnor.com.au

© Springer Nature Switzerland AG 2020

R. Brankaert and G. Kenning (eds.), *HCI and Design in the Context of Dementia*, Human–Computer Interaction Series,
https://doi.org/10.1007/978-3-030-32835-1_14

## 14.2 Color Design for People Living with Dementia: Why It Is Important

For the purpose of this discussion, color design in aged care and healthcare includes all color variations (hue, tonal value, and saturation) inherent in construction materials, fixtures, finishes, furnishings, textures, painted surfaces, and lighting. It is acknowledged that finishes and materials in these environments are often subject to regulations. However, these regulations do not necessarily need to hinder effective color design except where the variety and range of finishes and material products is limited in supply. Color design is one of many design factors that have the capacity to influence the effectiveness and enhance the interface between the built environment and people living with dementia, and dovetail with strategies to increase and improve engagement, and support orientation and wayfinding strategies.

Design in general is one of a range of factors that can support or hinder human evaluation and response to the built environment. Lewin (1967) conceptualized the environment–behavior interface as follows: where behavior is considered to be a function of the interactions between personal factors and the environment. Since the 1960s, an extensive body of environment–behavior literature exists that focuses on the physical design aspects of the built environment and the related impact on human response in terms of affective, cognitive, and behavioral response (Rapoport 2008). In terms of older people in general, an effective interface between the built environment and human response relies on the level of physical competency of an individual and environmental *press*—that is, the demands of a given environment or situation (Lawton and Nahemow 1973). A mismatch or shortfall on either side of this interface has an impact on any type of user in that environment. An ineffective interface between the built environment and people living with dementia can become highly problematic. Inappropriate environmental design is one of the two most common triggers for challenging behaviors in people living with dementia, the other being unidentified pain issues. The former is both a challenge and an imperative for the design of spaces for people living with dementia (Judd 2016).

Survey findings reported by Swaffer (2016) include a list of what people living with dementia want in regards to their residential care facility. In respect to environmental design, this list includes reablement, strategies, and support to enable independence, a creative environment, access to natural environments and the outside world, absence of visually apparent barriers and walls, personalized furnishings, and access to and use of technology. These findings add further weight to the ten design principles for dementia enabling environments (Fleming and Bowles 1987; Fleming et al. 2003):

1. Unobtrusively reduce risk: Safety is important but not at the cost of diminishing visual amenity, the joy of a view and access to the outdoors. Camouflage is recommended to unobtrusively reduce risk.
2. Provide a human scale: Ensure surroundings are at a homelike human scale as this scale is familiar to people with dementia. Large rooms with multiple distractions can negatively impact behavior.

3. Allow people to see and be seen: Allow clear visual access and ensure that people with dementia can see where they are and where they may want to go.
4. Minimize unhelpful stimulation: Unnecessary visual and auditory stimulation may distress and confuse those with dementia. Reduce excessive signage, visual clutter, and noise, and camouflage is recommended to obscure nonaccess doors.
5. Optimize helpful stimulation: Environmental cues such as color, visual landmarks, furniture and a view enable people with dementia to better find their way around and make environments more consistently meaningful.
6. Support movement and engagement: Arrange environments and seating to encourage people to use them, and for meaningful use and interaction.
7. Create a familiar space: Interior design, furniture, furnishings, colors, and fittings should be selected to provide a homelike and comfortable ambience.
8. Provide opportunities to be alone or with others: Provide a range of environments that allow for privacy as well as social interaction, inside and outside.
9. Provide links with the community: Meaningful links to the community can include a community garden or community events at the facility.
10. Respond to a vision for a way of life: Facilitate environments that respond to people's stories and allow them to continue with their interests in a meaningful way.

These guidelines for enabling environment remain of the utmost importance when creating smart responsive environments that include, for example, technology that responds to users through sensors. Color design and use, become no less important and links to a large proportion of these design principles and can support environmental and technology design that focuses on well-being, individual competency, personalization, and quality of life. For this approach to be meaningful, input regarding appropriate design from this particular cohort is imperative. However, prior to exploring this, it is helpful to understand the roles that color and contrast play in terms of general visual perception and specifically environmental visual literacy.

## 14.3 The Roles of Color and Contrast in Visual Perception

Color and, especially contrast, play key roles in visual perception, and these in turn support or weaken environmental visual literacy. Color data are also being input into databases and aggregated for wider use, for example, AI (Artificial Intelligence) start-up Norna.ai has built color trend software to elicit color preferences for applications across a range of sectors, including health industries. However, it will be some time before the outcomes of Norna's AI color research and application projects will be released. But, with the increasing interest in aged care and dementia care environments this suggests there may be opportunities to aggregate data from research studies that involve human-centered approaches to color design coupled with inclusive HCI approaches to provide greater insights. An understanding of this can then

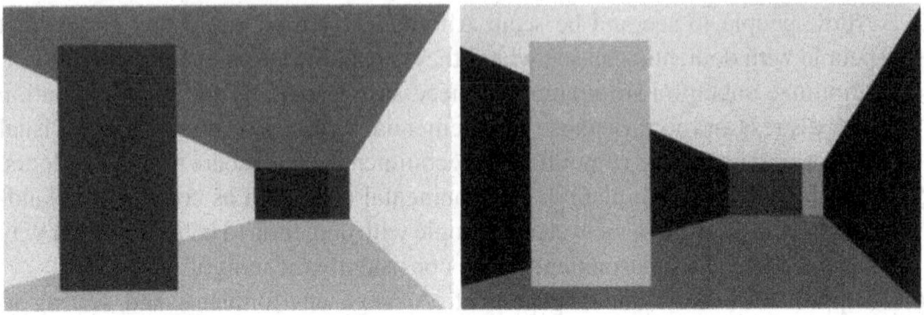

**Fig. 14.1** Color and contrast enhance environmental visual literacy

underpin and enhance color design across all sectors of aged care and healthcare in general and specifically in spaces designed for people living with dementia.

Incoming visual information travels to the brain via the optic nerve and it is commonly held that we construct what we see (Hoffman 1998). That is, visual perception occurs in tandem with cognitive processing and memory, and we perceive visual cues while simultaneously referring to memory and making evaluative judgements. We see geometric shapes and we begin to perceive this as walls, floors, and doors depending on our mental images of these in memory (Fig. 14.1). Color and contrast helps to underpin and reinforce this process. Specifically, strong contrast and movement attracts attention due to the fixational reflex as well as the tendency for the human eye to notice and focus on an object that is bright relative to its surroundings (Boynton 1979).

Visual perception also involves attention and this may be either directed or peripheral attention. The decision to apply direct attention relies upon the operation of saccades, which occur on a constant and ongoing basis during normal vision. Saccades are the microscanning movements that the eye makes when viewing a scene or performing an activity. It's estimated that the eye makes about three per second when viewing a scene and processing information to decide what's important in the scene and what's not. Eye-tracking studies indicate that during normal vision, movement and strong contrast catch the attention of saccades and are key variables in visual detection (McPeek et al. 1999; Shang and Bishop 2000). But, both color and contrast sensitivity decline from middle age onward. Contrast and especially light–dark contrast allow us to effectively differentiate contours, depth, shape, and objects in the environment. As a result, weak levels of contrast hinder our ability to effectively *read* visual imagery and environmental elements; this can be further hindered by poor ambient lighting.

## 14.4 Environmental Visual Literacy

In defining environmental visual literacy, reference is made to visual literacy, the ability to read and understand visual imagery. Environmental visual literacy extends the scope of visual literacy and refers to the ability to make sense of visual cues embedded in design and the built environment in a meaningful, functional, and effective way. Environmental visual literacy depends on functional visual perception, effective cognitive processing (including memory), and the functional capacity to read and interpret visual cues. Effective environmental visual literacy occurs when we can easily read and understand visual cues embedded in design and the built environment (O'Connor 2016, 2018).

An effective interface exists between the built environment and users, which underpins strategies to encourage and improve engagement, orientation, wayfinding, and the safe operation of daily activities. However, environmental visual literacy is negatively impacted by cognitive load, and this is of particular importance to people living with dementia. This cohort requires an optimal level of environmental stimuli that simultaneously supports them and minimizes visual distractions and unhelpful or unsafe levels of visual stimulation. For example, interior design that is characterized by excessive contrasts, patterning and design details translates into visual complexity, thereby adding to visual *noise* and unsafe levels of visual distraction. In terms of technology development and interface, development issues could arise from busy or cluttered screens, alarms, reminders and notifications, or use of low-contrast color palettes.

## 14.5 Cognitive Load—The Impact on Environmental Visual Literacy

Levels of cognitive load have an impact on visual perception and environmental visual literacy. When we are exposed to higher levels of environmental stimuli, we can experience difficulties processing all the visual information in our visual field, and this in turn can have an impact on the safe operation of daily tasks and activities. Cognitive load theory stems from research that suggests working memory capacity may have inherent limits and we are generally able to hold only seven plus or minus two units of information in short-term memory. Under cognitive load theory, we tend to differ in our processing capacity with some people less able to process effectively depending on experience and distraction levels. While cognitive load research was initially conducted among learners, this theory has relevance across all population cohorts and contextual settings.

Heavy cognitive load can result in error or misinterpretation of stimuli. Excessive visual stimuli (visual noise) negatively impacts environmental visual literacy and this tends to increase among older people. Therefore, optimal levels of environmental stimuli that support and enable people living with dementia are the ideal, especially given the visual challenges encountered by this cohort.

## 14.6 Variable Vision Needs and Visual Challenges of People Living with Dementia

In aged care and healthcare in general, declining visual capacity can negatively impact the effectiveness of color design and user experience of HCI, design, and the built environment. Aside from specific issues such as macular degradation, this decline in visual capacity tends to involve reduced luminance contrast and color contrast sensitivity. This is due to the changes which occur in the human visual system from middle age onward and are largely continuous (Fiorentini et al. 1996; Newacheck et al. 1990; Werner et al. 1990). Specifically, there are between 1.2 and 1.5 million retinal ganglion cells in the human retina which receive input from rods and cones; however, retinal ganglion cells decrease in number by about 25% from age 20 to 80 years. This is compounded by a decrease of about 50% in the lateral geniculate nucleus (LGN) from age 20 to 80 years. The LGN is the area in the thalamus that receives incoming visual information from the optic nerve before relaying it to the primary visual cortex of the brain. Visual perception of luminance contrast (light–dark contrast) and color contrast both decline in sensitivity with age thereby reducing the visual capacity among older people (Livingstone 2002). The impact for older people and people living with dementia is a decline in the capacity to perceive and understand environmental visual stimuli, potentially leading to anxiety, confusion, and aggression.

Aside from cognitive impairment, people living with dementia may experience a number of visual issues that impact their perception of their environment. From her experience living with dementia, Agnes Houston, author and dementia campaigner, summarizes the visual issues experienced by people living with dementia as 'your eyes see, but your brain doesn't interpret the information immediately' and provides the following specific visual perception challenges (Houston 2016, p. 4).

- Slower visual processing;
- Misinterpreting visual information;
- Sensory overload: double vision, ghosting;
- Visual hallucinations and difficulty discriminating between real scenarios and imaginary scenarios or dreams.

Declining cognitive capacity also impacts visual perception among people living with dementia. This means that visual perception issues may not be cognitively evaluated and contested by the individual, leading to an interface with the built environment that is negatively impacted. Color design strategies that aim to improve environmental visual literacy can positively address but perhaps not fully alleviate these visual challenges. In addition, HCI researchers and designers can work in consultation with people living with dementia to both understand their needs and assess design solutions from their perspective.

## 14.7 Color Design Strategies to Improve Environmental Visual Literacy

Fuggle (2013) advises a number of general design strategies for people living with dementia:

- Design very clearly defined spaces, prioritising what is most important;
- Provide much brighter light than normal and control sources of glare;
- Use strong tonal contrast between flooring, skirtings, walls, and doors;
- Use stronger colors;
- Use feature walls to make a room look more three-dimensional;
- Provide frequent cues, such as familiar objects and pictures.

While these strategies were developed in the context of interfacing with the environment, we might suggest that they are principles that may be applied in digital and virtual spaces. Well-considered and meaningful overall color design can provide optimal sensory stimulation (Chaudhury and Cooke 2014). However, there a number of specific color design strategies for people living with dementia that improve environmental visual literacy and hence enhance engagement and support orientation and wayfinding. These specific color design strategies include: 1. strong color contrast between design elements; 2. familiar residential *homelike* colors and design archetypes; 3. biophilia-inspired color design; and 4. circadian-colored lighting.

### *14.7.1 Strong Color Contrast Between Design Elements*

Due to the mechanics of human visual perception, strong light–dark contrast as well as hue contrast and saturation contrast have the capacity to attract directed attention and, in doing so, draw attention to key design variables in HCI and the built environment. In addition, contrast is especially important for many people living with dementia due to the reduced contrast sensitivity (Gilmore and Levy 1991; Grover et al. 2005). Lynch noted that color contrast as well as key visual and design cues in the built environment help to identify spaces and boundaries, create unique zones, and support orientation and wayfinding (Lynch 1960). Furthermore, across many areas of applied design, strong contrast (tonal value, hue, and saturation contrast) is referred to as the *Isolation Effect* and used to draw attention to specific design details.

This strategy boosts the effectiveness of intuitive design because it draws attention to key design elements quickly and overcomes language barriers (Van Dam et al. 1974).

Color contrast that exhibits at least 30% but ideally up to 70% differential between design details/objects and background color serves as a recommended contrast level. This level of color contrast provides the optimal contrast for improved legibility of environmental design details (Chaudhury and Cooke 2014; Pollock and Fuggle 2013; Russell-Minda et al. 2007; Nini 2006). Applying this contrast color strategy to resident doors, unique interior spaces/walls, and interior/exterior landmarks helps to support orientation and wayfinding strategies. In addition, color contrast can differentiate doors, flooring and hand rails from walls and is recommended for small-scale design details such as toilet seats, tapware, plates, placements, flatware, and cutlery.

### *14.7.2 Familiar Residential Homelike Colors and Design Archetypes*

Some people living with dementia can experience anxiety, stress, or distress in unfamiliar surroundings. This cohort is more able to use and enjoy places, spaces, furniture, fixtures, fittings, and objects that are familiar to them, because they may make associations with their earlier life and experiences. In this, familiar and homelike color design can help with maintaining dignity, competence, and a sense of joy through the use of familiar design archetypes, furniture, fittings, and colors (Chaudhury and Cooke 2014; Lawton et al. 2000; Day and Calkins 2002). Familiar color schemes tend to change over time with each generation cohort. Techniques that can identify familiar, homelike colors include: 1. survey color trends relevant to the formative years of individuals living with dementia and 2. conduct simple interactive surveys or interviews among people living with dementia.

### *14.7.3 Biophilia-Inspired Color Design*

The use of green foliage walls, views to nature, pot plants, and green painted or textured surfaces is a strategy aimed at supporting a connection with nature and enhancing a sense of well-being. This evidence-based approach is underpinned by universal preferences for biophilia to represent the strong attraction and sense of affinity for nature and living systems. Wilson posited the biophilia hypothesis, which suggests that we are hardwired to seek out connections with nature and other forms of life. Kaplan and Kaplan's research focused on the restorative effect of nature. The Kaplan's attention restoration theory proposed that people whose resources are depleted from attentional fatigue at work and associated stress can concentrate better after spending time in nature or viewing nature. More recent research suggests that nature may have a therapeutic impact for people living with dementia (Chalfont 2007). In this regard, a number of dementia residential care homes are designed to specifically reference nature including those by Jean Makesh, CEO and founder of the Lantern Group, who incorporates nature in a range of different ways: Green foliage walls and foliage installations, pot plants, nature-inspired green painted and textured surfaces and flooring, nature-inspired graphics and murals, digital sky installations that change lighting from daylight to nighttime, water features, and internal fountains and cross-ventilation breezes.

### 14.7.4 Circadian-Colored Lighting

In respect to circadian lighting, the Danish Dementia Research Centre (Samla 2016) has been researching the impact of lighting on the elderly using lighting-controlled facilities. Findings indicate a range of positive outcomes including improved sleep patterns. Circadian lighting uses different variations and intensities of colored light to mimic natural lighting across day and night, which might support people with dementia. Figure 14.2 features three circadian hallway lighting options installed in the ACC Senior Centre, Sacramento.

A key starting point is to minimize visual clutter and environmental stimuli which have the capacity to create visual distractions and add to cognitive load. Plus, avoid glare and minimize contrast at windows by adjusting the color and contrast of curtains, consider blinds and walls relative to the amount of natural and ambient lighting, and where costs permit incorporate circadian lighting.

Circadian-colored lighting mimics the color of light at different times of the day, from warm red/orange tones at sunrise and sunset, and blue tones during the daytime (HCD 2018). The circadian cycle is the 24-hour light–dark cycle that impacts

**Fig. 14.2** Circadian hallway lighting. *Image credit* ACC Senior Centre, Sacramento

our nonvisual responses to light, regulating our *body clock* and supporting normal sleeping and waking patterns. The presence of light suppresses the secretion of the hormone melatonin and this tends to peak at a spectral sensitivity of around 460 nm (blue light waves) in humans. Suppressed melatonin levels can shift the circadian cycle, impacting sleep quality and the body's ability to regulate blood pressure, glucose levels and body temperature. Interruptions to the circadian cycle lead to jetlag-like symptoms, and the presence of blue light at night can also shift the circadian cycle, leading to, for example, increased alertness. Other colored light waves, from red through orange, yellow, and green, have the least power to shift the circadian cycle (Rea and Figueiro 2018). Dementia can disturb the biological clock ageing (Lieshout-van Dal et al. 2019). In this context, circadian lighting can potentially improve the circadian rhythm, and have a positive impact on sleep patterns and overall well-being (HCD 2018).

## 14.8 The Role of HCI in Effective Color Design

In the past, design for people living with dementia occurred with relatively minimal interaction with that particular cohort. However, the imperatives of human-centered design and a greater focus on promoting respect, justice, inclusivity, and equality and well-being and quality of life have prompted new research methods focused on garnering input from people living with dementia.

HCI provides systems and tools to support and enhance this approach, which has similarities with reminiscence therapy. A recent research project, CIRCA (Computer Interactive Reminiscence and Conversation Aid), applied a similar approach. In this project, a number of interactive Quicktime VR (QTVR) environments were created. These environments were tested by people living with dementia to determine whether they would find the experience engaging, enjoyable and/or worthwhile. The findings from this project found that HCI can play a significant role in supporting older people with dementia-related cognitive impairment (Gowans et al. 2007).

More recently, Agnes Houston, a dementia campaigner diagnosed with early onset dementia in 2006 at the age of 57, has shown how people with early stage dementia remain observant, engaged and articulate (Houston 2016; Houston and Christie 2018). As such, people living with early stage dementia represent invaluable participants on design panels and research studies aimed at exploring color design strategies appropriate for spaces intended for people living with dementia. In such contexts, HCI systems and tools can forward input and recommendations from people living with dementia, ensuring that they are not only heard but included in research. A recent example is research led by Connie Samla at the ACC Care Centre in Sacramento. With a focus on human-centric lighting, Samla worked with three residents (people living with dementia) and staff members to evaluate the effectiveness of a circadian lighting intervention. This research showed that general well-being as well as sleeping patterns improved in tandem with a decrease in agitated behavior and falls (Samla 2016).

As HCI increasingly develops technologies in the support of people living with dementia it is important to understand not only their wants and needs but also the mechanics of how they engage with the environment and how the environment is designed and why. It is also important to understand that where HCI can benefit is not always in the direct interaction with people but in providing supportive environments such as sensor driven spaces that respond with circadian lighting, biophilic environments that are tended by sensor driven technologies and databases of *color palettes* for use in environments and interfaces.

Over time, a database of research results relating to specific color design strategies for people living with dementia can be harvested using machine learning specifically for AI applications. AI is currently being used for a range of applications in dementia context including Alzheimer disease diagnosis (Ding et al. 2019). In addition, tech start-ups like Norna.ai are developing machine learning database models to collect and analyze color and design data relating to individual preferences across a number of sectors. While such data is currently aimed at a mainstream market, in time the same techniques can be used for more specific applications such as dementia.

In conclusion, despite the best efforts of designers, color design strategies that are not underpinned by knowledge relating to environmental visual literacy and input gleaned from people living with dementia remain assumption-based design options that may or may not be appropriate for this cohort. HCI as well as AI provide the opportunity of systems, tools and technologies tailored to acknowledge and support people living with dementia. By involving people living with dementia at every step during the design process, color design strategies can be meaningful and effective, while also foregrounding respect, justice, inclusivity, and equality to improve well-being and quality of life.

## References

Boynton RM (1979) Human color vision. Holt, Reinhart & Winston, New York

Chalfont GE (2007) Wholistic Design in Dementia Care. J Housing Elderly 21(1–2):153–177

Chaudhury H, Cooke H (2014) Design matters in dementia care: The role of the physical environment in dementia care settings. In: Downs M, Bowers B (eds) Excellence in dementia care, 2nd edn. Open University Press, UK, pp 144–158

Day K, Calkins MP (2002) Design and dementia. In: Bechtel R, Churchman A (eds) Handbook of environmental psychology. John Wiley & Sons, New York, pp 2–53

Ding Y, Sohn JH, Kawczynski MG, Trivedi H, Hamish R, Jenkins NW, Lituiev D, Copeland TP, Aboian MS, Aparici CM, Behr SC, Flavell RR, Huang S, Zalocusky KA, Nardo L, Seo Y, Hawkins RA, Pampaloni MH, Hadley D, Franc BL (2019) A deep learning model to predict a diagnosis of Alzheimer disease by using F-FDG PET of the brain. Radiology 290(2):456–464

Elliott A, Fairchild MD, Franklin A (eds) Handbook of color psychology. Cambridge: Cambridge University Press

Fiorentini A, Porciatti M, Morrone MC, Burr DC (1996) Visual ageing: unspecific decline of the responses to luminance and color. Vision Res 36(21):3557–3566

Fleming R, Bowles J (1987) Units for the confused and disturbed elderly: development, design, programming and evaluation. Aust J Ageing 6(4):25–8

Fleming R, Forbes I, Bennett K (2003) Adapting the ward for people with dementia. NSW Department of Health, Sydney

Gilmore GC, Levy JA (1991) Spatial contrast sensitivity in Alzheimer's disease: a comparison of two methods. Optom Vis Sci 68:790–794

Gilmore Grover C, Groth Karen E, Thomas Cecil W (2005) Stimulus contrast and word reading speed in Alzheimer's disease. Exp Aging Res 31(1):15–33

Gramegna SM, Biamonti A (2017) Environment as non-pharmacological intervention in the care of Alzheimer's disease. Des J 20(1):S2284–S2292

Goldstein EB (1996) Sensation and perception. Brooks/Cole, Pacific Grove, CA

Gowans G, Dye R, Alm N, Vaughan P, Astell A, Ellis M (2007) Designing the interface between dementia patients caregivers and computer-based intervention. Des J 20(1):12–23

Hartig T, Mang M, Evans GW (1991) Restorative effects of natural environment experiences. Envir behavior 23(1):3–26

HCD (2018) White paper: Denmark—a dementia friendly society. Healthcare Denmark, Odense

Hoffman DD (1998) Visual intelligence: how we create what we see. WW Norton & Company, New York

Houston A (2016a) Dementia and sensory challenges. Life Changes Trust, Glasgow

Houston A (2016) Keynote speech. 2016 International Dementia Conference, Sydney

Houston A, Christie J (2018) Talking sense: living with sensory changes and dementia. Hammond Care, Sydney

Itten J (1973) The art of color. John Wiley, New York

Jackson GR, Owsley C, McGwin G (1999) Aging and dark adaptation. Vis Res 39(23):3975–3982

Judd S (2016) Mad, bad and dangerous to know. Opening address, International Dementia Care Conference, Sydney

Kolb H (2003) How the retina works. Am Sci 91(1):28–35

Lawton MP, Nahemow L (1973) Ecology and the aging process. In: Eisdorfer C, Lawton MP (eds) The psychology of adult development and aging. American Psychological Association, Washington

Lawton MP, Weisman GD, Sloane P, Norris-Baker C, Calkins M, Zimmerman SI (2000) Professional environmental assessment procedure for special care units for elders with dementing illness and its relationship to the therapeutic environment screening schedule. Alzheimer Dis Assoc Disord 14:28–38

Lewin K (1967) Field theory in social science: selected theoretical papers. Social Science Paperbacks, London

Dal Lieshout-van E, Snaphaan L, Bongers I (2019) Biodynamic lighting effects on the sleep pattern of people with dementia. Build Environ 150:245–253

Livingstone M (2002) Vision and art: the biology of seeing. Abrams, New York

Lynch K (1960) The image of the city. MIT Press, Cambridge

McPeek RM, Maljkovic V, Nakayama K (1999) Saccades require focal attention and are facilitated by a short-term memory system. Vis Res 39(8):1555–1566

Newacheck JS, Haegerstrom-Portnoy G, Adams AJ (1990) Predicting visual acuity from detection thresholds. Optom Vis Sci 67(3):184–191

Nini P (2006) Typography and the aging eye: typeface legibility for older viewers with vision problems. Retrieved August 30 2011 from http://www.aiga.org

O'Connor Z (2018) Environmental visual literacy: Examining the roles of color and contrast. Proceedings of the AIC2018, Interim meeting of the international color association, Margarida Gamito and Maria João Durão (Editors), AIC: Lisbon, pp 151–157

O'Connor Z (2016) Color/contrast strategies to improve environmental visual literacy, Universal Design Symposium, ANZ Viaducts Event Centre, Auckland, New Zealand

Pollock A, Fuggle L (2013) Designing for dementia: Creating a therapeutic environment. Nurs Residential Care 15(6):438–442

Rapoport A (2008) Environment-behavior studies: past, present and future. J Archit Planning Res 25(4):276–281

Rea MS, Figueiro MG (2018) Non-visual effects of colored light. In: Elliott A, Fairchild MD, Franklin A (eds) Handbook of color psychology. Cambridge University Press, Cambridge

Russell-Minda E, Jutai JW, Strong JG, Campbell KA, Gold D, Pretty L Wilmot L (2007) The legibility of typefaces for readers with low vision: a research review. J Vis Impair Blind, 402–415

Samla C (2016) Tuning the light in senior care. US Dept. of Energy, DOE SSL Healthcare Lighting webinar series

Shang H, Bishop ID (2000) Visual thresholds for detection, recognition and visual impact in landscape settings. J Envir Psychol 20(4):125–140

Swaffer K (2016) What people with dementia want from residential care homes. Aust J Dement Care, June/July

Van Dam G, Peeck J, Brinkerink M, Gorter U (1974) The isolation effect in free recall and recognition. Am J Psychol 87(3):497–504

Werner JS, Peterzell DH, Scheetz AJ (1990) Light, vision, and ageing. Optom Vis Sci 67(3):214–229

# Chapter 15
# Sharing a Virtual World with People Living with Dementia

**James Hodge and Kellie Morrissey**

## 15.1 Introduction

In recent years, Human–Computer Interaction (HCI) projects in sensitive contexts have considered how to best conduct and design research with people who might be regarded as *vulnerable* or positioned as part of marginalized communities such as people living with dementia (Waycott et al. 2015). With HCI research focused on research in *real-world* settings, researchers have responded by committing to work with *bottom-up* approaches, including experts and individuals within that community in the digital creation of tools to support participant empowerment (Olivier and Wright 2015). In this chapter, we discuss two studies working with families and individuals living with dementia. In these studies, we explored the opportunities and challenges of designing personalized media experiences that take into account an individual's history, interests, personality, desires, and their ecology of care (Ryan et al. 2009). Our first section discusses a vibrant and growing body of work in HCI that indicates a clear need for sensitivity in design for people with dementia, which concludes with a focus from cognition to an embodiment in new technologies. We then introduce a) an exploration into designing tailored Virtual Reality (VR) environments for people with dementia that places emphasis on reminiscence and b) a Research Through Design (RTD) methodology exploring media capture of meaningful experiences to support families living with dementia that questions whether approaches that rely on the person's ability to recognize or articulate past events is an appropriate activity to enhance emotional connection. We conclude this chapter by outlining directions for future research focusing on designing for recognition and

J. Hodge (✉)
Open Lab, Newcastle University, Tyne, UK
e-mail: J.Hodgel@ncl.ac.uk

K. Morrissey (✉)
University of Limerick, Limerick, Ireland
e-mail: Kellie.Morrissey@ul.ie

© Springer Nature Switzerland AG 2020

R. Brankaert and G. Kenning (eds.), *HCI and Design in the Context of Dementia*, Human–Computer Interaction Series,
https://doi.org/10.1007/978-3-030-32835-1_15

the aging body. Concluding with a reflection on our understandings of what it means to design for impact.

## 15.2 Moving Away from a Biomedical Deficit Model of Dementia

Traditional accounts of dementia often emphasize its biomedical origins (Leibing Annette 2006). Individuals living with dementia typically experience problems with language, memory, movement, and other abilities (Lindsay et al. 2012). As part of the changes that come with dementia, significant social ramifications can also cause people living with dementia's experience of the world to worsen (Hampson and Morris 2016). As dementia progresses, it often adds conflict between the person and their surroundings as they can become unfamiliar, and this can also cause difficulties with coexisting with others; this can happen in what was previously a familiar space such as a family home, a local community, or work place (Au et al. 2009; Langdon et al. 2007). Challenges within previously familiar surroundings can cause issues for the person living with dementia who may feel less able to express and explore their identity (John Killick Claire Craig 2012; Kontos 2005). As we live in a society that places a high value on cognitive ability, a diagnosis of dementia can put significant strain on meaningful interactions, relationships, and activities. Authors have argued that when a person has dementia, their cognitive dysfunction erodes our *being-in-the-world* (Hampson and Morris 2016), which adversely affects a sense of belonging and therefore, a sense of self.

Alternatively, Scheler and Merleau-Ponty (Gallagher 2010; Merleau-Ponty 1962; Spiegelberg 1965) recognized that individuals with a decline in cognitive abilities can continue to experience the world and create meaning (Hampson and Morris 2016). This view is further explored in the context of dementia by Kontos (Kontos et al. 2017; Kontos and Martin 2013) and Twigg (2013). This shift puts the body and embodied practices at the forefront of design. Given the overwhelming focus on cognitive deficits in dementia in design research to date (Lazar et al. 2017a), tasks which leverage creativity and expression can be valuable in allowing creative communication. Bauman and Murray (2014) further this notion by stating that we should consider the person as a whole, including the new experiences and skills which may come with what seem to be deficits:

> Being deaf is not automatically defined simply by loss but could also be defined by differences, and in some cases gain. (from Bauman and Murray 2014)

Bauman and Murray are addressing a social stigma of personal self-being lost within those who have cognitive/communication deficits (Bauman and Murray 2014). Murray further highlights the perspective of personhood as a shift away from the unity of sense, but toward social interactions of the person rather than their neurological changes.

## 15.3 Creativity with People Living with Dementia

Kitwood (1998) and others have followed person-centered approaches to dementia care that called attention to how we communicate with people living with dementia. Rather than questioning someone's cognitive abilities, person-centered approaches promote embodiment that brings attention to lived experiences of the body (Kontos and Martin 2013), and non-verbal communication is a key in ensuring the person living with dementia is able to experience their life to the fullest. Technology which focuses on cognitive decline, monitoring, and management may contribute to the feeling of stigmatization that can build social exclusion by depriving the person living with dementia of their personhood and changing their quality of life (Hampson and Morris 2016; Kontos et al. 2018).

However, an integral part of HCI work builds on this view for influencing the self and personhood of the person living with dementia. As a result, design has moved toward improving quality of life (Lazar et al. 2017a, b; Morrissey et al. 2016), supporting inclusion (McNaney et al. 2017; Welsh et al. 2018), evoking emotion (Wallace et al. 2012a, 2013a, b), and engagement through creativity which carefully crafts creative activities, to help foster a heightening of subjective wellbeing, maintaining skills, and providing social engagement. While many creatively oriented technologies have relied on the person's ability to recognize or articulate past events, as researchers have moved toward the inclusion of the voices of people living with dementia, recent research has similarly begun to question if reminiscence is an appropriate activity to enhance emotional connection. We discuss this in our first case study as one of the lessons learnt from designing personalized VR experiences. With designing for creativity becoming an important shift in design research (John Killick Claire Craig 2012; Morrissey et al. 2016), the potential for virtual or augmented reality environments for people living with dementia may come hand in hand with ways to experience and express creativity. Beyond the creative aspect of the technology, recent studies have begun to explore the way the benefits of the immersive quality of VR can be meditative and calming for people living with dementia (Hodge et al. 2018). While therapeutic uses offer great promises—and where it is of use in cognitive rehabilitation (Schultheis and Rizzo 2001)—more recent research has followed using immersive reality technology as an expressive and creative medium entirely separate from cognitive assessments.

This chapter presents two case studies that explore the use of VR and media experiences with people living with dementia. In our first study, we work closely with 7 participants living with dementia to design VR experiences of their choosing. Following this work, our second study worked with three families living with dementia, which explored how they could create immersive media experiences to capture moments in their lives.

## 15.4 Case Study One: Blending the Old with the New

Back in 2017, we began to look at the body of work associated with the use of virtual reality with/for people living with dementia. With consumer VR headsets quickly coming to the market, the technology was picked up by the entertainment industry, and in particular the gaming industry (Cipresso et al. 2018). With a significant focus on the recreational, it was surprising to see a focus on neurological rehabilitation when using VR technology with people living with dementia (Schultheis and Rizzo 2001). By focusing on the growing body of work that has concentrated toward evoking emotion (Olivier and Wallace 2009; Wallace et al. 2012a, 2013), and creativity through technology with people living with dementia, our study aimed to consider how VR experiences for people living with dementia might be sensitively designed to provide comfortable and enriching experiences. Working closely with a local dementia café charity known as Silverline Memories who showed interest in creating VR experiences, we recruited seven participants—three couples or family pairs where one person with living with dementia, and one older man who was attending the workshops on his own with a mild diagnosis of dementia. In this section, we discuss how we designed the VR experiences with our participants, and conclude with opportunities and drawbacks of how we conducted the research.

### *15.4.1 Designing Tailored VR Experiences*

To explore attitudes toward VR experiences with people living with dementia, we carried out workshops at a dementia café as part of the afternoon tea sessions on Mondays. Dementia Cafés are places where people living with dementia, their families, and friends can come along and be part of a supportive environment that encourages opportunities for sharing experiences. These workshops had been organized to be flexible to co-exist alongside other organized activities within the dementia café. The aim was to get to know the participant, and from getting to know one another, we would then seek to curate a set of tailored VR experiences that would be interesting for the café and its community after we had left.

With VR being relatively new to our participants, we began by introducing a simple VR *experience* which consisted of being placed in a virtual apartment as participants tried on a Google Cardboard headset. Our decision for an apartment VR experience was decided for its neutral nature; it did not give any low or high expectations for what to expect with VR technology. After participants tried the headset, we spoke about the type of places they would like to see through the VR headset. We used printouts of images to further these conversations, such as images of libraries, museums, forests, and beaches. During the first workshop, we spoke for an extended time with one couple, Thomas and Janet, where Janet was living with dementia. The couple told us about Janet's preferences for a VR environment that placed an importance on country music. From this, we decided on creating a personalized VR experience that was based on her love for Shania Twain. We also set out to design and develop environments for the dementia café. The first was a beach environment, and the second was a park that took inspiration from a local park which participants had reminisced about in the workshop. Thirdly, as briefly mentioned above, we sought to design a bespoke Shania Twain concert hall experience for Thomas and Janet.

We created all three VR environments in the Unity game engine. We carefully planned the design of our environments in terms of the field of view of the participant. We applied Mike Alger's (2015) concept of content zones that we have described in Fig. 15.1 to reduce risks of sickness or disorientation and to improve the overall experience for the individuals. At the time, designing realistic VR experiences was limited to using 360-degree cameras. As we wanted to create experiences that may not be available, such as a 360-degree Shania Twain concert, our design of the environment was based on low-poly art that not only can run on low-end hardware (a simple smartphone) but which also provides a very stylized and abstract view of the *reality*.

From the data collected from our first workshop, we created sketches based on the ideas and desires that individuals expressed. While we were unable to develop each participant an individual experience, some ideas had been combined into one environment. For example, one participant asked for us to 'take [her] back to Ireland, to see the beautiful castles again'. While we could not do that, we did create 3D designs of a traditional castle from Irish medieval architecture. We placed it in the park environment that many of the participants expressed interest in (see Fig. 15.2).

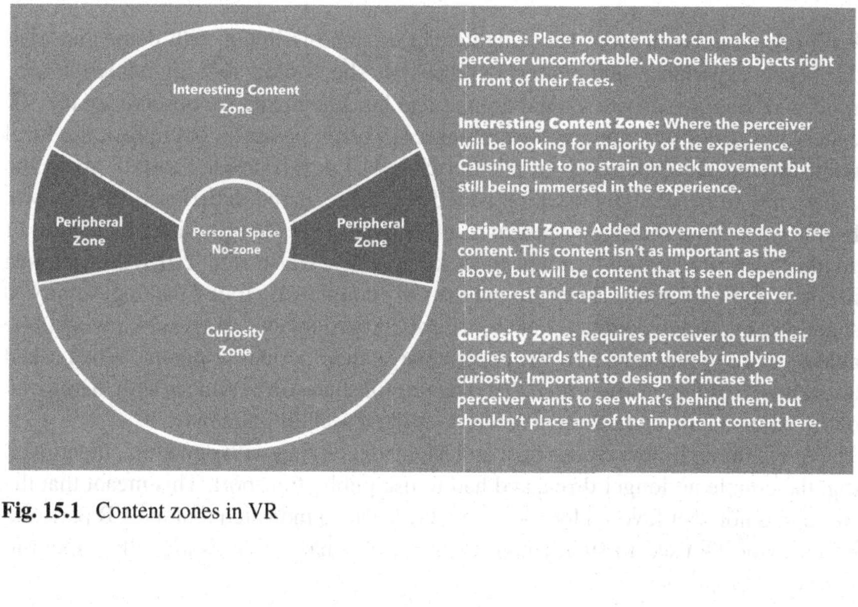


**Fig. 15.1** Content zones in VR

**Fig. 15.2** Park environment including an Irish castle

In our second workshop, we returned to the dementia café to try out our three different environments focused on the group at large: the beach with a horse running along the sand and a park based on the local park nearby. Both environments were completed with spatial audio captured from the locations the environments were based.

## *15.4.2 Lighthouse, Rocks, Sand, Sea, Boat!*

With encouragement from her daughter, Lucy, who is living with dementia, tried the beach experience and started listing what she could see—*'lighthouse, rocks, sand, sea, boat!'*—as she rotated around and became the active observer in the VR experience. Lucy was not a passive observer in her experience, but in fact, the focal point driving the experience in all its richness. Lucy continued to talk about the experience to her daughter, which added toward a shared experience for the two. In this way, the technology acted as a novel experience that provided an excuse or conduit for conversation—similar to 'ticket to talk' (Welsh et al. 2018) as discussed in Chap. 4 (Foley 2020). They are not the only couple who found the opportunity to share meaningful experiences. Many, if not all participants, expressed a wish to be able to share in the same *live* VR experience as their partner or parent. When asked about this, participants indicated that meaningful shared experiences with their loved one with dementia had changed recently or decreased in frequency.

For example, Linda, whose husband Michael is living with dementia, mentioned that the couple no longer drove and had to use public transport. This meant that the two could not visit favored locations together, and so indicated that the VR park and beach could be used to supplement their recreational activities and allow them to experience a semblance of the sorts of activities which used to mean very much to them. Having the carers experience the environment first allowed carers to help direct their loved one around the environment by being able to probe specific interactions in the environment that the person living with dementia may have missed. For example, one carer started asking questions around what they could see or if they saw the horse walk past on the beach. In addition to this kind of shared experience would be an external screen that displays the same view as the headset. Recently, with the increased interest of Facebook on VR headsets, with the Oculus series, being able to stream your headsets display to your phone is significantly more accessible than it was in 2017. A suggested interaction toward VR shared experiences would be for carers to be able to interact with the VR environments through their external display alongside the person living with dementia driving the experience from the VR headset. However, when designing aspects of training or testing into VR environments, they should be separate from those environments that aim to be recreational. To implement aspects of training or testing into these environments would mean returning to a medicalized view of the person with dementia as a set of deficits, rather than a fully realized person with needs and desires (Hodge et al. 2018).

### *15.4.3 Reflections and Outcomes*

From our initial workshops two years ago, our research into VR has continued to bring up themes and conversations around feeling isolated or the fear of looking *silly*. This tendency of feeling silly in VR is relatively common across many who have tried VR. While this is not focused purely on dementia, a diagnosis of dementia can heighten these feelings as dementia progresses. Nolan et al. (2006) reported examples of people living with dementia feeling embarrassment and shame if others became aware of their dementia. Nolan expands further that stigma and embarrassment become further apparent in fear of people *witnessing 'inappropriate behavior in public'*. With VR being isolating and looking *silly*, it is not surprising that we had participants feeling uncertain about taking part in activities, as a way to protect their dignity. Beyond the remarks of VR headsets looking silly, participants expressed concerns of comfortability and weight. In 2017, we used a Google Cardboard headset which is not comfortable, but many preferred to use this as it was lightweight and was comfortable to hold. Two years later, we have seen massive strides toward comfortable and attractive headsets, especially ones that do not require wires that connect to a computer. However, they remain moderately on the heavier side, and while attractive, they can tend to look remarkably futuristic and off-putting. Future designs could benefit from thinking about how headsets could fit into spaces and look normal—e.g., by embedding the display into a set of binoculars or a spectacle with a handle.

For the participants, VR was a novelty and technology they had not had the opportunity to experience. While the concerns above had participants reluctant to try the VR experiences, their view of the technology changed after they tried it.

In particular, our personalized design of the Shania Twain concert hall for Janet and Thomas had some initial concerns with Janet having '*the patience to hold the [headset] for a long time*'. As we set the VR experience up and handed it to Janet, Thomas initially aided her in holding the VR headset:

> Straight away [Janet] started to sing. She was singing to the tune and attempted to repeat the lyrics... [and] changed her body language completely. It went from rather static, to movements that captured the tempo of the music. Janet held up her hands to try to hold the Google Cardboard as well, which indicated she didn't want to stop the experience. [Afterwards], she seemed very happy and just from being around her, you could see her mood had changed completely. (Hodge et al. 2018)

While Janet's experience was heightened by her ability to recall the Shania Twain song, she got to experience it in a completely new way. While her verbal abilities are limited, other means of communicating became apparent. Janet's interests, body movement, and overall socialness in the café significantly changed after experiencing the concert hall. The bespoke design that placed Janet at the forefront of the design, and who could drive the experience, has a freeing effect that is pleasurable for participants who can engage in enjoying activities; lately, reflecting on the experience, Thomas mentions that Janet has '*always sang and whistled. She can sing along to songs as long as she remembers the words. The aesthetic of the theatre was a great idea and gave a great sense of space*'.

While we speak positively about the use of VR in this case study, it does not go without saying that this was trialed with a smaller group of participants. Similar to other research that places the participant at the forefront of the experience or is otherwise participatory in nature, this research did not seek to achieve clinical outcomes. Our experiences can be enjoyed by anyone and are not made necessarily for people living with dementia: by designing with people living with dementia, we can move toward design approaches that are more inclusive and move toward technology that does not stigmatize. Likely, Janet's enjoyment of the Shania Twain concert was not merely the use of the virtual reality technology; it was because we designed for her desires and choices. She wanted a Shania Twain concert, and that is what she experienced. In this context of research, we are designing for people—not focused on perceived cognitive deficits, but rather toward their present, ready to make use of a full spectrum of interactivity—including non-verbal communication and bodily movement.

## 15.5 Case Study Two: Media Capture of Meaningful Experiences

A key finding from our work above was that the environments provided a familiar experience that encouraged shared experiences with their loved ones. Motivated by previous findings, our next study explored the role of rich, personalized media experiences as a support for families living with dementia. Taking account of the ecology of care of the person living with dementia, which considers the person living with dementia, friends, and family, the experiences we created needed to be meaningful to the family—not just the person living with dementia. While prior work, including our own, have leveraged techniques such as reminiscence, we believe in some instances that this can limit the active participation of the person living with dementia in these design processes. While reminiscence can provide opportunities for engagement (Gowans et al. 2004; Yasuda et al. 2009), for some, it may merely be non-engaging or cause frustration when not being able to remember a specific memory from their past (Lazar et al. 2014). Another notable concern the first author had was lack of recognition and co-design from the first study. Researching under a culture of ethical 'protectionism' caused significant tension about formally acknowledging our participants as co-creators. While case study two was limited with anonymization of names for the research, there was flexibility to use the participant's faces and images as captured in the study. With the families wanting their photos to be used and not to be blurred, we sought to recognize and acknowledge participants as individuals who have contributed to the research and to ensure that their knowledge, experiences, and time are shared.

In this case study, we carried out a Research Through Design (RTD) methodology. Our study aimed to explore the opportunities and challenges of designing personalized multimedia experiences with people living with dementia and their families. The previous research focused on the concept of reminiscence, with the researchers developing the environments after the workshops. In this second study, the experiences of being in the moment are most important, and we aimed for the families to capture and 'design' the experiences themselves using 360-degree cameras. We worked with three families: two married couples, both with a wife living with dementia, and where the husbands had formed a close relationship through attending a support group. Our third family was a family of four, where the father was living with dementia. Similar to the work above, we worked closely with Silverline Memories Dementia Café. The families took part in day trips, which they co-planned, with data collection duration during these days providing insights into their shared social experiences. Following this, workshops were also held to personalize the experience of media created during these days out. Finally, our themes focused on individuality, relationships, and accepted changed realities.

### 15.5.1 *Designing* in the Moment *Experiences*

Working with Silverline Memories Dementia Café allowed this study to develop in two key ways. First, the way we design research with people living with dementia. Traditionally, individuals living with dementia typically experience deficits in memory, language, and other abilities (Bartlett and O'Connor 2007). Due to this, traditional research methods such as interviews are not appropriate or useful ways to gain insights into people's lives and experiences (Kontos and Naglie 2007; P. Kontos and Martin 2013). For this study, we were influenced by Silverline Memories, which prides itself on supporting its members (and families) with meaningful outings and day trips to engaging and stimulating locations. Our co-designed days out with the families was a way for us to bridge the gap in how we can engage in a more meaningful way through getting to know the history, personalities, and interests of each person in their ecology of care. Second, in working with the charity, we also followed their philosophy of living in the moment—'*[if] the present is all that person has, [then] that is their reality*'.

### *15.5.2 Days Out*

To begin conversations with families about participating in the project, we met families at one of the Silverline Memories days out. We used this as an opportunity to get to know the families, explain the research and purpose of it. For the families who were engaged in caretaking, we offered them a week to consider the type of location that held significance and value to them or a desirable destination for a future family outing. Four of our participants—The Fabulous Four—were John, Sarah, Lauren, Michael (see Fig. 15.3). Our first day out included both couples. The families had formed a close relationship over the last year from going to the same dementia-friendly community events. The two families decided on a **National Trust Site** north of Newcastle as this was a place that Michael and Lauren had become fond of over the past decade.

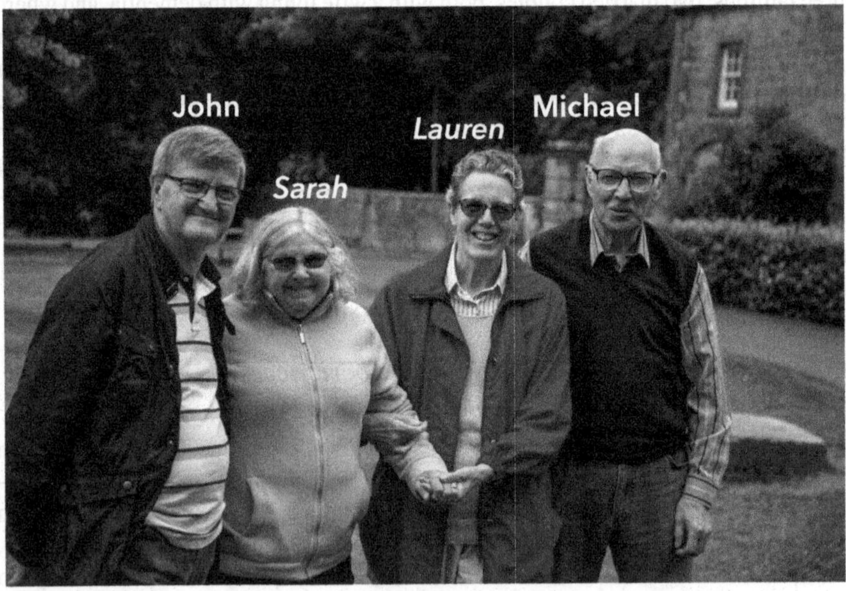


**Fig. 15.3** Anderson and Beckett family

**Fig. 15.4** Collection of pictures from their day out

The family directed our day out to capture moments that they would like to experience again through personalized media. These moments would be captured using photography, audio-recordings, as well as more contemporary technologies such as 360-degree video cameras. On the day out, researchers spent time with the family as more than just observers. They would take part in activities set out by the families, engage in conversations and help with capturing specific moments the families wanted throughout the day. The day out captured insights into each family's history, the families' care for the person with dementia, and meaningful interactions between the family members (Fig. 15.4).

Having captured a wide variety of content on the days out, we wanted to create ideas of how this content could be personalized and be used by the families. We invited families, designers, and dementia experts to individual family workshops to consolidate the personalization and to store the created moments from their days out. In the workshop, we shared pictures and VR videos to give each participant a perspective of the day out and to see the digital moments that the families had co-created. To structure this discussion of unfamiliar technological interactions, participants used a toolkit that consisted of cards and activities based on the interactions with the families before the workshop. The toolkit aimed to generate ideas and conceptualize technology interventions based on their past. Through our analysis of the data collected from the days out, and the workshops, we offer considerations that designers should consider when designing media experiences when working with people living dementia and their ecologies of care.

## 15.6 Future Directions for Designing Media Experiences

From this work, we offer two novel contributions: 1. a new model of practice for creating personalized media experiences for marginalized participants or those with special needs and 2. a series of future directions focusing on conflicting realities as dementia progresses, extended ecologies of personhood, and the aging body in immersive media. We will focus on contribution 2. for the remainder of this chapter.

### 15.6.1 Designing for Contested Realities

During our days out, it became apparent that the person living with dementia may slip in and out of realities which could then be contested by those around them, who may struggle with these conflicting accounts of reality. In particular, with one of the families we worked with, Michael would struggle to orient his wife, Lauren, to reality. Michael shared a story about how he struggled with always telling Lauren that her mother would not be coming over to see her, as she had passed away many years ago. Orienting the person living with dementia toward what we see as the *right* reality has minimal effect. The topic of lying or being deceptive is unsurprisingly controversial, but the use of therapeutic lying is somewhat questioned in what context it is being used (Casey et al. 2019; Elvish et al. 2010; Lorey 2019). Some researchers suggest that by lying, there becomes a sense of dishonesty, and once this occurs, trust is broken, which significantly moves away from person-centered approaches. While it is easy for researchers to engage in these types of moral debates, we are not usually the ones dealing with the challenging situations in care. Lying or the use of deception will continue to be a controversial topic, but when considering the use of deception, it comes entirely down to the situatedness of the moment. One must consider if the *truth* is the right or if it creates new grief for those involved. As researchers in the field, it is imperative to remember that a sense of self can come from more just an ability to recall and recount memories. Working with people living with dementia, we should reflect on what it means to design for this often-dreamlike state, depending on the stage of dementia. With this in mind, we should consider what it means to create media experiences for realities which may eclipse each other briefly rather than conflict with each other entirely (Hodge et al. 2019).

### 15.6.2 Every Person Has Personhood

In our second study, we aimed to design our media with not only the person living with dementia but to include their family members and friends. Traditionally studies often separate carers and people living with dementia as previous work expected different needs from one another. When carers are designed for/with, technologies typically have a focus on duties of care with direction toward assistive technology (Bennett et al. 2017; Bharucha et al. 2009; Gibson et al. 2015). Spending time with the ecology of care, and with a focus on memorable and pleasurable activities, the overall technology or activity tends to include a variety of interests and interactions that the ecology of care desire. *With many carers reporting high levels of burnout and burden, targeting carers as research participants worthy of digital interventions focusing on personhood (as much as we target those with dementia) means treating them with respect, and as whole persons, rather than defining them by their roles* (Hodge et al. 2019).

### *15.6.3 The Aging Body and Immersion*

As mentioned in previous literature and in particular, Nolan et al. work on stigma, people living with dementia have reported a feeling of lack of confidence when going out. As we age, our cognitive abilities are likely to change, similar to Janet, who communicated bodily when experiencing the Shania Twain concert (Hodge et al. 2018). Researchers in dementia, such as Kontos (2018; Kontos and Naglie 2007; Kontos and Martin 2013) and Twigg (Twigg and Buse 2013), describe interactions of participants less from the perspective of verbal communication, but toward their embodied potential. For instance, people in nursing homes being able to choose to dress in certain ways, getting their hair done, exploring the use of dance to improve social inclusion. Creating opportunities for a variety of way of communicating one's self, *we start to consider how we may represent aging bodies in respectful ways which represent their personhood and individuality* (Hodge et al. 2019). Engaging in this area of research, researchers must recognize the limitations of their way of communicating. We, therefore, must consider through co-design approaches, how participants may want to engage, and if this moves away from verbally, how can we design for communication through other means such as the body.

## 15.7 Conclusion

We have come a long way, and we have a long way to go. Over the past three years, our work has indicated tensions that arise in working within sensitive settings. As our work moved toward appreciating the importance of *being in the moment* in dementia care, it became apparent that the initial starting point of using virtual reality was not the critical part of the research. We have added guidance into designing media and VR experiences in this chapter. However, these future directions are guided toward designing for an individual, and not for a diagnosis for dementia. A collective contribution from the last 20 years of research around dementia is that someone living with dementia can still experience meaningful interactions, relationships, and activities at almost all stages of the condition (Kitwood 1998). But with over-protection, stigmatization, and emphasizing people's lack of ability, many believe that people living with dementia are poor at social contact, which can then prohibit many from interacting with people living with dementia (Christine Bryden 2005; Riley et al. 2014). We all interact with the world differently. We communicate, experience, integrate ourselves differently from one another. Through relationships and learning from one another, we can move toward a more inclusive relationship and understanding of how our neighbors and communities can create meaning in their day-to-day experiences—regardless of their diagnosis.

Although as researchers in the field, we may understand that every *person has personhood*, this does not always seem apparent in the real world. Our next steps are to consider what it means to be an inclusive society, what it means to do inclusive research and to question the infrastructures that surround and often hold up our work. For instance, as researchers, how can we ensure ethical review boards are reflexive and dynamic when they are evaluating research that seeks to design in *sensitive* settings? Our two case studies stress that we should take a more empathetic approach to our work which is echoed by others working in the field (Foley et al. 2019a, b; Lazar et al. 2017a; Morrissey et al. 2016; Wallace et al. 2012b, 2013; Welsh et al. 2018). To build upon the consensus of designing ***with*** people living with dementia, as researchers, we should aim to consider how we engage with the community from the very start of the research. In terms of those working in dementia, we should be engaging with advocates outside of HCI, such as organizations similar to Dementia Enquirers (*Dementia Enquirers—DEEP*, s. d.). Working with organizations similar to this can help to ensure that research agendas are more closely aligned with the needs of the population, thus moving toward a more inclusive approach to design and society. Ensuring our research designs are rooted in participant-led agendas can contribute to ethically engaged research impact.

Finally, when we consider our impact, it is important to note that technology offers opportunities for meaningful engagement as well as create challenges relating to robustness and longevity when the project ends. Typical strategies to overcome these challenges could be to ensure a longer lifespan and technology support if anything goes wrong. Alternatively, we can aim for technology to become a part of a community and create meaningful relationships with our participant groups and research ecologies. This pertains to participatory and community-based research, personalization, recognition, and meaning. In this way, it is clear that technology alone does not hold any value; it is the relationships and experiences it creates and mediates.

## References

Alger M (2015) Visual design methods for virtual reality. Personal Website, September, 98

Au A, Lai M-K, Lau K-M, Pan P-C, Lam L, Thompson L, Gallagher-Thompson D (2009) Social support and well-being in dementia family caregivers: the mediating role of self-efficacy. Aging Ment Health 13(5):761–768. https://doi.org/10.1080/13607860902918223

Bartlett R, O'Connor D (2007) From personhood to citizenship: broadening the lens for dementia practice and research. J Aging Stud 21(2):107–118. https://doi.org/10.1016/j.jaging.2006.09.002

Bauman L, Murray J (2014) Deaf gain: raising the stakes for human diversity. University of Minnesota Press

Bennett B, McDonald F, Beattie E, Carney T, Freckelton I, White B, Willmott L (2017) Assistive technologies for people with dementia: ethical considerations. Bull World Health Organ 95(11):749–755. https://doi.org/10.2471/BLT.16.187484

Bharucha AJ, Anand V, Forlizzi J, Dew MA, Reynolds CF, Stevens S, Wactlar H (2009) Intelligent assistive technology applications to dementia care: current capabilities, limitations, and future challenges. Am J Geriatr Psychiatry, 17(2):88–104. https://doi.org/10.1097/JGP.0b013e318187dde5

Casey D, Lynch U, Murphy K, Cooney A, Gannon M, Houghton C, Hunter A, Jordan F, Smyth S, Felzman H, Meskell P (2019) Telling a 'good or white lie': the views of people living with dementia and their carers. Dementia, 147130121983152. https://doi.org/10.1177/1471301219831525

Christine Bryden (2005) Dancing with dementia: my story of living positively with dementia. Jessica Kingsley Publishers, London, United Kingdom

Cipresso P, Giglioli IAC, Raya MA, Riva G (2018) The past, present, and future of virtual and augmented reality research: a network and cluster analysis of the literature. Frontiers Psychol, 9. https://doi.org/10.3389/fpsyg.2018.02086

Dementia Enquirers—DEEP (s. d.) Consulté 17 novembre 2019, à l'adresse. https://www.dementiavoices.org.uk/dementia-enquirers/

Elvish R, James I, Milne D (2010) Lying in dementia care: an example of a culture that deceives in people's best interests. Aging Ment Health 14(3):255–262. https://doi.org/10.1080/13607861003587610

Foley S, Pantidi N, McCarthy J (2019) Care and design. In: Proceedings of the 2019 CHI conference on human factors in computing systems—CHI '19, pp 1–15. https://doi.org/10.1145/3290605.3300840

Foley S, Welsh D, Pantidi N, Morrissey K, Nappey T, McCarthy J (2019) Printer pals. Proceedings of the 2019 CHI conference on human factors in computing systems—CHI '19, 1–13. https://doi.org/10.1145/3290605.3300634

Gallagher S (2010) Merleau-Ponty's phenomenology of perception. Topoi 29(2):183–185. https://doi.org/10.1007/s11245-010-9079-y

Gibson G, Dickinson C, Brittain K, Robinson L (2015) The everyday use of assistive technology by people with dementia and their family carers: a qualitative study. BMC Geriatr 15(1):89. https://doi.org/10.1186/s12877-015-0091-3

Gowans G, Campbell J, Alm N, Dye R, Astell A, Ellis M (2004) Designing a multimedia conversation aid for reminiscence therapy in dementia care environments. In: Extended abstracts of the 2004 conference on human factors and computing systems—CHI '04, p 825. https://doi.org/10.1145/985921.985943

Hampson C, Morris K (2016) Dementia: sustaining self in the face of cognitive decline. Geriatrics 1(4):25. https://doi.org/10.3390/geriatrics1040025

Hodge J, Balaam M, Hastings S, Morrissey K (2018) Exploring the design of tailored virtual reality experiences for people with dementia. Proceedings of the 2018 CHI conference on human factors in computing systems—CHI '18, 1–13. https://doi.org/10.1145/3173574.3174088

Hodge J, Montague K, Hastings S, Morrissey K (2019) Exploring media capture of meaningful experiences to support families living with dementia. In: Proceedings of the 2019 CHI conference on human factors in computing sys*tems*—CHI '19, pp 1–14. https://doi.org/10.1145/3290605.3300653

John Killick Claire Craig (2012). Creativity and communication in persons with dementia: a practical guide. Jessica Kingsley, London, UK

Kitwood, T. (1998). Toward a theory of dementia care: ethics and interaction. J Clin Ethics 9(1):23–34

Kontos PC (2005) Embodied selfhood in Alzheimer's disease. Dementia 4(4):553–570. https://doi.org/10.1177/1471301205058311

Kontos PC, Naglie G (2007) Expressions of personhood in alzheimer's disease: an evaluation of research-based theatre as a pedagogical tool. Qual Health Res 17(6):799–811. https://doi.org/10.1177/1049732307302838

Kontos P, Grigorovich A, Dupuis S, Jonas-Simpson C, Mitchell G, Gray J (2018) Raising the curtain on stigma associated with dementia: fostering a new cultural imaginary for a more inclusive society. Critical public health 30:1–12. https://doi.org/10.1080/09581596.2018.1508822

Kontos P, Martin W (2013) Embodiment and dementia: Exploring critical narratives of selfhood, surveillance, and dementia care. Dementia 12(3):288–302. https://doi.org/10.1177/1471301213479787

Kontos P, Miller K-L, Kontos AP (2017) Relational citizenship: supporting embodied selfhood and relationality in dementia care. Sociol Health Illn 39(2):182–198. https://doi.org/10.1111/1467-9566.12453

Langdon SA, Eagle A, Warner J (2007) Making sense of dementia in the social world: a qualitative study. Soc Sci Med 64(4):989–1000. https://doi.org/10.1016/j.socscimed.2006.10.029

Lazar A, Edasis C, Piper AM (2017a) A critical lens on dementia and design in HCI. In: Proceedings of the 2017 CHI conference on human factors in computing systems—CHI '17, pp 2175–2188. https://doi.org/10.1145/3025453.3025522

Lazar A, Edasis C, Piper AM (2017b) Supporting people with dementia in digital social sharing. In: Proceedings of the 2017 CHI conference on human factors in computing systems—CHI '17, pp 2149–2162. https://doi.org/10.1145/3025453.3025586

Lazar A, Thompson H, Demiris G (2014) A systematic review of the use of technology for reminiscence therapy. Health Educ Behav, 41(1_suppl):51S–61S. https://doi.org/10.1177/1090198114537067

Leibing Annette LC (2006) Thinking about dementia: culture, loss, and the anthropology of senility. Rutgers University Press, New Jersey, US

Lindsay S, Brittain K, Jackson D, Ladha C, Ladha K, Olivier P (2012) Empathy, participatory design and people with dementia. In: Proceedings of the 2012 ACM annual conference on human factors in computing systems—CHI '12, p 521. https://doi.org/10.1145/2207676.2207749

Lorey P (2019) Fake bus stops for persons with dementia? On truth and benevolent lies in public health. Isr J Health Policy Res 8(1):28. https://doi.org/10.1186/s13584-019-0301-0

McNaney R, Vines J, Mercer J, Mexter L, Welsh D, Young T (2017) DemYouth. In: Proceedings of the 2017 CHI conference on human factors in computing systems—CHI '17, pp 1313–1325. https://doi.org/10.1145/3025453.3025558

Merleau-Ponty M (1962) Phenomenology of perception. Éditions Gallimard, Routledge

Morrissey K, Wood G, Green D, Pantidi N, McCarthy J (2016) I'm a rambler, I'm a gambler, I'm a long way from home. In: Proceedings of the 2016 ACM conference on designing interactive systems—DIS '16, pp 1008–1020. https://doi.org/10.1145/2901790.2901798

Nolan L, McCarron M, McCallion P, Murphy-Lawless J (2006) Perceptions of stigma in dementia: an exploratory study item type report perceptions of stigma in dementia: an exploratory study the school of nursing and midwifery trinity college Dublin. Alzheimer Society Of Ireland, Dublin, Ireland

Olivier P, Wallace J (2009) Digital technologies and the emotional family. Int J Human Comput Stud 67(2):204–214. https://doi.org/10.1016/j.ijhcs.2008.09.009

Olivier P, Wright P (2015) Digital civics. Interactions 22(4):61–63. https://doi.org/10.1145/2776885

Riley RJ, Burgener S, Buckwalter KC (2014) Anxiety and stigma in dementia. Nurs Clin North Am 49(2):213–231. https://doi.org/10.1016/j.cnur.2014.02.008

Ryan EB, Bannister KA, Anas AP (2009) The dementia narrative: writing to reclaim social identity. J Aging Stud 23(3):145–157. https://doi.org/10.1016/j.jaging.2007.12.018

Schultheis MT, Rizzo AA (2001) The application of virtual reality technology in rehabilitation. Rehabil Psychol 46(3):296–311. https://doi.org/10.1037/0090-5550.46.3.296

Spiegelberg H (1965) The phenomenology of essences: max scheler (1874–1928). In: The Phenomenological movement. Springer Netherlands, pp 228–270. https://doi.org/10.1007/978-94-015-7394-8_6

Twigg J, Buse CE (2013) Dress, dementia and the embodiment of identity. Dementia 12(3):326–336. https://doi.org/10.1177/1471301213476504

Wallace J, McCarthy J, Wright PC, Olivier P (2013) Making design probes work. In: Proceedings of the SIGCHI conference on human factors in computing systems—CHI '13, p 3441. https://doi.org/10.1145/2470654.2466473

Wallace J, Thieme A, Wood G, Schofield G, Olivier P (2012a) Enabling self, intimacy and a sense of home in dementia. In: Proceedings of the 2012 ACM annual conference on human factors in computing systems—CHI '12, p 2629. https://doi.org/10.1145/2207676.2208654

Wallace J, Thieme A, Wood G, Schofield G, Olivier P (2012b) Enabling self, intimacy and a sense of home in dementia. In: Proceedings of the 2012 ACM annual conference on human factors in computing systems—CHI '12, p 2629. https://doi.org/10.1145/2207676.2208654
Wallace J, Wright PC, McCarthy J, Green DP, Thomas J, Olivier P (2013) A design-led inquiry into personhood in dementia. In: Proceedings of the SIGCHI conference on human factors in computing systems—CHI '13, p 2617. https://doi.org/10.1145/2470654.2481363
Waycott J, Wadley G, Schutt S, Stabolidis A, Lederman R (2015) The challenge of technology research in sensitive settings. In: Proceedings of the annual meeting of the Australian special interest group for computer human interaction on—OzCHI '15, pp 240–249. https://doi.org/10.1145/2838739.2838773
Welsh D, Morrissey K, Foley S, McNaney R, Salis C, McCarthy J, Vines J (2018) Ticket to talk. In: Proceedings of the 2018 CHI conference on human factors in computing systems—CHI '18, pp 1–14. https://doi.org/10.1145/3173574.3173949
Yasuda K, Kuwabara K, Kuwahara N, Abe S, Tetsutani N (2009) Effectiveness of personalised reminiscence photo videos for individuals with dementia. Neuropsychol Rehabil 19(4):603–619. https://doi.org/10.1080/09602010802586216

# Chapter 16
# Bridging the Gap: Design for Intergenerational Engagement in Dementia Care

**Sarah Foley and Daniel Welsh**

## 16.1 Introduction: Intergenerational Design and Technology

While the increasing access to media has resulted in hyper-personalised content consumption, it has also led to more isolated interactions with technology. For people with dementia, who are at risk for social isolation and stigma, the need to engage socially is paramount to both quality of life and access to meaningful media, which has the potential to enrich social engagement with those invested in their care. Expanding the role younger people can play in the dementia care ecology has the potential to greatly enrich the lives of people living with dementia (Gawande 2014). In the past, these two groups have been seen as separate or two populations considered 'vulnerable' in research processes and therefore avoided. In our experience supporting these two groups in design processes can lead to mutually engaging interactions, which are mediated and supported by technologies (Welsh et al. 2018). The need to support all participants through this process requires careful consideration. In this chapter, we discuss two case studies, which involved designing for intergenerational engagement between younger people and people with dementia. We first discuss the existing literature in HCI which examines the role of experience in design and the potential of HCI research to counteract stigma through supporting intergenerational engagement. We then introduce Ticket to Talk and Printer Pals, describing their design and evaluation, and their role in mediating meaningful interactions between younger people and people with dementia. Finally, we discuss the

S. Foley (✉)
University College Cork, Cork, Ireland
e-mail: Sarah.Foley@ucc.ie

D. Welsh
Open Lab, Newcastle University, Newcastle, UK

© Springer Nature Switzerland AG 2020

R. Brankaert and G. Kenning (eds.), *HCI and Design in the Context of Dementia*, Human–Computer Interaction Series,
https://doi.org/10.1007/978-3-030-32835-1_16

implications of design in widening the dementia ecology of care and the role of technologies in bringing people together, in a return to more traditional forms of socially oriented media consumption.

## 16.2 Background and Related Literature

The experience of living with dementia is associated with changes in cognitive function, often resulting in a number of social consequences such as isolation and stigmatisation (Cowdell 2010; Mitchell et al. 2009; O'rourke et al. 2015). These changes may include transitioning into residential care, increased reliance on others for physical care and general confusion and worry. The compound result of these changes can lead to decreased opportunities for active participation and contribution in their social circles. This lack of opportunity to actively engage socially is viewed as a key contributor to the reported 'loss of self' experienced by people with dementia (Nyqvist et al. 2013; Theurer et al. 2015).

When research does not include people affected by dementia, it can lead to results that offer a skewed understanding of the varied experience of dementia (Swaffer 2014). Similarly, a lack of inclusion of people with dementia in research has resulted in a skewed understanding of the varied experience of dementia. Research within HCI, and more generally, has traditionally responded to dementia and ageing as a deficit, viewing older people as uninterested, afraid of and incapable of using technology (Lazar et al. 2017; Vines et al. 2015). In their review of discourse used to describe older users in the HCI literature, Vines et al. capture the negative positioning of the user group:

> In much of the data that embodies the deficit discourse of ageing, researchers talk of how older people are 'slower' at completing tasks, have 'very obvious' signs of difficulty mastering certain tasks, and are less accurate than younger people. Furthermore, familiarity with technology is also a potential deficit for older people—particularly as technology becomes an increasingly important feature of everyday life. (p. 15) (Vines et al. 2015).

Within design, people with dementia have typically been positioned as passive users in need of monitoring, assistance and management (Cruz-Sandoval et al. 2018; Kamada et al. 2017; Mulvenna et al. 2010). However, we have recently seen a shift in HCI and design research which focused on the experience (McCarthy and Wright 2007; Morrissey et al. 2017) and the role of technology and design in enriching the interpersonal and social experiences of people with dementia (Foley et al. 2019a; Kenning and Treadaway 2018; Welsh et al. 2018). In order to further support and enrich the social lives of people with dementia, our work has focused on intergenerational design processes and highlighted the role of younger people in the dementia ecology of care.

Supporting young people and people with dementia to engage socially has many potential benefits, particularly within the field of HCI. While much work has been done on the carer/cared-for relationship, younger people are somewhat on the outskirts of the dementia ecology of care, but as highlighted by McNaney et al. (2017)

are often willing and are important figures in the lives of people with dementia and may offer an important outlet to create more inclusive environments and break down the stigma around dementia. As early career researchers, our intergenerational approach was two-fold. Not only was the focus of our research trying to support intergenerational processes, but we were also navigating the generation gap ourselves, something which came to be a key strength of our research. In the following section, we present two case studies we have designed with a view to supporting intergenerational engagement.

## 16.3 Case Study One: Ticket to Talk

An example of one of the technologies we have developed to stimulate intergenerational interaction is Ticket to Talk (Welsh et al. 2018). This is a co-designed mobile application that gives younger people conversation topics to use with their older relative living with dementia through photos, sounds and videos related to their relative's life. This technology comes from co-design workshops exploring young people's experience of dementia care. Design concepts were developed addressing some of their issues regarding dementia care. One of the major themes discussed by young people was that despite having a strong desire to engage in positive social interactions with relatives who have dementia, a perceived generational gap created difficulties in initiating and maintaining conversations. These workshops began to explore how a curated set of assorted media can form conversational 'ins', allowing younger family members to engage with an older relative with dementia (McNaney et al. 2017). The Ticket to Talk idea was then developed into a mobile application in collaboration with young people from a local youth charity, utilising different media formats and portability of mobile devices.

### *16.3.1 Implementation*

The final iteration of Ticket to Talk offers young people the chance to create personalised talking points around a curated set of personalised media such as photos, videos and songs. Younger people are asked to create a simple profile of their older relative. This profile contains an optional photo of the relative, basic biographical information, and a description of their condition. The young person can then invite other people (i.e. family, friends or carers) to contribute to this profile, giving them access to the tickets they will create, but also allowing the rest of the care circle to upload theirs (Fig. 16.1).

After creating a profile of their relative, young people can upload media that they think might make an interesting conversational 'in'. However, this poses the same problem the younger person faces during a conversation of not knowing what a good 'in' might be. Ticket to Talk scaffolds this with its inspiration feature. The application

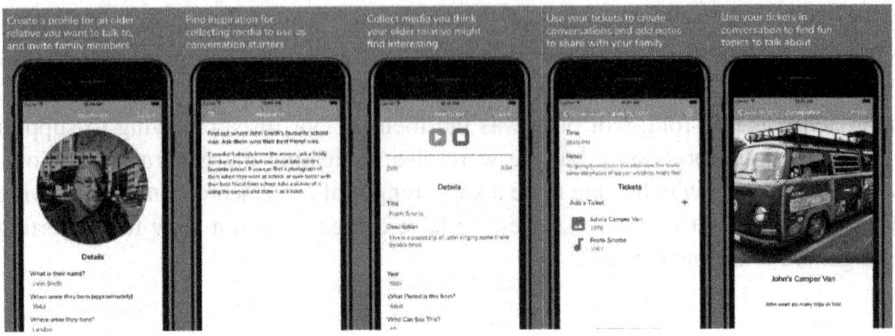


**Fig. 16.1** Ticket to talk application

contains a list of generic prompts, which are personalised from their older relative's profile. Inspiration prompts typically invite the young person to research the life history of their older relative, and to create media associated with major life events in their older relative's history. For example, "Steven was 18 in 1940, can you find a picture of London at that time?"; and "Stephen was 25 in 1947, try and find out the number 1 news story for that year." The events featured in the inspiration's aim to explore memorable experiences, occurring mainly during early adulthood. This capitalises on the effect of the 'reminiscence bump' in the older relative (McKeown et al. 2010), focussing on big events such as marriage and building a household.

Ticket to Talk also aims to encourage preparation and reflection on conversations with older relatives living with dementia. To facilitate this, younger people can create a collection of tickets, called a 'conversation' within the app, which mimics a music playlist. They can also add a description, a time and notes to this conversation. This allows the younger person to prepare tickets and already have an idea of conversational 'ins' before the conversation begins, allowing them to bridge conversational gaps even without the application in some cases. Once a conversation has finished, users can log their reflections and share this to their relative's wider care ecology to give advice on fruitful or ineffective topics. These conversations are shared between all those who contribute to a person with dementia's profile, allowing for the older relative's children to make conversations for their grandchildren or family members to make conversations for care workers. In comparison to more traditional forms of displaying meaningful media, such as Life Story Books, the app allowed for continued development of content, encouraging new intergenerational engagement.

### *16.3.2 Use of Ticket to Talk*

This application was evaluated in a number of different environments, firstly within families as the application was originally intended for, but also between younger people and people living in residential care with dementia to determine its efficacy in the wider dementia care ecology. Given the diversity of its deployment environments there were many different use cases for Ticket to Talk. There were some common themes across these environments; however, one of the most prominent being the redistribution of agency in social settings including a person living with dementia. This came from Ticket to Talk being used as a tool to preserve the experiences of the older relative living with dementia, meaning that in social situations people with dementia were positioned as the leaders in conversation, where other interlocutors would prompt the person living with dementia and aid them in sharing a story. In some families this story was immediately recorded, whereas others used tickets to encourage their older relative to share a story they had already heard.

This use of Ticket to Talk naturally influenced the media used to stimulate conversation. Media was often centred around the past, mirroring a record of their older relatives' memories and life. In a critique of Ticket to Talk with older people who have an interest in dementia, they noted how the use of future facing tickets might be more engaging than ones centred around the past, encouraging the older relative to take more of an interest in the younger person's current engagements. One issue with relying solely on tickets orientated towards the past is it invites comparison between the past and current selves of the person living with dementia. It may give the view to the younger person that there is a degradation in self when comparing the current and past abilities of the person with dementia, rather than viewing dementia as an overall change instead of worsening.

We felt it was important to move away from the past when encouraging intergenerational interaction as for most the details and knowledge of past events of the older person's lives may be inaccessible (Brankaert et al. 2019; Hodge et al. 2018). While photos and memories are often associated with memories we found that using media to incite challenge and competition removes the focus on the past, and encourages interaction with the present instead. We explore this in another technology, Printer Pals.

## 16.4 Case Study Two: Printer Pals

Printer Pals is a media-generating printer, comprised of a cylinder casing which holds a Raspberry Pi, receipt printer and speaker [4]. It is used to facilitate storytelling and quizzes and is connected to a local server in which we can upload questions, riddles, images and audio to be used with residents in care homes.

Printer Pals is the result of a three-year ethnographic design study carried out in 'Oakfield House'. This project initially involved the first author (Sarah) engaging with residents in care with a view to understanding the ways in which people with dementia co-create meaning and communicate their experience through embodied actions, subtle participation and interactions of care (Foley et al. 2019b). We quickly understood the importance of creating opportunities for people with dementia in care to take a more active role in contributing to meaningful social engagement and set up a student design project to create opportunities for intergenerational engagement. This phase of the project involved ten undergraduate students working closely on projects with residents that had dementia, using methods of design to explore personhood, life stories and the collective history of the city they both shared (Cork, Ireland). This work aimed to re-configure the role of the person with dementia as an expert, both in their lived experience and the history of the city that the students shared with them. In terms of mutually beneficial engagement, the students expressed the development of a greater understanding of what it means to live with dementia, and an empathy for the residents in care. Below one of the students discusses their new understanding:

> I didn't have any experience about dementia beforehand. I mean I knew what it was, from books, and we had that module on Ageing… and we went through dementia and it was like 'oh it's all concrete'. It's all like funnelled into one… disorder. Whereas then you come in here and it's like, everyone is completely different in the way that they act and some days they're bad, some days they're good… some days you could see they have dementia and then other days you're like 'don't see what's wrong with them whatsoever.'

As well as engaging the students and residents in mutually beneficial interactions, this work also indicated the key role of media, such as old photographs, videos and audio in aiding communication between the students and residents. While access to Wi-Fi and online resources was extremely limited in the care home, the students would pull up resources on their phones or bring back printed pictures that they had found on the Internet. The findings from the student design project were the basis of the design and implementation of Printer Pals, which then facilitated further intergenerational engagement.

Printer Pals was designed iteratively based on the sensibilities of Experience-centered Design [8]. As such, we focused on the felt-experience, and the potential of technology to enrich experience in this context. From the student project, we were aware that residents were cautious of any technology that looked fragile and were much more engaged with resources such as paper. In response to this, we created a device which could produce cheap, accessible resources such as a receipt, which the residents were familiar with already. The prototype was encased in laser cut cardboard, giving it a robust exterior to encourage residents to engage with the tactile nature of the device. We later created versions in metal and plastic to explore how material shaped the interaction (see Fig. 16.2). When introducing the prototype to the residents for initial evaluation, we were surprised at their interest in the physical components of Printer Pals, such as the Raspberry Pi:

> We introduced the Printer Pals, and they commented very enthusiastically about the colour. Daniel explained how he made it; 3D printing, sanding, painting. We showed them the inside parts, they thought I was breaking it as I took it apart. Surprisingly they remarked parts like the speaker and board were 'Cute' especially when Kate compares it to her speaker, which is much bigger. They all laughed at this.

Printer Pals facilitated a number of sessions based on quizzes, sing-alongs and sharing life experience. Based on some of the initial sessions which were more competitive in nature, we also added more challenging questions, riddles and jokes to Printer Pals. In the following example, Sarah read out a riddle produced by Printer Pals:

**Fig. 16.2** Printer pals

> 'I travel around the world but stay in one corner, what am I?' I repeated it on request, and the residents began to shout out answers. We all complimented them on their guesses and gave them some hints; that it was small, and cheap and there would be more around at Christmas. One lady got close with a post-card so we told her she was the closest. Eventually one person a lady got it right and shouted out 'Stamp.' We all gave her a cheer. She said she thought that was very clever. I give her the receipts and tell her to quiz the staff on the war. 'Sure I have two from before' she says referring to earlier sessions. From then, anytime a new person comes in she asks them the question. One man rolls in his wheelchair and she tells him she has a question. 'He'll get it, he's a genius' the women beside me says. 'It's simple' the woman with the receipt tells him. Kathleen says 'You're only saying that because you know it now' and everyone laughs. The man gets in very fast. 'A stamp,' he says. Everyone gives him a cheer. He smiles at everyone. A few minutes later the manager of the care home comes up to talk to Kate. Before she goes, the lady tells her to come here, she has a question. 'See will you get this now, he got it in two seconds.' 'I'm very proud of myself there now,' he says and he looks it. The manager takes a few guesses and eventually she gets it too. They give her a cheer as well.

Quizzes and asking questions to people with dementia is a contested idea, as it can be seen to further highlight their cognitive decline. However, our sessions with the students, in which the residents and students were part of a team and the nature of questioning which was light-hearted and from Printer Pals rather than a clinician or researcher, highlights the abilities of people with dementia to be active in the process of co-creative sense-making. Through the gentle pushing of boundaries of what we suppose are suitable activities for people with dementia, we can design technologies which challenge the narrative of deficit and disengagement associated with dementia and technology. This advancement in the type of technologies design with people with dementia requires careful ethical decision-making, which in this case was supported by the staff and residents of the care home, as well as the understanding gained through long-term engagement. It was also important for us to capture the subtly of participation, demonstrating the varied ways in which engagement with the media was demonstrated:

> May is usually very quiet and non-responsive. When a country music song came on there was immediately a change about her. She announced the name of the singer and started mouthing the words. She started to smile and brought her hands together, swaying them along with the music. I had never seen her so animated. I looked over to Carmel to see her smiling and we caught each other's eye as she gestures towards her. She continues to sing and sway along to the music until it stops. I smile at her and she smiles back. As soon as the song is over, she resumes her usual position. But for a moment she was completely engrossed in this song.

This project demonstrates the use of design processes and technology to bridge both the generational and technological gap that can exist in dementia care and design. The intergenerational engagement provides opportunities for people with dementia to be supported in a more active role in their community and engage in meaningful interactions. The project also indicates the role of technology in mediating these interactions.

## 16.5 Reflections: Configuring Roles of Technology and People

Our case studies demonstrate the types of meaningful intergenerational exchanges which can be meditated and supported by appropriate technologies. While both technologies focused on creating access to suitable and personalised media, they differed in the types of interactions and the configuration of the people using them. Below we discuss some of our reflections on these interactions, with a view to examining the potential of technology and design to further support intergenerational engagement.

Many of the interactions with Ticket to Talk encourage younger relatives to preserve a version of their older relative in the application. The design and inspirations are often rooted in past events to ease the level of entry for younger people when finding conversation topics, but users rarely created tickets around the present or future. In many cases, these past-oriented tickets were successful and created meaningful conversations, but in some cases, it can create pressure for the person living with dementia to recall an event, especially when the media is so personal towards them. For people who find difficulty in recollection, this could emulate the stigma of dementia they may experience in wider society, where cognition is one of the most heavily used indicators of a person's worth (Taylor 2008).

In comparison to this highly personalised approach, Printer Pals provided opportunities for different modes of interaction. In terms of socially oriented technologies, Printer Pals reflects the first wave paradigm of HCI, with many people sharing one device, closely reflecting technologies older people might recognise, such as sitting around a television together or listening to a radio and discussing the content. In comparison to the highly personal and intimate use of Ticket to Talk, in which the 'success' of the technology depended on the abilities of the person with dementia to remember events of their past, the responsibility for the success of the technology and a positive interaction is diffused amongst the group, allowing different levels of participation. The use of Printer Pals as an indifferent, objective 'quiz master' also removes social pressure, as answers do not have to be successful and players have no consequence of not being able to recall specific memories.

One of the key reasons Printer Pals was successful in use was due to our sensitivity towards the types of questioning and activities which were appropriate for the group we worked with. In essence Printer Pals is a 'blank canvas' which means there is a heavy reliance on the people using the technology to appropriate its use. Used in another way, it could draw more attention to the memory of the person with dementia or exclude them from the social interactions, which is ethically unfair and so it is important to discuss its intended use with participants and staff to ensure everyone is comfortable with the types of interactions. For example, Ticket to Talk scaffolds the possible conversations, which can help younger people in their use of the technology with the person with dementia, while Printer Pals requires a certain level of understanding of dementia in order to use the device to challenge stigma around dementia and create inclusive environments. In this sense, finding a balance between supporting engagement and allowing for the creation of new experiences that are not reliant on the autobiographical memory of the person with dementia is an important consideration for design here. Similarly, the contrast between digital preservation of memories on Ticket to Talk, and the dispensable receipts, which are viewed as inexpensive and mundane, creates a different type of engagement, both of which result in different engagements with the technology and subsequent social interactions.

## 16.6 Design Implications

Through these projects, we have come to understand the need to support intergenerational processes, and the role of technology in creating cohesion and shared experiences. Widening the ecology of care to include younger people can create additional support to all those in care. Much of the feedback we received from carers during this process is that while they value highly light-hearted, playful engagement, their time is restricted by other care demands. Intergenerational engagement can fill this gap, providing space and time for meaningful, enjoyable interactions as part of the care experience.

The intersection between social and technological interactions has the potential to draw on media, as well as the technology itself to scaffold and enrich relationships in care. In terms of the role of technology in mediating social engagement, it can inspire conversation, aid communication and offer an outlet for capturing, exploring and expanding meaningful interactions. Introducing technologies into the care home setting for playful, social use can also counteract the stigma attached to technologies and older people (Vines et al. 2015). Including people with dementia in the design process can counteract the narrative that people with dementia and older people are disengaged with technology and move towards more appropriate and accessible design which speaks of the abilities and interests of people with dementia and their need for social inclusion (Kitwood 2002; Theurer et al. 2015). Creating technologies which challenge the perception of dementia can not only counteract stigma, but also provide opportunities for further development of skills and building intergenerational relationships through the learning process.

## 16.7 Conclusion

Design processes and technologies that mediate and support intergenerational engagement have the potential to preserve and develop the social roles of people with dementia within their families and communities. Designing for accessible and inclusive interactions with technologies can further challenge our perceptions of both the types of technologies and social engagements that are suitable in the care context. Both Ticket to Talk and Printer Pals demonstrate the use of design and technologies to explore the relationships between younger people and people with dementia fostering creative and meaningful engagement. Creating technologies which bring people together in socially orientated and enriching environments has the potential to create more inclusive communities for people with dementia and those invested in their care.

## References

Brankaert R, Kenning G, Welsh D, Foley S, Hodge J, Unbehaun D (2019) Intersections in hci, design and dementia: inclusivity in participatory approaches. Published in companion publication of the 2019 on designing interactive systems conference 2019, San Diego, CA, USA

Cowdell F (2010) Care of older people with dementia in an acute hospital setting. Nurs Stand 24(23)

Cruz-Sandoval D, Penaloza CI, Jes #250, Favela S, Castro-Coronel AP (2018) Towards social robots that support exercise therapies for persons with dementia. In: Paper presented at the proceedings of the 2018 ACM international joint conference and 2018 international symposium on pervasive and ubiquitous computing and wearable computers, Singapore

Foley S, Pantidi N, McCarthy J (2019) Care and design: an ethnography of mutual recognition in the context of advanced dementia. In: Proceedings of the 2019 CHI conference on human factors in computing systems—CHI '19 May 04, 2019, Glasgow, Scotland UK. ACM, New York, USA

Foley S, Welsh D, Pantidi N, Morrissey K, Nappey T, McCarthy J (2019) Printer pals. In: Proceedings of the 2019 CHI conference on human factors in computing systems—CHI '19, pp 1–13. https://doi.org/10.1145/3290605.3300634

Gawande A (2014) Being mortal: medicine and what matters in the end: Metropolitan Books

Hodge J, BalaamM, Hastings S,Morrissey K (2018) Exploring the design of tailored virtual reality experiences for people with dementia. In: Proceedings of the 2018 CHI conference on human factors in computing systems—CHI '18. ACM Press, New York, USA, pp 1–13 https://doi.org/10.1145/3173574.3174088

Kamada S, Matsuo Y, Hara S, Abe M (2017) New monitoring scheme for persons with dementia through monitoring-area adaptation according to stage of disease. In: Paper presented at the proceedings of the 1st acm sigspatial workshop on recommendations for location-based services and social networks, Redondo Beach, CA, USA

Kenning G, Treadaway C (2018) Designing for dementia: iterative grief and transitional objects. Des Issues 34(1):42–53. https://doi.org/10.1162/DESI_a_00475
Kitwood T (2002) Malignant social psychology. Understanding care, welfare, and community: a reader, 225
Lazar A, Edasis C, Piper AM(2017) A critical lens on dementia and design in HCI. In: Proceedings of the 2017 CHI conference on human factors in computing systems—CHI '17. Denver, ACM Press. https://doi.org/10.1145/3025453.3025522
McCarthy J, Wright P (2007) Technology as experience. The MIT Press, Cambridge, MA
McKeown J, Clarke A, Ingleton C, Ryan T, Repper J (2010) The use of life story work with people with dementia to enhance person-centred care. Int J Older People Nurs 5(2):148–158. https://doi.org/10.1111/j.1748-3743.2010.00219.x
McNaney R, Vines J, Mercer J, Mexter L, Welsh D, Young T (2017) DemYouth. In: Proceedings of the 2017 CHI conference on human factors in computing systems—CHI '17, pp 1313–1325. https://doi.org/10.1145/3025453.3025558
Mitchell SL, Teno JM, Kiely DK, Shaffer ML, Jones RN, Prigerson HG, Hamel MB (2009) The clinical course of advanced dementia. N Engl J Med 361(16):1529–1538
Morrissey K, McCarthy J, Pantidi N (2017). The value of experience-centred design approaches in dementia research contexts. In Proceedings of the 2017 CHI conference on human factors in computing systems—CHI '17. Denver, ACM Press. https://doi.org/10.1145/3025453.3025527
Mulvenna MD, Nugent CD, Moelaert F, Craig D, Dröes R-M, Bengtsson JE (2010) Supporting people with dementia using pervasive healthcare technologies. In: Supporting people with dementia using pervasive health technologies. Springer, pp 3–14
Nyqvist F, Cattan M, Andersson L, Forsman AK, Gustafson Y (2013) Social capital and loneliness among the very old living at home and in institutional settings: a comparative study. J Aging Health 25(6):1013–1035
O'rourke HM, Duggleby W, Fraser KD, Jerke L (2015) Factors that affect quality of life from the perspective of people with dementia: a metasynthesis. J Am Geriatr Soc 63(1):24–38
Swaffer K (2014) Dementia: stigma, language, and dementia-friendly. In: Sage Publications Sage UK, London, England
Taylor JS (2008) On recognition, caring, and dementia. Med Anthropol Q 22(4):313–335
Theurer K, Mortenson WB, Stone R, Suto M, Timonen V, Rozanova J (2015) The need for a social revolution in residential care. J Aging Stud 35:201–210
Vines J, Pritchard G, Wright P, Olivier P, Brittain K (2015) An age-old problem: examining the discourses of ageing in HCI and strategies for future research. ACM Trans Comput-Hum Interact 22(1):1–27. https://doi.org/10.1145/2696867
Welsh D, Morrissey K, Foley S, McNaney R, Salis C, McCarthy J, Vines J (2018) Ticket to talk. In: Proceedings of the 2018 CHI conference on human factors in computing systems—CHI '18, pp 1–14. https://doi.org/10.1145/3173574.3173949

# Part IV
# Design In the Field: In the Context of Dementia

# Chapter 17
# Designing Sentic: Participatory Design with People Living with Dementia

**Myrte Thoolen, Rens Brankaert, and Yuan Lu**

## 17.1 Introduction

Over the past years, we have seen a shift in the approach toward dementia care, moving from the medical perspective focused on care-oriented processes, schedules, and staff efficiency toward a person-centered approach that elevates individual and personal experiences in care (Fazio et al. 2018). At the same time, in the field of HCI research, there is a growing interest in providing technology that follows similar philosophies and incorporates person-centered approaches, and is developed in ongoing dialog with people living with dementia and their extended care network (Lindsay et al. 2012; Wallace et al. 2013; Morrissey et al. 2017). These approaches take into account context, embodiment, sensorial experiences, and emotional experiences (Lazar et al. 2017). Using these developments, we can design for dementia care to enable participation in pleasurable activities (Meiland et al. 2017), improve quality of life, and provide meaningful participation (Lazar et al. 2016). The experiences of dementia can widely vary, and different personal and social factors play a role. These differences are not always considered in design for and with people with dementia (Gibson et al. 2018; Nygård and Starkhammar 2007).

M. Thoolen (✉) · R. Brankaert · Y. Lu
Department of Industrial Design, Eindhoven University of Technology, Eindhoven, The Netherlands
e-mail: M.E.Thoolen@tue.nl

R. Brankaert
e-mail: R.Brankaert@fontys.nl

Y. Lu
e-mail: Y.Lu@tue.nl

R. Brankaert
School of Allied Health Professions, Fontys University of Applied Sciences, Eindhoven, The Netherlands

© Springer Nature Switzerland AG 2020

R. Brankaert and G. Kenning (eds.), *HCI and Design in the Context of Dementia*, Human–Computer Interaction Series,
https://doi.org/10.1007/978-3-030-32835-1_17

In this chapter, we report on an inclusive design process for creating a tangible music interface which is directly accessible to people with dementia. Using this process, we designed *Sentic*: a physical and digital music player combined to promote independence when listening to music (Thoolen et al. 2019). It consists of two parts: a record player base and a mobile application (see Fig. 17.1). The record player base has an interchangeable tangible interaction component that can be tailored to the user's abilities and allows users to access a range of audio files and create a playlist together with their family members and caregivers. The musical playlist is connected to a tangible token with corresponding color that acts as an interface. The mobile application allows for the creation of a personal profile by collecting personally meaningful audio files related to life events of the person with dementia (see Fig. 17.2). However, the mobile application will not be discussed in detail in this chapter, which will focus mainly on the inclusive design process of the record player base.

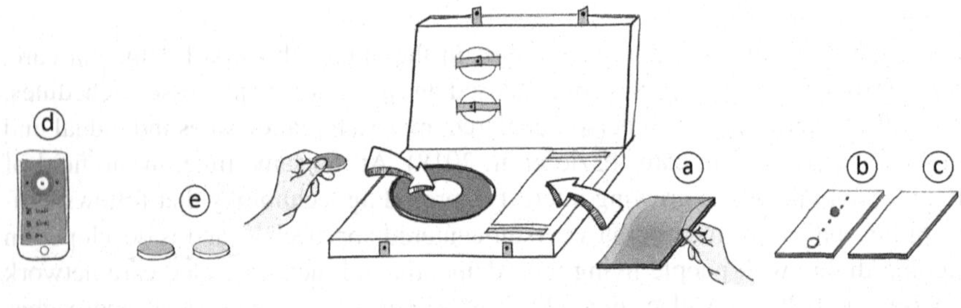


**Fig. 17.1** Sketch of the *Sentic* design concept that provides a record player base with three interchangeable interfaces: **a** *Sentic*.**play** with an explorative soft interface, **b** *Sentic*.**touch** with a discrete interface, or **c** *Sentic*.**listen** without interface. The provided music can be tailored through: **d** a mobile application that allows for the creation of musical playlists, which is connected to **e** a tangible token

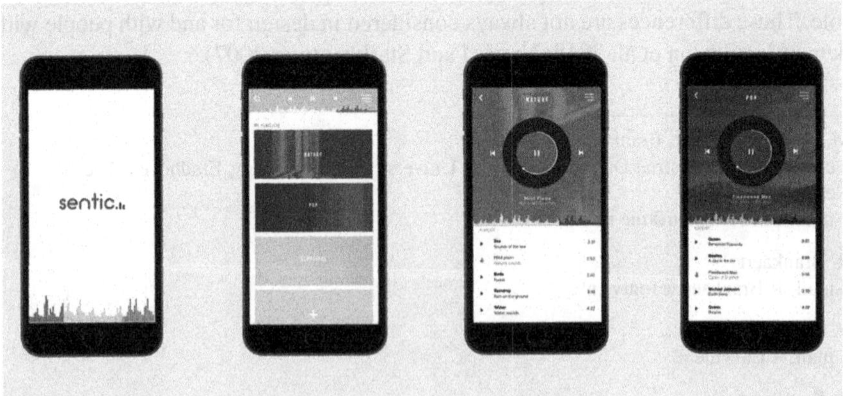


**Fig. 17.2** Mobile application that makes it easy to create unique playlists of personally meaningful music. The color of each playlist corresponds to the color of the physical tokens

We will discuss the design process of *Sentic* through a series of participatory design workshops with people living with dementia to (a) explore individual differences in abilities in dealing with interfaces and technology in general and (b) understand which associations and aesthetics people with dementia relate to and how interaction design can leverage this. This involved working with a group of ten people with dementia in smaller subsets and obtaining their reactions to existing interfaces, products, and prototypes iteratively, in order to evolve design ideas culminating in the final *Sentic* prototype. Individual differences in response due to personality and changing stages of dementia led the designers to provide multiple *adaptive* options for the interface.

This chapter contributes to the growing literature in HCI and the design of everyday technologies for people living with dementia. First, we outline an inclusive design process in which we highlight and exemplify the value of designing with people with dementia. In these workshops, physical and sensorial experiences were explored to provide concrete leads to enable people with dementia to reconnect both with their own personal history and with the present moment through both the music and the interface. Secondly, we show the potential of tailored tangible interaction design to support the maintenance of autonomy of people living with dementia and allow access to technology and discuss how it promotes positive wellbeing and supports their sense of self. To conclude, we reflect on the design of *Sentic* and envision future opportunities for tailored user interfaces in design for people living with dementia.

## 17.2 Related Work

In this section, we introduce key considerations in designing tailored user interfaces for people living with dementia.

### *17.2.1 User-Sensitivity in Design*

Technology has focused on providing support in carrying out daily activities by designing assistive technologies that address the *gap* that can occur in the cognition of people with dementia (Branco et al. 2017). However, recent work in design and dementia has shifted focus to a more holistic perspective that makes use of the skills still present in the person (Lazar et al. 2016; Morrissey et al. 2017), and focuses on what the individual can do by interpreting the contextualized meaning of these actions, rather than on focusing on deficits (Lazar et al. 2017). Every person is different, the skills and challenges people face vary and affect their ability on an individual level (Kitwood 1997). In dementia care, this approach is also referred to as the new care paradigm of *person-centered care* (Branco et al. 2017). In parallel, there is a growing body of research in the field of HCI that incorporates this person-centered approach in the design of new technologies for people living with dementia. This research suggests that when designing for people with dementia, HCI researchers should pay attention to individual perspectives and take into account personality, uniqueness (Branco et al. 2017; Wallace et al. 2013), and the changing nature of needs and characteristics of people with dementia (Newell et al. 2011). Research highlights the importance of seeing every experience and interaction as an opportunity for engagement, even when dementia is at its most severe, each unique and complete person can experience joy and live a life with meaning and dignity (Fazio et al. 2018). With this aim, participatory design approaches are being used to involve people with dementia as codesigners in the creation of new technologies (Foley et al. 2019; Hendriks et al. 2014; Hodge et al. 2018; Wallace et al. 2013), as mediators in the use of artifacts (Houben et al. 2019; Wallace et al. 2013), and in open approaches that focus on personalization (Branco et al. 2017; Hodge et al. 2019). This shift in HCI embraces the personal aspects of interaction with technology in everyday life (Lazar et al. 2017), and is valuable for developing user-sensitive design and technologies.

### *17.2.2 Personal Dynamics in Dementia*

With dementia, continuous physical, sensorial, and emotional changes affect each individual differently and can influence one's sense of self and self-reliance (Cerejeira et al. 2012). Changes in ability are related to decreased confidence and loss of motivation for involvement in activities (Górska et al. 2018). Deterioration in a person's ability makes it challenging for people with dementia to understand everyday technologies, which makes it increasingly difficult to maintain access to activities of daily living (Meiland et al. 2017; Nygård and Starkhammar 2007), and they then require increasing support. There is a growing body of research that explores the effect of losses in both cognitive and physical skills in the technology use of people with dementia (Nygård and Starkhammar 2007; Riikonen et al. 2013; Smith and Mountain 2012). However, research has also shown that even in later stages of dementia people can interact meaningfully and engage when prompted (Gowans et al. 2007; Thoolen et al. 2020). Furthermore, current research has sparked new interest in designing technologies to foster interaction, understanding, and empathy between people with diverse cognitive abilities (Lazar et al. 2017). More research is needed to determine how these different cognitive abilities can be considered in the design.

### *17.2.3 Music for Meaningful Participation*

Music can enable people with dementia to participate in an activity that is enjoyable and personally meaningful (McDermott et al. 2014). Research has shown that an individual listening to music can result in a more personalized experience, which is beneficial for improving mood and relieving agitation (Kulibert et al. 2018). Besides, self-selected music activates different parts of the brain and positively affects the lived experience, more effectively compared to when it is chosen by caregivers or relatives (Blood and Zatorre 2001). While most of the research in music has focused on the effect of music as a therapeutic intervention, the role of design in having personal access to individualized listening to music in everyday life is still unexplored (Sixsmith and Gibson 2007). One of the main problems of individualized listening to music is the person's inability to use music player interfaces. People with dementia are often dependent on caregivers to access their personal music through commercially available music players (e.g., CD player or Spotify); however, these are often too difficult to use. Additionally, research has shown that problems in accessing music go beyond the usability of the equipment and involve the importance of considerations on aesthetics and appearance (Sixsmith and Gibson 2007). Accordingly, access to music is dependent on multiple factors influencing a person's individual, social, and physical environment. Numerous commercially available music players are attempting to address this market and are sold to private parties such as the Simple Music Player by 1958LLC,[1] the Memory Loss One Button Radio from GeriGuard Solutions,[2] and the Unforgettable Music Player and Radio from LiveBetterWith.[3] All of these systems claim to be adaptable to all individuals, although few are designed for specific cases (Sixsmith and Gibson 2007) and take the changing needs of people with dementia over time into account (Newell et al. 2011). Additionally, supporting listening to music together is often seen as an additional and less important activity by caregivers (Kulibert et al. 2018).

### *17.2.4 Tangible and Customizable Interactions in Dementia*

Tangible interactions can stimulate tactile senses and can enhance people's bodily coordination and sensorimotor skills (Huber et al. 2019). Haptic direct manipulations, in which users can grab, move and feel the relevant elements, can invite users to interact with objects by appealing to their sense of touch, providing joy and playfulness (Hornecker and Buur 2006). Previous work by other researchers has shown that haptic user interfaces for therapeutic use can encourage active participation and improve the evocation of positive emotions in people with dementia (Morrissey et al. 2017; Murko and Kunze 2015). Lazar et al. (2016) generated design recommendations for the design of recreational systems that can support activities for people living with dementia, and described the meaningfulness of integrating a personal approach as people with dementia may forget how to use the system as their condition progresses. Research has suggested that looking more fundamentally at what constitutes an intuitive control related to the person themselves may help to design appropriate technology (Orpwood et al. 2010). Moreover, presenting only a subset of available options in applications and content can meet diverse needs and provide

[1] http://www.dementiamusic.co.uk/.

[2] https://designability.org.uk/projects/products/one-button-analogue-radio/.

[3] https://dementia.livebetterwith.com/products/unforgettable-music-player-digital-radio.

a way to access recreational systems. These examples demonstrate the potential for a personally tailored approach, which can be realized through customization and adaptability in HCI and show the prospect of more suitable user interfaces for people living with dementia. In this chapter, we explore how to design systems that are customizable or can be tailored to specific needs—and investigate how aesthetics and tangible interactions enable users to maintain individual access to these systems.

## 17.3 Study Approach

We intended for our design process to be recognizable and directly usable for those with dementia. The process was based on a three-stage, iterative design process covering: *Exploration, Design*, and *Evaluation* (Brankaert 2016). The study took place over the course of 11 months from early 2017 to late 2017. We investigated the associations and aesthetics that people with varying stages of dementia appreciate and relate to, and the interaction modalities that could facilitate accessibility. We conducted an iterative design process (Branco et al. 2017) using collaborative ways of designing for and with people with dementia to design an individualized recreational activity (Cui et al. 2017; Newell et al. 2011). It explored possible interactions and functionalities with people with dementia via a series of engagement workshops (Morrissey et al. 2017) and investigated initial reactions to technology via group sessions (Hynes et al. 2016). We then organized a series of six engagement workshop sessions in which observations and informal interviews were conducted. To open the dialogs, we used existing products, mockups, and specifically developed prototypes to solicit reactions from participants to various interactions, aesthetics, and functionalities in the design process (Foley et al. 2019; Hendriks et al. 2013; Wallace et al. 2013). Each workshop was followed by a design iteration conducted by the first author based on the insights gathered.

### *17.3.1 Participants and Ethics*

We collaborated with Vitalis care organization, in Eindhoven, the Netherlands. Care professionals selected a total of ten participants who met the following criteria: they had a formal diagnosis of dementia, varying from early- to late-stage dementia and attended a day center at least once a month (so that staff had sufficient time to get familiar with the participant). Ethical approval was gained from the university and the care organization. Written consent was initially obtained from the participants with dementia themselves, and verbal assent was sought before and during each interview session to remind participants about the purpose of the research and their right to withdraw at any time. A family member signed the consent form in cases where participants were not able to do so.

### *17.3.2 Deployment in day care center*

This research took place in familiar surroundings within a daycare setting, where people who live at home visit a day program during working hours, and in which a long-standing and trustworthy relationship is established between the participants and the care professionals (i.e., sharing private information). It is important that the care professional is familiar with the life history and preferences of the participant for selecting the personal music content for the study. Care professionals of the involved care organization recruited participants in early to late stages of dementia who regularly visit the day care facility. Care professionals who were familiar with the participants divided them into two smaller groups of not more than five persons per group in which the different stages of dementia were represented: a group composed of five people with early-stage dementia and a group of five people with moderate-to-later stages of dementia. The majority of the participants were not in the advanced stage of dementia since they still live at home. We carried out the workshop sessions with both of the groups as part of the morning program of the daycare facility, which was allocated for brain training activities. The workshops were designed to be reciprocal and to offer participants the opportunity to engage and to experience *in the moment* pleasure (Kenning 2018), as part of a positive experience.

## 17.4 An Inclusive Design Process for Iterative Feedback

In the workshop series a process of iterative feedback was applied which focused on trying to develop a holistic understanding of people with dementia's individual differences in abilities in dealing with interfaces and technology in general and which associations and aesthetics people with dementia relate to and how interaction design can leverage this.

### *17.4.1 Workshop 1 and 2: Associations and Aesthetics in Design (Exploration Phase)*

We started the process with a design activity in which two prototypes were developed to observe interactions and enabled researchers to gather insights into how the design affects behavior and their engagement. In the first workshop, the researchers introduced themselves to both groups and participated in the regular morning activity. Then two prototypes were introduced with which participants could engage with and respond to. This was visual and tactile stimuli to prompt a response. The workshop ran for approximately one-and-a-half-hours per group. Each participant was given a prototype one after the other to explore the interaction capabilities and motor skills of the particular group, starting with the cube (see Fig. 17.3). As the prototypes were

**Fig. 17.3** Tangible prototypes as prompts. *Left* cube corresponding cards, *Right* playful disc mapping

unrelated to each other, transference of learning between prototypes was unlikely. The first prototype was based on *matching the shapes* (Sheppard et al. 2016), resulting in a simple cube probe with six different sides corresponded to six same-sized surfaces with silhouettes of the objects (see Fig. 17.3, left). The second prototype was based on a playful ring interface, on which participants could *map* disc objects into corresponding slots (see Fig. 17.3, right).

During the exploration, the participants demonstrated the ability to match shapes in both prototypes. However, the forms of interaction greatly varied per person. People within the early-stage group found the rather playful interactions childish and showed no engagement. Conversely, people within the moderate-to-later stage dementia group became enthusiastic about the playful interactions and were actively engaged in discovering the possibilities of the prototypes. All participants, clearly showed that the physical *negative* space on the prototype (i.e., the cutlery shape on the cube that need to be matched with the similar shape) seemed to increase the ability to understand the interaction and allowed them to interact with the prototypes individually.

From this first explorative workshop, we concluded: (1) clearly defining expectations in form and appearance provoked users to interact with an artifact across all stages, and (2) to be careful with playful interactions as these can be perceived as a negative experience and rather *childish*.

A second explorative workshop was organized, involving a card sort session to identify participants' know-how of audio products and understand how they related to them. The same participants as the first workshop were provided with cards depicting audio devices, such as radios, stereos, record, and players. We asked them to arrange cards in order of *makes sense* to *does not make sense* and reflect on the results.

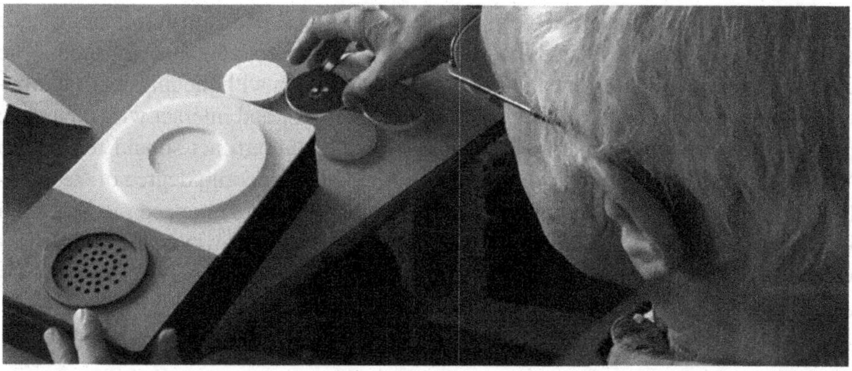

**Fig. 17.4** The first conceptual prototype of a record player-inspired music device

We found that music products from the past were generally recognized. Many participants were reminded of pleasant moments, and all participants still understood some elements on how these systems worked in detail. More modern music-playing devices were not always known (i.e., discman, iPod shuffle, and Spotify). In these sessions, we applied the principle of error-less learning. We did not correct participants, but rather discussed their perspective to maintain or boost self-esteem and motivate people to engage in the workshop actively (Cotter et al. 2018).

Based on findings the record player proved a promising metaphor for interaction suitable for people with dementia. All participants related the record player to treasured moments of their past life and stimulated recollection of personal stories. The insights from workshops 1 and 2 (exploration phase) were translated into a first design proposal of a new type of music player for people living with dementia (see Fig. 17.4). The prototype was designed with a calm aesthetic (clean white look) and a wooden speaker. By placing colored sound discs on the white platform, sound files could be played.

### 17.4.2 *Workshop 3: User-Sensitivity in Design (Design Phase)*

To explore the potential of the design proposal, we evaluated the music player prototype (see Fig. 17.4). Care professionals selected three participants from the first workshops, with diverse characteristics to maximize variation, who were willing to engage in a one-on-one session with the first author and were physically able and verbally articulate enough to use the prototype and create narratives. Two participants with early-stage dementia and one participant with moderate-stage dementia were asked to observe the prototype, try to use it, and play a song by placing a sound disc on the platform by themselves.

The aesthetic appearance of the prototype did not reference a music-playing device at all, they, for example, stated that the 'system was unrecognizable' for them. The chosen aesthetics and designed interaction did not match with the physical and cognitive frame of reference to allow them to make sense of and interact with the music player. The participants mentioned that the form of the artifact should not be too 'different' in relation to music devices and should have a certain degree of 'recognition' in the audio device; therefore, it appeared that the more nuanced insights from workshop 2 were not translated well in the design proposal. However, the sound discs worked well; the participants appreciated their tactility and recognized them as CDs or records.

### *17.4.3 Workshop 4: Personal Diversity in Interaction (Exploration Phase)*

Based on our findings in workshop 3, we stepped back from the prototype (*design phase*) and continued to discover more about the interaction and recognition preferences of the participants (*exploration phase*). In this workshop, we brought several audio devices (i.e., old-fashioned radio, iPod shuffle, and Discman) to the same participants as in workshop 1 and observed the interaction with them. We facilitated discussion on the personal associations with objects to understand how people related to the audio devices (see Fig. 17.5). While exploring the audio devices, participants expressed their associations for music related to the aesthetics of a record player and shared stories from the past about listening to vinyl together with friends or their family. Interaction with the audio devices varied among the participants. Participants were not able to operate the audio devices. The first authors therefore observed the touch-related interactions with the devices to get a better understanding of appropriate interactions for the skills of different people with dementia. We concluded that

**Fig. 17.5** Exploring interaction with existing audio devices in a group session and discussing their personal associations with these devices

the physical interaction ability of individuals varied considerably among the participants, across different stages, ages, and backgrounds; however, most devices were recognized as audio devices. Based on these observations, we found that it would be challenging to design a single interaction paradigm suitable for this group, while it would be possible to design a single recognizable aesthetic. This led to the concept of tailoring the interface to different users and their abilities.

### 17.4.4 Workshop 5: Tailoring the Interface (Design and Evaluation Phase)

We developed a second design proposal with a modular interface to respond to the individual differences between people with dementia (see Fig. 17.6). The proposal had (1) a discrete interface with a volume knob and song selection, (2) a more explorative fabric interface to play music, and (3) no interface for passive listening. The prototype was designed to be reminiscent of a record player, and was evaluated with the same ten participants as in the first workshops through a *Wizard of Oz* evaluation method (Kelley 1984).

**Fig. 17.6** *Top* a discrete interaction interface, *Bottom* a more explorative soft interface. Each caters to a different type and ability of interaction with the device

The researcher observed the participant's behavior and personal preferences from which recommendations were established. The evaluation indicated the importance of a flexible interface that can be adjusted to personal abilities appropriate to individual strengths. For example, one participant with advanced dementia discovered the interface through tactile senses by touching the soft surface and became enthusiastic when a song changed to a different tune, after which he raised his thumb to fellow participants (see Fig. 17.6, top). Another participant with mild dementia found it more pleasant to use the discrete and rotating knob (see Fig. 17.6, bottom). Participants with varying stages of dementia expressed comfort and interest in using the customizable interface and indicated the potential of personalized access to audio. The findings from this evaluation session resulted in our final design proposal: *Sentic.*

## 17.5 Sentic: A Personal Adaptable Music Player

*Sentic* is designed to address the issue of lack of accessibility in currently available audio devices for people with dementia experiencing condition-related changes in physical and cognitive abilities (see Fig. 17.7). The aim of *Sentic* is to provide a tangible interface that can be adjusted to the individual capabilities and skills still present within a person living with dementia. The tangible interface of the record player base can be configured by a caregiver by plugging in the module to allow people with dementia to directly engage and intuitively invite the user to

**Fig. 17.7** The final design of Sentic

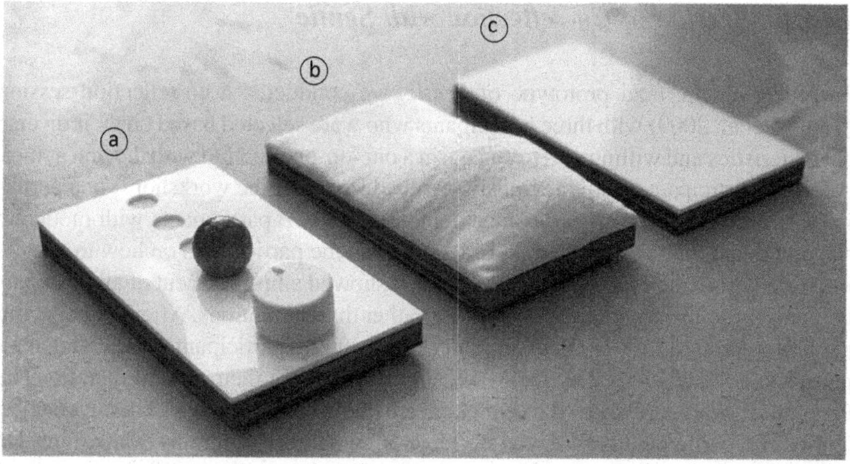


**Fig. 17.8** The adaptable interfaces of *Sentic* in its current implementation: **a** *Sentic*.**touch**, **b** *Sentic*.**play**, and **c** *Sentic*.**listen**

interact with the controls of the system and use it. *Sentic* in its current implementation provides three interchangeable interfaces: (1) *Sentic*.**touch** with a discrete interface, (2) *Sentic*.**play** with an explorative soft interface, or (3) *Sentic*.**listen** with no interface. The design itself is reminiscent of a record player, and sound discs (i.e., tangible tokens) can be placed on the r*ecord player* to play personal music lists. The overall aesthetic is designed as a suitcase, common in record players of the fifties, with a smooth wooden finish that people appreciated and recognized. *Sentic* includes speakers to play the music and has headphones that can be connected.

*Sentic*.**touch** is a *discrete interface* (see Fig. 17.8a) that allows to select songs and adjust volume. The song can be selected by moving the ball object between five points on the interface. These reference points indicate that the music token contains five songs. At the bottom, the volume can be controlled with a volume knob.

*Sentic*.**play** is an *explorative soft interface* (see Fig. 17.8b) that is equipped with a soft fabric surface to adjust volume and go to the next song. A song can be selected by touching the soft surface, which divided into five areas vertically corresponding to the five songs. The volume can be controlled by stroking over the surface.

*Sentic*.**listen** is the third interface, which removes the interaction to control the volume and switch to the next song (see Fig. 17.8c). It therefore emphasizes the interaction with the sound discs and listening to the playlist that plays songs one after another.

### 17.5.1 Session 6: Co-reflection with Sentic

To reflect on the final prototype of *Sentic*, we conducted a co-reflection session (Tomico et al. 2009) with three participants who were selected based on their diverse characteristics and willingness to engage in a one-on-one session with the first author. All three participants were previously involved in one of the workshops; one participant was diagnosed with early stage dementia and two participants with moderate stage of dementia. The first author did not advise the participants on how to use the interface before the evaluation. The reflection showed empowerment of all three participants through accentuation on abilities rather than limitations. After experiencing the prototype (see Fig. 17.9), short interviews with the participants revealed that all participants were amazed by their own ability to control their preferred audio. The first author, who performed the user engagements, noted a change in the interaction ability of a participant with moderate stage of dementia during this evaluation: 'He placed his hand on the *Sentic*.**play** interface and made small movements over it, and the volume turned up. All of a sudden, his eyes were filled with tears. His attention was drawn and his interest to keep interacting with it was encouraged' While his interactions throughout the day were initially not very energetic nor independent, he markedly changed when touching the *Sentic* interface. The modularity, because of customizable interactions, helped each participant in their own way to interact independently with the system. The participants showed changes in mood and more positive emotions. As expressed by a participant with early-stage dementia: 'Since I tried *Sentic*.**touch**, I can listen repeatedly to the most beautiful song on earth. Just by a simple movement with the little ball.' The participant expressed that *Sentic*.**touch** was his favorite interface (see Fig. 17.10). This finding indicates that a simple operation that fits the individual-specific preferences and strengths is successful in supporting the ability to interact independently and contributes to the perceived usefulness of the technology. In another example, two participants began to tell stories from their past, making associations with the music played. They had not told such detailed stories in the previous sessions. For example, a participant with moderate dementia had difficulties with speaking, but when he touched *Sentic*.**play** for the first time he

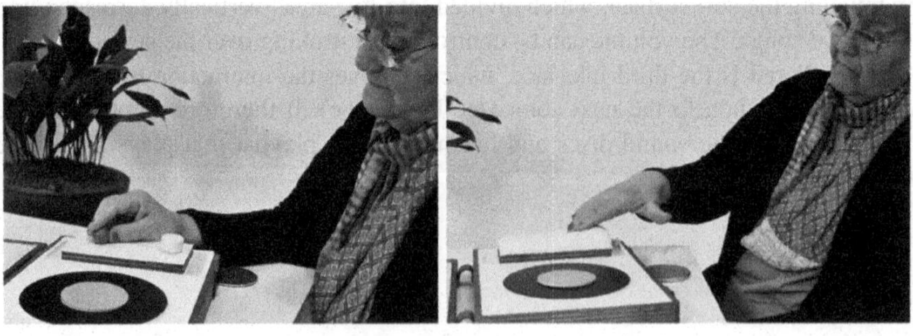

**Fig. 17.9** Participant engaging with Sentic

**Fig. 17.10** User evaluation in Vitalis with a participating resident listening to his favorite song

spoke softly: 'How beautiful, and incredible …' repeatedly. Engaging with the system, highlighted an ease of interacting with technology and music. The participant kept touching the interface, which made the smile on his face grow bigger. It seemed as if he were becoming more comfortable with using the system independently and taking control of it. Through the evolving nature of use, it demonstrated to be an effective interface for this particular participant.

By supporting appropriate inclusion for people with dementia in using *Sentic*, all participants showed an emotional and physical response to varying degrees to one of the interfaces. For two participants, diagnosed with moderate stage of dementia, the soft interface was preferred, and for the participant with early-stage dementia the discrete interface was preferred. The evaluation showed that by providing a personally tailored interface it gives people with dementia personal access to their favorite music tracks. Besides this, it also demonstrated how the design could support communication and contribute to a meaningful and inclusive experience for people living with dementia.

## 17.6 Discussion

Our case study demonstrates an inclusive design process with people living with dementia that iteratively shaped the development of *Sentic*. This work shows how we used artifacts and prototypes to engage participants with dementia and explore various forms of interaction with technology. Our major finding from the design process was that people with dementia have diverse needs, independent of the phase of dementia and age, which we cannot entirely address by a generic solution. The *Sentic* design showcases an interface that can be tailored, which caters to diversity and personalization in people living with dementia, and facilitates direct access to technology. With the possibility to select a specific user profile. This case study can open up the potential for the design of adaptable and adaptive interfaces that respond to the heterogeneity of people with dementia in terms of needs, preferences, and capabilities and address the need to include them in technology design in the HCI field (Lazar et al. 2017; Morrissey and Mccarthy 2015; Morrissey et al. 2016).

This study showed the benefits of an adaptable user interface that can give users more control over the appearance and the way of interaction with the user interface. However, for some users it can be difficult to customize the interface due to, for example, lower levels of ICT literacy (Gullà et al. 2015). In order to support them, an adaptable interface with system support can be an efficient outcome for developing suitable user interfaces for people living with dementia.

In addition to this, the case study provides design researchers with insights and new perspectives on how to include people with dementia in engagement workshops and how responses could be to technology, interactions, and aesthetics. The *Sentic* design proposal is based on a familiar association with a record player, adopting its aesthetic to increase association and appreciation by people living with dementia.

### 17.6.1 Design Considerations

Adaptable user interfaces have great potential as an approach to design for people living with dementia, to cater for diversity and change, this section presents design considerations for future design and research. The reasons for individual preference can vary and depend on the unique frame of reference, needs, or stage of dementia. Adapting and tailoring technologies for different abilities is considered challenging (Hodge et al. 2018); however, with current developments in technology, this is increasingly more feasible. Previous work emphasizes the importance of both appealing (Alm et al. 2007) and adaptive systems (Leong 2017) for people with dementia; however, this is rarely realized in physical product design. Also, recommendations for the design of recreational systems are still very much in development (Lazar et al. 2016). Throughout the design process of *Sentic*, we also found that the aesthetic of *Sentic* should match with the associations of people living with dementia to invite direct engagement and facilitate improved access. We argue that associations and familiarity can be enabled through aesthetics.

In our case study, we applied the notion of tailored interface design to an audio device. This principle could also be applied in other application domains such as household products (e.g., coffee machine, washing machine, stove), recreational systems (e.g., television, computer, mobile phone), or everyday environments (e.g., kitchen, living room, bathroom). With this approach, we can contribute to one of the pressing challenges in designing person-centered technologies and services for people living with dementia (Brankaert 2016; Cui et al. 2017; Foley et al. 2019; Hodge et al. 2019; Lazar et al. 2017; Wallace et al. 2012). However, further research is required to examine suitable areas and levels of adaptability (Górska et al. 2018), both in terms of technology as well as care efforts.

Through an inclusive design process, we managed to create *Sentic*, which contributes to providing a rich interaction that stimulates tactile senses tuned to the particular needs of the person and allows for active participation. In the current design of *Sentic*, the three options of tangible interfaces are manually plugged into the system by caregivers or family members, but with more advanced prototypes we could automate this through human-aware or context-aware intelligent technologies. More research is needed to discover the possibilities of such intelligent and adaptive systems, and explore the balance between automation and manual control, desired and required in interaction design.

## 17.7 Conclusion

In this chapter, we covered the design process of *Sentic,* which is designed as a novel concept with a user interface that can be tailored toward people with dementia to enable personalized access to music. Our design process included multiple probes and prototypes in user engagements and showed an example of how to design with and for people with dementia and provide them with the possibility to configure their own (preferred) experience. Current technology often still requires a relatively high level of cognitive and functional ability, making it difficult for people with dementia to access. As dementia progresses, stimulating tactile senses can contribute to the maintenance of autonomy in interaction and add to a feeling of self-reliance and encourages positive health. Our final session showed how the customizable interaction modules gave participants with different stages of dementia access to their preferred music. The design of *Sentic* and the inclusive process reported in this chapter inspire new directions for interaction design for people with dementia and broaden the approach of designing with and for people with dementia. *Sentic* shows that it is possible to design for people with dementia in ways that are accessible, meaningful, and aesthetic appealing.

**Acknowledgements** We thank all participants and care staff from the care organization Vitalis for participating in this study, as well as sharing their time, activity, and experiences. We gratefully acknowledge the care organization for providing a space for the workshops and the design of the *Sentic* system.

## References

Alm N, Dye R, Gowans G, Campbell J, Astell A, Ellis M (2007) A communication support system for older people with dementia. Computer 40(5):35–41. https://doi.org/10.1109/MC.2007.153

Blood AJ, Zatorre RJ (2001) Intensely pleasurable responses to music correlate with activity in brain regions implicated in reward and emotion. Proc Nat Acad Sci 98(20):11818–11823. https://doi.org/10.1073/pnas.191355898

Branco RM, Quental J, Ribeiro Ó (2017) Personalised participation: an approach to involve people with dementia and their families in a participatory design project. CoDesign 13(2):127–143. https://doi.org/10.1080/15710882.2017.1310903

Brankaert R (2016) Design for dementia: a design-driven living lab approach to involve people with dementia and their context. University of Technology Eindhoven

Cerejeira J, Lagarto L, Mukaetova-Ladinska EB (2012) Behavioral and psychological symptoms of dementia. Frontiers Neurol 3(May):1–21. https://doi.org/10.3389/fneur.2012.00073

Cotter VT, Gonzalez EW, Fisher K, Richards KC (2018) Influence of hope, social support, and self-esteem in early stage dementia. Dementia 17(2):214–224. https://doi.org/10.1177/1471301217741744

Cui Y, Shen M, Ma Y, Wen SW (2017) Senses make sense: An individualized multisensory stimulation for dementia. Med Hypotheses. https://doi.org/10.1016/j.mehy.2016.11.006

Fazio S, Pace D, Flinner J, Kallmyer B (2018) The fundamentals of person-centered care for individuals with dementia. The Gerontologist. https://doi.org/10.1093/geront/gnx122

Foley S, Welsh D, Pantidi N, Morrissey K, Nappey T, McCarthy J (2019) Printer pals: experience-centered design to support agency for people with dementia. In: Proceedings of the 2019 CHI conference on human factors in computing systems—CHI '19. ACM Press, New York, USA, pp 1–13. https://doi.org/10.1145/3290605.3300634

Gibson G, Dickinson C, Brittain K, Robinson L (2018) Personalisation, customisation and bricolage: how people with dementia and their families make assistive technology work for them. Ageing and Soc, 1–18. https://doi.org/10.1017/S0144686X18000661

Górska S, Forsyth K, Maciver D (2018) Living with dementia: a meta-synthesis of qualitative research on the lived experience. Gerontologist 58(3):e180–e196. https://doi.org/10.1093/geront/gnw195

Gowans G, Dye R, Alm N, Vaughan P, Astell A, Ellis M (2007) Designing the interface between dementia patients, caregivers and computer-based intervention. Des J 10(1):12–23. https://doi.org/10.2752/146069207789318018

Gullà F, Ceccacci S, Germani M, Cavalieri L (2015) Design adaptable and adaptive user interfaces: a method to manage the information. In: Research trends in media informatics, pp 47–58. https://doi.org/10.1007/978-3-319-18374-9_5

Hendriks N, Huybrechts L, Wilkinson A, Slegers K (2014) Challenges in doing participatory design with people with dementia. In: Proceedings of the 13th participatory design conference on short papers, industry cases, workshop descriptions, doctoral consortium papers, and keynote abstracts—PDC '14, vol 2. https://doi.org/10.1145/2662155.2662196

Hendriks N, Truyen F, Duval E (2013) Designing with dementia: guidelines for participatory design together with persons with dementia. Lecture Notes in Computer Science (Including Subseries Lecture Notes in Artificial Intelligence and Lecture Notes in Bioinformatics), 8117 LNCS(PART 1), 649–666. https://doi.org/10.1007/978-3-642-40483-2_46

Hodge J, Balaam M, Hastings S, Morrissey K (2018) Exploring the design of tailored virtual reality experiences for people with dementia. In: Proceedings of the 2018 CHI conference on human factors in computing systems—CHI '18. ACM Press, New York, USA, pp 1–13. https://doi.org/10.1145/3173574.3174088

Hodge J, Montague K, Hastings S, Morrissey K (2019) Exploring media capture of meaningful experiences to support families living with dementia, 1–14. https://doi.org/10.1145/3290605.3300653

Hornecker E, Buur J (2006) Getting a grip on tangible interaction. In: Proceedings of the SIGCHI conference on human factors in computing systems—CHI '06. ACM Press, New York, USA, p 437. https://doi.org/10.1145/1124772.1124838

Houben M, Brankaert R, Bakker S, Kenning G, Bongers I, Eggen B (2019) Foregrounding everyday sounds in dementia. In: Proceedings of the 2019 on designing interactive systems conference—DIS '19. ACM Press, New York, USA, pp 71–83. https://doi.org/10.1145/3322276.3322287

Huber S, Berner R, Uhlig M, Klein P, Hurtienne J (2019) Tangible objects for reminiscing in dementia care. In: Proceedings of the thirteenth international conference on tangible, embedded, and embodied interaction—TEI '19. ACM Press, New York, USA, pp 15–24. https://doi.org/10.1145/3294109.3295632

Hynes SM, Field B, Ledgerd R, Swinson T, Wenborn J, Di Bona L, … Orrell M (2016) Exploring the need for a new UK occupational therapy intervention for people with dementia and family carers: Community Occupational Therapy in Dementia (COTiD). A focus group study. Aging Ment Health 20(7):762–769. https://doi.org/10.1080/13607863.2015.1037243

Kelley JF (1984) An iterative design methodology for user-friendly natural language office information applications. ACM Trans Inf Syst 2(1):26–41. https://doi.org/10.1145/357417.357420

Kenning G (2018) Reciprocal design: inclusive design approaches for people with late stage dementia. Des Health 2(1):142–162. https://doi.org/10.1080/24735132.2018.1453638

Kitwood T (1997) The experience of dementia. Aging and Ment Health 1(1):13–22. https://doi.org/10.1080/13607869757344

Kulibert D, Ebert A, Preman S, McFadden SH (2018) In-home use of personalized music for persons with dementia. Dementia. https://doi.org/10.1177/1471301218763185

Lazar A, Edasis C, Piper AM (2017) A critical lens on dementia and design in HCI. In: Proceedings of the 2017 CHI conference on human factors in computing systems—CHI '17. ACM Press, Denver. https://doi.org/10.1145/3025453.3025522

Lazar A, Thompson HJ, Demiris G (2016) Design recommendations for recreational systems involving older adults living with dementia. J Appl Gerontol, 073346481664388. https://doi.org/10.1177/0733464816643880

Leong T-Y (2017) Toward a collaborative AI framework for assistive dementia care. AAAI work—shop—Technical Report, WS-17-01-. https://doi.org/10.1006/cres.1998.0128

Lindsay S, Brittain K, Jackson D, Ladha C, Ladha K, Olivier P (2012) Empathy, participatory design and people with dementia. In: Proceedings of the 2012 ACM annual conference on human factors in computing systems—CHI '12 (pp. 521–530). New York, USA, ACM Press. https://doi.org/10.1145/2207676.2207749

McDermott O, Orrell M, Ridder HM (2014) The importance of music for people with dementia: the perspectives of people with dementia, family carers, staff and music therapists. Aging Ment Health 18(6):706–716. https://doi.org/10.1080/13607863.2013.875124

Meiland F, Innes A, Mountain G, Robinson L, van der Roest H, García-Casal JA, … Franco-Martin M (2017) Technologies to support community-dwelling persons with dementia: a position paper on issues regarding development, usability, effectiveness and cost-effectiveness, deployment, and ethics. JMIR Rehabilit Assistive Technol 4(1):e1. https://doi.org/10.2196/rehab.6376

Morrissey K, Mccarthy J (2015) Creative and opportunistic use of everyday music, 295–298

Morrissey K, McCarthy J, Pantidi N (2017). The value of experience-centred design approaches in dementia research contexts. In: Proceedings of the 2017 CHI conference on human factors in computing systems—CHI '17. ACM Press, Denver. https://doi.org/10.1145/3025453.3025527

Morrissey K, Wood G, Green D, Pantidi N, McCarthy J (2016) "I'm a rambler, I'm a gambler, I'm a long way from home": the place of props, music, and design in dementia care. In: Proceedings of the 2016 ACM conference on designing interactive systems—DIS '16, vol 32. ACM Press, New York, USA, pp 1008–1020. https://doi.org/10.1145/2901790.2901798

Murko P, Kunze C (2015) Tangible memories: exploring the use of tangible interfaces for occupational therapy in dementia care

Newell A, Gregor P, Morgan ME, Pullin G, Macaulay C (2011) User-sensitive inclusive design. Univers Access Inf Soc 10(3):235–243. https://doi.org/10.1007/s10209-010-0203-y

Nygård L, Starkhammar S (2007) The use of everyday technology by people with dementia living alone: Mapping out the difficulties. Aging Ment Health 11(2):144–155. https://doi.org/10.1080/13607860600844168

Orpwood R, Chadd J, Howcroft D, Sixsmith A, Torrington J, Gibson G, Chalfont G (2010) Designing technology to improve quality of life for people with dementia: user-led approaches. Univers Access Inf Soc 9(3):249–259. https://doi.org/10.1007/s10209-009-0172-1

Riikonen M, Paavilainen E, Salo H (2013) Factors supporting the use of technology in daily life of home-living people with dementia. Technol Disabil 25(4):233–243. https://doi.org/10.3233/TAD-130393

Sheppard CL, McArthur C, Hitzig SL (2016) A systematic review of montessori-based activities for persons with dementia. J Am Med Direct Assoc 17(2):117–122. https://doi.org/10.1016/j.jamda.2015.10.006

Sixsmith A, Gibson G (2007) Music and the wellbeing of people with dementia. Ageing Soc 27(01):127–145. https://doi.org/10.1017/S0144686X06005228

Smith SK, Mountain GA (2012) New forms of information and communication technology (ICT) and the potential to facilitate social and leisure activity for people living with dementia. Int J Comput Healthc 1(4):332. https://doi.org/10.1504/IJCIH.2012.051810

Thoolen M, Brankaert R, Lu Y (2019) Sentic: a tailored interface design for people with dementia to access music. In: Companion publication of the 2019 on designing interactive systems conference 2019 companion—DIS '19 companion. ACM Press, New York, USA, pp 57–60. https://doi.org/10.1145/3301019.3325152

Thoolen ME, Brankaert R, Lu Y (2020) AmbientEcho: exploring interactive media experiences in the context of residential Dementia care. In: Proceedings of the 2020 on Designing Interactive Systems Conference—DIS '20

Tomico O, Frens JW (2009) Co-reflection: user involvement for highly dynamic design processes, (June 2014). https://doi.org/10.1145/1520340.1520389

Wallace J, Thieme A, Wood G, Schofield G, Olivier P (2012) Enabling self, intimacy and a sense of home in dementia. In Proceedings of the 2012 ACM annual conference on human factors in computing systems—CHI '12 (vol. 47, p 2629). New York, New York, USA, ACM Press. https://doi.org/10.1145/2207676.2208654

Wallace J, Wright PC, McCarthy J, Green DP, Thomas J, Olivier P (2013) A design-led inquiry into personhood in dementia. In: Extended abstracts on human factors in computing systems—CHI EA '13 (p 2883). New York, ACM Press. https://doi.org/10.1145/2468356.2479560

# Chapter 18
# Insights from an Exergame-Based Training System for People with Dementia and Their Caregivers

**David Unbehaun, Konstantin Aal, Daryoush Daniel Vaziri, Rainer Wieching, and Volker Wulf**

## 18.1 Introduction

Even though dementia can be considered a progressive phenomenon, the progression is often an unpredictable cycle of improvement and deterioration of individual conditions. Dementia not only results in physical limitations but also affects the social life of people with dementia as well as their relationship with their family members. The behavioral changes of people with dementia represent an organizational and emotional challenge for relatives and the social environment. Relatives, family members and friends often take over responsibilities and decisions for people with dementia in their daily life, which they have not been previously responsible for. On an emotional level the usual exchanges and mutual support is lacking; family members often put their own needs and emotions aside in order to take care of their loved ones. As a result, caring relatives often overexert themselves emotionally and physically (Schulz and Martire 2004; Brodaty and Donkin 2009; Schorch et al. 2016).

Information and communication technologies (ICT) to support people with dementia and caring relatives are widely used in health promotion, disease prevention and healthcare support and can initiate care services in households and care

D. Unbehaun (✉) · K. Aal · R. Wieching · V. Wulf
Information Systems and New Media, University of Siegen, Siegen, Germany
e-mail: David.Unbehaun@uni-siegen.de

K. Aal
e-mail: Konstantin.Aal@uni-siegen.de

R. Wieching
e-mail: Rainer.Wieching@uni-siegen.de

V. Wulf
e-mail: Volker.Wulf@uni-siegen.de

D. D. Vaziri
University of Applied Sciences Bonn-Rhein-Sieg, Sankt Augustin, Germany
e-mail: Daryoush.Vaziri@h-brs.de

© Springer Nature Switzerland AG 2020

R. Brankaert and G. Kenning (eds.), *HCI and Design in the Context of Dementia*, Human–Computer Interaction Series,
https://doi.org/10.1007/978-3-030-32835-1_18

facilities in the future (Brankaert et al. 2019; Marston and Samuels 2019). Studies in relation to ICT used in the context of people with dementia have shown that technologies can promote personal relationships, social wellbeing and physical performance of people with dementia and their caregivers (Foley et al. 2019; Hodge et al. 2019). However, there is limited research investigating the potential of such technologies that promote activity and reinvigorate social interaction and collaboration between people with dementia and others in their social environment, such as relatives, informal and professional caregivers (Anderiesen 2017). Literature and systems that integrate different activities from various disciplines like sports science, cognitive training and established interventions from everyday treatment or that have integrated people with dementia and their caregivers into the design and evaluation process in an inclusive approach are scarcely available.

In the following, we present results from a design case study that describes the process of exploring, designing and evaluating an ICT-based platform and illustrates the related individual and socio-collaborative impacts and benefits of a video game-based assistive system for people with dementia and their caregivers. We report on results from a four-month evaluation study with a videogame-based prototype to support people with dementia in physical, cognitive and social activities. The system and the related exergames were developed and selected from the fields of sport science, sport gerontology and nursing science and, for the first time in ICT design research for people with dementia, it considers different design ideas grounded on evidence-based and interventions from across various disciplines (Liu-Ambrose et al. 2008). The goal of the study was to investigate the effects of ICT-based exergames on the daily and social lives of people with dementia and their caregivers and to what extent such systems may support that target group in their individual and social needs.

## 18.2 Background

Information and communications technology can be a significant key technology for the technical development and integration of age-appropriate assistance systems for health, safety, care and communication. Over the past decade, research and design in HCI and ICT have provided technological solutions that suggest improvements in areas such as social participation, personal autonomy and improved the quality of life of older adults and people with dementia (Mokhtari et al. 2015; Martínez-Alcalá et al. 2016; Morrissey et al. 2017; Pinto-Bruno et al. 2017; D'Onofrio et al. 2017; Lazar et al. 2018). In the context of people with dementia, assistive technologies for the smart home, telecare and low-level technologies are considered the most accessible assistive technologies on the public market. In addition, assistive technologies for people with dementia and their families are specifically designed to support daily activities, safety monitoring, as a memory aid, prevent social isolation and to facilitate everyday life (Schorch et al. 2016; Martínez-Alcalá et al. 2016). The so-called *Serious Games* are game applications that go beyond only gaming by combining information, skills and knowledge in an entertaining way. For this purpose, different physical or cognitive exercises, computer games and new technology is combined with a gamification approach into ICT and applied to a broad spectrum of application domains such as training, education, sports and health. Video games focusing especially on involving physical exercise into a virtual game environment are called *exergames*. Exergames have become increasingly visible in the field of HCI and health prevention and the support of physical activity in older adults in the last few years (Freyermuth et al. 2013; Smeddinck et al. 2015; Ogonowski et al. 2016; Vaziri et al. 2016). Advantages of exergames are that the playful aspects of a videogame encourage users to train both their physical abilities and at the same time, their cognitive skills. Exergames range from controllers with built-in sensors, such as the Nintendo Wii, to pressure sensors, such as the Nintendo Wii Balance Board, to camera systems, such as the Microsoft Kinect and the Sony PlayStation EyeToy, which are controlled by gestures (van Diest et al. 2013). An example of the applications used for exergames is the interactive TV system "iStoppFalls." It is based on Microsoft Kinect and designed for older people to prevent falls (Aal et al. 2014; Ogonowski et al. 2016; Vaziri et al. 2016). In the context of dementia, McCallum and Boletsis (2013) have suggested that exergames that aim to improve physical performance can positively influence several different factors among people with moderate Alzheimer dementia and mild cognitive impairment, including gait, balance and motor control. Notably in our own work, exergames have been shown to have the potential to improve health and wellbeing in older adults with dementia (Unbehaun et al. 2020a, b; Unbehaun et al. 2018a, b, c).

## 18.3 Methods and Study Setup

This study deals with the effects of prototypically developed ICT-based systems to support the individual and social everyday life of people with dementia and their relatives. This design case study was formulated as per studies originally articulated by Wulf et al. (2011, 2015, 2018), which consists of three phases: (1) a pre-study focus with an empirical analysis of existing individual and social practices in a specific field; (2) design of innovative ICT-based artifacts related to the findings from the pre-study; and (3) investigation of the interaction with and appropriation of the designed technical artifact over a longer period of time. Owing to the limited space available in this chapter, we will focus on the interaction, appropriation and user experience in the findings section.

The pre- and design-study took place in the first and second phase of the presented work, the aim being to take a closer look at the existing social context of the research field. This involved researching existing practice and identifying the individual needs of people with dementia, their relatives and caregivers. For this purpose, guideline-based semi-structured interviews were conducted. The pre-study was followed by the design phase and the design of the exergame prototype and its underlying technical infrastructure. The prototype was adapted on the basis of the data collected from the preliminary study and initially used in day care and care facilities in the area of Siegen in Germany. There was a continuation of the participant observation from the preliminary study, in which we could observe early interactions of people with dementia with the exergames and their environment. The design iterations carried out in this phase with all actors in a participatory manner enabled further development of the prototype, so that in the evaluation phase study, the prototype could be rolled out in private households and a day care centre as part of a four-month pilot study.

In the third phase, we deployed the prototype in the day care setting and in households. The observation protocols for data collection were also carried out in the third phase. For this purpose, the researchers conducted moderated group sessions with people with dementia twice a week in a day care facility and once or twice a week in the households. The moderated group sessions in the day care centre were performed in groups of 4–5 permanent participants and 2–3 visiting guests. In the home care settings, where relatives were the caregivers, 3 people living with dementia and their caregivers participated. Within the day care, one of two large group rooms, usually used for activities such as singing, crafting or creativity, was used for the recurring session with the system and the semi-structured interviews. To provide a routine for people with dementia the workshops always took place in the same room and at the same time, around 2 pm in the afternoon. Participants were guided by professional caregivers and the researcher in the group room. As illustrated in Fig. 18.1, the participants sat in a semicircle in front of the system. A researcher sat between the system and the participants without disturbing the view of the system. At least two researchers with two different roles were assigned to carry out the workshops. One of the roles included leading the workshops with setting up and operating the technology as well as supervising and motivating the participants. If the workshops took place in the households, the focus was more on motivation and support of the participant and their caregiver. The other researcher was also responsible for setting up the technology and also observed the participants'

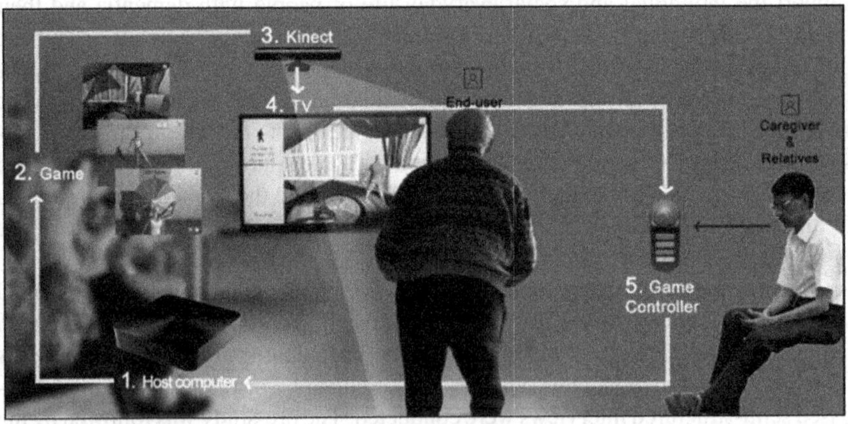


**Fig. 18.1** Participant interacting with the system

interaction with the technology and the effect the technology had on people with dementia during the workshops. The impressions of both researchers were recorded in observation protocols as data, which formed the basis of the participant observation.

We present results that describe how the usage behavior and interaction was perceived in relation to the people with dementia and their caregivers. In particular, we illustrate the related individual and socio-collaborative impacts and benefits of a videogame-based system, designed with people with dementia and their caregivers. Specifically, we seek to address the following research questions: (1) To what extent does the prototype exergame have an impact on the physical and cognitive condition of people with dementia and, (2) which social phenomena can be observed in the social environment of people with dementia through the introduction of the system?

To answer these questions, different data collection methods were used, such as conducting qualitative interviews and participating observation during the study in the home settings and care facilities. The subsequent processing of the data was based on qualitative content analysis as according to Mayring (2000). Overall, the study included nine people with early to mid-stage dementia (as confirmed by medical professionals) who were aged 65 years and over, including six informal caregivers. Ethical approval was given by the ethics committee of the University of Siegen. The inclusion criteria were that the participants should have frequent access to a high-definition TV with a HDMI port, located in a room with at least three square meters of space in front of the TV, so that they would be able to use the system without risk of injury. No financial compensation was offered to the participants.

## 18.4 System Overview

The videogame-based training system is based on a prototype for fall prevention in older adults which was further developed in collaboration with people with dementia and their caregivers (Gschwind et al. 2015; Vaziri et al. 2017). The system consists of several technical components. The technology is centered around the TV to provide an easy and familiar route through which it can be accessed. The ICT-based training system runs on a space-saving and quiet mini-computer. Currently, a MS Kinect is used to detect the movements of the participant when interacting with the system. Recognition of the movements detected by the Kinect is reflected in their visual representation, providing comparable and measurable movement definitions and movement sequences. To simplify the interaction with the overall system, a tablet and a PlayStation 3 Buzzer were used. The tablet displays the current exercise plan, the results of the different games and educational material about dementia, which are saved in a secure online storage. The Buzzer, with its big colorful buttons, is used as a simple input device during the games, such as choosing an answer during a quiz. Over time, the system automatically increases the difficulty level of the exercises. To counteract the progression of dementia and to help people to remain autonomous and less dependent upon caring relatives, specific exercises and games, as well as performance assessments, were developed and selected by project partners from the fields of sport science, sport gerontology and nursing science (see Fig. 18.2).

To strengthen the upper and lower limbs and muscles, prominent exercise programs such as the Otago exercise program were implemented. The training includes exercises such as knee extensors, strengthening the front thigh muscles; knee bends, strengthening the rear thigh muscles; sideways leg raises, for the lateral thigh muscles; toe-stands, for the calf muscles; elbow bends, for the upper arm muscles; and front raises, for the shoulder muscles. The focus of the balance and coordination games is to solve percipience, improve balance and reaction and for the tasks to be done in a playful fashion. For instance, in the so-called *Apple Game* the participant has to harvest virtual apples from a tree and put them in the basket next to them. In a second game, participants have to raise their knees in turn while walking through a park. In a third game, they have to perform sideways and forward steps to hit moles. The creativity and cognition aspect cover a variety of games that combine movement and cognitive tasks. In the game *Wheel of Fortune* participants raise their hands and spin a wheel. Afterwards, they have to solve different types of tasks, such as letter games; mental arithmetic; classification and completion of rhymes, verses and poems; and remembering music titles. In another game, traditional and folk music is played while the player walks on the spot. If they stop, the music fades and they have to start the music again by walking.

## 18.5 Results

In the following, we present findings in relation to the impacts and benefits for people with dementia and their caregivers using the exergames over a longer period of time (Fig. 18.2).

### *18.5.1 Sociality and Group Interaction*

Here we present the results related to social interaction and group dynamics. This includes how people with dementia interact in day care, how groups can act as motivators or intimidators and comment on how harmonious moments unfolded with the support of each other and in moments of discussion. In the day care center, it could be said that with increasing and regular numbers of participants, a group-dynamic is developed in relation to the continuous interaction with the system. For example, the participants gave each other tips for the execution of certain movements of play and praised actions by cheering. We could observe that in games, in which only one person was active, the whole group could be involved by singing, supporting or guessing answers, in the game *Wheel of Fortune*. These were, according to their own statements, the games that people with dementia preferred to play. Beside games

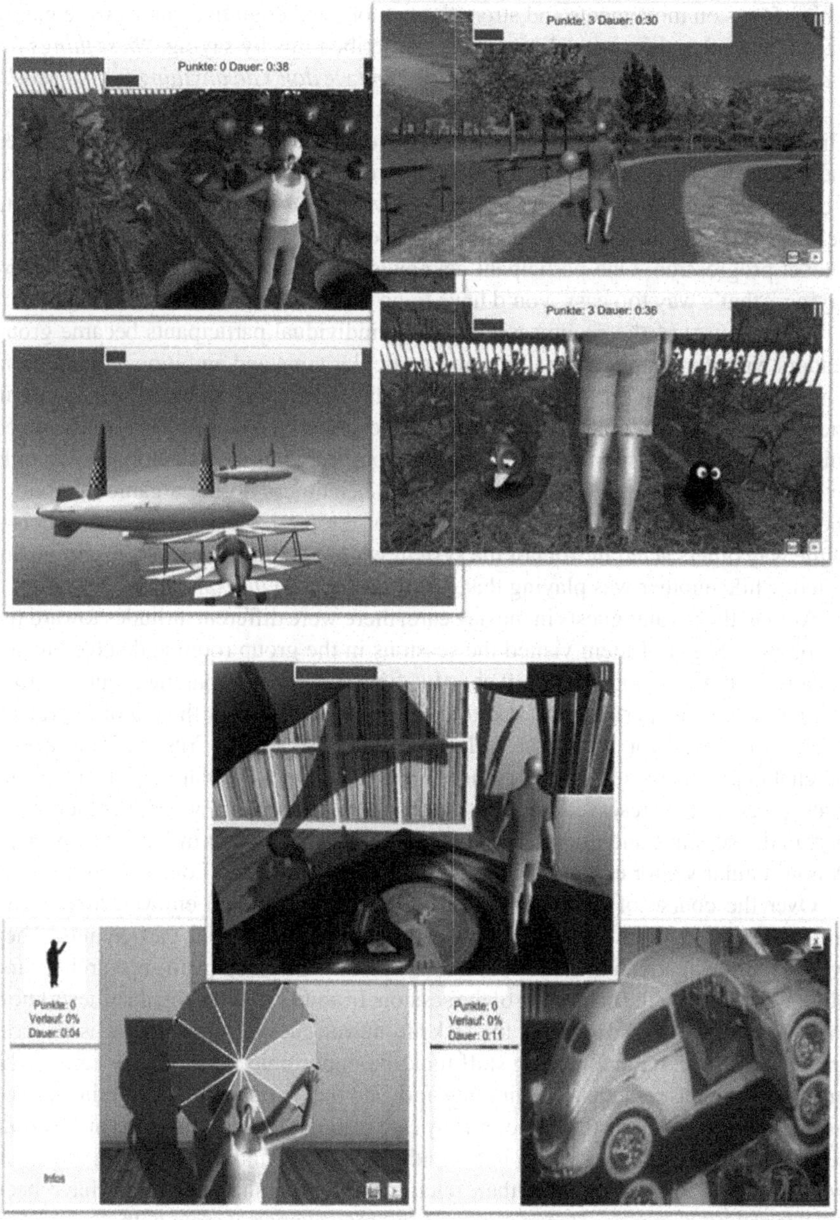


**Fig. 18.2** Coordination, balance and creativity games

with a focus on movements and strength, memory and cognitive games were gladly played and often asked for. A participant described this by saying, "*best things for the head. We can run, we can do gymnastics, but we don't do anything for the head.*"

A few games turned out to be too easy for some participants in the day care. They were able to quickly recognize repetitive questions as a group and expressed their thoughts about the level of difficulty. For example, a participant explained after a certain question appeared on the screen, "we've had the question with the cobra before." Building upon this the participants were also aware that the system offered a level progression. One participant acknowledged a less-challenging question by saying, "that's way too easy, you'd have to go one level higher."

In the course of the group sessions, some individual participants became group leaders with dominant personalities and particular aims and ambitions. In addition, it was observed that participants supported the cognitively weaker participants in the sessions. For example, the tasks during the game *Wheel of Fortune* were solved jointly in the group. On the one hand, the group acted as a motivator, for example by commenting on a participant who showed her fitness during a game in front of the group by unintended movements. Some of the participants expressed criticism at the way others acted in front of the system while playing the games. A participant noted, while another was playing that, "*no, she can't do that anymore*."

Among the regular guests in the day care, there were different attitudes toward the exergames. Some of them visited the sessions in the group room and stayed to see what was going on, and others left shortly after recognizing what the group sessions were about. Some participants also told different guests about the ongoing project. "Yes, I did enroll for it because I always enjoy it so much…Yes, we're always a bit challenged there, so I like to go here," was stated by a regular participant. Some guests were rather reserved and not interested in the system, whereas others took part in the sessions and told their friends in the day care about the research project. A non-regular visitor explained that, "I think it's nice too, but I don't need it."

Over the course of four months, some of the guests who enjoyed taking part in the sessions and interacting with the system became regular participants. They were usually already in the room before the system was set up by the researchers and already waiting for the beginning of the session. In addition, these regular guests knew most of the tasks and explained the tasks to newer guests and provided assistance. In addition, professional nursing staff took the opportunity to show day care onsite guests during the sessions. The findings indicate that people with dementia enjoyed using the system in both, the home and day care setting. Many participants in the home setting took the opportunity to connect with their grandchildren by playing together, which actively helped to strengthen relationships that otherwise might have been challenged by dementia. Hence, this synergy may support people with dementia in readopting social roles and facilitate communication and interaction across different generations. Observations and interviews indicated that such aspects helped people with dementia to maintain social responsibilities and aided reintegration into familiar structures, their daily life routines and respective social roles.

### 18.5.2 Attitude to the System and Individual Perception

The focus here is on the daily performance of people with dementia, their attitude toward the system and memories that are evoked during the interaction with the system. It could be observed that the results achieved by people with dementia in the games were strongly dependent on their daily wellbeing. On some days, dementia, as illness was more present, result in a decrease in cognitive abilities, which in turn affected the participants and their performance in the games. However, there were some moments when individual participants remembered beautiful moments from the past through the games. While playing the walking game, one participant made an association, "Yes, I can walk and run. I was a track and field athlete and had a 12.2 s time at the 100-m sprint."

Participants, their caregivers and their relatives expressed their opinion on the system and assessed whether they would like to continue using it. Overall, the relatives affirmed that they saw potential in the exergames and would continue to use. A relative even stated that she would recommend an improved, more stable version of the system to other people. Some people with dementia, on the other hand, expressed themselves differently about the system. A participant refused to continue using the system because there was no interest for them in playing it. "Actually not. No, because I have many other interests. So, playing, no. I'm also not like that, that you always have to play." However, another person would use the system to have more daily activities, and with regard to long-term use, a participant said that "I would say yes. I also need that…Because I normally just sit here…and have nothing to do. Then I always have a little activity." In addition, participants specified the advantages and disadvantages of the system from their point of view. The general attitude of the participants toward the system was very positive and the idea was perceived as good. One relative stated that he used the system himself and that the games and exercises were physically good for him and more entertaining than gardening, for example. In comparison to a sports course, the exergames performed better with the participants. The reason given was that sports courses had to be based on fixed times and that the training times could not be arranged individually. In addition, you would have to leave the house to get to the sports hall. A relative explained that, "it is easier to use such a system at home than it is to have to leave the house again and to have a greater risk of falling." Another relative describe the advantages in her perception, "especially for people in our age, I find the training at home better than in the Gymnastics club."

The conversation with the professional nursing staffs showed that the day care guests were looking forward to the workshops and found it a pleasant change of pace. The nursing staffs were positive about the system and could imagine a long-term installation of the system. A professional caregiver noted this by explaining, "just don't get the idea to stop." Newcomers were also invited to the group sessions by the caregivers. According to the nursing staff, the research project with the exergame was of great importance for the day care guests. As mentioned before, people with dementia were looking forward to the next session. This was mentioned by a professional caregiver, "so you got an enormous importance for our guests, who really don't want to have a lunch break, because those from the university are coming soon."

The system affected also the relationship with the family and friends on a social basis in the settings. One relative in the ambulatory setting emphasized that after using the system, she generally wanted to play more games with her grandmother, "Yes, I will now try that I also play more with my grandmother. So, between three and four o'clock, because she also likes to play Rommeé." The caregivers found that the introduction of the system and the sessions encouraged the formation of group that continued even beyond the sessions. A newly formed group met in day care center outside the use of the exergames and asked the caregivers about the timing of the next workshop. Because of such positive experiences, group sessions became a recurring event in the day care setting, where participants connected to each other and had fun together. A representative of a care institution expressed a desire to integrate the system and its games into the daily schedule of group activities, because people with dementia enjoyed using the system so much.

## 18.6 Conclusion and Outlook

The aim of this work was to find out what effects a prototypically developed ICT system has on the individual and social life of people with dementia and their relatives. The results of this work show that the system primarily affects the social environment of people with dementia. The participants of the system looked forward to the contact with the researchers and the other people with dementia who played together. The results also showed that people with dementia in both nursing homes and households played the games with great intent and tried to help and support other participants. The results illustrate that the games were particularly well received by people with dementia and that movements could be associated with positive events from the past. With regard to the type of games played, people with dementia showed more interest and more motivation in improving social interaction, having joyful moments and improving wellbeing rather than physical fitness. In the course of the study, dominant personalities emerged, and cognitively stronger participants supported people with advanced dementia in interacting with the system. Some guests participated in the session and became regular participants over the period of the study. In addition, it was found that friendships formed between some guests through using the system have continued after the training was over. Relatives reported that they operated the system themselves or had it operated by professional nursing staff. On average, the system was used one to three times a week for a period of about half an hour to one hour.

Overall, the attitude toward the system was described as positive and the relatives in particular saw its high potential. The nursing staff of the day care center also assessed the system positively and would agree to a long-term installation of a stable prototype in the day care center. According to professional caregivers, people with dementia were looking forward not only to engage with the system but also with the researchers on the research project. The relatives at home stated that they did not feel any relief during the system usage, whereas the sessions in the day care center were a relief for the day care nurses. In terms of the home environment, only a few effects of the system on the social contact between people with dementia and their relatives were reported. As shown the potential for ICT and exergames especially with people with dementia is good and needs further investigation. Here, the focus should lay on group settings and social interactions in-between the participants.

In relation to the related work focusing only on combining exergames and physical activity, our presented work and system in the field of motion-based technologies for people with dementia resulted in facilitating social health and wellbeing of people with dementia. Beyond the previous findings in these areas, the results of this work show that in this research context the motivation lies with the system itself and does not originate from a desire for improved physical strength and the activity of playing the system itself. The use of the system was contextualized into the community of people with dementia, and therefore represents a social enrichment. As a result, in our case study a large part of the motivation of the use of the system can be traced back to the social component, which may help researchers and developers in the field of human–computer interaction and beyond to benefit from and improve in the design of appropriate technologies for people with dementia and their caregivers.

Finally, our results indicate that a successful and sustainable implementation of technology in the daily life of people with dementia and their social environment depends on many factors. Owing to the diverse and complex social process, technology appropriation can only succeed if the technology is embedded in the social context of people with dementia's everyday activities and care-processes. The social process of technology mediation and appropriation were found to be critical for success, with this opening up new possible arenas for technology-based solutions to support care settings for people with dementia and their caregivers. Thus, the complex daily and institutional challenges involved in living with dementia cannot be faced through a technically oriented one-sided perspective. Instead, design solutions have to be developed in and with the all actors in the related social care network. In this respect, we argue from a design and technology perspective that technology in the dementia context leads to social innovations, and thus contributes to needs-based and practice-oriented solution models for professional and private care.

## References


Aal K, Ogonowski C, von Rekowski T et al (2014) A fall preventive iTV solution for older adults. In: ACM international conference on interactive experiences for television and online video. Figshare

Anderiesen H (2017) Playful design for activation: co-designing serious games for people with moderate to severe dementia to reduce apathy. Delft University of Technology, The Netherlands

Brankaert R, Kenning G, Welsh D et al (2019) Intersections in HCI, design and dementia: inclusivity in participatory approaches. Companion publication of the 2019 on designing interactive systems conference 2019 companion—DIS '19 companion. ACM Press, San Diego, CA, USA, pp 357–360

Brodaty H, Donkin M (2009) Family caregivers of people with dementia. Dialog Clin Neurosci 11:217–228

D'Onofrio G, Sancarlo D, Ricciardi F et al (2017) Information and communication technologies for the activities of daily living in older patients with dementia: a systematic review. J Alzheimers Dis 57:927–935. https://doi.org/10.3233/JAD-161145

Foley S, Pantidi N, McCarthy J (2019) Care and design: an ethnography of mutual recognition in the context of advanced dementia. In: Proceedings of the 2019 CHI conference on human factors in computing systems—CHI '19. ACM Press, Glasgow, Scotland, UK, pp 1–15

Freyermuth GS, Gotto L, Wallenfels F (eds) (2013) Serious games, exergames, exerlearning: for transmedialization and gamification of knowledge transfer. Transcript, Bielefeld

Gschwind YJ, Eichberg S, Ejupi A et al (2015) ICT-based system to predict and prevent falls (iStoppFalls): results from an international multicenter randomized controlled trial. Eur Rev Aging Phys Act 12. https://doi.org/10.1186/s11556-015-0155-6

Hodge J, Montague K, Hastings S, Morrissey K (2019) Exploring media capture of meaningful experiences to support families living with dementia. In: Proceedings of the 2019 CHI conference on human factors in computing systems—CHI '19. ACM Press, Glasgow, Scotland, UK, pp 1–14

Lazar A, Toombs AL, Morrissey K et al (2018) HCIxDementia workshop: engaging people living with dementia. In: Press ACM (ed) Extended abstracts of the 2018 CHI conference on human factors in computing systems—CHI '18. ACM Press, Montreal, QC, Canada, pp 1–7

Liu-Ambrose T, Donaldson MG, Ahamed Y et al (2008) Otago home-based strength and balance retraining improves executive functioning in older fallers: a randomized controlled trial: home exercise program and cognition. J Am Geriatr Soc 56:1821–1830. https://doi.org/10.1111/j.1532-5415.2008.01931.x

Marston H, Samuels J (2019) A review of age friendly virtual assistive technologies and their effect on daily living for carers and dependent adults. Healthcare 7:49. https://doi.org/10.3390/healthcare7010049

Martínez-Alcalá CI, Pliego-Pastrana P, Rosales-Lagarde A et al (2016) Information and communication technologies in the care of the elderly: systematic review of applications aimed at patients with dementia and caregivers. JMIR Rehabil Assist Technol 3:e6. https://doi.org/10.2196/rehab.5226

Mayring P (2000) Qualitative content analysis. Forum Qual Sozialforschung (Forum Qual Soc Res) 1

McCallum S, Boletsis C (2013) Dementia games: a literature review of dementia-related serious games. In: Ma M, Oliveira MF, Petersen S, Hauge JB (eds) Serious games development and applications. Springer, Berlin, pp 15–27

Mokhtari M, Endelin R, Aloulou H, Tiberghien T (2015) Measuring the impact of ICTs on the quality of life of ageing people with mild dementia. In: Bodine C, Helal S, Gu T, Mokhtari M (eds) Smart homes and health telematics. Springer International Publishing, Cham, pp 103–109

Morrissey K, Lazar A, Boger J, Toombs A (2017) HCIxDementia workshop: the role of technology and design in dementia. In: Proceedings of the 2017 CHI conference extended abstracts on human factors in computing systems—CHI EA '17. ACM Press, Denver, Colorado, USA, pp 484–491

Ogonowski C, Aal K, Vaziri D et al (2016) ICT-based fall prevention system for older adults: qualitative results from a long-term field study. ACM Trans Comput-Hum Interact 23:1–33. https://doi.org/10.1145/2967102

Pinto-Bruno ÁC, García-Casal JA, Csipke E et al (2017) ICT-based applications to improve social health and social participation in older adults with dementia. A systematic literature review. Aging Ment Health 21:58–65. https://doi.org/10.1080/13607863.2016.1262818

Schorch M, Wan L, Randall DW, Wulf V (2016) Designing for those who are overlooked—insider perspectives on care practices and cooperative work of elderly informal caregivers. ACM Press, pp 785–797

Schulz R, Martire LM (2004) Family caregiving of persons with dementia: prevalence, health effects, and support strategies. Am J Geriatr Psychiatry Off J Am Assoc Geriatr Psychiatry 12:240–249
Smeddinck JD, Herrlich M, Malaka R (2015) Exergames for physiotherapy and rehabilitation: a medium-term situated study of motivational aspects and impact on functional reach. In: Proceedings of the 33rd annual ACM conference on human factors in computing systems—CHI '15. ACM Press, Seoul, Republic of Korea, pp 4143–4146
Unbehaun D, Aal K, Vaziri DD et al (2018a) Facilitating collaboration and social experiences with videogames in dementia: results and implications from a participatory design study. Proc ACM Hum-Comput Interact 2:1–23. https://doi.org/10.1145/3274444
Unbehaun D, Vaziri DD, Aal K et al (2018b) Video-game based exergames for people with dementia and their caregivers. GROUP '18: Proceedings of the 2018 ACM Conference on Supporting Groupwork. https://doi.org/10.1145/3148330.3154506
Unbehaun D, Vaziri DD, Aal K et al (2018c) Exploring the potential of exergames to affect the social and daily life of people with dementia and their caregivers. ACM Press, pp 1–15. https://doi.org/10.1145/3173574.3173636
Unbehaun D, Taugerbeck S, Aal K et al (2020a) Notes of memories: fostering social interaction, activity and reminiscence through an interactive music exergame developed for people with dementia and their caregivers. Int J Hum-Compute Interact. https://doi.org/10.1080/07370024.2020.1746910
Unbehaun D, Aal K, Vaziri DD et al (2020b) Social technology appropriation in dementia: investigating the role of caregivers in engaging people with dementia with a videogame-based training system. ACM Press. https://doi.org/10.1145/3313831.3376648
van Diest M, Lamoth CJ, Stegenga J et al (2013) Exergaming for balance training of elderly: state of the art and future developments. J NeuroEng Rehabil 10:101. https://doi.org/10.1186/1743-0003-10-101
Vaziri DD, Aal K, Gschwind YJ et al (2017) Analysis of effects and usage indicators for a ICT-based fall prevention system in community dwelling older adults. Int J Hum-Comput Stud 106:10–25. https://doi.org/10.1016/j.ijhcs.2017.05.004
Vaziri DD, Aal K, Ogonowski C et al (2016) Exploring user experience and technology acceptance for a fall prevention system: results from a randomized clinical trial and a living lab. Eur Rev Aging Phys Act 13 https://doi.org/10.1186/s11556-016-0165-z
Wulf V, Müller C, Pipek V et al (2015) Practice-based computing: empirically grounded conceptualizations derived from design case studies. In: Wulf V, Schmidt K, Randall D (eds) Designing socially embedded technologies in the real-world. Springer London, London, pp 111–150
Wulf V, Pipek V, Randall D et al (eds) (2018) Socio-informatics: a practice-based perspective on the design and use of IT artifacts, 1st edn. Oxford University Press, Oxford, United Kingdom
Wulf V, Rohde M, Pipek V, Stevens G (2011) Engaging with practices: design case studies as a research framework in CSCW. ACM Press, p 505

# Chapter 19
# Working with Experts with Experience: Charting Co-production and Co-design in the Development of HCI-Based Design

**Kristina Niedderer, Dew Harrison, Julie Gosling, Michael Craven, Alethea Blackler, Raquel Losada, and Teresa Cid**

## 19.1 Introduction

The chapter discusses the design process and how the decision-making and development undertaken in creating the *Let's meet up!* system was interwoven with participant activities in the UK, Germany, the Netherlands and Spain. These events informed the research and facilitated co-design and effective design development and decision-making by and for the users (Hendriks et al. 2015; Sanders and Stappers 2014). The rationale for this research was the understanding that people with

K. Niedderer (✉)
Manchester Metropolitan University, Manchester, UK
e-mail: K.Niedderer@mmu.ac.uk

D. Harrison
University of Wolverhampton, Wolverhampton, UK
e-mail: Dew.Harrison@wlv.ac.uk

J. Gosling · M. Craven
Nottinghamshire Healthcare NHS Foundation Trust, Nottingham, UK
e-mail: Julietgosling@hotmail.com

M. Craven
e-mail: Michael.Craven@nottingham.ac.uk

A. Blackler
Queensland University of Technology, Brisbane, Australia
e-mail: A.Blackler@qut.edu.au

R. Losada · T. Cid
INTRAS, Valladolid, Spain
e-mail: Rld@intras.es

T. Cid
e-mail: Tcb@intras.es

© Springer Nature Switzerland AG 2020

R. Brankaert and G. Kenning (eds.), *HCI and Design in the Context of Dementia*, Human–Computer Interaction Series,
https://doi.org/10.1007/978-3-030-32835-1_19

dementia need and often want to maintain social connections, interaction and physical activities and that these are important for maintaining cognitive abilities, emotional well-being, and quality of life (Mendes de Leon et al. 2003; Ylvisaker et al. 2005). However, social engagement becomes more challenging for people living with dementia. This is due to a combination of functional issues (e.g. memory and attentional problems), behavioural and psychological symptoms of dementia (e.g. depression, aggression), and social issues (e.g. perceived stigma of dementia) (Baddeley et al. 2002; Ylvisaker et al. 2005), which may lead to their withdrawal from social interaction. The lack of these abilities has a particular impact on the independence of people with early to mid-stage dementia who wish to continue living at home for longer.

Common issues for people with dementia include mobility, where, for instance, orientation becomes a challenge and driving and cycling may no longer be possible (Blackman et al. 2003; Marquardt 2011; Taylor and Tripodes 2001). A caregiver or other support person may not always be available to accompany them (e.g. Zwaanswijk et al. 2013). While the mobility issues are not necessarily caused by dementia, they are compounded by dementia, in that it may make it more challenging to drive or because of license restrictions (Taylor and Tripodes 2001). Technological options are available for orientation support such as using a Satnav when driving (Wallace 2010), and when walking, there are digital devices available to help with wayfinding (Grierson et al. 2011; Tchang et al. 2008; Teipel et al. 2016) or with safekeeping (e.g. Daniels 2008; Milne et al. 2014). In the UK, the Dementia Dog scheme has pioneered the use of trained dogs to act as companions not only to aid with finding the way but also to remind people of meal times (Design Council 2012).

Another common issue for people with dementia is social support. Social support is available in various forms and levels across different countries. In terms of social opportunities, in Germany, a person with dementia can apply for several hours of support per week for someone to spend time with and to accompany them on any activity including social and leisure activities (Bracke et al. 2016). In the UK, non-state-sponsored support includes Alzheimer's cafes and day-care groups which provide opportunities for social interaction (Alzheimer Europe 2013). In the Netherlands, the Humanitas scheme offers students with learning difficulties free accommodation in return for contact and support time for care home residents; however, this approach is not without its critics (Jansen 2015).

In terms of making and maintaining social connections outside of such formalized support or social groups, Facetime and Skype are increasingly being used (e.g. Evans et al. 2015). But, as yet, there are few Apps available which are specifically developed for people with dementia (e.g. My House of Memories[1]), and even fewer that allow them to connect to others (e.g. Cuomo, MyLife, Care and Connect: Dementia Friendly Places). Most Apps are directed at caregivers, and those available for people with dementia are generally complex and can be a challenge to navigate even for people without dementia.

[1] All available on the App store.

This brief overview of available support indicates two main points: Firstly, that personal social support is impacted by the country's national support system and its local organizations, and this varies greatly from country to country. Secondly, problems with support are diverse and need to be addressed on an individual basis. So, the availability of an individual's network and how to facilitate ongoing connections in a sufficiently user-friendly way is vitally important. To address this second point, we developed the *Let's meet up!* electronic system through a co-production approach with people with dementia. In the following, we first describe the design development process including the different phases of co-production and the co-design activities. We then provide a critical discussion on the inter-relationship of research, co-production and co-design processes, and draw out insights and recommendations for best practice.

### *19.1.1 Research Process: Co-designing 'Let's Meet Up!'*

The social role of design is rarely acknowledged in the context of dementia support. More commonly, design aspects are subsumed under the label of 'assistive technology', addressing predominantly functional issues relating, for example, to stimulating memory, personal safety, enabling independence, and orientation (e.g. Guss et al. 2014). Furthermore, assistive technologies are often technology-driven and developed with and for use by caregivers of people with dementia. Where technology developments involve people with dementia, they tend to adopt an arts-based approach (e.g. Lazar et al. 2017) or focus on the expression of experience (e.g. Morrissey et al. 2017). By contrast, our research is on the development and use of design for its socially transformative and empowering qualities involving people with dementia actively in the development process.

Our research process has taken a novel approach in that we have involved people with early to mid-stage dementia throughout the research process from beginning to end; from the data collection, scoping and decision-making phases right through to the design concept and prototype development. Methods have included interviews and focus groups in Germany, The Netherlands and Spain as well as a one full-day consultation with the European Working Group of People with Dementia (EWG-PWD), and working locally with groups of experts with experience (GEE) groups in the UK[2] and in Spain, at various points throughout the project. Altogether over 70 people with dementia participated in the study.[3] Our design research process can be broken down into four overlapping phases (Fig. 19.1):

---

[2]The UK specific term for GEE used by the National Health System (NHS) is 'Public and Patient Involvement' (PPI). However, for unity with European terminology, we are using the term GEE throughout.

[3]Ethics approvals and informed consent where sought and observed in line with European and local guidelines by the relevant partner organizations.

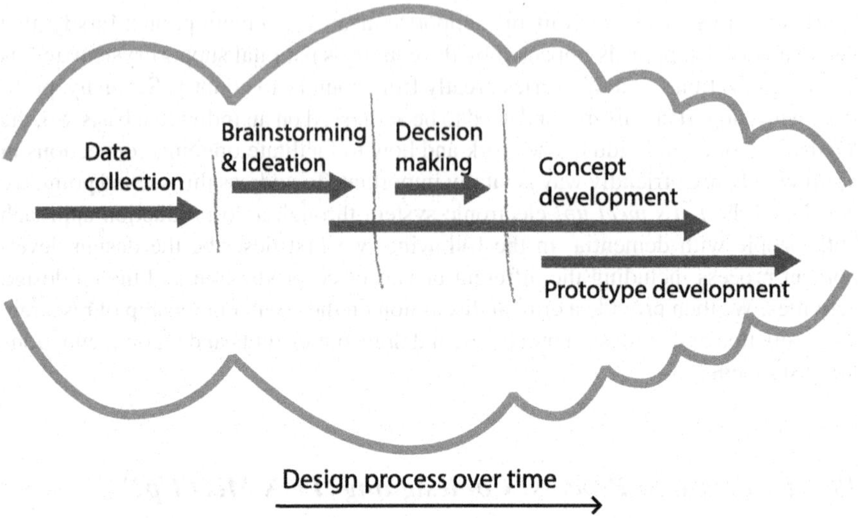


**Fig. 19.1** Design research process in four overlapping phases

1. Data collection with people with dementia, which resulted in a number of 'MinD themes'.
2. Brainstorming and ideation where themes were addressed by designers and critically reviewed with a GEE representative, leading to the identification of 'Transition Areas'.
3. Idea development and decision-making for potential prototypes from the transition areas.
4. Concept development, design specification and prototype development.

**Phase 1—Data collection: Understanding what people with dementia want and need**
The data collection, undertaken with people with dementia, sought to gain insights into their wants and needs in relation to their subjective well-being, self-empowerment and social engagement. The data collection methods were used to elicit details about issues and challenges related to well-being and self-empowerment in everyday social contexts from the view of the person with dementia with the aim of identifying situations for design innovation. The data collection methods and instruments included qualitative interviews with individuals and focus groups using visual cards with images related to everyday, social and leisure activities to support discussion in interviews, and visual probes—a design method used to collect experiential information visually and to complement the data collected in interviews. Visual probes provide insights into individuals' personal context including their social, aesthetic and cultural environment as well as needs, feelings and attitudes (Hendriks et al. 2015; Mattelmäki 2006; Sanders and Stappers 2014). The MinD probes included, for example, pop-up paper houses and Kilner storage jars with prompt questions, which

acted as visual metaphors designed to promote memory and initiate conversations about the everyday life and needs of a person with dementia. These probes are more fully described in Garde et al. (2018).

Groups of care professionals (psychiatrists, gerontologists, care workers) and researchers conducted the data collection and analysis with people with dementia and caregivers in Germany, The Netherlands and Spain. The transcripts from the interviews were translated and passed to the designers as sets of themed quotes for them to work with. The analysis of the quotes revealed nine content-related themes to focus the design innovations, plus two generic themes (familiarity and continuity) to provide further guidance for designers (Fig. 19.2). In the figure, the themes are related to the five stages of change experienced during the progression into dementia: pre-symptomatic, mild cognitive impairment, and early, moderate and late stages of dementia (Caldwell et al. 2015: 67). The nine content-related 'MinD themes' provided the basis for brainstorming and design ideation in the next phase.

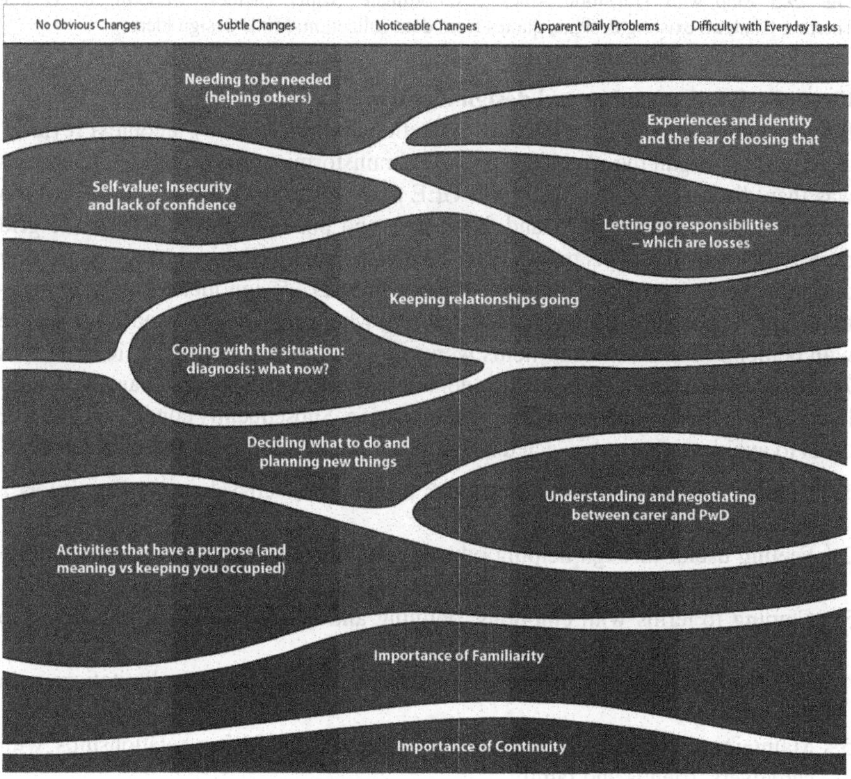


**Fig. 19.2** 9 + 2 MinD Themes

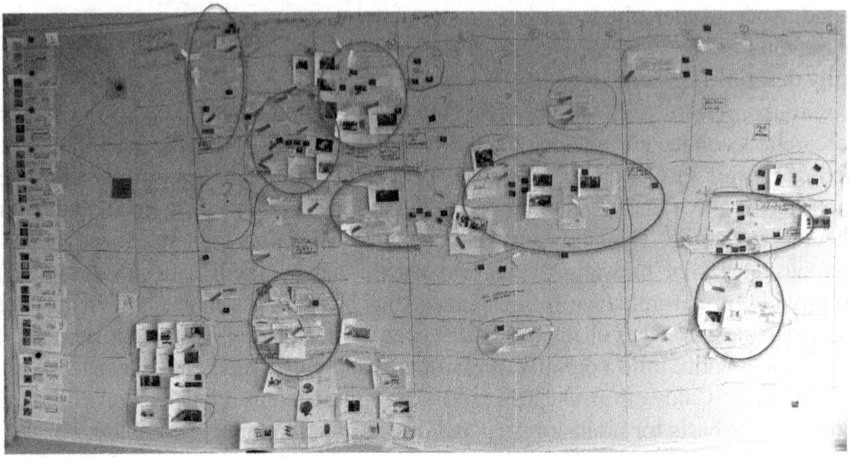

**Fig. 19.3** Map with Transition Areas. X-co-ordinate: MinD Themes; Y-coordinate: Design Themes; Content: existing designs, quotes from data collection, MinD design ideas

**Phase 2—Brainstorming and design ideation**

Based on the 'themes' from the data collection and informed by a context review,[4] the designers began the ideation work with brainstorming and sketching. Each idea was then discussed by the team with GEE representation according to the criteria of mindfulness, functionality and feasibility, and positioned on a large-scale grid map as a data matrix. This matrix (Fig. 19.3) was populated with images of existing designs, quotes from the data collection and 'MinD' design ideas. Our map highlighted particular areas of concern (circled red) where support was needed for people with dementia but no existing items were available. Seven areas were identified as *Transition Areas* where people with dementia experience specific changes in their lives and which are suitable for design intervention. Subsequently condensed into five areas to avoid overlaps, they acted as briefs for the development of the prototypes:

1. Coming to terms with the diagnosis: acceptance, self-value and identity as a person with dementia
2. Feeling useful through helping others: sustaining self-worth and positive emotions
3. Coming to terms with emotions: defining and valuing yourself, in relation to others (later subsumed under point 2)
4. Self-realization through purposeful activities: compensating for limitations with new activities
5. Maintaining social participation: autonomy in continuing relationships with caregivers, friends and family

[4]The context review was conducted during 2016–2017 by colleagues of the MinD team. It surveyed existing design products and services with applications in the dementia context to provide an overview of the state of the art of design practice in this area against which to evaluate any new design ideas from the Mind project.

6. Keeping relationships going: empathy in planning, decision-making and in negotiation with caregivers, friends and family
7. Negotiation and communication: when planning activities (later merged with point 6)

**Phase 3—Idea development and decision-making.**
The initial design ideas were developed in more detail in relation to the *Transition Areas*, and to personas and scenarios. The latter were developed as fictional entities based on real data from the data collection, bringing together typical characteristics and offering representative examples to work with (see Niedderer et al. 2017; Carroll 2000; Williams et al. 2014). Ideas were then presented in short form (Fig. 19.4) to different professional and user groups in Germany and Spain in an iterative feedback process. Those judged to be useful, relevant and appropriate for taking forward were then presented to a group of people with dementia and caregivers in the UK, and one representative from the European Working Group of People with Dementia (EPWPWD) who joined via Skype. Overall, design ideas were discussed with a total of 26 MinD design and healthcare colleagues, external healthcare experts, caregivers and people with lived experience of dementia and memory problems to indicate, understand and acknowledge their preferences.

Based on the collated feedback, the MinD management group decided which design ideas were to be taken forward for prototyping: the Good Life Kit (not discussed in this chapter) and the *Let's meet up!* system (based on the Social Engagement

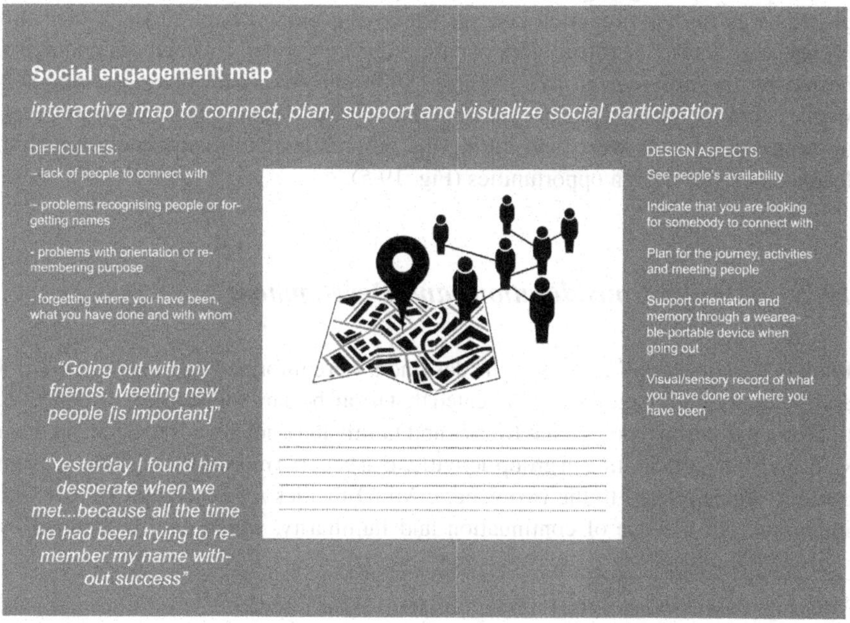


**Fig. 19.4** Social Engagement Map 'Let's meet up!'—short form presented for discussion

Map) were selected. This chapter reports on the latter. The following section presents the prototype co-development activity leading to the creation of the system.

**Phase 4—Concept development, design specification and prototype development**

Having provided insights into the processes and development plans used in the 'MinD' project we will now provide an overview of the 'Lets meet up!' design and describe the process through which it was developed. *Let's meet up!* is an electronic system for social engagement that aims to empower people living with dementia. It encourages people with dementia to stay in touch with their loved ones and to remain physically and socially active by arranging joint activities through a simple, user-friendly, tangible interface. It seeks to empower people with dementia by helping them to plan and prepare for going out and by giving them the confidence to initiate these activities.

## 19.2 Design Development Process

This section is organized into three parts: an overview of the design considerations and development, a brief description of the participatory co-design processes, and a summary of the final design. After the decision-making was completed, the development process continued as an iterative process, which is a generally acknowledged characteristic of designing (Sanders and Stappers 2014). The iterative development process was further supported and shaped by the grant scheme under which this project was funded[5]: Project work occurred during regular 2-weekly secondments, hosted by the different project partners. Different groups of visiting researchers worked first on the design concept development and later on the prototype development. GEE events were held during the secondments to facilitate consultation, feedback and co-design opportunities (Fig. 19.5).

### *19.2.1 Design Considerations and Development*

For the 'Lets meet up!' prototype the designers were informed by *transition areas* 4 and 5 (see previous page) which indicated that it can be hard for people with dementia to keep relationships going, that friends and family may not always understand them well, and that participating in group activities can become more difficult. Other design considerations related to the two generic MinD themes referenced previously: the importance of a sense of continuation and familiarity, which can be attained by

[5]The project was funded under the Horizon 2020, Marie Sklodowska Curie, Research Innovation and Staff Exchange grant, which seeks to promote staff upskilling through working on a collaborative research project.

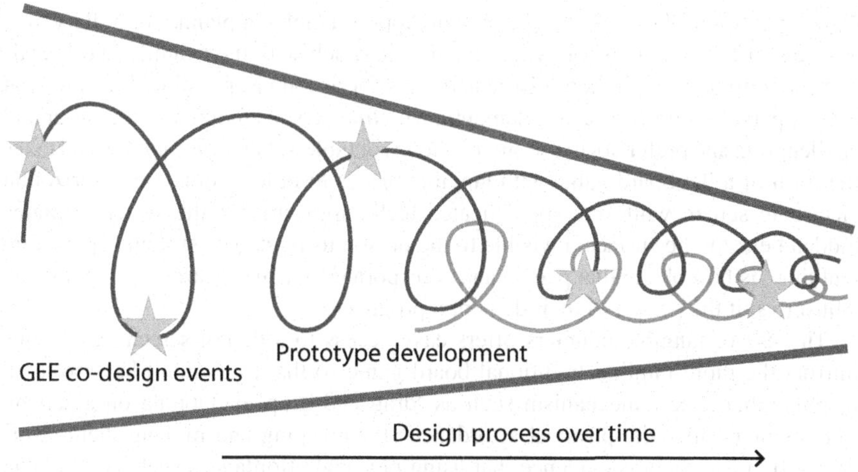


**Fig. 19.5** Iterative design concept and prototype development process

attending the same regular activity events, with the same people or using familiar things. The data revealed that although people with dementia might be happy to let go of activities if they found them difficult, they would not be so willing to give up activities they found pleasurable and gave them a sense of independence, purpose or achievement, even if this caused anxieties for the caregiver who perceived those activities as a risk. Therefore, the design needed to offer ways of encouraging motivation and confidence while offering new pastimes, which might compensate for the necessary loss of some activities.

There are currently a large number of people living with dementia who are not 'digital natives' having been born into an analogue generation. As these people are less familiar with new technological devices and can find the interfaces somewhat complex, cognitive simplicity was considered essential for the prototype in line with the theme: familiarity. While there are a number of mobile phones and tablets with helpful Apps available, they are not necessarily the first choice of users with dementia and caregivers as they usually need training to use them, which is possible but can be difficult. Feedback from the GEE groups reinforced this and indicated people's varied preferences for paper diaries, email or iPads for using Skype. In addition, electronic devices presented difficulties with remembering passwords or with the layered structure of Apps and Programs. In bringing the two aspects of familiarity and cognitive simplicity together, the design developed an interactive format that offered a more simplistic interface than existing solutions, essentially in a 'hybrid' format integrating digital and analogue elements drawing on familiar concepts and processes.

Based on these considerations, the designers agreed on an electronic system in the form of an interactive map presented in the style of a board game with counters to move in order to play. The aim of the *game* is to facilitate the person with dementia to connect, plan, support and visualize social participation. The social engagement electronic system *Let's meet up!* is not an App or a tablet, a planner or a diary, it is a means of keeping a person with dementia in touch with their family and friends and for continuing with their leisure activities for as long as possible. It is aimed at elderly persons with early-stage dementia who find new technologies unfamiliar and challenging, and prefer not to use smart-phones or tablets. *Let's meet up!* instead takes the form of a flat board game with tangible pieces to move around on a horizontal electronic screen while the sophisticated technology driving the system remains hidden beneath the surface, invisible to the person using it. The system is played in real time, is bespoke to that person and incorporates machine-learning so that it can adjust to suit the person as their dementia progresses.

The use of tangible counters offers easy access to a digital screen in that this mirrors the more familiar traditional board game so that users don't have to learn or remember a new mechanism such as 'drag and drop' or tapping on a screen. The counters offer the physical affordances for grasping and moving them (Norman 2013) and there is evidence that using physical affordances such as these can make interfaces more intuitive for people living with dementia, following principles described in Chap. 10 (Thea Blackler et al.). In addition, they have longevity in people's memories—common physical affordances are learnt in childhood and reinforced throughout the lifespan. So they are more familiar and potentially more robust in the face of dementia compared with other interface features, especially newer features and conventions, that many people in their 70s and older have limited familiarity with (Lawry et al. 2019).

## *19.2.2* Let's Meet Up! *Co-design and Co-production*

In order to fully involve people with dementia as co-designers, some mutual capacity building was required to surmount common apprehensions and preconceptions and build confidence in working together within multidisciplinary teams in the co-design sessions. One way of achieving this was to begin each session with a joint convivial and creative social task loosely related to the session theme. These tasks allowed people to get to know each other, share feelings and experiences, and celebrate common experiences as well as diversity. The sessions were then able to offer a safe space each time where participants were comfortable with each other, felt accepted, valued and able to speak up as illustrated in Chap. 2 (Kenning 2020). Two examples of these collaborative tasks are given below; the first focusses on developing shared experiences, the second concerns co-design working.

**Example of developing a safe co-production space**
This was an exercise around creative space where all participants were asked to pick an object of their choice from a 'magic suitcase' (Fig. 19.6). Participants then worked in groups telling each other who they were and why they had selected 'their' object before working together to create a joint storyline in which all the objects were embedded. To create a convivial atmosphere, each group then told their story to the

**Fig. 19.6** Capacity building for creative partnerships in decision-making

others, and finally, joined together to reflect on what they had learned about themselves, the other participants and about working together creatively. These sessions took about one hour in total.

**Example of developing co-design processes to facilitate moments of co-production**
During the design phase for *Let's meet up!* one of the co-design workshops introduced a series of tasks around everyday objects, where all the participants were asked to bring along an object of their choice such as a diary, watch, map or tablet. For these tasks, the participants worked in mixed groups to explore how we use such objects, how they help us organize and manage our everyday lives, and to see where they might not work so well, the space where new products could be envisaged. Based on the observations and insights from the tasks, participants were able to conceptualize what improvements or variations might be useful for 'Let's meet up!'. A large amount of material was gathered from these workshops, which helped to inform the next iteration of the design process.

In the examples given, all participants shared personal information about themselves: people with dementia, caregivers, designers and clinicians completed the tasks in groups. A redistribution of roles and power was enabled along mutual mindful explorations of the personal worlds of others, as co-workers with and without dementia discovered how much they had in common and helped to create a team spirit where all felt included, enabled and empowered.

### *19.2.3* Let's Meet Up! *Design Specification and Prototype*

The final system design is the output from the co-design process. It uses a single 40-inch screen placed on a (coffee) table where the person with dementia (player) will usually sit to rest and relax. Accompanying the screen is a round, transparent counter or *puck* 8.5 cm in diameter and an A4 sheet of instructions (Fig. 19.7). The screen is activated by sensors, which are triggered when the player sits down near the table. It then *comes to life* and shows a number of round images moving slowly

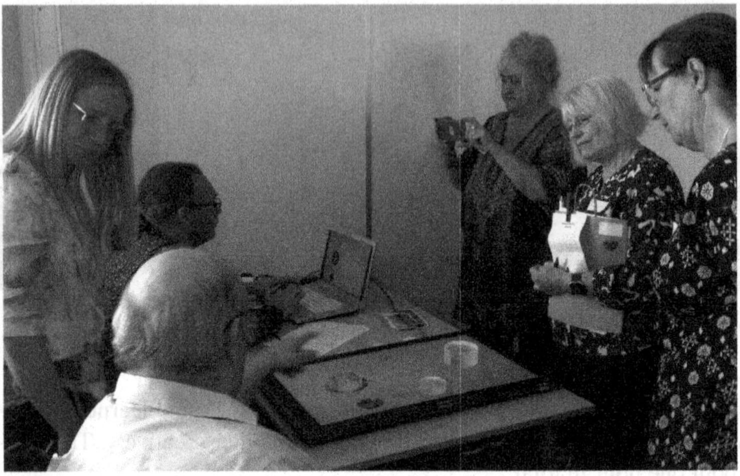

**Fig. 19.7** Trying out and evaluating the Let's meet up! experiential prototype with GEE participants in Nottingham, UK

around the screen. The images are either of the face of a friend or family member with their name and relationship printed at the top or an image of them with the person with dementia enjoying an activity together with the activity's name at the bottom. Some of the images are large and clear, seemingly at the screen's surface, others are smaller and faded, as if below the surface. The clear images indicate who and what activities are available at that time, the faded images indicate unavailability. The 'face' images are on the left side of the screen, and the 'activity' images on the right. The screen of labelled faces and activities is to remind people of who they know and what they do. They can then follow through a small set of actions ending with a video call to make an arrangement to meet and undertake an activity.

**Using Let's meet up! involves the following steps:**
First select one of the large clear images by placing the *puck* on it. This action *sets* the image by *stamping* a coloured ring around it (Fig. 19.8), holding it still while most of the other images fade and shrink in size leaving the next set of selection choices available to be *stamped* (Fig. 19.9).

The second *stamped* image (Fig. 19.9) causes the others to fade as before, but also generates up to three information circles as conversation prompts at the bottom of the screen (Fig. 19.10).

At this point one of the two *stamped* and colour-ringed images (face/activity) is circled by an animated ring, encouraging the player to place the *puck* on it for a second time (Fig. 19.10). This action tells the system to call the chosen person directly and if it is a video call, the person called will appear in a central circle between the two faces and the activity images, with the three previously selected information circles visible below to act as conversation prompts (Fig. 19.11).

**Fig. 19.8** Let's meet up!—first 'entrance' screen

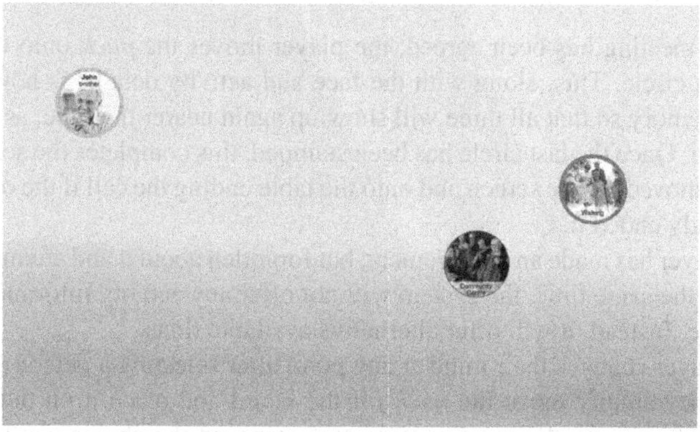

**Fig. 19.9** Let's meet up!—second screen

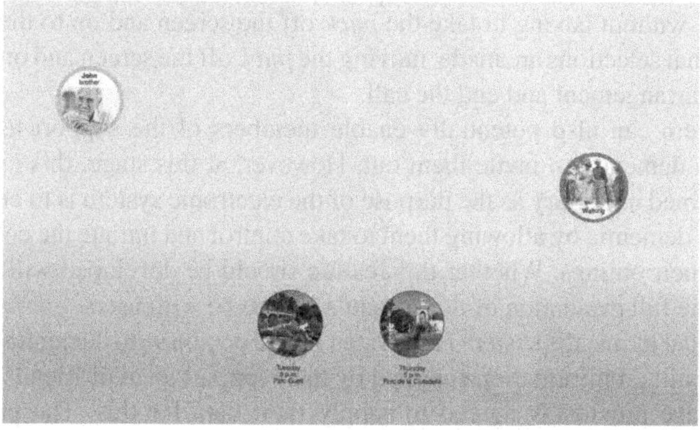

**Fig. 19.10** Let's meet up!—third screen

**Fig. 19.11** Let's meet up!—fourth screen

When a meeting has been agreed, the player moves the *puck* onto the relevant information circle. This, along with the face and activity details, is now set in the system's memory so that all three will show up again nearer the time, as a reminder to the player. Once the last circle has been stamped, this completes the sequence and the *puck* is moved off the screen and onto the table ending the call if the other person hasn't already ended it.

If the player has made an arrangement, but forgotten about it and attempts to make another for the same time, the system will not offer any activity information circles for that time. Instead, it will offer alternative available times.

If the player changes their mind at any point after selecting a person and activity and date, they simply move the *puck* off the board and place it on the table. The system then reverts to the previous selection step and the choice can be re-taken. However, if the final information circle has been selected and needs to be changed, the *puck* can be moved instantly on to another information circle taking the orange ring with it, without having to take the *puck* off the screen and on to the table first. When the final selections are made, moving the *puck* off the screen and onto the table will set the arrangement and end the call.

The system can also potentially enable members of the support team for the person with dementia to invite them out. However, at this stage, this extra facility was not deemed necessary as the purpose of the electronic system is to empower the person with dementia by allowing them to take control and initiate the conversations to arrange their outings. Whether this feature should be developed will be decided following the full evaluation of the system's prototype with users.

In technical terms, the system is activated by the person with dementia but runs on a database built on information supplied by their support team of friends and family who will have previously agreed to supply their data for this. The programmed system and database are invisible to the person with dementia. The support team members need to input personal details such as names, relation to the person with dementia, time slots when they are available to be called, and face and activity images, separately. They can also edit their data if, for example, they need to change their face image or their available time slots. The support team needs to ensure between them that someone is available for the person with dementia during the daytime time slots. When no one is available, for example, throughout the night, no large clear images are offered to the player during those hours. During day times, the player simply moves the *puck* to select the clear circular images.

The system is designed for easy play. There are only three levels and never more than three options for the player to choose from at each level. The aim is to enable the person with dementia to use the device on their own, as their caregiver may not always be at hand, to promote autonomy for as long as possible. The prototype created exists in its basic form of contact and engagement, and other affordances could be programmed in as required. One example is to include a means of recording the event for memory enhancement and savouring pleasant moments. Each system is uniquely bespoke for its owner and may begin with a much wider social sphere than the one demonstrated in this prototype; however, as the dementia progresses, the machine-learning aspect of the system will work with the user to reduce the scale of the social sphere and its complexity accordingly.

## 19.3 Conclusion and Recommendations

In this chapter, we have discussed the development of the *Let's meet up!* electronic system designed with and for people with early to mid-stage dementia. In response to data collected at the start of the project, the system was developed as a means of enabling people living with dementia to stay active and socially engaged.

A key aspect of this design project has been putting people with dementia at the centre of an open-ended design process, not predefined by technology. It was therefore essential to involve people with dementia at all stages of the research and design process. This engagement has taken different forms through the different phases of the project, and for different purposes. For both the data collection and the evaluation stages, traditional interview and focus group techniques were used, while for the iterative design process, the GEE was seminal in getting people with dementia to share their experiences and offer valuable feedback and input. The GEE was also essential when helping to devise and review the research tools using appropriate formats, content and language.

The co-design process made it clear that it is paramount that designers work directly with the user group to better understand the feelings and lived experiences of people with dementia, and to provide efficient and appropriate designs. The key to this process is an understanding of what form of involvement is most useful at what point in the design process. This means designers moved away from their role of providing consultation and advice, to that of co-designer and co-producer where they enable people with dementia to contribute. The benefit of this process was direct real-life experience and input for the designers and a sense of satisfaction and empowerment for people with dementia in being able to contribute directly to the design outcomes of the project.

This kind of working needs careful consideration with regards to communication and feedback to those involved, researchers, designers and healthcare workers as well as to people with dementia. When working with a large group of people on a design project like that of MinD, which included over 50 researchers and many more participants, it needs to be understood that decisions have to be made and that they cannot be made by everyone. Even though an individual's contribution may have been crucial to the development of the design, their ideas and voice may not be explicitly evident in the end result. Therefore, it is important to be explicit about the decision-making process and to manage expectations while at the same time communicating to everyone involved in the project that their input has been important and highly valued, regardless of how much they contributed or in what stage of the process they contributed.

**Acknowledgments** This project has received funding from the European Union's Horizon 2020 research and innovation programme under the Marie Skłodowska-Curie grant agreement No 691001. This document reflects only the authors' view and the Research Executive Agency is not responsible for any use that may be made of the information it contains.

This chapter is one of the outcomes of the MinD project, and we wish to thank all external partners, research participants, and especially GEE participants in Nottingham, UK, and Valladolid, Spain, who were engaged in the process of the data collection, design idea, concept and prototype development as well as MinD project researchers, including

MinD Design & ICT—Tom Barrington, Elena Bellini, Ben Bokkers, Kathrin Büter, Christopher Dennett, Gara Escobar, Daniil Garayzuev, Alex Hogan, Armagan Karahanoğlu, Mathilde Lamotte, Lisa Lüneburg, Sebastian Lorenz, Alessia Macchi, Jordi Paris, Hiran Patel, Zuzana Prochazkova, Daniil Razdyakonov, Ben Salter, Jens Krzywinski, Jochem Wilson, Christian Wölfel.

MinD GEE & data collection—Afsaneh Abrilahij, Yolanda Bueno Aguado, Rosa Almeida, Guillermo Benito, Michaelle Bosse, Andreu Catala, Tom Dening, Ana Diaz, Martha Diaz, Julia Garde, Dianne Gove, Vjera Holthoff-Detto, Jennifer Lim, Geke Ludden, Kathryn Powell, Thomas van Rompay, Tina Smith, Isabelle Tournier, Mascha van der Voort, Michele Zanasi, Berit Ziebuhr.

Further project information: www.designingfordementia.eu

## References

Alzheimer Europe (2013) Social inclusion and psychosocial support. Accessed http://www.alzheimer-europe.org/Research/European-Collaboration-on-Dementia/Social-Support-Systems/Examples-of-good-practice/Social-inclusion/(language)/eng-GB?#fragment2 [15 August 2017]

Baddeley AD, Kopelman MD, Wilson BA (2002) Handbook of memory disorders. Wiley, Chichester

Blackman T, Mitchell L, Burton E, Jenks M, Parsons M, Raman S, Williams K (2003) The accessibility of public spaces for people with dementia: a new priority for the 'open city'. Disabil Soc 18(3):357–371. https://doi.org/10.1080/0968759032000052914

Bracke J, Ott-Meyer H, Söngen S, Petri R, Selle-Uersfeld A, Haas B (2016) Leistungen der Pflegeversicherung mit den neuen Regelungen durch das Pflegestärkungsgesetz, Wiesbaden, DE, Amt für Soziale Arbeit. Available from: https://www.wegweiser-demenz.de/fileadmin/de.wegweiser-demenz/content.de/downloads/08_gesetzliche_leistungen/161208_Leistungen_Pflegeversicherung_Internet.pdf [12 May 2019]

Caldwell CC, Yao J, Brinton RD (2015) Targeting the prodromal stage of Alzheimer's disease: bioenergetic and mitochondrial opportunities. Neurotherapeutics 12:66–80. https://doi.org/10.1007/s13311-014-0324-8

Carroll JM (2000) Five reasons for scenario-based design. Int Comput 13:43–60

Chang Y-J, Tsai S-K, Wang T-Y (2008) A context aware handheld wayfinding system for individuals with cognitive impairments. In: Proceedings of the 10th international ACM SIGACCESS conference on computers and accessibility, Halifax, Nova Scotia, Canada—October 13–15. ACM, New York, USA, pp. 27–34. https://doi.org/10.1145/1414471.1414479

Daniels S (2008) Ring of freedom: tagging and tracking helps keep patients with dementia safe. Nurs Stand 22 (33):28 + . *Health Reference Center Academic*: https://go.galegroup.com/ps/anonymous?id=GALE%7CA179032353&sid=googleScholar&v=2.1&it=r&linkaccess=abs&issn=00296570&p=HRCA&sw=w [Accessed 12 May 2019]

Council Design (2012) Living well with dementia. Design Council, London, UK

Evans S, Bray J, Evans S (2015) How iPads can support people with dementia living in care homes. A study by the University of Worcester, working with Anchor. An evaluation report. University of Worcester, Worcester, UK. Available from: https://anchorv3dev.s3.eu-west-2.amazonaws.com/public/PDFs/How%20iPads%20can%20support%20people%20with.pdf [12/5/2019]

Garde JA, van der Voort MC, Niedderer K (2018) Design probes for people with dementia. Proceedings of DRS 2018 international conference: Catalyst 6:2607–2621. Available: https://www.scribd.com/document/382347614/DRS2018-Vol-6

Grierson LEM, Zelek J, Lam I, Black SE, Carnahan H (2011) Application of a tactile way-finding device to facilitate navigation in persons with dementia. Assist Technol 23(2):108–115. https://doi.org/10.1080/10400435.2011.567375

Guss R, Middleton J, Beanland T, Slade L, Moniz-Cook E, Watts S, Bone A (2014) A guide to psychosocial interventions in early stages of dementia. The British Psychological Society, Leicester, UK

Hendriks N, Slegers K, Duysburgh P (2015) Codesign with people living with cognitive or sensory impairments: a case for method stories and uniqueness. Codesign-Int J Cocreat Design Arts 11(1):70–82. https://doi.org/10.1080/15710882.2015.1020316

Jansen TR (2015) The nursing home that's also a Dorm. CityLab. Accessed: http://www.citylab.com/housing/2015/10/the-nursing-home-thats-also-a-dorm/408424/ [23/8/2017]

Lawry S, Popovic V, Blackler A, Thompson H (2019) Age, familiarity, and intuitive use: an empirical investigation. Appl Ergonomics 74:74–84

Lazar A, Edasis C, Piper AM (2017) A critical lens on dementia and design in HCI. In: Proceedings of the 2017 CHI conference on human factors in computing systems (CHI '17), pp 2175–2188. https://doi.org/10.1145/3025453.3025522

Marquardt G (2011) Wayfinding for people with dementia: a review of the role of architectural design. HERD Health Environ Res Des J 4(2):75–90. https://doi.org/10.1177/193758671100400207

Mattelmäki T (2006) Design probes. Publication Series of the University of Art and Design Helsinki, Helsinki

Mendes de Leon CF, Glass TA, Berkman LF (2003) Social engagement and disability in a community population of older adults: The New Haven EPESE. Am J Epidemiol 157(7):633–642

Milne H, van der Pol M, McCloughan L, Hanley J, Mead G, Starr J, … McKinstry B (2014) The use of global positional satellite location in dementia: a feasibility study for a randomised controlled trial. BMC Psychiatry 14 (160). https://doi.org/10.1186/1471-244x-14-160

Morrissey K, McCarthy J, Pantidi N (2017) The value of experience-centred design approaches in dementia research contexts. In: Proceedings of the 2017 CHI conference on human factors in computing systems (CHI '17), pp 1326–1338. https://doi.org/10.1145/3025453.3025527

Niedderer K, Tournier I, Coleston-Shields DM, Craven MP, Gosling JA, Garde J, … Griffoen I (2017) Designing with and for people with dementia: developing a mindful interdisciplinary co-design methodology. In: Paper presented at the Seventh International Conference of the International Association of Societies of Design Research (IASDR), Cincinnati, USA. https://scholar.uc.edu/concern/documents/db78tc00b

Norman D (2013) The design of everyday things: revised and expanded edition. Basic books, New York, US

Sanders EB-N, Stappers PJ (2014) Probes, toolkits and prototypes: three approaches to making in codesigning. CoDesign 10(1):5–14. https://doi.org/10.1080/15710882.2014.888183

Taylor BD, Tripodes S (2001) The effects of driving cessation on the elderly with dementia and their caregivers. Accid Anal Prev 33(4):519–528

Teipel S, Babiloni C, Hoey J, Kaye J, Kirste T, Burmeister OK (2016) Information and communication technology solutions for outdoor navigation in dementia. Alzheimer's Dementia: J Alzheimer's Assoc 12(6):695–707. https://doi.org/10.1016/j.jalz.2015.11.003

Wallace D (2010) The perspective of a person with dementia. In: Hughes J, Lloyd-Williams M, Sachs G (eds) Supportive care for the person with dementia. Oxford University Press, Oxford, UK

Williams I, Brereton M, Donovan J, McDonald K, Millard T, Tam A, Elliott JH (2014) Int J Sociotechnol Knowl Devel 6(2):17–35

Ylvisaker M, Turkstra LS, Coelho C (2005) Behavioral and social interventions for individuals with traumatic brain injury: a summary of the research with clinical implications. Semin Speech Lang 26(4):256–267

Zwaanswijk M, Peeters JM, van Beek APA, Meerveld JHCM, Francke AL (2013) Informal caregivers of people with dementia: problems, needs and support in the initial stage and in subsequent stages of dementia: a questionnaire survey. Open Nurs J 7:6–13. https://doi.org/10.2174/1874434601307010006

# Chapter 20
# Using Design to Engage Stakeholders to Explore the Quality of Life of Families Living with Dementia

**Chih-Siang Wu, Chen-Fu Yang, and Yuan Lu**

## 20.1 Introduction

As the aging population increases globally, the impact of dementia on population health also grows (Prince et al. 2016). Taiwan exemplifies this. Since 2018, Taiwan has become an aged society as the older adults above the age of 65 comprise 14% of the population. It will become a super-aged society by 2026 with more than 20% of the population above the age of 65 (Lin and Huang 2016). In Taiwan, more than 80% of people with dementia were resident in their home environment cared for by their family members (Liu et al. 1991), rather than living in care homes or similar institutions. In response to the World Health Organization report *The Global Action Plan On The Public Health Response To Dementia* 2017–2025 (WHO 2017), the Ministry of Health and Welfare (2017) and Taiwan Alzheimer Disease Association (TADA) (2018), and the formal member of Alzheimer's Disease International in Taiwan have collaboratively proposed policies that focus on improving the quality of life, especially psychological issues and emotional pressures of families living at home with people with dementia.

Research has shown that professional and informal caregivers of persons with dementia experience diverse rates of physical and mental stresses (Brodaty and Donkin 2009; Ritchie and Lovestone 2002). In Taiwan, there is an enormous pressure on the family caregiver, i.e., the informal care system. Chiao et al. (2015) advised that

C.-S. Wu · C.-F. Yang
DreamVok, Taipei, Taiwan
e-mail: Mikewu@dreamvok.com

C.-F. Yang
e-mail: Chenfu0510@dreamvok.com

Y. Lu (✉)
Department of Industrial Design, Eindhoven University of Technology, Eindhoven, The Netherlands
e-mail: Y.Lu@tue.nl

© Springer Nature Switzerland AG 2020

R. Brankaert and G. Kenning (eds.), *HCI and Design in the Context of Dementia*, Human–Computer Interaction Series,
https://doi.org/10.1007/978-3-030-32835-1_20

family caregivers often do not receive enough support from others and feel they are fighting a long battle. These issues may not only lower the quality life of the family, but also cause serious health problems. While many experts and professional organizations have proposed the idea of conducting non-pharmacological interventions or planning leisure time for family caregivers, without support, such as applicable tools or accessible resources, from their social networks; these ideas are likely to fail in practice (Bahramnezhad et al. 2017).

Many family caregivers understand the importance of non-pharmacological interventions to alleviate symptoms of dementia, mediate behavior change, and reduce stress for caregivers. But, without suitable methods, tools, knowledge, and resources, family caregivers struggle at home. For example, focusing on planning leisure time TADA (2018) urged the society to put more effort into allowing the families of people with dementia to have access activities to improve quality of life, such as family travel. But, without suitable places, programs, and specifically designed itineraries it is hard for families with people with dementia to plan and travel together. By involving stakeholders from other areas to collaborate to find deliverable and accessible new solutions for family caregivers, travel can be facilitated that will maintain their quality of life.

Design thinking is increasingly used as an open human-centered problem-solving process for problems that are difficult to solve because of incomplete, contradictory, and changing requirements that are hard to recognize (Melles et al. 2012). According to Johannsson-Skoldberg et al. (2013), design thinking can be a suitable approach for maintaining quality of life for families living with dementia, not least because it has shared philosophical approaches with person-centered care highly valued in dementia care (Brooker 2003). Firstly, Brown (2008) promoted design thinking in non-traditional design fields because of designer's creative inputs and their ability to take action for and with multiple stakeholders. This is beneficial for the innovation processes, not only at the process level but also for innovative results. Design thinking enables stakeholders to co-observe, co-learn, and co-develop during the design process and establish a shared vision toward new solutions (Yang et al. 2014). Secondly, *designerly* references how professional designers' practices and tools, such as visualization, customer experiences journey, and inspiration cards, can lead the discussion of design directions with stakeholders (Yang and Sung 2016). So, by applying these practices and tools, the designer's role may be that of director or facilitator of the design process.

Maintaining the quality life of families with dementia requires support from various stakeholders. Therefore, this study suggests that the area of dementia is an ideal ground to explore the role and results from designers and various stakeholders in the design thinking process, and especially how these roles contribute to explore and develop the quality life of families living with dementia. There are many different design thinking processes used in practice; in this chapter, we will demonstrate two case studies on design using the 4D process (Discover, Define, Develop, Deliver) from UK Design council.

## 20.2 Related Work

We will begin by summarizing related work with regards to the current design strategies for non-pharmacological interventions for dementia care, the 4D design process, the benefits of culture probes and prototypes in design processes, and the competencies of designers and stakeholders in designing for complex societal problems. Then, we will report on two design case studies related to the design of two non-pharmacological interventions for dementia care with specific focus on lowering the stress of the informal caregivers. Finally, we will identify important strategies to design for non-pharmacological interventions for dementia care led by designers together with a multi-stakeholder network.

### *20.2.1 Dementia, Non-pharmaceutical Care, and Leisure Time Activities*

People living with dementia experience a gradual decrease in cognitive functioning, expression, and increasingly more changed behaviors (Lyketsos et al. 2000). These symptoms were associated with a reduced quality of life, an increased caregiver burden, and increased dementia care costs (Moore and Hollett 2003). In a systematic review by (Olazarán et al. 2010), some specific strategies of applying non-pharmaceutical interventions were identified that benefit people with dementia, caregivers, or both by alleviating some symptoms of dementia and enhancing the relationships and interactions between the caregivers and the people with dementia. Non-pharmaceutical interventions refer to those that support persons with dementia without the use of drugs. (Berg-Weger and Stewart 2017; Cohen-Mansfield 2018; Douglas et al. 2004; Dyer et al. 2018).

From an economic perspective, Donnelly et al. (2008) argue that it is better to provide interventions at home in the early stages of dementia. However, relying on the impact on home-based informal care is not necessarily sufficient to help people living with dementia more generally (Graff et al. 2008). While family caregivers can benefit from the knowledge that already exists in professional and institutional care, these approaches are not tailored toward the home context. As a result, there is a need to balance the knowledge and efforts at home care and professional care for people with dementia (Mountain and Craig 2012).

Teri and Logsdon (1991) suggested that people living with dementia with increased pleasurable activities experienced decreased levels of depression. Daily activities, especially social and leisure activities, are very meaningful to the people living with dementia (Droes et al. 2006; Dupuis et al. 2012; Phinney 2006; Smits et al. 2007; Wherton and Monk 2008). Nevertheless, people living with dementia have decreasing ability to continue or create their own enjoyable activities to remain independent and socially connected (Topo and Östlund 2009). Similarly, dementia caregivers often experience depressive symptoms and stressed relationships (Richard and Williamson 1991). Au et al. (2015) found that pleasurable activities could also contribute to the well-being of the dementia caregivers. Therefore, there is a need to provide leisure activities to people with dementia and their caregivers to help them to deal with the emotional pressure and depression. This requires a close collaboration between the service providers of pleasure activities for both people with dementia and their informal caregivers.

### *20.2.2 Design Thinking, Designers, and Stakeholders*

Societal challenges call for a human-centered design thinking approach (Buchanan 1992; Melles et al. 2012) in which designers and stakeholders take collective actions in co-creating innovation. Designers can take an active role in initiating such changes and invite related stakeholders to join the innovation efforts and practice the so-called design-directive and invitational approach (Cross 2001; Sloane 2011; Tomico et al. 2011). However, designers can also take a facilitator role to support different stakeholders in co-creating innovation. Sanders and Stappers (2008) highlighted the changing landscape of co-design, encouraging designers to move closer to future users and stakeholders and to co-design with them. Literature suggests that designers should be able to inspire, inform, and facilitate different stakeholders to be personally engaged in the realization of the desired societal transformation (Gardien et al. 2014). When designing solutions for the quality life of families living with dementia, stakeholders may include people with dementia, their caregivers, and related professions from different fields. Due to the reduced cognitive function of people with dementia, the already existing stresses among caregivers, and needing to engage related multidisciplinary stakeholders, the co-design process is challenging and worthy of further research.

There are many different design thinking processes; they have in common that convergent and divergent thinking are embedded in the process to create choices and make decisions. In the case studies reported in this chapter, we applied the 4-D design thinking process from Design Council UK: *Discover insight into the problem, Define the area to focus upon, Develop potential solutions and Deliver solutions that work* (Design Council, n.d).

When designers are involved in the process together with other stakeholders, they can take different roles and actions. Sloane (2011) suggested a co-creation approach that can follow four different models based on two factors; how the innovation is initiated, and how participants are involved. These include suggestive and directive models on how topics of innovation are initiated, and how the participants are initially involved. It implies that when designers are initiating the innovation, they can be directive or suggestive toward stakeholders in the direction of innovation while stakeholders can be invited or participative on free will. In this chapter, we will analyze the roles of designers and stakeholders in two design cases for non-pharmacological interventions for dementia home carers from the lens of Sloane (2011) and learn how designers and stakeholders collaborate and give useful recommendation for future co-creation teams when initiating and participating in such collaborations.

## 20.3 Case Background

Taiwan Alzheimer's Disease Association (TADA) collaborates with the government to build a dementia-friendly community and empower informal caregivers with training and tools. However, while increasing supports for home care and informal caregivers are established, the resources mainly focus on providing support for physical illness rather than psychological challenges such as emotional pressure of people living with dementia. Two case studies initiated by Dreamvok, a design consultancy from the Industrial Technology Research Institute (ITRI) will be discussed here. The aim of these projects was to create non-pharmaceutical solutions to improve the quality of life of people living with dementia and reduce the stress of their informal caregivers, in both indoor and outdoor contexts.

### *20.3.1 Designing Indoor Social Leisure Activities for People Living with Dementia*

In this project, DreamVok worked closely with ChungHwa Senior Care Co. (CSCC) and 5% Design Action. CSCC mainly offers high-quality senior care services including home helpers, personal services, dementia care, and cancer care. Recently, in order to provide holistic care experiences to the seniors to enhance their quality of life, CSCC has dedicated themselves to creating a *one-stop* service platform by integrating resources with cross-industry partners, for example, in relation to food and housing. 5% Design Action is a social enterprise, which runs a platform to encourage stakeholders and designers to donate 5% of their time as volunteers and participate in social innovation (Yang et al. 2014; Yang and Sung 2016). 5% Design Action assumes that by matching the interests, expertise, and resources of the volunteers with those of public sectors such as Non-Profit Organizations and Non-Government Organizations (NPOs and NGO)s, and companies' Corporate Social Responsibility (CSR) projects, it is possible to inspire innovative and practical solutions for social challenges.

The aim of the first case was to enable the family caregiver to conduct non-pharmacological interventions with people with dementia more frequently in the home context, to alleviate symptoms of dementia and enhance the relationships and interactions between the caregivers and the people with dementia. The design challenge was to design tools and activities for non-pharmacological interventions for family caregivers, who do not have professional skills to interact with people with dementia. The design thinking process, the action of the designers and stakeholders are summarized below:

**Discover**

The purpose was to explore innovative opportunities. The designers applied generative tools such as probes (Fig. 20.1) to stimulate the stakeholders (e.g., family caregivers, managers of CSCC, doctors) to reveal their expectations. Applying generative tools in this way was a design-invited approach, since it enabled participants to share hard to express expectations. For example, most of the participants picked the pictures related to interaction, talking, working together, rather than staying in bed, or using medical devices. They told the designers that "caring is only a part of their life, and they really hope to have fun, work out something, and create precious moments with each other." This statement inspired the stakeholders from medical professions to propose ideas to incorporate interesting daily activities and tools in the non-pharmacological intervention. Since there are many positive effects of allowing people with dementia and family caregivers collaboratively join in certain daily activities (e.g., cooking, pealing fruit, shopping), the design challenges were jointly defined by the designers and the stakeholders as redesigning the daily activities and embedding the core functions of non-pharmacological interventions to achieve the quality interaction. Thus, the designers and the participants collaboratively identified the characteristics of additional stakeholders who should be involved (e.g., people who have a background in teaching homemade food or homemade artwork). Lastly, designers promoted the defined design challenges through 5% Design Action platform and received a number of volunteers.

**Define**

The goal was to define a value proposition to enable the participants to identify their roles in creating the proposition and make commitments to the final implementation. Here, the design is more directive and participants are invitational, since designers need to lead the participants in the communication and collaboration. Firstly, they set up a value proposition workshop (Fig. 20.2) to allow the participants to share their ideas toward the design challenge, learn from each other, and find the opportunities for using the core resources of all participants to create a value proposition together. The participants were asked to share their services, so that others could understand and

**Fig. 20.1** Generative tools

Exchanging core resource of the stakeholders
Value proposition alignment


**Fig. 20.2** Value proposition workshop

collaboratively explore the possibilities for new non-pharmacological interventions for home settings. For example, after experiencing food making, a doctor who has experience in non-pharmacological interventions found that activities of picking up food, mixing the ingredients, or decorating cupcakes are similar to the cognitive skills of non-pharmacological intervention programs, but more fun and interactive. Thus, through these activities of learning, exploring, and reflecting, the participants gradually came up with the idea of designing modularized steps and tools, which incorporate the programs of non-pharmacological interventions with food making activities. They named the new concept as FooKit, a homemade food DIY Kit that can inspire people to interact, while experiencing the benefits of non-pharmacological interventions. After realizing the idea of FooKit, the participants found roles for each participant; for example, some needed to design recipes and food DIY toolkits, others needed to develop instructions for the non-pharmacological intervention. This result inspired the participants to form a core team to realize the concept, since their core competences were properly integrated.

**Develop**

After identifying the concept, the main goal was to empower the stakeholders to collaboratively develop the details. The term "empower" emphasizes the role of designers as facilitating the stakeholders to put more effort into realizing the concept, so that they may learn how to collaborate in the future. The design became a directive as the designers orchestrated the development process and stakeholders participated in following the guidelines and filling in the contents. For example, the designers applied the experience journey map as a framework for participants to illustrate the process of the interactive activities within FooKit, how these activities are incorporated with non-pharmacological interventions, and what are the tools that should be provided. The stakeholders considered that the experience journey map was useful, since it allowed them to think through the details of every touchpoint and how the experience should be embedded. In order to make FooKit fun, interactive, and easy, the stakeholders incorporated the food DIY process into six modularized steps (e.g., mixing the ingredients, decorating). It included instructions, tools, and tips for the non-pharmacological intervention. In this way, they hoped to allow the caregivers to apply these modularized steps to collaboratively make the food with

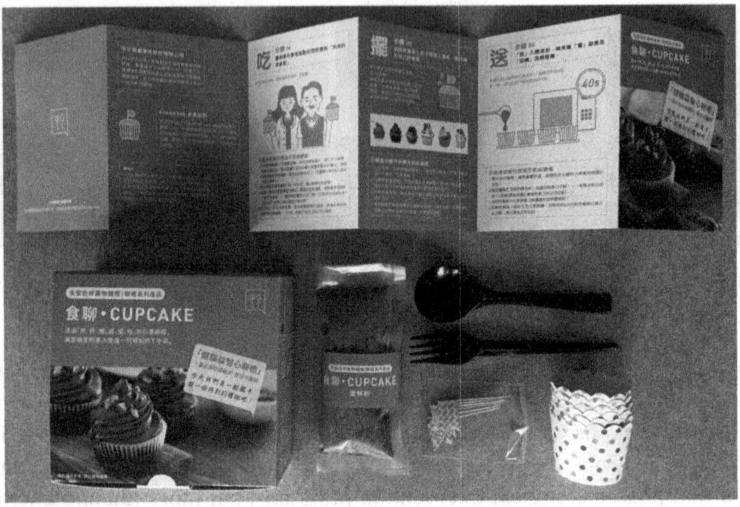


**Fig. 20.3** The prototypes of FooKit

people with dementia. Finally, through the guidance from the designers, the stakeholders developed prototypes of FooKit. With the establishment of prototypes, the stakeholders had more confidence and commitment toward collaboration (Fig. 20.3).

**Deliver**

The main aim was to realize the concept and collaboration in the real world. Thus, the stakeholders became active and participated as they needed to, to collaboratively implement the FooKit. The stakeholders firstly held educational workshops (Fig. 20.4) to train the family caregiver to use the design. After that, 20 families living with dementia were invited to use the tools and practices of FooKit at home (Fig. 20.4). The design was suggestive and the designers became observers. In both workshop and home-usage testing, the designers did not get involved or interrupt, but observed how the families experienced the concept and what feedback was given to the stakeholders. Most of the family caregivers appreciated the concept of FooKit, and this motivated the stakeholders to commit themselves to a commercial realization. Therefore, FooKit did not remain as a concept, but gradually became a realized product. Currently, FooKit has been launched in the market and is used by families and home care corporations.

The interplays between the role of designers and stakeholders of case 1 are summarized in Table 20.1.

**Fig. 20.4** Applying FooKit in workshop and homecare services

**Table 20.1** The interplays between the role of design and stakeholders of case 1

| Stage | Discover | Define | Develop | Deliver |
|---|---|---|---|---|
| Designers | *Suggestive* To use generative tools to facilitate stakeholders to express opinions | *Directional* To apply design professional skills to lead stakeholders to collaborate | *Directional* To develop experience journey for stakeholders to follow | *Suggestive* To observe how the result work in the real context |
| Stakeholders | *Invitational* To provide opinions of expectations, needs, and pains | *Invitational* To follow designers' instructions to find collaboration opportunities | *Participative* To fill-in the content based on professions and experience journey | *Participative* To collaboratively deliver the results into the context |

### *20.3.2 Designing Outdoor Social Leisure Activities for People Living with Dementia*

The second case study focusses on *Respite tourism for dementia family*. It integrates various activities that are based on the core values of the Leofoo Tourism Group (LTG), to allow the families living with dementia to have a chance to travel together and create a positive memory together. Here, Dreamvok worked closely with Leofoo Tourism Group, CSCC, Professional Animal-Assisted Therapy Association of Taiwan, Physical therapists, art therapists, music therapists, and an accessible transport company. Leofoo Village Theme Park is the first recreation area in Asia that combined both amusement park and Werribee Open Range Zoo. In order to offer a better experience for all age customers, Leofoo Village Theme Park has committed to developing an accessible environment and services for people with different physical or mental needs. The design process leading up to this case, the action of the designers, and stakeholders are summarized below.

**Discover**

The designers explored the challenges and expectations of families living with dementia. They found caring in an outdoor environment is difficult as there is a lack of activities dedicated to people with dementia and their families. The staff at LTG explained that they did not have training on serving families living with dementia and did not know how to deliver the services in an appropriate way. For example, staff may use words used with children and apply them to people with dementia, or focus on children and neglect the older adults. As a result, together with the LTG, the designer proposed a value-exploring workshop and invited stakeholders including experts in dementia caring to identify the values of the services in LeoFoo Village Theme Park for it to be redesigned for the families living with dementia.

**Define**

Through the connection from ITRI and 5% Design Action, the designers had connected to several experts who were willing to participate. They went to the Leofoo theme amusement park and identified possible opportunities (Fig. 20.5). The experts found that the theme park had a lot of assets (e.g., fun activities and shows, relaxing atmosphere, cute animals, etc.) that were suitable for the families living with dementia. Moreover, they proposed that the existing services and activities could be redesigned to engage people with dementia and their families and at the same time create shared memories. For example, Leofoo theme amusement park has different animals and many different characteristics relating to human experience and stories. This content could be developed into a complete story to inspire the members of families living with dementia to interact with each other. In addition, redesigning a program of non-pharmacological interventions (e.g., animal-assisted therapy or art therapy) and incorporating this within the services of the Leofoo theme amusement park could provide a more meaningful traveling experience. After the visit, the designers, the experts, and the Leefoo managers agreed with the ideas and started to work for the new service together as a team.

**Develop**

The tools and the interaction of the new animal-assisted therapy based on the ideas of enabling the members of families living with dementia to interact with each other, while conducting non-pharmacological interventions, the designers played a directive role and orchestrated the experience of the whole itinerary and planned the route. This provided guidelines for the stakeholders to develop detailed contents for every activity. For example, the animal-observing activities were redesigned to incorporate the program of animal-assisted therapy. Instead of training the animals to assist non-pharmacological interventions, the therapist and the zookeepers collaboratively developed the new animal-assisted therapy, which could include the content of the park and tools to facilitate people to observe the animal in new ways. The new content could be used to stimulate the people with dementia to talk, act, and recall memories

Fig. 20.5 Ideation at Leofoo theme amusement park

while observing the movements of animals. In addition, the tools were designed to facilitate the interaction of the family living with dementia. As shown in Fig. 20.6, family members could pull out the pages and read with the people with dementia at the same time. The service providers can then use the contents on the pages to assign tasks (e.g., searching for animals, imitating animals' movements) to the family members collaboratively. Furthermore, the art and music therapy were designed to use elements from the animals (e.g., animal silhouette making, music of animal sounds performing) to allow the families to capture their memories of the zoo.

**Deliver**

The stakeholders acted as a team and started to provide the service to the families living with dementia. Meanwhile, the designers played the suggestive role in observing how the family living with dementia responded to the new services. They found that the families living with dementia did not only enjoy the interaction and relaxation during the services, but also used the pictures taken in the Leofoo theme amusement park as tools to talk with the people with dementia at home. It allowed the family to extend these precious moments. With these feedbacks, the stakeholders believed that there were potential opportunities on the market, so they actively established a sustainable business model to deliver the service to the market for people living with dementia and their families.

The interplays between the role of designers and stakeholders of case 1 are summarized in Table 20.2

Fig. 20.6 The tools and the interaction of the new animal-assisted therapy

**Table 20.2** The interplays between the role of design and stakeholders of case 2

| Stage | Discover | Define | Develop | Deliver |
|---|---|---|---|---|
| Designers | *Suggestive* To interview with families living with dementia to find the pain and gains of traveling | *Suggestive* To collect opinions from the experts for redesigning the itinerary | *Directional* To develop experience journey of itinerary and the route for stakeholders to follow | *Suggestive* To observe how the new service in the real context |
| Stakeholders | *Invitational* To provide pain and gain of the travel experience in the past | *Invitational* To provide professional ideas and suggestions | *Participative* To develop the new content for the travel experience | *Participative* To collaboratively deliver and sustain the service |

## 20.4 Discussion and Conclusion

The two case studies presented in this chapter clearly demonstrate how designers play different roles to initiate, lead, and facilitate a design thinking process together with stakeholders and experts from related fields when designing for and with people from dementia. Truly believing that non-pharmaceutical interventions can improve the quality of life of people living with dementia and with a strong focus on reducing the stress of informal caregivers, the designers teamed up with experts and stakeholders who could contribute to the potential solutions. Step by step, the stakeholders were supported to co-create the intended solutions. Throughout the process, they moved from passive participation to active exploration. For example, initially they were recruited to contribute to a societal problem that may be beneficial to the development of their businesses. Gradually the stakeholders took over the process and clearly defined what they could do in order to overcome the hurdle of the family caregivers and improve the pleasure of the people living with dementia. Eventually they worked out in detail what needed to happen in order to realize the intended solutions. Users including people with dementia and their families participating in co-creating future solutions by actively using the implemented solutions as the stakeholders and designers learned together. They were not only providing feedback based on prototypes, but were experiencing the products and services in real-life contexts. From the experiences gained, the designers were able to improve the design and the stakeholders were able to improve their implementation further. The participation of the core stakeholders, commercial companies such as Leefoo, CSCC, ITRI, social companies such as 5% design action, and volunteers helped the designers to iterate their designs in the wild. These cases showed a societal participation with designers as the conductor of an orchestra of experts and stakeholders with different resources and expertise to support people living with dementia.

## References

Au Alma, Gallagher-Thompson Dolores, Wong Meng Kong, Leung Jess, Chan Wai Chi, Chan Chun Chung, Hui Jing Lu, Lai Man Kin, Chan Kevin (2015) Behavioral activation for dementia caregivers: scheduling pleasant events and enhancing communications. Clin Int Aging 10:611–619

Bahramnezhad Fatemeh, Chalik Raheleh, Bastani Farideh, Taherpour Masoumeh, Navab Elham (2017) The social network among the elderly and its relationship with quality of life. Elect Phy 9(5):4306–4311

Berg-Weger M, Daniel B Stewart (2017) Non-pharmacologic interventions for persons with dementia. Missouri Med 114(2):116–119

Brodaty Henry, Donkin Marika (2009) Family caregivers of people with dementia. Dialogues Clin Neurosci 11:217–228

Brooker Dawn (2003) What is person—centred care in dementia? Rev Clin Gerontol 13(13):215–222

Buchanan Richard (1992) Wicked problems in design thinking. Des Iss 8(2):5–21

Chiao CY, Wu HS, Hsiao CY (2015) Caregiver burden for informal caregivers of patients with dementia: a systematic review. Int Nurs Rev 62(3):340–350

Cohen-Mansfield Jiska (2018) Non-pharmacological interventions for persons with dementia: what are they and how should they be studied? Int Psychogeriatr 30(3):281–283

Cross N (2001) Designerly ways of knowling: design disciplines versus design science 17(3):49–55

Design Council UK (n.d) The design process: what is the double diamond? |Design Council. Retrieved May 6, 2019 https://www.designcouncil.org.uk/news-opinion/design-process-what-double-diamond

Donnelly MP, Chris DN, David C, Peter P, Maurice M (2008) Development of a cell phone-based video streaming system for persons with early stage Alzheimer's disease. In: 2008 30th annual international conference of the IEEE engineering in medicine and biology society. IEEE, pp 5330–5333

Douglas Simon, James Ian, Ballard Clive (2004) Non-pharmacological interventions in dementia. Adv Psychiatr Treat 10(3):171–177

Droes RM, Ellen CC, Boelens-Van Der Knoop, Joke B, Lucinda M, Teake PE, Debbie LG, Frans H, Jacomine L, Carla JM, Schãlzel-Dorenbos (2006) Quality of life in dementia in perspective: an explorative study of variations in opinions among people with dementia and their professional caregivers, and in literature. Dementia 5(4):533–558

Dupuis Sherry L, Whyte Colleen, Carson Jennifer, Genoe Rebecca, Meshino Lisa, Sadler Leah (2012) Just dance with me: an authentic partnership approach to understanding leisure in the dementia context. World Leisure J 54(3):240–254

Dyer Suzanne M, Harrison Stephanie L, Laver Kate, Whitehead Craig, Crotty Maria (2018) An overview of systematic reviews of pharmacological and non-pharmacological interventions for the treatment of behavioral and psychological symptoms of dementia. Int Psychogeriatr 30(3):295–309

Gardien P, Tom D, Caroline H, Aarnout B (2014) Changing your hammer: the implications of paradigmatic innovation for design practice. Int J Des 8(2)

Graff, ML., Eddy MM, Adang Myrra JM. Vernooij-Dassen, Joost Dekker L Jönsson Marjolein Thijssen, Willibrord HL Hoefnagels, Marcel GM. Olde Rikkert (2008) Community occupational therapy for older patients with dementia and their care givers: cost effectiveness study. BMJ 336(7636):134–138

Johansson-Sköldberg Ulla, Woodilla Jill, Çetinkaya Mehves (2013) Design thinking: past, present and possible futures. Creat Innov Manage 22(2):121–146

Lin Yi Yin, Huang Chin Shan (2016) Aging in taiwan: building a Society for Active Aging and Aging in place. Gerontologist 56(2):176–183

Liu H-C, Lin K-N, Tsou H-K, Lee K-M, Yan S-H, Wang S-J, Chiang BN (1991) Impact of demented patients on their family members and Care-Givers in Taiwan. Neuroepidemiology 10:143–149

Lyketsos Constantine G, Steinberg Martin, Breitner John C S, Tschanz Joanne T, Norton Maria, Steffens David C (2000) Mental and behavioral disturbances in dementia: findings from the cache county study on memory in aging. Neurobiol Aging 21:244

Melles Gavin, Howard Zaana, Thompson-Whiteside Scott (2012) Teaching design thinking: expanding horizons in design education. Proc Soc Behav Sci 31:162–166

Ministry of Health and Welfare (2017) World Alzheimer's Day: September 21, 2017 Ministry of health and welfare called on creating a dementia friendly community ~ Maintain the brain health for you and your family ~. Taiwan. Retrieved 13 April 2020 (https://www.mohw.gov.tw/cp-3425-37619-2.html)

Moore Theresa F, Hollett Jane (2003) Giving voice to persons living with dementia: the researcher's opportunities and challenges. Nurs Sci Quart 16(2):163–167

Mountain Gail A, Craig Claire L (2012) What should be in a self-management programme for people with early dementia? Aging Ment Health 16(5):576–583

Olazarán Javier, Reisberg Barry, Clare Linda, Cruz Isabel, Peña-Casanova Jordi, del Ser Teodoro, Woods Bob, Beck Cornelia, Auer Stefanie, Lai Claudia, Spector Aimee, Fazio Sam, Bond John, Kivipelto Miia, Brodaty Henry, Rojo José Manuel, Collins Helen, Teri Linda, Mittelman Mary, Orrell Martin, Feldman Howard H, Muñiz Ruben (2010) Nonpharmacological therapies in Alzheimer's disease: a systematic review of efficacy. Dement Geriatr Cognit Disord 30(2):161–178

Phinney Alison (2006) Family strategies for supporting involvement in meaningful activity by persons with dementia. J Family Nurs 12(1):80–101

Prince M, Gemma CA, Maëlenn Guerchet A. Matthew Prina, Emiliano Albanese, Yu Tzu Wu (2016) Recent global trends in the prevalence and incidence of dementia, and survival with dementia. Alzheimer's research and therapy 8(1)

Richard Schulz, Williamson Gail M (1991) A two-year longitudinal study of depression amongst Alzheimer's care-givers. Psychol Ageing 6(4):569–578

Ritchie Karen, Lovestone Simo (2002) The dementias. The Lancet 360(9347):1759–1766

Sanders Elizabeth B N, Stappers Pieter Jan (2008) Co-creation and the new landscapes of design. CoDesign 4(1):5–18

Sloane P (ed) (2011) A guide to open innovation and crowdsourcing : practical tips advice and examples from leading experts in the field. Kogan Page

Smits Carolien H M, De Lange Jacomine, Dröes Rose Marie, Meiland Franka, Vernooij-Dassen Myrra, Pot Anne Margriet (2007) Effects of combined intervention programmes for people with dementia living at home and their caregivers: a systematic review. Int J Geriatr Psychiatr 22(12):1181–1193

Taiwan Alzheimer Disease Association (2018) The association suggests the government to put effort on encouraging friendly travel service for dementia. Retrieved September 9, 2019 (http://tada2002.ehosting.com.tw/tada_event_detail.aspx?pk=1719)

Teri L, Logsdon RG (1991) Identifying pleasant activities for Alzheimer's disease patients: the pleasant events schedule-AD. Gerontologist 31(1):124–127

Tomico O, Yuan L, Paula L, Ehsan B, Tuija H (2011) Designers initiating open innovation with multi-stakeholder through co-reflection sessions work or workout? view Project. In: Diversity and unity: proceeding of IASDR2011, the 4th world conference on design research, PJ Roozenburg, NFM, Chen LL (eds). Stappers. Delft

Topo P, Östlund B (eds) (2009) Dementia, design and technology: time to get involved. IOS press, Amsterdam, Netherlands

Wherton Joseph P, Monk Andrew F (2008) Technological opportunities for supporting people with dementia who are living at home. Int J Human Comput Stud 66(8):571–586

WHO (2017) Global action plan on the public health response to dementia 2017–2025. Geneva. Licence: CC BY-NC-SA 3.0 IGO

Yang CF, Wu CS, Ho SS, Sung TJ (2014) '5% design action': cancer screening service innovation in Taiwan. Touchpoint 6(2):44–49

Yang Chen-Fu, Sung Tung-Jung (2016) Service design for social innovation through participatory action research. Int J Des 10(1):21–36

# Chapter 21
# Supportive Technologies for People with Dementia: A Closer Look into an Interdisciplinary Field

**Sandra Suijkerbuijk, Henk Herman Nap, and Mirella Minkman**

## 21.1 Introduction: The Active Involvement of People with Dementia in Technology Development

Earlier literature reviews, mainly focused on research in healthcare settings, highlight how important it is to involve people with dementia and their informal caregivers in the development of new supportive or assistive technologies (Meiland et al. 2017; Span et al. 2013; Topo 2009). The most common type of involvement, which occurs in the evaluative phase, results in insights into the effectiveness, usefulness, and acceptability of the developed devices. In the majority of these reviewed studies, people with dementia have had a passive role in the development, at best serving as an object of study or informant. Few studies found in the medical and healthcare databases (Cochrane library, PubMed, EMBASE, and CINAHL database) report on the involvement of people with dementia throughout the entire development process of technology, as an equal partner or co-designer. Co-design is defined by Sanders and Stappers (2008) as the 'creativity of designers and people not trained in design working together in the design development process' (p. 2). This working together

S. Suijkerbuijk (✉) · H. H. Nap · M. Minkman
Centre of Expertise Long-Term Care, Vilans, Utrecht, The Netherlands
e-mail: S.Suijkerbuijk@vilans.nl

H. H. Nap
e-mail: H.Nap@vilans.nl

M. Minkman
e-mail: M.Minkman@vilans.nl

S. Suijkerbuijk · H. H. Nap
Human Technology Interaction, Eindhoven University of Technology, Eindhoven, The Netherlands

M. Minkman
TIAS School for Business and Society, Tilburg University, Tilburg, The Netherlands

© Springer Nature Switzerland AG 2020

R. Brankaert and G. Kenning (eds.), *HCI and Design in the Context of Dementia*, Human–Computer Interaction Series,
https://doi.org/10.1007/978-3-030-32835-1_21

on equal grounds stimulates collaboration and serves to enhance the qualities of the engagement of all partners involved. The lack of creatively working together in the development of supportive technology is noteworthy since co-design carried out from the start of the development process can have an impact positive, long-term consequences on the user experience of the eventual design outcome (Sanders and Stappers 2008). Co-design with people with dementia can promote an enhanced sense of control in participants (Hanson et al. 2007) and can ultimately lead to a more empathic understanding of the user group (Lindsay et al. 2012). Empathic understanding enables designers and developers to gain relevant and intimate user insights needed for more meaningful and suitable technology development. However, involving people with dementia as co-designers in development can be challenging due to the characteristics of the syndrome, which might vary between the different types of dementia with specific behavioral, cognitive, and emotional consequences. Being a co-designer might require levels of sensory, cognitive, and motor abilities to be involved in the process that includes using methods and tools to acquire contextual knowledge and to create and visualize new viable solutions together with others. These aforementioned skills needed are often compromised in a person with dementia (Hendriks et al. 2015), and this can result in insecurity about one's own capabilities and challenges the partnership. The large variation in how people are impacted with dementia adds to the overall challenges of successful co-design with this user group, as different people might need different methods of participation.

There is still a lack of specific knowledge about the research methods and materials needed to actively involve people with dementia throughout the entire development process of supportive technologies. We need to be cautious about method-ism as suggested in Chap. 2 (Hendriks et al. 2020), as the different contexts of design research with different people living with dementia cannot result in a singular or universal methodology (Hendriks 2019), so, it is important to share insights gained from the use of different methods and materials over the entire process of technology development.

A review by Suijkerbuijk et al. (2019) showed that there is a growing number of research projects that aim to develop supportive technologies for people with dementia. Compared to earlier work (Span et al. 2013), there is an increase in studies eliciting an active involvement of people with dementia. By including studies from the Human–Computer Interaction (HCI) and Design fields, the review undertaken by Suijkerbuijk and colleagues outlined a more balanced view of where in the development process people with dementia can be involved. Not only are people with dementia able to evaluate technology, but they can also play an important role in the generative phase of development and steer the design of supportive technology earlier in the process. Considerable attention is now being given, in the HCI community, to designing with people living with dementia (Brankaert et al. 2019; Lazar et al. 2018; Morrissey et al. 2017). The HCI community is moving the research focus away from considering only the medical concerns of dementia, toward a broader view that includes context, values, and the situatedness of technology use. Involving people with dementia as co-designers in the development of technology is deemed challenging, but not impossible. However, even with the updates in this expanded review, what is generally missing are extensive reports on the methodology and evaluation of the experiences of people with dementia themselves. This makes understanding and further improvement of active involvement and co-design difficult.

## 21.2 Examples of Technology Development

Designers, researchers and developers with different backgrounds, different languages, different motives, and different ways of working need to collaborate in the process of developing supportive technologies in order to create solutions that are desirable, feasible, and viable. This complex collaboration creates obvious difficulties that sometimes seem to stand in the way of prioritizing the voice of the end-user in the development process. This might result in low acceptance and usefulness of currently available supportive technologies (Evans et al. 2015) and of technologies such as eHealth in general (Wouters et al. 2018). What follows in this chapter are stories of two Active and Assisted Living (AAL—a technology innovation funding program of the European Union) projects in which the authors have been actively involved; *FreeWalker* and *eWARE*. These projects exemplify the challenges experienced in collaborating on development projects.

**Case 1: Working within an international and multidisciplinary project team**
The project *FreeWalker* (https://www.freewalker-aal.eu n.d.) is a European consortium of eight partners from three different countries (Austria, Switzerland, and The Netherlands) working together to develop a dynamic GPS-based safety zone for people with dementia and their (in) formal caregivers. The FreeWalker project was based on a proposal with a workplan developed ahead of the pre-design and generative phases. This implies that the project goals, main functionalities of the supportive technology, and evaluation methodology are defined to a great extent at the project start. While, the project intentions are positive and iterative co-design is key, Research and Development (R&D) projects such as these rarely start with end-users needs. For the purposes of this chapter, it reveals two interesting project phases for discussion: firstly, the requirements analysis phase within an interdisciplinary consortium, and secondly, the involvement of the primary end-users, 'people with dementia'.

In *FreeWalker*, people with dementia were not involved in the pre-design and generative phases and took part only in the evaluative phase after *FreeWalker* had been developed. It is debatable as to what extent it is necessary to include people with dementia in the design of GPS software and hardware, although, it should be noted that the implications of the technologies on their lives can be quite significant. *FreeWalker* can increase freedom of movement, but also limit the perception of freedom due to the tracking and localizing functionalities. Overall, the person with dementia has no control over the dynamic safety zone and the algorithm deciding the shape and size of their GPS-based safety zone. However, a large part of this project was assigned to the technical challenges of development, and so as the application might be very abstract to actual end-users, the consortium recognized difficulties with involving people living with dementia in the concept development if they were to stay with the time planning of the original proposal.

Another interesting aspect of the project was the *end of requirement* phase. Once requirements had been gathered in multiple co-design rounds with formal and informal caregivers, it transpired that not all these requirements could be met, due to incompatibility with some constraints such as the overall project goals; time and funding limitations; technical feasibility; and cultural or national differences in needs of the potential market. By rating requirements these constraints via a MoSCoW analysis (Clegg and Barker 1994), with *Must-have*, *Should-have*, *Could-have*, and *Would-have* functionalities, a ranked list was made with functionalities to be developed within the project constraints. The MoSCoW process was transparent and the interdisciplinary consortium partners were able to vote based on their perspectives. But, this approach provides limited room for end-user involvement in the process and may fail to acknowledge end-users' needs whenever they are incompatible with, for example, the predefined project goals or funding requirements.

**Case 2: From Generative to Evaluative Phase**

The goal of the *eWARE* project was to introduce a novel ecosystem to support the well-being of people with dementia and their informal caregivers. In the project, existing supportive technologies were integrated and adapted for people with dementia who live alone at home (about 70% of people affected by cognitive impairments). These supportive technologies included a lifestyle monitoring system and social support robotics, which together could provide context-relevant responses needed in daily living (Zwierenberg et al. 2018). Four different end-user organizations in four different countries are currently taking part in the project.

In the generative phase of the project, it was mostly informal and formal caregivers involved (Casaccia et al. 2019), as the participating end-user organizations found it difficult to involve people with dementia this early in the process. It was doubted whether people with dementia could express their needs on the integration of lifestyle monitoring and social robots. Some of the needs that were generated in the generative phase, were categorized as *Would-have* functionality (the MoSCoW analysis was also used in this project to prioritize requirements). The project partners decided the functionality was outside the scope of the integration of the two systems as it did not seem to be the most relevant requirements at that phase of the project. However, during the alpha trials in the evaluative phase it appeared that people with dementia needed additional functionalities to start and keep motivated in using the *eWARE* system. For example, the social robot as a stand-alone has functionalities such as playing the radio. This was deliberately left out of the *eWARE* project to simplify the scope of the project. The participants from the test mentioned that they wanted more *interaction* and more *fun* elements. It was decided to frame the functionalities of the system differently in the remainder of the project and the *eWARE* system, for example, was programmed to provide *compliments*, not *reminders*.

In this project, different researchers have deployed the research to be carried out according to the project proposal. Research partners with a medical background were eager to include a clinical test in the questionnaires and so in the project meetings, a lot of time was spent discussing this. From the care-organization perspective, clinical testing was not desirable as this would impact the requirements phase and it was expected that it would negatively impact the experiences of participants with the *eWARE* system. Furthermore, the HCI researchers did not see how these insights would help further developments of such a system. To find a way of valuing the individual perspectives of the participants and find a measure for outcomes on effectiveness, the research partners decided to use the *Goal Attainment Scale* (Turner-Stokes 2009). This is a measure that uses a personal situation standardized across research participants. The standardized measures could be used to see the effect on all participants. With this measure, different research perspectives could be combined and the *Goal Attainment Scale* is currently used on the remainder of the project.

## 21.3 Challenges for Active Involvement

To further understand the challenges we experienced in involving people with dementia in the development of supportive technologies, we conducted in-depth interviews in 2018 with eleven Dutch researchers. We used a convenience sampling method by inviting existing contacts to take part. To further understand the interdisciplinary field, we aimed for a wide variety of experiences across the interview participants who differed in fields from design, engineering, and psychology and in years of experience from 1-year PhD to 9 years of being a professor. Interviews ($n = 11$) lasted approximately 1 h and were recorded with permission and transcribed verbatim. The semi-structured interviews covered three questions:

1. What are the experiences of the researchers with different methods and materials used to involve people with dementia?
2. What are the most valuable lessons that researchers gain from working in collaborative projects to develop supportive technologies for people with dementia?
3. How do researchers obtain and share relevant knowledge within this field?

For this chapter, we decided to focus on the outcomes of the first two questions only.

### *21.3.1 Experiences of Active Involvement*

All interview participants stated that they involved people with dementia multiple times throughout their projects. Four interview participants explicitly mentioned a specific iterative approach (e.g., co-design) that they aim for in their projects. It was a shared insight that keeping people with dementia involved throughout a project is challenging and time-consuming (keeping in contact with participants, also outside of research activities) but highly relevant for the development of meaningful supportive technologies. One of the interview participants mentioned that people were not asked to participate in the entire project from the start, as this might be experienced as overwhelming and therefore discouraging. This highlights one of the challenges in continuous involvement of people with dementia. From the interviews, we gained several insights that support findings of previous work (Astell et al. 2009; Brankaert et al. 2015; Hendriks 2019; Mayer and Zach 2013) such as, the need for interviews and focus groups to have clear time constraints in order to not overburden participants with dementia. Below we highlight a number of specific new insights.

Several interview participants highlighted the importance of using existing knowledge, for example, by doing literature reviews ($n = 6$). One of the interview participants spoke about a large needs study that her research group performed. In that study, a total of 236 interviews were conducted with people with dementia and the outcomes of this large study have been the foundation of all subsequent development projects for this research group. However, one of the interview participants with a design background pointed out that not all relevant information can be gained from reading literature. One of the biggest challenges that interview participants referred to is the translation of everyday needs to market-ready solutions for a larger group of people. This is an important phase in the design practice and might be experienced by researchers from different backgrounds as being a non-scientific *black box* situation. It raises interesting questions about how this impacts the involvement of the people living with dementia themselves within this *intellectual property* development phase of the design process. Do all participants take part as equal partners, as precondition of co-design, and is that even possible?

With respect to materials used in research, the interview participants explained that a variety of prototypes were tested throughout their projects. The fidelity of these prototypes ranges from paper prototypes in the generative phase to fully functional prototypes in the evaluative phase. In line with previous research (Orpwood et al. 2004) it was pointed out that it is very important to think carefully about what to test with people with dementia, and even more so than when testing with users without cognitive problems. However, the reasons given by our interview participants were diverse. One of the interview participants talked about the importance of problem-free testing. This interview participant recounted that she uses a regular group of enthusiastic people with dementia, which meets frequently in order to increase the accessibility of new innovations for the user group, she noticed that the group became reluctant to test new versions of prototypes when they had experienced *troubles* earlier. This is an important insight when including the same users over the course of one or multiple projects.

Other reasons for reconsidering testing prototypes with people with dementia are that some prototypes of technologies can be quite harmful and risky to the end-user when tested in real-life contexts (such as navigation support systems). Other prototypes might be too costly so that only a few people can be included in real-life testing. All of these reasons need to be given consideration during prototype testing with people with dementia and can influence the outcomes of formative evaluations.

One of the recurring themes in the interviews was in relation to researching the effectiveness of supportive technologies for people with dementia. The interview participants ($n = 5$) who talked about quantitative measurements all underscored that Randomized Controlled Trials (RCT) are not feasible in projects developing technology, even though this is still a common part of many project proposals. Not only do funding agencies still ask for trials with a large group of people, dementia care organizations also want to know whether technology truly supports the life of people with dementia and assists informal and professional caregivers. However, the time for setting up an effect study cannot be incorporated within the mean of three years that is common in supportive technology development projects. In addition, the traditional RCT designs do not fit within the field of technology; technology always needs updates and randomizing by way of a placebo is nearly impossible. This opens up the debate on how to dynamically approach an outcome such as effectiveness, as the earlier example within the *eWARE* project shows. One of the interview participants mentioned that more anthropological research to fully understand how technology can be supportive in the everyday lives of people with dementia creates more relevant rich data that will help the field to move forward. More research on how to hand-over such experiences is highly relevant (Smeenk et al. 2018).

## 21.4 Working in Multidisciplinary Teams

As involving people with dementia throughout a project is regarded as an essential prerequisite for successful technology development, the entire team should be open to investing time in this. One of the interview participants stated that she has an intrinsic motivation to work from the perspective of users and create positive outcomes in their lives and that of relevant others. This was helpful for convincing other stakeholders (such as developers) in the team and the research participants to take part. People with dementia and their informal caregivers are more willing to share their insights when researchers are enthusiastic. Three of our interview participants explicitly mentioned that developers need to be open to different outcomes during a project, as the iterative human-centered design approach can create unexpected outcomes. In addition to that, developers should have some interest in the user group as well. One interview participant explains,

> Sometimes these development projects give interesting insights about older adults without the actual technology being valuable. For technical partners this can be regarded as a failed project. That cannot be the case, we do not want to stimulate a technology-push.

Interview participants explained that maybe more than in the development of non-technological interventions, project partners were very dependent on each other. Developers and designers have very different skills to some of the researchers. This makes it difficult to fully understand the capabilities and resources needed before the actual start of a project, in particular when the design brief is more open than a developers brief might be. Also, the aims of different project partners can vary, for example, between researchers and designers. Two design interview participants explained that there is always a need for finding a balance between doing reliable research activities and getting actual practical insights in the context of use to steer the development and design in the right direction. In the case of involving people with dementia, it is also highly relevant to not overburden the participants, and to adapt the methods to the situation at hand. Another example of different aims between partners is that of Small and Medium Enterprises (SMEs) or business partners and designers, as acknowledged in the *FreeWalker* example given earlier in this chapter. Overall, our interview participants underscored the importance of having a business partner for developing viable outcomes. However, in the pre-design and generative phase of technology development there is a high need for creativity, which, to one of the interview participants, can be affected when thinking about costs early on.

Two interview participants defined solutions on how to overcome the differences between partners involved in the development of supportive technologies. One of the interview participants explained the process of *educating* each other throughout the project on the common paradigms and methods used in their own disciplines which can lead to more interdisciplinary teamwork. Close collaboration, by literally sitting and working next to each other, is deemed necessary to integrate research, design, business, and development. Another solution given in our interviews was to involve people with an interdisciplinary profile (such as HCI professionals) who can facilitate the communication between dementia researchers and technology developers, since translating insights from research into technology development goes beyond simply understanding each other.

Despite having an intention to actively involve people with dementia iteratively throughout a project, the different interview participants from the various fields experienced similar challenges, such as researching needs, translating these into actual designs and first prototypes, as well as exactly *how* to involve people with dementia in the process. The difficulties in collaborating on funded projects with different partners and with different aims and studying the effectiveness of the developed supportive technologies are highlighted by the project examples given earlier in this chapter with existing human-centered design projects. They are also reflected in work by Span and colleagues (2017) who argue that funders should consider the extra time required for meaningful participation of people with dementia within these complex projects.

## 21.5 Conclusion: Implications for Co-designing Technologies

The increasing number of people with dementia worldwide creates a need for meaningful support in independent living and overall well-being in daily life. Large national and international programs for developing supportive technologies reflect the growing interest in the potential for technologies to improve dementia care, although the uptake of these technologies is still limited to technologies such as lifestyle monitoring (see, Zwierenberg et al. 2018). There seems to be a mismatch between products produced and the *real* needs and abilities of people with dementia.

Active involvement of people with dementia is complex, due to the characteristics of the dementia syndrome, the limited of knowledge on useful research methods and materials and the inherent need for multidisciplinary engagement that accompanies these development projects. The projects described in this chapter exemplify these difficulties. To apply for funding that aligns a consortium of partners with different backgrounds and from different countries and cultures needs a detailed proposal before a project is started. This inherently affects the balance within the project between users, designers, and researchers, as people with dementia usually do not take part in the writing of project proposals. While funding agencies, such as ZonMw in the Netherlands (ZonMw, n.d.), increase the use of panels of users to review proposals, how to include a variety of people with dementia on these reference panels remains largely unknown. Designers and researchers within the field need therefore to find suitable ways of including people in pre-project phases.

Furthermore, when defining user requirements from user research perspectives, it is not only desirability that must be accounted for, but viability and feasibility also needs to be considered. People with dementia usually do not have a direct voice in the prioritizing of requirements, unlike the business partners and developers, which may result in the requirements being aimed more toward project and product viability, effectiveness, and feasibility. Moreover, when designing new technologies, it is challenging to invite people with dementia onto the project in the early stages. While we have learned from our systematic literature review that people with dementia can be part of the generative phase in the development process, from our experiences in *FreeWalker* and *eWARE*, requirements are more easily drawn from the perspectives of informal and formal caregivers. This shortcut affects outcomes later in the process such as the need for redesigning technology to better match the needs of people with dementia. Overall, it remains challenging to strike a balance between desirable, feasible, and viable designs for supportive technologies. A clear vision at the start of the project of how the project partners want to involve people with dementia and an action-based process evaluation might overcome the temptation to choose the quickest way. Moreover, sharing honest reflections of designers and researchers within the field on the process and the materials and methods used is highly valuable to strengthen the ways we undertake to co-design with people living with dementia (Brankaert and Ijsselsteijn 2019).

**What Does Co-design Mean in Developing Supportive Technologies?**
In this chapter, we took a closer look at the different disciplines and challenges involved in the development of supportive technologies for people with dementia. The methods and materials that various disciplines are acquainted with influence the role that people with dementia can play in the development of technology. Merely involving people in evaluating ideas, concepts, and prototypes does not create the equal partnership that is required for a genuine co-design process, as described in the beginning of this chapter. More knowledge needs to be shared about how designers use the creative capacity of people with dementia and actively involve them in the pre-design and generative phases of technology development. The collaboration

between partners in the development of supportive technologies can be challenging, due to different backgrounds and cultures. Our examples show that the level of involvement of people with dementia in the pre-design and generative phases of supportive technology development can, despite the growing interest in the field, still be improved. Furthermore, more attention is needed in how people with dementia appraise their involvement and how this can be guided toward their desired role by means of appropriate research and design methods.

Future research needs, therefore, to continue to focus on and show how research methods and materials can be shaped, chosen, and applied. This does not need to interfere with the explorative nature of design activities in the pre-design and generative phases, for example, by writing detailed method stories of these design activities with different people with dementia (Hendriks et al. 2015). In line with person-centered dementia care (Brooker and Latham 2015), the research methods and materials need to consider users' changing individual strengths and vulnerabilities and give people with dementia their desired role in the development of supportive technology. Only when people with dementia have gained a sense of having some control, will designers, developers, and researchers gain the necessary empathic understanding to create meaningful and suitable technology. This is beautifully described by one of the participants in the development of the DecideGuide by Span and colleagues (Span et al. 2017):

> Research is important. Only by participating you forge ahead with the development of things. I am into technology. When there are technical aids then you should try them. It is a pity not to do it. As long as I can participate I will do so. That is useful… (Person with dementia)

**Acknowledgments** We owe a great debt to the work of Barbera Bongaards, which was used as input for this chapter. Furthermore, we would like to thank all participants for their time and valuable insights. We also gratefully acknowledge support from the European Active and Assisted Living (AAL) Programme. In particular, the work reported here has been supported by the AAL *FreeWalker* and *eWARE* project.

## References

AAL Programme (n.d.) Retrieved October 23, 2018, from https://www.aal-europe.eu/

Astell A, Alm N, Gowans G, Ellis M, Dye R, Vaughan P (2009) Involving older people with dementia and their caregivers in designing computer based support systems: some methodological considerations. Uni Access Inf Soc 8(1):49–58. https://doi.org/10.1007/s10209-008-0129-9

Brankaert R, Ijsselsteijn W (2019) Dementia lab 2019—making design work: engaging with dementia in context. In R Brankaert, W IJsselsteijn (eds), 4th conference, D-Lab 2019. Springer, Eindhoven. https://doi.org/10.1007/978-3-030-33540-3

Brankaert R, Kenning G, Welsh D, Foley S, Hodge J, Unbehaun D (2019) Intersections in HCI, design and dementia: inclusivity in participatory approaches. In Companion publication of the 2019 on designing interactive systems conference 2019 (pp 357–360). https://doi.org/10.1145/3301019.3319997

Brankaert R, den Ouden E, Brombacher A C (2015) Innovate dementia: the development of a living lab protocol to evaluate interventions in context. ISM-Info 17(4):40–52. https://doi.org/10.1108/info-01-2015-0010

Brooker D, Latham I (2015) Person-centred dementia care: making services better with the VIPS framework, 2nd edn. Jessica Kingsley Publishers, London

Casaccia S, Revel GM, Scalise L, Bevilacqua R, Rossi L, Paauwe RA, … Nap HH (2019) Social robot and sensor network in support of activity of daily living for people with dementia. In R Brankaert, W Ijsselsteijn (eds), 4th conference, D-Lab 2019 (vol 1, pp 128–135). Springer, Eindhoven. https://doi.org/10.1007/978-3-030-33540-3

Clegg D, Barker R (1994) Case method fast-track: a RAD approach. Addison-Wesley Longman Publishing Co., Inc

Evans J, Brown M, Coughlan T, Lawson G, Craven M (2015) A systematic review of dementia focused assistive technology. Lecture notes in computer science (Including Subseries Lecture Notes in Artificial Intelligence and Lecture Notes in Bioinformatics) 9170:3–12. https://doi.org/10.1007/978-3-319-20916-6

Hanson E, Magnusson L, Arvidsson H, Claesson A, Keady J, Nolan M (2007) Working together with persons with early stage dementia and their family members to design a user-friendly technology-based support service. Dementia 6(3):411–434. https://doi.org/10.1177/1471301207081572

Hendriks N (2019) The involvement of people with dementia in the design process. KU Leuven

Hendriks N, Slegers K, Duysburgh P (2015) Co-design with people living with cognitive or sensory impairments: a case for method stories and uniqueness. Co-design 11(1):70–82. https://doi.org/10.1080/15710882.2015.1020316

https://aal-eware.eu/wp/ (n.d.)

https://www.freewalker-aal.eu (n.d.)

Lazar A, Toombs AL, Morrissey K, Kenning G, Boger J, Brankaert R (2018) HCIxDementia Workshop: Engaging People Living with Dementia. In Extended Abstracts of the 2018 CHI Conference on Human Factors in Computing Systems (CHI EA '18). ACM, pp 1–7

Lindsay S, Jackson D, Ladha C, Ladha K, Brittain K, Olivier P (2012) Empathy, participatory design and people with dementia. CHI '12 extended abstracts on human factors in computing systems. https://doi.org/10.1145/2207676.2207749

Mayer JM, Zach J (2013) Lessons learned from participatory design with and for people with dementia. Proceedings of the 15th international conference on human-computer interaction with mobile devices and services—MobileHCI '13, 540. https://doi.org/10.1145/2493190.2494436

Meiland F, Innes A, Mountain G, Robinson L, van der Roest H, García-Casal JA, … Franco-Martin M (2017) Technologies to support community-dwelling persons with dementia: a position paper on issues regarding development, usability, effectiveness and cost-effectiveness, deployment, and ethics. JMIR Rehabilit Assis Technol 4(1):e1. https://doi.org/10.2196/rehab.6376

Morrissey K, Lazar A, Boger J, Toombs A (2017) HCIxDementia workshop: the role of technology and design in dementia. In Proceedings of the 2017 chi conference extended abstracts on human factors in computing systems (pp 484–491) https://doi.org/10.1145/3027063.3027083

Orpwood R, Bjorneby S, Hagen I, Maki O, Faulkner R, Topo P (2004) User involvement in dementia product development. Dementia 3(3):263–279. https://doi.org/10.1177/1471301204045160

Sanders EB-N, Stappers PJ (2008) Co-creation and the new landscapes of design. Co-design 4(1):5–18. https://doi.org/10.1080/15710880701875068

Smeenk W, Sturm J, Terken J, Eggen B (2018) A systematic validation of the empathic handover approach guided by five factors that foster empathy in design A systematic validation of the empathic handover approach guided by five factors that foster empathy in design. Co-design 0882:1–21. https://doi.org/10.1080/15710882.2018.1484490

Span M, Hettinga M, Groen-van de Ven L, Jukema J, Janssen R, Vernooij-Dassen M, … Smits C (2017) Involving people with dementia in developing an interactive web tool for shared decision-making: experiences with a participatory design approach. Dis Rehabil 0(0):1–11. https://doi.org/10.1080/09638288.2017.1298162

Span M, Hettinga M, Vernooij-Dassen M, Eefsting J, Smits C (2013) Involving people with dementia in the development of supportive IT applications: a systematic review. Ageing Res Rev 12(2):535–551. https://doi.org/10.1016/j.arr.2013.01.002

Suijkerbuijk S, Nap HH, Cornelisse L, De Kort YAW, Ijsselsteijn W, Minkman MMN (2019) Active involvement of people with dementia: a systematic review of studies developing supportive technologies. J Alzheimer's Dis 69(4):1041–1065. https://doi.org/10.3233/JAD-190050

Topo P (2009) Technology studies to meet the needs of people with dementia and their caregivers. J Appl Gerontol (vol 28). https://doi.org/10.1177/0733464808324019

Turner-Stokes L (2009) Goal attainment scaling (GAS) in rehabilitation: a practical guide. Clin Rehabil 23(4):362–370. https://doi.org/10.1177/0269215508101742

Wouters M, Swinkels I, van Lettow B, de Jong J, Sinnige J, Brabers A, … van Gennip L (2018) E-health in verschillende snelheden. eHealth-monitor 2018. Den Haag en Utrecht

ZonMw (n.d.) Patiëntenpanel. Retrieved October 31, 2019, from https://www.zonmw.nl/nl/onderzoek-resultaten/palliatieve-zorg/patienten-en-naastenparticipatie/patientenpanel/

Zwierenberg E, Nap HH, Lukkien D, Cornelisse L, Finnema E, Med AD, … Sanderman R (2018) A lifestyle monitoring system to support (in)formal caregivers of people with dementia: analysis of users need, benefits, and concerns. Gerontechnology 17(4):194–205. https://doi.org/10.4017/gt.2018.17.4.001.00

# Part V
# Closing

# Chapter 22
# Where from and Where Next?—HCI and Design in the Context of Dementia

**Rens Brankaert and Gail Kenning**

## 22.1 Reflecting on HCI, Design and Dementia

### *22.1.1 Challenges*

*HCI and Design in the context of dementia* presents contributions from a wide range of experts across a range of fields and disciplines to share the latest HCI research and practice in relation to dementia care. We have focused on the *how*, *when* and *where* the fields of HCI and design can support people living with dementia and showed examples of *what* HCI and design can do to improve their quality of life. All of the projects discussed seek to empower people living with dementia by supporting their ability, maximizing their potential, and using participatory and inclusive approaches. In the introduction, we located *design for dementia* in relation to contemporary challenges of dementia care within the context of an ageing population, framed within the philosophical and practical changes in health and dementia care (Chap. 1). We highlighted the many different, multidisciplinary approaches needed in design, HCI and research in general; the wide range of stakeholders invested in dementia care; the multi-faceted relationships that exist; the different environments in which

R. Brankaert
School of allied health professions, Fontys University of Applied Sciences, Eindhoven, The Netherlands
e-mail: R.Brankaert@fontys.nl

Department of Industrial Design, Eindhoven University of Technology, Eindhoven, The Netherlands

G. Kenning (✉)
Ageing Futures Institute, University of New South Wales, Sydney, Australia
e-mail: Gail.Kenning@unsw.edu.au

Faculty of Arts and Social Sciences, Faculty of Engineering and IT, University of Technology Sydney, Ultimo, Australia

© Springer Nature Switzerland AG 2020

R. Brankaert and G. Kenning (eds.), *HCI and Design in the Context of Dementia*, Human–Computer Interaction Series,
https://doi.org/10.1007/978-3-030-32835-1_22

people with dementia and their caregivers live; the many fields and disciplines that are implicated; and the complexities related to dementia care.

### 22.1.2 *Inclusivity*

The respectful inclusion of people with dementia in research and design practices is a recurring theme, highlighting the importance of working with people with dementia, caregivers, family members, care staff and organizations, researchers, designers and practitioners. Great consideration is given to the perspectives of those participating in the research and design projects (Frost et al., Chap. 6 and Unbehaun et al., Chap. 18) as reflected in the focus on reciprocity (Kenning, Chap. 2), need for personalization in compassionate design (Treadaway, Chap. 4), and calls for authentic engagement and participation (Frost et al., Chap. 6). The echoes of 'nothing about us, without us' from disability discourse, can be heard clear and strong in many of the contributions and in particular from those with younger onset dementia (Frost et al., Chap. 6). HCI researchers and designers foreground the need for change in how research and design is conducted particularly when engaging with marginalized groups (Hendriks et al., Chap. 7, Branco et al., Chap. 8, Blackler et al., Chap. 10 and Astell et al., Chap. 11). They provide concrete examples of projects which highlight the sensitivities that come with research and practice that includes people with dementia respectfully in the design process (Fennell, Chap. 5, Thoolen et al., Chap. 17 and Niedderer et al., Chap. 18). The stakeholders included in projects ranged from the local, family member, caregiver, care staff, to the wider network of industry partners and social innovation platforms (Chih-Siang et al., Chap. 20 and Suijkerbuijk et al., Chap. 21).

The projects discussed offer a counterbalance to the once dominant biomedical perspective of dementia that focused on disability, loss and deficits, often framed within a stigmatizing view of ageing that is seen as synonymous with being frail and helpless (this is particularly addressed in Hodge and Morrissey, Chap. 15 and Foley and Welsh, Chap. 16). The contributions show how HCI, technology and design research contribute to the development of meaningful lives, affirming older age, and achieving the best quality of life possible for those living with dementia or caring for them (IJsselsteijn et al., Chap. 3 and throughout Sect. 3 and 4).

### 22.1.3 There Is no One Way

We see there are many ways of approaching design for dementia and contributing to the dementia care space and the lives of people with dementia and stakeholders in their care. Working with HCI and design in the complex and sensitive context of dementia calls for understanding of the context, engaging in multidisciplinary or interdisciplinary collaborations, being flexible and innovative, and being open to a range of approaches, methods, methodologies and perspectives. These approaches involve relational ways of working, sometimes one on one or in small groups of three to four people (Hendriks et al., Chap. 7, Frohlich et al., Chap. 12, Houben et al., Chap. 13, Hodge and Morrissey, Chap. 15, Foley and Welsh, Chap. 16, and Thoolen et al., Chap. 17). In other approaches we also see the search for new principles, methods and methodologies (Hendriks et al., Chap. 7, Ramos et al., Chap. 8, Blackler et al., Chap. 9 and Astell et al., Chap. 10), the application of tools, methods and methodologies, used successfully in other areas, adapted and applied to design in the context of dementia (Blackler et al., Chap. 19, and O'Connor, Chap. 14). Some chapters have provided valuable reviews and insights into existing literature, projects and approaches to show the scope and potential for HCI research and design (For example, Ramos et al., in Chap. 3), and call for new ways of working in HCI and design (IJsselsteijn et al., Chap. 3 and throughout Sect. 3 and 4).

The range of projects contribute to well-being and extend research through design in context of dementia through artefacts (Frohlich et al., Chap. 12, Houben et al., Chap. 13, Foley and Welsh, Chap. 16, Thoolen et al., Chap. 17), novel services (Chih-Sian et al., Chap. 20), the critical review of projects and assistive technologies (Ramos et al., Chap. 9), the appropriation of theories and approaches to new contexts (Frohlich et al., Chap. 12, and Blackler et al., Chap. 19). Giving consideration to context, participants, and appropriateness, and taking time for reflection can be achieved in various ways and a strong theme that is embodied throughout the book.

### 22.1.4 Transferability

When we reflect on the many ways of working, approaches used, and methodologies in addition to findings, recommendations and conclusions we begin to see how HCI and design can support people living with dementia and stakeholders in their care. The role of HCI and design to address societal challenges will only increase over the next couple of years. We see how the approaches, methods and tools, and the knowledge, skills and practices from the contributions in this book that come from working in context are transferrable to other domains as well.

The challenges around inclusion in HCI and design impacts everybody as increasingly we move beyond simply being *users* of services and technologies, and start to understand that being included reflects our daily expectations. From this work, we can extract important lessons to guide future designers and researchers when working with people in networked, complex and sensitive areas such as dementia. These inclusive approaches are appropriate for working with populations who have particular access needs to enable them to participate and let their voices be heard; in the health care domain this might mean working with people who are non-neurotypical, have mental health concerns, are impacted by injury or trauma, or have other chronic conditions such as Parkinson's disease.

## 22.2 Future Design and HCI in the Context of Dementia

There are some more general guiding principles that we can take from the many HCI and design projects in collaboration with designers, researchers, people with dementia and other stakeholders in this book, and the various overviews, experiences, studies, examples and observations too. Each chapter in this book provides their own richness and insights, reflections and contribution in detail. Here we will cover themes and ideas that can guide future design work, and thereby encourage HCI researchers and designers to design in context; we suggest there are three considerations. These can be described in terms of *1. Conditions, 2. Approach and 3. Design.*

***Conditions***—This prompts us to consider what are the conditions to be taken into account before starting a project in context of dementia, and in which context will the design artefact or service ultimately operate. For example, what is the environment, who are the people, what are the relationships, what will the artefact do, and importantly is it wanted or needed, and does it contribute, support and empower people? A prerequisite to designing for and with people living with dementia and stakeholders in their care is the recognition of the person first and not the condition. This leads to an inclusive, respectful and individualized way of working that is considerate of the people involved. The sensitivity of the context needs to start from the people themselves, and ensure they are partners in the research or design project. In this, the researchers and designers have to move beyond only fulfilling their own goal, toward reciprocal and meaningful engagement and shared goals, or separate goals that can co-exist.

***Approach***—Here consideration needs to be given to how a research or design project will be introduced, explained and understood by the stakeholders involved, such as users, caregivers, organizations but also the designers and researchers. This means carefully considering how people are included, and how much information is appropriate to share and when. For example, to what extent would information about the entire project be clarifying and welcome information or become burdensome and be dismissed. Also, when engaging with people living with dementia for a research or design purpose how do we present opportunities for participants to have a strong voice in the work conducted? This takes careful thought and planning by researchers and designers as to why and how someone is involved at a particular stage of a project and why they may be excluded at other times. Researchers can build on their relationship with participants to explore, understand and navigate these research challenges. Co-design methods can be used to structure and facilitate the inclusion of people living with dementia and be considerate of the wider care network, including partners, family, friends, caregivers and others involved.

**Design**—An important aspect in the participatory design of projects, artefacts, or services in complex societal settings is to collaborate with people that bring a range of perspectives, experiences and expertise. Each person involved in the collaboration has expertise to offer, this is what we may call a 360-degree expert approach. For example, people with dementia have expertise because of their lived experience, and care staff have expertise in the act of caring. In addition, the expertise of the designer and researcher can come to the fore in acknowledging and reconciling differences and shared concerns of all stakeholders partnering in the design process. The designer and researcher can engage with people for their individual wants and needs and individuals' uniqueness, and recognize, for example, that wants and needs may change over time for people with dementia as their condition progresses. The designer as expert can recognize abilities, as opposed to disability, contribute to a meaningful experience and engage with the full range of senses to increase acceptance and to enable the qualities and uniqueness of the individual to increase the user experience of design interventions. Working in this way designers can use their expertise to design for autonomy, empowerment and self-reliance and contribute to increase the quality of life of people living with dementia and stakeholders in their care.

## 22.3 Where Next?

Much has been achieved in the area of design for dementia over the last few decades. Recognizing people with dementia as individuals with wants, needs, abilities and potential in this area is a direct response to the calls of Kitwood to recognize the people and not the condition and to overcome the stigma of having dementia. We recognize the important work being carried out. There are, however, 'gaps' that need to be addressed in HCI and design to increase the impact on this field. These are opportunities for future researchers and designers.

Multi-stakeholder design is complex, particularly in areas such as dementia. Several chapters in this book address the challenges of designing in a multi-stakeholder context. However, the nuances, implications and best practices of working with stakeholders with varying degrees of economic and emotional investment, with competing aims and ambitions, differing regulatory, reporting, and funding restrictions, and diverse beliefs, philosophies and understandings have been under addressed in research. These qualities are often only investigated in terms of the user and the technology or service, and sometimes with informal and formal caregivers, but rarely on the level of the wider stakeholder network that operates around people living with dementia or taking multiple lenses into account. The multi-stakeholder aspects of the research and design in sensitive settings do not get enough attention in HCI and design, as opposed to its appearance in systems and soft systems thinking and in business and organizational literature. In addition to the diversity of stakeholders, the topic of teams deserves attention too, often teams are brought together to realize a project in a complex situation such as dementia. However, what roles are needed, and how can people best work together in terms of design, setup and evaluation, is often neglected as a research topic. What disciplines are needed, how are they involved in a research process, and how can the main guiding principles from this book be transferred toward different disciplines?

Another issue that has not been extensively addressed in the projects discussed throughout this book is scalability. With the ageing population and increased incidences of dementia there is a likelihood that more people than ever before will be living with dementia. We have discussed in detail the need for reciprocity, personalization, inclusivity and direct engagement with potential users. But inherent in this approach is the need to research and design on a societal scale. How then do research and design prototypes and outcomes reach more people as products, services, and make a significant change? Some of the projects discussed here provide leads to tackle the issue of scalability of approaches, artefacts and services, and are engaging in knowledge transfer. However, there is scope for further development in HCI and design.

Similarly we are also seeing disappointingly few artefacts and services 'getting to market' and becoming products that can make a difference to many people. This is obviously not always the purpose of research projects; however, there is the inevitable lag between research, design and product. This is partly impacted by the project-based funding that supports many of these research projects. Funding is often allocated for a set amount of time with specific outcome requirements. So, while funding may be awarded for innovation in technology and design, less funding is available to develop the technologies or design into a sustainable product. While it may need entrepreneurs and private funding to achieve this, there is great variation with regard to how this can be achieved from country to country. More research is needed to operationalize and implement research and design findings in the everyday environment to have a long-lasting impact. How to achieve this could be investigated further within the area of HCI and design.

Dementia is a condition that has been and still is stigmatized by society, this is partly because the greatest risk for dementia is old age but other factors play a role as well since it affects a person's identity, ability and sense of self. The stigma is impacted by the close relationship with old age and the ageism that exists in many westernized countries. HCI and design can contribute to the de-stigmatizing of dementia, but this also needs to happen at a larger political, sociological and economical level. To influence society on a systemic level, HCI researchers and designers will need to rethink and adapt practices and engage as social innovation platforms to kick start the debates around these topics, and put research efforts into them going forward. In addition, while throughout the book there is a call to work at a local level, to engage with individuals and embrace personalization, there remains a need for both global and cross-cultural, approaches, and the need to go deeper into communities to be inclusive to ensure that there is a diversity of engagement with underrepresented cultural groups.

## 22.4 Conclusion

To conclude, this book brought together leading researchers in the field of design, HCI, and dementia, working to understand and improve the lives of people living with dementia and stakeholders in their care. From these contributions, valuable lessons can be learned that apply to many fields and sensitive contexts.

Much work is still to be done in HCI and design to positively impact people who are living daily in a disadvantaged position. But by working together, as researchers and designers, we can make a change in the lives of those who need it most. Using inclusive practices can contribute to an open and equal society. At this broader level, many of the approaches and insights in this book are important as many people who the systems and services are intended for do not yet have a say in how and why they are developed. HCI researchers and designers that are addressing the social and societal challenges of our day need to ensure that all of those impacted have an opportunity to be included in finding answers and ensure the steps are in place to enable them to do so.

Printed in the United States
by Baker & Taylor Publisher Services

Printed in the United States
by Baker & Taylor Publisher Services